The Complete Book of Children's Theater

The Complete Book
of
Children's Theater

Vernon Howard

Illustrated by Doug Anderson
and others

DOUBLEDAY & COMPANY, INC.
GARDEN CITY, NEW YORK

Library of Congress Catalog Card Number 69–10951
Copyright © 1955, 1956, 1957, 1959, 1960, 1961, 1962,
1964, 1969 by Sterling Publishing Co., Inc.
All Rights Reserved
Printed in the United States of America

The author wishes to thank G. Dobbelaere and P. Sara-goussi for the use of material from Techniques of Expression, *originally published by Presses d'Île de France, Paris*

Contents

The Complete Book of Children's Theater

Section 1

Before You Begin

A full knowledge of what is in this section is just about all a good actor or pantomimist needs to know to launch himself on a career in the theater—not the children's theater or the "little theater" alone, but the professional stage.

It is not necessary to read this section of the book *now*—but it is a good idea. If you find it goes more deeply into acting than you want to go at the start, skip to Section 2, but remember that this section is here for you to come back to—and back you will come, time and again, if you are going to be a worthwhile actor or dramatist. For, in this section are all the clues and hints, the dances and games and exercises that will loosen up your body and your mind and your tongue so that you act freely and spontaneously.

Don't underestimate the importance of being "natural" and acting spontaneously.

Now read on as far as you want in this introductory section, leave it when it stops being fun, and dip into the pantomimes and charades, the monologues and play acting. Act out a few pieces, and then come back and read more here, play more games from this section, and then see how much you have improved when you put on your next act before an audience.

FACIAL EXPRESSIONS AND GESTURES

A player secretly thinks of an object of any kind. He then stands before some guessers and answers their questions about the object—not out loud, but with pantomime movements. The questions need not necessarily be of the kind that can be answered with a *yes* or *no;* the audience can ask any question which the actor can answer with a pantomime movement. Here is how the

9

questions and answers might go if the actor's secret object were a *merry-go-round*.

"Is it large or small?" (*player holds his hands out wide*)

"Is it found in the house?" (*player shakes head*)

"Does it have moving parts? (*player nods*)

"How does it move?" (*player spins forefinger in flat circle*)

"Does it carry things?" (*player nods*)

"What does it carry?" (*player indicates audience and himself*)

"Is it a bus?" (*player shakes head*)

"Where is it usually located?" (*player gestures in several directions*)

"Is it used for amusement?" (*player nods*)

"Is it a merry-go-round?" (*player nods*)

If desired, the audience may be required to guess the object within twenty questions.

The game being played might be called "Pantomime Answers." As you participate in this and other pantomime games presented in this book, you will find that you can say a great deal merely using facial expressions and hand gestures. For, pantomime is a fascinating and basic form of dramatic art. Practice in pantomime will help you not only in silent acts, but in speaking roles also, for gestures and expressions are highly important as you speak and laugh and play and have fun acting.

One of the best ways for a person to bring out his natural abilities is through expressing his thoughts with actions—with laughter and tears, with grunts and groans. The different dramatic ideas suggested in this book will give you the chance to express yourself in many ways—whether on the stage in front of an audience, at home in your family circle, or just in socializing with your friends. As you try various stunts and skits, you will discover with growing excitement that they are challenging your creative powers, that you are beginning to portray emotions and feelings you never thought you could express. And as you go on and get better at pantomime and acting, you will find that you act spontaneously. You see, the more spontaneously you act and react in situations, the more successful you will be on stage. But what exactly do we mean by "spontaneous"?

In order to be spontaneous, you must feel at ease and confident when moving about and acting, and do what comes naturally, what is fun for you to do. Find a comfortably heated and quiet room for yourself and your group. If there is no leader in your group with experience, you or any player can take charge. If you are the leader, help the other players, the new actors and actresses to express themselves freely. Inspire their confidence by avoiding destructive or non-objective criticism, and do everything yourself that you ask of your group.

Confidence will develop as each player thinks out his own part without interfering with the work of others.

Keep your acting simple at first, so that you are not hampered by thinking technically as you begin to express yourself spontaneously. Concentrate on doing and don't worry about what effect your act will have. If you have a speaking part, go off by yourself and rehearse several times until you play the part naturally and with humor. If pantomiming *or* speaking, practice in front of a mirror, watching your facial expressions and gestures as you perform. Then try your presentation in front of your family and friends.

If your group is performing a play or skit and rehearsal time is limited, or the performance is informal, you and the other players can read your parts. Hold the book in one hand and gesture with the other. Reading the lines instead of memorizing them will help you produce spontaneous gestures, facial expressions and tone of voice, rather than focusing on remembering. All first group rehearsals should begin by reading aloud. It's a good idea to follow with music and dancing.

USING MUSIC

The following suggestions will help you to experiment with musical rhythms and instruments, which you can later use to accompany your skits.

Warming Up

Play for the group a few records that are purely rhythmic, such as African percussion instruments, modern jazz or drums.

This first session should make everyone aware that sounds which are simply rhythmic can also be effective music.

Offer the members of the group as large a choice as possible of percussion instruments, from triangle to tom-tom; from old-fashioned washboard to maracas; from empty tin cans to cymbals; from blocks of wood to drums.

Then let each player try out the various instruments and choose one.

Accompaniment of a Rhythm

The leader starts a continuous rhythm, either by tapping it out, or by some mechanical means such as using a metronome or record, a windup toy, or even by turning a bicycle wheel with a card hitting the spokes.

Against this background the members of the group create variations or rhythmic counterpoints. They accompany each other or alternate with each other as the spirit moves them.

Individual Creativity

Each of you must discover the possibilities inherent in your instrument, as well as its shortcomings. By experimenting you will learn whether you are tapping it too hard or not hard enough, too far from the middle or at just the right spot, in order to find rhythms and patterns of sound that are both right and precise. You can vary the results by using different drumsticks or batons to beat with.

These rhythmic measures can be written down through some simple but imaginative method of notation. The Morse code symbols, for instance, would make a fine graphic system for long and short sounds.

Group Encore

Each one plays his version of the measures for the group who, as they listen, form ideas of which instruments "talk" to each other and which go well together.

Once again the group listens to the background rhythm of the metronome or whatever is being used, and each one then accompanies it according to the sequence he has developed.

Orchestral Creation

Now you are ready to conduct a joint work and record it on a tape recorder. For inspiration choose a simple dramatic sequence, such as waiting, impatience, joy of meeting, separation, and finally sadness; or the succession of the seasons, etc.

Each member of the group tries to find a suitable way to illustrate or accompany each movement with his instrument. Then the group selects the most pleasing measures and records them on tape until the entire composition is complete.

Variations on a Theme

There are a great many ways to lengthen and improve a composition:

1. Add a melodic instrument to the rhythm orchestra.
2. Add a reader or a singer to perform against the background of rhythm.
3. Add a dance you have created to go with the music the group created.
4. Venture into the field of experimental music with the aid of mechanical or electronic devices.

Group activities and experiments such as just described obviously require several sessions to complete. Members of the group should practice or experiment at home if they can, find a way or time which will not disturb the family or others nearby. Perfect your rhythm simply by tapping a plank with a stick. Even a pencil and an empty box will allow you to develop precise rhythm.

It is a good idea to take down the improvisations on a tape recorder at each session. Playing them back at the end allows the group to judge individual performances with a view to improvement. Replaying them is a good way to start a new session.

DANCING SPONTANEOUSLY

You can do any dance, any movement of the body that you want in this game. If you are the leader, take care not to criticize. Suggest that the dancers "do more," never "do better." The dance, even more than the other exercises in this chapter, requires the right setting. Warm enthusiasm is necessary for the freest of expression involving the entire body of the performer. We all have definite ideas of what the dance is like, whether classical or folk dancing, the waltz or rock 'n' roll, so it may be unnerving to be offered complete liberty and freedom of movement. In any event, it will be fun.

Listening to a Recording

Choose a recording which will best support improvising. It must combine several characteristics. It must be melodic and the rhythm must not be too rapid for beginners to dance to. On the other hand, it must not be slow.

The first time the group listens to the record, the players should not be looking for forms of expression, but just absorbing the general idea of the music. Be sure to play the record only once, or your dancing will not be spontaneous.

Without any discussion after the first hearing of the record, the leader tells the members of the group to improvise on the music using only their legs. They can jump, walk, turn, run, etc., but must not use their arms.

After a few moments, without stopping the music, the leader tells the dancers to lie down on the floor and continue to improvise without getting up again. They may use arms, legs, and heads, but must stay on the floor.

Next the leader tells them to arise and, while standing in one place, to improvise solely with movements of the head, then the arms alone, then head and arms. Next, trunk movements may be added, and finally legs.

The purpose of this exercise is to acquaint the players with the entire range of possibilities offered by their bodies.

In Search of a Theme

Having become familiar with the recording, not only through the medium of ears but also of the body, the players should now try to work out a theme for the music.

The theme may be "abstract," such as sorrow, joy, etc. They can quickly choose obvious or simple images.

The theme may be concrete, such as Springtime, Return of the Fishermen, The Tower of Babel, etc. Here you should avoid detail that reduces the theme to mere anecdote.

Play the record once again, and now the players, using all the bodily means at their disposal, attempt to illustrate the chosen

14

theme. Although they are dancing together in the same area, it is a case of "each man for himself." However, it is likely that, during the course of this exercise, chance meetings or involuntary pairings will occur. From these meetings, new improvising will stem.

MOVING SPONTANEOUSLY

After you have warmed up with dancing and music, the next group of active exercises and games will make you use your body spontaneously and also help you to improvise or "ad lib" not only in actions, but in words. There is not much difference between an improvised pantomime (such as in our first game) and a pantomime skit—only that a skit is usually longer and is a public show, possibly with music, costumes, and settings.

Improvising is the spontaneous outward expression of a feeling or thought for your own satisfaction. What matters is that you express yourself "honestly"—the sincerity of your expression tends to disappear when you try to repeat something again and again. When you are improvising, treat the other players not as spectators, but as interested parties to an act in which they are as deeply involved as you are.

Games and Exercises

Free Association Pantomime Place a variety of objects on the floor in the middle of a circle of players. The players must pretend not to know the normal use of the objects—but should proceed to try out all the possible uses which the *shape* of the objects suggests.

Whenever the players have an inspiration, they can rise and pantomime an action with the object, then sit down again. A ladle, for instance, might become a telephone, a golf club, a lorgnette, etc.

Chain Game This game is derived from the preceding one. The leader gives an object to one of the players—a stick, for example. The player must improvise an action with the stick—for instance, it might become a fishing rod. The next player then gets up and interrupts the action. He might be a policeman

15

(game warden) who indicates that fishing is against the law. The fisherman returns to his seat, and the policeman who now has the stick must find a new use for it. It might become a gun. But the next player rises in his turn, and is wounded by a shot from the gun. The policeman sits down, abandoning the stick, which the new actor now uses for a crutch. The next player then becomes a doctor and uses the stick for . . . and on it goes.

In case a player cannot quickly and spontaneously think up something to do, he gives his turn to the next player, but he has to pay a forfeit—perhaps to mime something called out by one of the group.

Lost Objects The leader presents the players with a variety of articles, such as a hat, an umbrella, a pot, a glove. These objects have been found in a public place. By whom were they lost? The players chime in with answers: The hat belonged to a gangster, the umbrella to a minister, the pot to a cook, the glove to a woman.

The leader now distributes these roles. The designated players leave the room. They have a few minutes to organize together a scene which shows wordlessly the circumstances under which the objects were lost.

The Living Photograph Game This game is derived from the previous one. The leader shows a photograph of someone in action, or of a landscape. If it is a landscape, the players must by gestures tell how they would provide it with people. If it is a person, they must imagine the circumstances leading up to its being taken, and the people involved, and what they did afterwards.

The Career Game Each one must explain to the others, by gestures alone, a profession or kind of work. In this game, the players should try to follow this pattern:
- Choose a role.
- Describe (by gestures) the scene where it takes place.
- Perform the action.
- Conclude the action.

16

The Pairing-Up Game   The director makes up two series of cards, A representing easily typified people, and B representing associated people or things, such as:

A	B
Toreador	Bull
Nurse	Baby
Bricklayer	Wall

After the cards have been distributed among the players, one of the A players performs actions intended to reveal his character. The holder of a B card who recognizes that he is the associate of that character gets up and joins him. Together they improvise a suitable action.

SPEAKING SPONTANEOUSLY

The following games are to help you become more forceful in the use of language. Try to use words that will *really* express what you are thinking, and avoid triteness and vulgarity.

Games and Exercises

The Question Game   The leader asks the players to decide in their minds on either a question or an answer. The questions must be general such as, "What to you is love?" or "What is life all about?" The players have to think of an answer that is definite but poetic, such as a warm field of wheat, a loving puppy, a summer sky, a dead tree, etc.

Each time someone thinks of a question, he raises a fist. Each time someone imagines an answer, he raises an open hand.

The leader of the game chooses a questioner at random, and a respondent to speak. The unexpected combinations often give astonishing results.

The Poem Game   The leader provides a few drawings and asks the players to call out various titles which come to their mind for the pictures, but the titles should be imaginative. It would be rather pointless to call a winter scene merely "Snow"

17

when one could think up titles that represent an association of ideas, such as "Purity" or "Dominoes" or even "Death of Autumn," etc.

The leader calls on those who have titles to contribute, and when the answers have been exhausted, he goes on to other activities. During this time, however, someone has been writing down at random the most striking titles. When the game is over, he quickly places verbs in between the titles in such a way as to form coherent sentences. The result is a free verse poem, which he then reads aloud, to everyone's amusement. Spontaneity combines naturalness with surprise.

The Lost Story The leader starts to tell a story which he makes up as he goes along. At a certain point he says, "I forget what comes next." He designates one of the group to tell how he thinks the story might continue, and then at a sign from the leader, he says, "I've forgotten the rest." He points to someone else to continue until such time as the leader gives him the signal to interrupt himself. This continues until all have taken part, and an incredible humorous story told.

Strangers Meet Two players each assume an identity, either that of a specific historical personality or of a cowboy, nurse, etc. Each player tries to discover the identity of the other by asking questions which can be answered only by yes or no. The questions must be indirect, aimed at finding out about the other person rather than simply guessing.

Improvising to a Theme The theme may be based on one or several snapshots. Work alone or in small teams. The object is to build an imaginary story involving the subjects in the pictures. The story is then told to the whole group.

A short item from the newspaper could also be used as the theme. The object is to tell a story which might follow from the newspaper account.

What do these vocal games do for you? They merely stir up your thinking apparatus regarding words and thoughts, so you can say things without hesitation or embarrassment.

YOUR SENSES

After you have done some spontaneous experimenting, you will want to develop some more techniques of acting. As you learn more bodily gestures, you will become more aware of how the senses of your body work and this will in turn help you interpret your surroundings. The more you enlarge the range of your sight, smell, taste, touch, and hearing, the more you will be able to contribute to your range of silent expressions. Try the following to increase the use of your senses.

1. Sight

Ask someone to put ten or twelve different objects on a table. Observe the table for one minute, and then look away and see how many you can remember. Repeat the game, each time increasing the number of objects and decreasing the observation time as your faculty for visual attention develops.

2. Hearing

Standing quite still in a busy street, sitting in a restaurant, or in a field in the country, try to record mentally all the sounds that you hear, from the loudest to the softest. After you get used to this kind of observation, try the same exercise while listening to recordings, going from the most simple to the most complicated and trying to identify the instruments. In the case of classical music, for instance, you could go from a sonata to a trio, to a quintette and then a concerto.

3. Touch

Our tactile sensations are not as keen as they could be. Try to increase your ability to recognize temperature, weight, and size of an object by touch alone. Here is an exercise: Blindfolded, feel an object and then try to reproduce it with modeling clay.

Still blindfolded, concentrate on a variety of materials, and try to appreciate the weave of cloth, the grain of paper, the satin of polished wood.

19

4. Smell

While walking through a food market, fix your attention on the variety of aromas. If you have never tried this, you will be absolutely amazed at the richness of the sensations you discover.

The sense of smell is without doubt the least used of our senses. The Japanese, for example, have far more refined olfactory senses than most Westerners. To deprive ourselves of this faculty is to miss a great deal indeed.

5. Taste

Why does a good cook try to bring out the taste of food so that, even with eyes closed, you can appreciate how delicious it is? What good is the wonderful variety of tastes in fruits and vegetables if you gulp them down without paying attention to what you eat? Form the habit of becoming more aware of each food you eat every meal.

Besides becoming more aware of the world through a heightened use of your senses, consider how you are responding to the information your senses gives you. As you perform each movement, note how it can be made simpler and more precise. Work on finding your own "tempo" and rhythm while performing simple actions, and then transfer this rhythm to your pantomiming and gestures. Perform your movements spontaneously and gracefully. Then try to put different movements together smoothly, such as beating out a rhythm with one hand on a thigh, and tapping the floor with one foot. Another exercise is to pat your head up and down with one hand and to rub your stomach in a circular movement with the other. Can you do it?

A familiar movement that we hardly ever stop to analyze is walking. Think for a few moments of the way you walk. Look at yourself in the mirror. Does your head move? Is your upper body pitched forward? Do you lean sidewards when you turn? Perhaps you sway slightly. Each one of us has a particular way of walking, and that way can express your character to a great extent. When you are playing a particular role, it is important that your walk fit the role. Here are a few things that a walk can tell:

– A rigidly held head indicates an obstinate person.
– Rolling shoulders may indicate a woman or a sailor.
– Swinging arms are usually the sign of an athlete.
– The chest held upright gives a noble appearance.
– The abdomen pushed forward may indicate illness.
– Legs which bear down hard might indicate a military person.
– The body held back is a sign of a cowardly character.
– The body held forwards portrays courage and aggressiveness.

Many other movements will also express your personality. For example, how do you shake hands? Do you give a limp, weary squeeze or a brisk, firm one? How do you wave goodbye? Or express your sympathy? Pantomime will lead you to question yourself on all your everyday movements, perhaps leading you to change your movements in real-life situations as well as on stage.

Here are some suggestions that will help you to develop freer movements and more imaginative actions on stage.

ANALYSIS OF MOVEMENTS

Walking

Walk with stiff legs, bent legs, holding your body rigid, bending from the waist. Invent new ways of walking, even the most unnatural-seeming positions. They will be extremely useful when incorporated into the act you prepare.

Running

Run just as you usually do, but make your body as weightless as possible. To do this, concentrate on nimble, neat foot movements. Do not let your arms follow behind while the upper part of your body pitches forward at a 45° angle to the ground.

Vary your steps. Run with the highest leaps possible at each step, and then try for the longest possible steps as you run. Next run with a double step, or a step and a hop, first on your left foot only, then the right foot only. With every new way of running you invent, experiment with various speeds.

21

Tumbling

You can experiment with falling or tumbling, starting from a standing position or an in-between position, such as kneeling. You can land on a shoulder, a hip, stretched out, or rolled up like a ball. Create different ways of standing up again after each fall.

Jumping

Jump with one leg or two. Try for height or distance. Jump in one place, forwards, backwards or to either side. Move your arms with each leap, then jump with your legs alone. Even move your upper torso into the jump. Execute a quarter turn as you leap, then complete about-face. You will find a great variety of jumps possible, and you will have fun inventing new jumps.

Turns

Take a few leaps and then start turning. See how much variety you can put into this simple action. Turn in many different ways without leaping: simple turns, reverse turns, multiple turns, etc. Let your arms pull you through the turns, then just the upper half of your body. Turn on one foot or two, with knees straight or bent, etc.

Balancing

Hold your balance on one foot or two, on the balls of your feet or your toes, in motion or on a fixed point.

POSITIONS AND TONE OF VOICE

When engaged in a speaking role, you will want to consider the use of your voice as well as body movement. Be sure to place yourself in a position where everyone can both see and hear you.

When you practice speaking now, try to use only those gestures which go along naturally with the words. Any extraneous gestures will detract from the meaning of what you are saying.

Regulate the tone of your voice, making it loud enough for the audience to hear, but not so loud that it is uncomfortable for both you and your listeners. Using a microphone will help you, especially if you are performing in a large auditorium. Experiment with the volume of your voice by speaking at various distances from the microphone.

If you have trouble getting the audience's attention at first, speak softly so that they will have to quiet down to hear you.

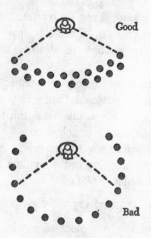

When you have their attention, raise your voice to a louder level, always leaving a reserve of volume to stress certain words to the audience. You will find in the Monologues and Duologues sections, for example, italicized words that should be stressed. If there are other words you want to emphasize, underline them in your working script before you begin practicing your act.

Remember that when you are speaking you must speak slowly enough for the audience to grasp what you are saying. If you are reading something, establish "rapport" with the audience by looking up occasionally from the reading and gazing at them. Watch the public speakers on television and notice that the most successful ones look at the camera most or all of the time.

After working by yourself on spontaneous expression and technique before a mirror, you can then try performing with your group. As you and your group perform for an audience, be on the lookout for small signs which will tell you how the audience is responding to you. The more aware you are of the audience's responses, the more successful a performer you will be.

PANTOMIME

The Action

Once the theme of your pantomime is clear in your mind, illustrate it with an action. This action must show clearly what you will present—just enough to make it easy for your audience to understand, but not enough to destroy the interest of the performance which follows.

If you are in a group acting out a number of situations, one will lead naturally to the next. Audience response to situation A provokes situation B, which leads to a third circumstance, C, until you reach a satisfactory conclusion.

In the next few pantomime themes, you may find you can use some as models for working out your own pantomimes rather than copy them as complete skits.

An Example of Free Improvising

This time after listening to a piece of music, have the members of the group tell what sort of atmosphere it suggests to them individually, and then settle on one theme. Play the music a second time and help them imagine the characters to go with the theme.

Now during a third playing of the music, concentrate on the characters within their setting, letting a suitable situation develop in your minds. Ask yourselves the familiar questions: Who? When? Where? Why? How?

"We are in a railway station."

"But what sort of a station is it?"

"It's a suburban station."

"What people are there?"

"A man in a hurry, a sad young girl, a soldier home on leave."

"What time is it?"

"Evening."

"What season?"

"Wintertime. It is very cold."

"What are they doing there?"

"The young girl is engaged to the soldier, who has been recalled

24

to his regiment. The stationmaster keeps disturbing them. The man in a hurry interferes with them."

"What is going to happen?"

Just think of all the possibilities each character can bring to his part. Choose the solutions which seem to offer the richest potential and weave them together into a whole.

Work out an improvisation like this without using music. A poem, a painting, or the text of an essay or novel can just as easily serve as your point of departure.

A Pantomime with a Concrete Theme

Start with a rather specific theme this time. For example, you might decide to use a county fair as the background for a love affair. Remember, though, that it is not necessary to stick slavishly to reality. Try to suggest rather than represent, to transpose rather than imitate.

The attractions at a small county fair are at the disposal of two young couples. The four lovers roam happily about the fair, riding the cars and coasters, spinning about on the various rides, feeding the animals, eating ice cream or candy. Suddenly a band of hoodlums invades the fair, jostling the young lovers as they take over.

The hoodlums single out the lovers and chase them, but the lovers take refuge inside the House of Glass. The roughnecks follow them into the labyrinth, but they become separated from each other. They lose their self-assurance and, one by one, slink out of the maze as best they can, disorganized and vulnerable.

A Theme from Literature

After reading, for example, John Steinbeck's story "The Pearl," extract its theme: Money does not in itself solve all problems, and in fact often brings unhappiness.

The action follows Steinbeck's plot. In a Mexican village a small child lies sick. His father goes to call the doctor, who refuses to come for fear he will not be paid. The man goes fishing in dangerous surf, but when he is successful and returns from his expedition with a beautiful pearl, his child is dead.

In the village, the pearl excites curiosity, then jealousy, then greed. Robbers attack the man. He returns to his home badly

25

wounded. He has saved the pearl from his attackers, but his wife seizes it and throws it back into the sea.

To limit pantomime to the strictly concrete would needlessly limit it. As in painting and literature, the pantomime is an art that can translate abstract ideas as well.

An Example of an Abstract Theme

Starting with the abstract idea, "Men pass, but ideas remain," here is an example of one symbolic way to interpret it.

A journalist who is working at his typewriter is visited by an idea, which is personified. He presents the idea to the editor who accepts it and prints it. When the paper appears on the newsstand it causes dissension. Two groups form and fight for and against it. The journalist's side is overwhelmed by the opposition, which is larger, and he is killed. After the battle, the idea comes up again and finds a surviving journalist who will continue to support the idea in his turn.

HOW TO PREPARE FOR A PANTOMIME

After the theme of the pantomime has been translated into a plan for action, it is time to distribute the roles. Each member of the group should ask himself:

"Who am I?"

"Where am I?"

"When is this taking place?"

"Why am I here?"

"How should I act?"

The answers each actor formulates to these questions will guide his conduct and his actions. Play your part with as much sincerity as possible. Outlining the action is merely the beginning of the job, and each player must make the most of his situation, extracting a wealth of rich detail to make the character come alive. However, this is a group enterprise, and through the group you will mold your individual actions and personalities. Express to each other what you are and what you desire.

The importance of this group contact is not just in technique. Working with a group will help you to think like, act like, and *be* another person. It is really an exercise in brotherhood and understanding.

PRODUCING THE PANTOMIME

To some extent, the production of a pantomime depends on the stage or space at your disposal, and also the entrances and exits available. The number of people in the group also influences the pantomime. In fact, you must take both factors into account when you break down the script into the individual sequences of action.

The entrances of each player for each particular sequence, as well as his exits, must be clearly marked in the script. An important rule to remember is that a player who enters the stage from the right must leave from the right. This rule can be broken occasionally, but too many exceptions create a feeling of confusion in the audience.

Pantomime has its own special vocabulary. Let us study the principal elements of this vocabulary.

Guide Lines

Vertical lines give an impression of spaciousness, power, of active expectation. *Examples:* A man standing upright in a sturdy stance or a man coming onstage from the rear and moving straight toward the proscenium (the arch which frames the front of the stage as seen by the audience).

Horizontal lines suggest balance and calmness. *Examples:* a group of people lying down, or a player moving slowly across the stage from side to side.

Diagonal lines are a sign of movement, life, effort. *Example:* a group of men standing quite still will give these effects if they are off balance, leaning to the front or the rear.

Broken lines convey uncertainty and agitation. *Example:* a subject crossing the stage in fits and starts, changing his direction a few times.

In planning each action sequence, choose the lines of direction which will best establish your mood and intention.

Patterns and Tempo

As the pantomimers move onstage, or across the stage, instead of taking random positions, let them gather in groups which

27

form patterns—squares, circles, or stars. Point out that each pattern has its own significance. Under the law of contrast: a straight line emerges from a curve; a square opposes a circle, a man opposes a group.

By the same token, slow movements are emphasized by contrast with spirited movement.

Remember that what is downstage (that is, nearest the audience) is more important than what takes place upstage (that is, at the rear of the stage). The action taking place on one side is often eclipsed by what is going on at the other side. In writing and performing on the stage, it is far better not to have simultaneous action in both places, but alternate the action.

Fixed Points

During the pantomime there are many moments when the action should pause momentarily. For the audience, these can be moments of active attention which serve to clarify in their minds the action they have just witnessed. The players, under the direction of the leader, should work out their actions, paying particular attention to the fixed positions of the individuals, or the group during these pauses. After the plan has been worked out and agreed upon, chart the lines and the fixed positions of each sequence according to this kind of illustration:

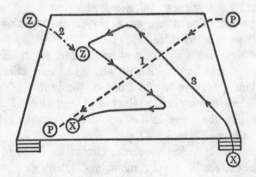

Gestures

Gesture is the first and most important consideration in pantomime. A gesture is most effective when introduced by a

28

momentary pause, a sort of mute "click" which gives it force and precision. This pause is like using "The" before a proper noun—without it, you are too abrupt.

It is possible to amplify gestures with real accessories or "props" (stage properties). More often than not, you will find that props interfere with the exaggeration of the pantomime. Instead of hampering your group with many props, you will find it not only easier but far more effective to suggest the props through pantomime.

The art of hand movement is the forte of the mime. As you already know, there are several tricks of the trade which will enable you to create and sustain illusion of a created object. Your hands should be able to preserve the object which you have created.

For example, indicate that you are holding a stick of wood, and show its size. Turn it in your fingers, put it down, pick it up, be sure to remember it is in your hands when it is supposed to be. Repeat the exercise with a coin, a ball, etc.

If you are creating the illusion of props in space, make sure that they remain fixed. If you are dancing around a pole, be sure that the hand you place on the pole remains where the pole is supposed to be, and check to see that your hand does not budge from it. If you have created a table out of thin air, make sure that the table retains its height. Put your hand on it, take something off of it, replace the object on the table, and check to make sure the table has not moved, or grown, or shrunk.

On the other hand, as a mime you can alter space or change the size of your imaginary props at will. Here are a few exercises:

–A carpenter is sawing a log, but the log gets thicker and thicker. He saws with more and more difficulty. He must take several steps backwards to drag his saw, and brace his feet in order to push it.

–A tailor is trying a suit on a customer, but the customer grows smaller and smaller until he is only a few inches high.

–A bookkeeper is trying to write figures in a ledger, but his pen grows larger and larger, until it is the size of a tree.

(Try exercises, too, in which you can speed up or slow down your movements with great exaggeration.)

In gestures which involve great effort in handling an imaginary weight, you can show "counterbalance." Let us analyze the motion of picking up a heavy weight:

– Show that you are preparing for the effort.
– Imagine the object and pantomime its weight and volume.
– Demonstrate the muscles you will need in the effort.
– Seize the imaginary object and manage to lift it with as much tiring effort as if it really weighed a great deal.

Counterbalance: Make believe that the weight of the imaginary object is so real that immediately your entire body must react, perhaps by staggering. The weight imposed upon one part of your body is so great that only by a counterweight will your balance be re-established. However, since there has not really been a weight imposed on your body, using the imaginary counterweight serves to unbalance you in the opposite direction. It follows that this real loss of balance must be compensated for (remember your physical laws of nature!) by parts of the body which normally would not come into play in the actual lifting of a real object. That is one of the many benefits of playing in pantomime. It brings about new muscular patterns and breaks old, routine patterns, with excellent results.

DEVELOPING THE PANTOMIME IN DEPTH

Simple pantomimes need to be thought out, but a group pantomime that is to be staged needs development. An outline of the action, staging, etc., is necessary to start rehearsals, but it is not enough to create a good pantomime. An outline is a fleshless skeleton, but without it, the players would become too concerned with what they have to do next to transform themselves into the characters they are creating.

At the start, your outline may still be fairly fluid. Use it as an aid to the players, not as a limit, and make necessary changes now. For instance, if a player is worried about his actions, and how they fit into the whole, this should be discussed and brought into harmony. However, there should be fewer changes at each rehearsal as the players adapt themselves little by little to the outline which they will follow at a finished performance.

Each player should strive, moreover, to translate his inner feelings about the character he has become for the charade with the greatest possible economy. Simple gestures are the most telling, while a complex series of detailed actions will often confuse and dismay the audience.

Remember that when pantomiming, you are playing not only for yourself, but also for an audience with whom you wish to share the intimate emotions you feel.

One way to make sure that the audience clearly reads your actions, your attitudes or poses is to turn either your face or your back directly to them, rather than your profile.

A slow pace will help to make the gestures pointed as well as meaningful. However, speed is relative, and you cannot perform all your motions at the same rate. Your important motions, performed slowly, will stand out against the background of your faster, less important actions. Besides, the general pace of your performance should change as the action progresses. Like a passage of music, it may start slowly, work up speed as the climax approaches, and then slow down again. This or a different pattern will hold true for each sequence. These rhythmic patterns must be worked out in relation to each individual character and his actions and also in relation to any group action.

However, all the tricks in the pantomimer's book will be wasted if you forget the primary quality of a good mime: sincerity. Exaggerate each action, but beware of too-easy grimaces and too-obvious gestures. They will not fool your audience for a minute.

STAGING TECHNIQUES

It is traditional to present a pantomime with the greatest possible seriousness, no matter how humorous it may be.

A musical background is helpful. It emphasizes the pantomime and enriches the atmosphere. The rhythm must be delicate, for if it is too pronounced, the actors will unconsciously follow it and turn the pantomime into a sort of dance.

The decor should be sketchy. It must not call attention to itself by being more realistic than the pantomime.

The same thing is true of the costumes, which should be simple, workable, and designed to underline the gestures, walking and motions. Avoid ridiculous effects. Long skirts or billowing pants

31

hide a play of the legs. Also, do not costume all the players in skin-tight costumes.

As for accessories, "Neither too many nor too few" is the rule. It is not necessary to lose ten minutes in making the audience understand that you are opening an umbrella when you can use a real one, especially if the umbrella itself is unimportant to the action. A real struggle with an umbrella might be enhanced by "using" an imaginary umbrella.

Remember, however, that style is one thing, the liveliness of the performance is another. Talent is like elegance—it is not real unless it goes unnoticed! So, use accessories or props if they are necessary, but make sure they do not cloud the poetic art of the pantomime, and do not confuse them with the props of a circus clown.

Lighting for a pantomime is a different story. In view of the stripped-down stage settings, costumes and props of all kinds, lighting plays a very important role in pantomime.

You can get excellent lighting even with humble means, provided that the sources are well placed and easily controlled. You can light from direct front or silhouette the players against the source of light. Light up from below or down from above, spotlight from a single source, or diffuse the stage with soft-hued light. All the many possibilities of stage lighting are possible and recommended only if they *serve* the action of the pantomime and the actors themselves.

Section 2

This amusing stunt will teach you to use all of your faculties for expressing a particular action or mood. Once you see that you need only to use freely those faculties which you *already have,* there will be no stopping you!

Players stand in a circle. The leader then reads the following movements which express certain actions and attitudes. Players then act them out in pantomime. The leader can greatly assist by first showing his own exaggerated version.

1. Say with your palm, "Stop!" (raise palm up and outward)
2. Say with your head, "Yes." (nod head)
3. Say with your shoulder, "I bumped the door." (bump shoulder vigorously against imaginary door)
4. Say with your eyes, "I don't understand." (raise eyebrows and blink eyes in bewilderment)

5. Say with your foot, "I'm waiting." (keep heel down, tap toes against floor impatiently)

6. Say with your ear, "I hear a songbird." (tilt ear upward and look up sideways)

7. Say with your waist, "I'm dancing." (sway hips)

8. Say with your jaw, "I'm surprised." (suddenly drop jaw)

9. Say with your tongue (no words), "I like this cake." (roll tongue around lips)

10. Say with your finger, "Come here." (beckon coyly with finger)

11. Say with your arms, "I'm running." (wildly churn arms as if running)

12. Say with your fingertips, "This potato is hot!" (touch imaginary potato, jerk away from it)

13. Say with your nose, "I smell fresh pie." (sniff in appreciation)

14. Say with your chest, "I'm relaxed." (take a deep, relaxing breath)

15. Say with your legs, "I'm slipping!" (slip, but catch yourself before falling)

ADD AND ACT

Here is pantomime fun for the entire group. The play leader starts things off by making a movement of any kind, such as shaking his left knee. The group must imitate the movement. The leader then makes a second motion, perhaps that of nodding his head. The group then performs both movements in order. The leader continues new actions without repeating those that went before, and the players must add the new action to the series. The fun lasts for as long as players can remember the actions in the right order, beginning with the first one.

IMITATIONS

Four players leave the room. The others (two or more) decide upon a fairly simple pantomime movement, such as setting a dinner table or planting a garden. The first of the four players, A, returns to the room where a member of the group acts out the selected pantomime for him. Player B then returns to the room where he witnesses the pantomime as imitated by player A. Next, player B acts it out for returning player C, then C repeats it for player D. At the end, let the original player act it out a second time. It is interesting to see how the original act has become distorted by the time it gets to the last imitator.

Try this stunt several times.

SWEET PANTOMIMES

In sweet pantomimes, each performer portrays a rich food or ingredient. A player assigned to *frosting* could pretend to frost a cake; a player could reveal *coconut* by pretending to climb a tree to pick a coconut. The game leader can assign the following:

1. frosting
2. coconut
3. syrup
4. pudding
5. taffy
6. spice
7. sugar
8. jam
9. cake
10. chocolate
11. vanilla
12. marshmallow
13. jelly
14. pie
15. doughnut
16. mint
17. honey
18. molasses
19. cookie
20. ice cream

YES AND NO PANTOMIMES

The game leader asks a series of questions on a level with the knowledge of the players. (See samples below.) The questions should be of the kind that can be answered either *yes* or *no*. Before each question the leader gives instructions, such as, "If the answer is *yes*, raise your left arm; if the answer is *no*, do nothing," or, "If the answer is *yes,* pat your head; if the answer is *no,* do nothing." A different movement should be requested with each question. Players must answer questions quickly without stopping to puzzle out the answer. If a player acts when he should do nothing, or if he does nothing when he should act, he drops out of the play. The final player wins the stunt. Sample questions:

1. Is the dime smaller than a nickel? (yes)
2. Does the sun rise in the west? (no)
3. Is *d* the third letter of the alphabet? (no)
4. Is Nevada one of our fifty states? (yes)
5. Is *re* a higher note than *do?* (yes)

ANIMAL ACTIONS

Players are secretly assigned the names of animals. In turn they act out the characteristic movements of these animals while the other players try to identify them. Players should be reminded that they may act out the sounds—such as the barking of a dog or the roaring of a lion—but they must do so in silence.

The listed animals (with obvious suggested actions) are especially suitable for this beginning stunt.

1. tiger (pace, growl)
2. beaver (swim, chew imaginary tree)
3. monkey (leap, scratch)
4. horse (gallop, buck)
5. bear (waddle, hug)
6. rabbit (hop, munch)
7. goat (charge, ram)
8. lion (roar, claw)
9. dog (bark, sit up)
10. kangaroo (hold limp paws, hop)
11. squirrel (dart, crack nuts)

12. seal (swim, flap fins)
13. wolf (howl, slink)
14. crocodile (swim, snap teeth)
15. gorilla (strut, beat chest)
16. bull (snort, paw ground)
17. cat (lap milk, curl up)
18. deer (tilt head, race lightly off)

PRODUCTS IN PANTOMIME

Each player selects one of the well-known products listed below. Then he acts out a scene in pantomime in which he uses the product in some way.

1. glass	11. copper
2. sponge	12. wool
3. tin	13. feathers
4. leather	14. gold
5. silk	15. aluminum
6. oil	16. cotton
7. lumber	17. ivory
8. iron	18. lead
9. cork	19. fur
10. rubber	20. silver

The audience attempts to guess the product. As soon as it is correctly identified, another performer goes onstage.

MR. MUSCLEMAN

An announcer introduces a performer as "Mr. Muscleman, the world-famous expert on physical culture." The announcer explains that Mr. Muscleman is here to lead the group in some physical exercises which will develop mighty muscles for all.

As Mr. Muscleman strides powerfully onstage (flexing his arm muscles) the announcer continues, "For the first exercise Mr. Muscleman will show you how to develop and expand the muscles in the lower part of your upper left elbow. Please do exactly as does Mr. Muscleman!" The performer then makes a number of nonsensical movements as if exercising his elbow, such as jerking it swiftly up and down or spinning his elbow in a circle. The audience imitates his peculiar actions.

The announcer then calls out other sensible or strange exercises which are illustrated by Mr. Muscleman and imitated by the audience. The performer can lead the audience, for example, in wriggling ears, shaking a foot back and forth, and in exercising the jaw muscles, nonverbally, of course. The stranger the action the better.

HOW IS THE WEATHER?

A player selects one of the weather conditions listed below. He acts it out as he crosses the stage, as if he were actually experiencing the weather condition. There are many ways in which each of the listed states of weather can be revealed through pantomime movement. For instance, the player experiencing hail could react as if struck by the icy pellets, while the performer caught in the thunderstorm could clap his hands over his ears while glancing upward.

The state of weather can be announced before or at the end of each act, or the audience can be left to guess.

1. hail
2. thunder
3. windy
4. foggy
5. clear and sunny
6. snowing lightly
7. heavy rain
8. tornado
9. icy and slippery
10. burning hot
11. lightning
12. blizzard
13. drizzle
14. freezing
15. hurricane
16. humid and sticky

BALANCED PANTOMIME GAME

All performers line up. Each balances a book on his head as the fun begins. The leader calls out the listed pantomime movements one at a time, and the players act them out with at least moderate speed. Those who lose their books during an action drop from the stunt. The last player to remain with a book on his head is crowned champion of the day. If players still remain by the time the list is completed the leader can start over again while calling for speedier movements.

1. Wave goodbye with both arms.
2. Lift hands overhead and lower them.

3. Take two steps forward.
4. Tickle both of your own ears.
5. Turn head to left and back again.
6. Stand on tiptoes for a moment.
7. Kick with right leg.
8. Shrug shoulders.
9. Stand on one leg for a moment.
10. Crouch and touch both knees.
11. Pantomime a hearty laugh.
12. Turn around twice.
13. Lean as far as possible to the left.
14. Walk heel-to-toe for five steps.
15. Bend knees and touch floor with both hands.

OPEN IT

In this guessing game the players pantomime the act of opening something, revealing to the audience the package by their actions—either by how they open it or what they do with the contents, or both.

Take a few minutes to practice your pantomime. Then come onstage, one at a time, and let the audience guess the object which you are opening. If necessary, a player can repeat his act once or twice.

1. package of flower seeds
2. safety pin
3. wallet
4. candy bar
5. can of paint
6. Chinese fortune cookie
7. watermelon
8. photograph album
9. bottle of catsup
10. walnut
11. letter
12. jar of glue
13. umbrella
14. box of crackers
15. package of cough drops
16. woman's purse
17. can of shoe polish
18. safe
19. jar of vitamins
20. package of butter
21. cupboard
22. box of stationery
23. jar of peanut butter
24. tool box
25. first aid kit
26. filing cabinet
27. package of cheese
28. sewing kit
29. doctor's bag
30. box of laundry soap

LOST AND FOUND

As many players as desired can take part in this comical pantomime stunt, although only two of them are onstage at a time.

The audience is told that the action takes place in the lost-
and-found department of a police station. At the start of the
performance a policeman (or policewoman) is on duty at a
desk. One by one the players come onstage to tell the officer
what has been lost. Describe the lost object by pantomime. Try
to find various actions that will describe the object, rather than
just one obvious action.

The audience continues to guess until it names the lost object
correctly. You can use the following items or make up your
own.

1. a toy balloon	16. a television aerial
2. a canoe	17. a pet goat
3. a railroad ticket	18. a penny
4. a dog collar	19. a towel
5. a blanket	20. a thermometer
6. a flashlight	21. a mirror
7. an anchor	22. a postage stamp
8. a flute	23. a clock
9. a can of sardines	24. an automobile tire
10. a door hinge	25. a cash register
11. a baby's bottle	26. a beehive
12. a bowl of goldfish	27. a mop
13. a mask	28. a king's crown
14. a puppet	29. a statue
15. a flag	30. a block of ice

SPELL IT

A pair of performers select a secret word. Start out by using
4-letter words. They take turns in acting out other words which
start with the letters in the secret word. If the secret word
happened to be *cake,* the first player could act out a word that
begins with the letter *c,* for example, *chair.* The other player
would then act out the second letter, *a.*

As each letter is guessed, someone writes it down on a blackboard or on a large sheet of paper. Before long the audience
will be ready to guess longer words.

FIND YOUR PARTNER

This is a lively pantomime stunt which can be used to form partners for other games. It is also fun for its own sake. The leader goes around the room and secretly assigns pantomime movements, giving the same movement to two players only. At a signal, everyone moves quickly about the room in the assigned manner. When a player sees another performing in a similar manner he knows he has found his partner. The partners then line up along the side of the room, while the others continue to act and seek. The first pair of players to make contact can be assigned to leading the next pantomime act.

THE TALKERS

A pair of performers face each other onstage. They talk to each other in pantomime, varying their gestures, body actions and facial expressions. A speaker's mouth may move as if talking, but of course he must not make sounds.

The talkers try to reveal to the audience their subject of conversation. The audience watches their pantomime movements in an effort to guess what it is. The viewers continue to make guesses throughout the performance until the actors inform them of a correct guess.

The selected topic should be one that offers a wide range of pantomime action. Here are fifteen that will serve the purpose:

1. clothing	9. the sea
2. airplanes	10. candy
3. the weather	11. school
4. music	12. jewelry
5. sleep	13. the time
6. gardening	14. flowers
7. dancing	15. an athletic contest
8. money	

ODD GREETINGS

This one can be as funny as it is silly. The idea is for a pair of players to enter from opposite sides of the stage, walk toward each other, greet one another in the oddest and funniest fashion they can think of, and then walk off. To make the stunt more comical, perform it very soberly, if you can. The leader pairs off all the players, who are then allowed a few minutes to work up their pantomime greetings. Here are a few suggestions which will help to spark off ideas:

1. Greet by clasping hands, then turning around in circles several times with hands still clasped.

2. Play patty-cake.

3. Bow and curtsy with greatly exaggerated respect as if they were mighty monarchs.

4. Pretend to stamp on each other's foot several times.

5. Twist left ears and then the right.

6. Brush off each other, using fingers as brush.

7. Place soles of right shoes together, shake up and down as if feet were in a handshake.

8. Do arm and leg exercises in unison, end with handshake.

9. Player A holds arm out near floor while player B jumps over it, followed by A jumping over B's arm.

10. Players touch forearms and elbows and shake them up and down.

CATCHY PANTOMIMES

A pair of players face each other onstage, several yards apart. They pantomime the act of tossing and catching an object, while the viewers try to guess the object. The players toss and catch in ways which reveal what it is. For instance, if it were an elephant, players could pat it, make a great show of strength when trying to pick it up, and stagger when catching it.

WHO WANTS WHAT?

Two players take the stage. One of them makes pantomimed requests of the other, and the other answers it. The audience tries to guess who wants what. Both actors contribute toward making the requests clear.

1. Man wants to borrow money from reluctant banker.
2. Young man wants girl to accept his marriage proposal.
3. Son wants help with his homework from father.
4. Salesman wants to sell vacuum cleaner to customer.
5. Mother wants child to study music lesson.
6. Backseat driver tries to command actual driver.
7. Frantic man wants fireman to save his home.
8. Employee wants raise from employer.
9. Woman orders fancy style from hairdresser.
10. Sergeant wants soldier to march properly.
11. Lawyer wants to persuade judge.
12. Child wants mother to buy candy.
13. Customer wants to buy automobile at lower price.
14. Motorist tries to talk policeman out of traffic ticket.
15. Wife wants tired husband to fix leaky faucet.

YOU ARE!

You now have had some experience in expressing yourself without using your voice. Here is one feeling at a time for you to imaginatively portray.

1. You are *happy* while playing catch.
2. You are *hungry* for lunch.
3. You are *surprised* at receiving a birthday present.
4. You are *sad* after dropping a glass.
5. You are *tired* after playing hard.
6. You are *puzzled* over a strange sound.
7. You are *cheerful* as you sweep the floor.
8. You are *peaceful* as you see the blue sky.
9. You are *not interested* in a television program.
10. You are *wondering* at your dog's disappearance.
11. You are *sleepy* as you go to bed.
12. You are *cold* as you stand in the snow.
13. You are *hot* as you stand in the sun.
14. You are *gay* as you hear peppy music.
15. You are *excited* over a ball game.

BEST MAN WINS

This stunt starts with two players standing alongside each other onstage. A third player is the director and he asks them to assume an emotional mood, perhaps that of *shock* or *amazement*. The player giving the most effective expression of the mood, in the opinion of the director, remains onstage, while the other player is replaced by the director, who becomes the next performer. These two compete by assuming another emotion, perhaps that of *joy* or *confusion*. Once more the best man in the opinion of the new director (a fourth player), wins. The competition continues for as long as necessary in order to give each actor and actress an opportunity to be director and player.

The audience can help with the stunt by suggesting to the director the various emotions to be acted out by the competing couples.

ACTION BELOW

Here is good body movement practice as well as fun. Two assistants hold a sheet in front of the performer (who can be seated or standing) at a height which reveals only his or her legs. The actor then performs one of the listed actions or one which he thinks up for himself, and the audience tries to guess what is going on.

1. Jumping rope.
2. Diving.
3. Boxing.
4. Kicking a football.
5. Driving a car.
6. Doing knee bends.
7. Waiting in line.
8. At bat in baseball.
9. Putting a golf ball.
10. Playing hopscotch.
11. Crossing a stream on rocks.
12. Walking on deck of ship in storm.
13. Watching a movie.
14. Eating dinner.
15. Cutting toenails.
16. Eating at a lunch counter.
17. Listening to music.
18. Holding hands.

MIXED EMOTIONS

The audience takes part in this stunt. Two performers come on-stage. One of them silently acts out one of the paired words listed below, while the other performer acts out the other word. The audience is told that the emotions that they are to guess are opposites, such as gay and sad. Some of them will be easy for the audience to guess, while others will make them think twice. If the viewers do not guess both emotions within a reasonable time, the actors exchange words with each other and act them out again.

1. gay and sad
2. calm and excited
3. interested and indifferent
4. frightened and confident
5. hot and cold
6. energetic and tired
7. friendly and angry
8. peaceful and worried
9. certain and puzzled
10. relaxed and tense
11. nonchalant and surprised
12. fascinated and bored

MOVING AROUND

Each performer is allowed about one minute in which to move around in a circle in as many different ways as possible. For instance, a player might skip, stumble, run. The player with the cleverest performance might be awarded a prize. The instructor can assist his group to get the idea by reading aloud the following types of movement: skip, stumble, run, fall, trip, walk slow motion, slide, dance, tiptoe, stamp, hop, leap, jump backward, side-step, waddle, walk apelike, walk stiff-legged, walk heel-to-toe, crawl on hands and knees.

IN THE DARK

The idea is for a performer to pretend that he is groping in the dark. Actually he can see where he is going but he pretends to stumble, to bump into things and so forth. Each player thinks up two separate things to do—or that happen to him. Practice by closing your eyes while you perform the action, to feel what it is like to actually do it in the dark. They need not necessarily be funny events, but they should be as interesting as possible.

The audience is told whether the act is taking place indoors or outdoors. Here are good examples of both:

1. He bumps into a door and bangs his nose.
2. He falls into a swimming pool.
3. He finds his coat and puts it on upside-down.
4. He plunges his hand into a sticky pie.
5. He stubs his toe on a cat which he picks up and pets.
6. He tries to thread a needle but misses by a foot.
7. He tries to eat but misses his mouth constantly.
8. He bumps into a freshly painted wall.
9. He tries to iron clothes.
10. He turns on the water sprinkler and gets wet.

The actor performs his actions as clearly as possible. When he finishes, the audience tries to guess what they were. Sometimes this is the most laughable part of the act.

CROSS-COUNTRY

Make your movements as definite and informative as possible as you try this stunt.

A player crosses from one side of the stage to the other, pretending to meet and overcome two separate obstacles or perils. The obstacles are those one might meet while hiking or riding through the countryside. A player may make up his own obstacles or use the suggestions listed below.

As an actor finishes, the play director leads the observers in a brief review of the performance. They try to guess the pair of acted-out obstacles.

1. Jump over a high fence.

2. Wade through a waist-high stream.
3. Trudge exhausted through deep sand.

4. Run up a steep hill.
5. Fight your way through thick woods.

6. Climb over boulders.
7. Slip and slide on ice.

48

snow.

g a narrow mountain trail.
r low-hanging trees.

your class that is _n_
nt to the department
_n_ stating that you will

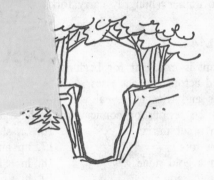

_t_, please check with t'
not, please tell the st _ent rapids._
m Audit to Credit _tree across a deep ravine._

GOING PLACES

As a player crosses the stage he reveals that he is going to a particular place. He does this by actions and attitudes which are in keeping with his destination, and he can add to his art by wearing or carrying an object which is associated with his destination. For instance, a player going to bed could sleepily rub his eyes and carry a clock.

The narrator may introduce a series of stunts by saying: "We are about to see a number of folks who are going places. Let's try to find out where they are going." Players may then cross the stage one after another with only a brief pause between each. As soon as a player exits the narrator might say something like: "That was Sleepyhead Sam—looks like *he's* going to *bed*."

Players can work out their own destinations or use the listed ones.

1. to bed (sleepily carry clock)
2. to work (briskly carry brief case)
3. to the beach (gaily bounce beach ball)
4. to a wedding (mischievously open box of rice)
5. to a picnic (bouncily carry picnic basket)
6. to a fire (quickly drag hose)
7. to school (happily carry books)
8. to church (solemnly carry prayer book)
9. to a party (humorously wear comic hat)
10. to dinner (hungrily carry fork)

WHERE AM I?

This stunt is excellent for beginners, but just as much fun for advanced actors and actresses. A player selects one of the listed locations and tries to reveal where he is to the audience. The act may be serious or comical, or perhaps a mixture of both.

1. in a submarine	16. on shipboard
2. on roof	17. up an apple tree
3. in a gold mine	18. in a kitchen
4. on parade	19. in a courtroom
5. in a jewelry store	20. in the hospital
6. in a bank	21. on a picnic
7. in a zoo	22. in the desert
8. in a printing shop	23. on a space ship
9. in a lighthouse	24. in an aquarium
10. in a theater	25. in a closet
11. on a train	26. in a shoe shop
12. in a café	27. in a taxi
13. in a museum	28. behind a ticket booth
14. in a library	29. in a canoe
15. in a fire station	30. on a mountaintop

TRAVELERS

A player pantomimes the act of traveling in a particular manner and the audience tries to guess the method of travel. Make your act interesting as well as informative. What happens if your raft has too much weight on one side? If the roller coaster gets stuck at the top of a hill?

1. elephant-back
2. raft
3. covered wagon
4. tractor
5. motorized lawn mower
6. diving bell
7. roller coaster
8. helicopter
9. camel-back
10. elevator
11. speedboat
12. dog sled
13. ski lift
14. merry-go-round
15. basket of balloons

DO ANYTHING!

A player stands before the rest of the group. A number of people in the audience shout out letters of the alphabet. The performer does not tell which letter he has selected, and pantomimes actions which start with one of the letters called. For instance, if the letter is *w* the actor could walk, whirl, wriggle, and whisper. For the letter *g* he could grin, grab, gulp, and gargle. He can do anything he likes as long as the acts start with the same letter. The audience may guess an act, without guessing the letter. The player continues to perform acts until the letter is guessed.

TELEVISION PANTOMIMES

There is no better way to start learning the art of pantomime than this. It is a method that can be used by anyone for building both self-confidence and dramatic skill.

The actor or actress sits on a chair in the middle of the stage, facing the audience. He pretends that he is watching television by acting out facial expressions and making gestures that he might experience if he were actually watching a program.

Exaggeration will help you draw out fully your powers of self-expression, help you to realize how much emotion you really have inside, ready for release to the outside. Also, a broad expression helps the audience recognize clearly the *kind* of feeling which you are supposed to be experiencing. Start your performance while seated, but leap up on occasion and go through any movements that will make the action *look* exciting. Let yourself go when expressing laughter or surprise or any other emotion.

For the first time around, each performer should demonstrate a wide variety of reactions as he pretends to watch television. For the second round, each performer selects one of the listed types of programs and responds accordingly. Players should be allowed sufficient time for thinking over and planning their pantomimes. Here are various television programs calling for specific reactions.

1. mystery show
2. Western
3. weather report
4. political speech
5. comedy show
6. love and romance
7. spy thriller
8. travel film
9. news report
10. dancing instruction
11. cartoon show
12. quiz contest
13. animal adventure
14. football game
15. detective show
16. inspirational sermon
17. children's program
18. band music
19. baseball game
20. space-travel film

PURSES AND POCKETS

You can never tell what strange things you will find in a woman's purse or a man's pocket—especially in this pantomime stunt.

An actress stands onstage and withdraws all sorts of odd and startling things from her purse. (She may set her purse down after each withdrawal in order to free both hands for pantomime action.) An actor does likewise by withdrawing objects from his pockets. The more out-of-place the objects, the more interesting your act will be.

Here are enough ideas to get performers off to a good start.

1. Withdraw cake and knife, slice a piece, replace cake and knife, eat slice.

2. Withdraw bow and arrows, fire a few shots, carefully replace bow.

3. Withdraw a typewriter, set it on table (a real table may be used as a stage property), type a letter, seal it, pretend to drop it in mailbox, replace typewriter in purse or pocket.

4. Withdraw telephone, dial, talk excitedly for a few seconds, hang up and replace phone.

5. Withdraw salad vegetables, dressing, seasonings, and a bowl, prepare and eat salad, replace items in purse or pocket.

DISGUISES

This pantomime stunt for a large group will test your ability to disguise your identity as well as offer you acting practice. Half the players go off by themselves to put on clothing for disguising themselves. All items should be simple to put on and wear, such as overcoats, veils, and hats. The boys can change jackets to create confusion.

One at a time the players cross the stage in view of the

other group, each performer in disguised movements, as well as clothing. The audience tries to identify players as they cross. As soon as all the players have been recognized the other group goes off to disguise themselves. The degree of difficulty in identification will depend on the age group, the costumes available, and the cleverness of the performers.

HANDY PANTOMIMES

Each player performs one of the listed actions while the others try to guess what is being done. Although hands and arms are the principal means of expression other faculties should also be used. The purpose of this performance is *clarity of action*. It contributes to clarity to have players briefly bow their heads just before and just after their performances; otherwise the viewers will think that the exits and entrances are part of the act.

1. Paste stamp on letter.
2. Open and close door.
3. Pick up and dial telephone.
4. Feed crumbs to birds.
5. Sail a glider.
6. Cut paper with scissors.
7. Clean a window.
8. Trim a hedge with large shears.
9. Open drawer, remove object, close drawer.
10. Play marbles.
11. Balance a stick on palm.
12. Place sheet in typewriter and type.
13. Take books from shelf, replace them.
14. Play a piano.

15. Fill glass from pitcher or faucet, drink.
16. Pick up and pet cat.
17. Hang a picture on wall.
18. Unscrew light bulb, replace it with new one.
19. Wind up and toss a toy top.
20. Select key from ring, unlock door.
21. Attach flag to rope, raise it.
22. Set nail on box, hammer it in.
23. Polish both shoes.
24. Take coins from pocket, count and replace them.
25. Wrap a package.
26. Adjust a television picture.
27. Catch and reel in a fish.
28. Dab brush in paint, paint a picture.
29. Lower bucket into a well, pull it up.
30. Briefly read several pages of a newspaper.
31. Pick up telescope, peer in several directions.
32. Play a trombone.
33. Pick up rug, shake and replace it.
34. Slice cake, eat a piece.
35. Trim a tree with Christmas ornaments.
36. Set a dinner table.
37. Sharpen a pencil, write.
38. Hang clothes on line.
39. Fly a kite, pull it in all the way.
40. Place saddle and bridle on a horse.

THE LATEST FASHIONS

With a bit of imagination, you can have a hilarious pantomime show that will run for at least ten or fifteen minutes. A dozen or more performers can model their fashions, one after another.

Help the players develop the pantomime movements into a humorous routine, using startling poses, awkward steps and funny facial expressions.

The costumes should be as peculiar as possible. Here are some suggestions:

1. A coat worn backward.
2. A cereal box with a feather on it as a lady's hat.
3. An actor made up as a visitor from outer space.
4. A skirt made from newspapers.
5. Two male actors sharing a large coat.
6. Boots worn with a party frock.
7. A ripped and shabby suit.
8. A dress decorated with real leaves.
9. A paper bag mask with holes cut out for seeing.
10. A suit with imitation paper money pinned all over.
11. A grocery carton worn as a short coat.
12. A ghost costume consisting of an old white sheet with eye holes cut out.
13. A mixed uniform, such as Indian feathers and a policeman's badge.
14. A woman's hat and a man's coat.
15. Shoes worn on the hands.
16. A beautiful dress with a witchlike mask.

17. An actress carrying as a handbag a cardboard grocery carton.

18. A suit or dress with newspaper headlines pinned all over.

19. Actors with long beards.

20. A costume representing an animal or bird.

An announcer can introduce each performer just before he or she enters. The announcement should contribute to the player's act, so have the announcer think up and rehearse his witty comments beforehand.

If music is available, suitable selections could be played in the background.

THE WISHING WELL

Clever actors and actresses can build this idea into a highly entertaining pantomime stunt. As a stage property, a model of a well (wooden or cardboard) is set in the center of the stage. A sign identifies it as the WISHING WELL. One by one the actors enter and make their wishes before the well, then reach down to get whatever the well produces. The objects taken from the well are imaginary and are revealed to the audience by means of pantomime.

The actor's role is divided into two parts:

1. Letting the Wishing Well (and the audience, too) know exactly what is wanted.

2. Getting and revealing the actual gift obtained from the well.

As an example, a player could enter, shabbily dressed, and hold an empty wallet or pocket toward the well, thus making it clear that he wants money. He then reaches down in great expectation, grasps the gift, looks at it in astonishment, shrugs goodnaturedly, then peels and eats his gift—a banana.

The main idea is to turn everything that comes from the well into a laugh or a surprise. In the case of very young or inexperienced performers, the objects taken from the well can be real.

SECRET WISHES

Players can act out secret desires for others to guess. The more comical they are and the further from the character who is dreaming, the more entertainment they will give the audience. For example, a timid old lady secretly wishes to be a circus acrobat. You can use the listed subjects or think up your own.

1. To pick money off trees.
2. To be a circus acrobat.
3. To catch a fish twelve feet long.
4. To fly like a bird.
5. To become a king or queen.
6. To haunt a house.
7. To ride in a flying saucer.
8. To be ten feet tall.
9. To eat pies one after another.
10. To become a powerful orator.
11. To rock a crying baby to sleep.
12. To become a fortuneteller.
13. To catch your own shadow.
14. To own a pet gorilla.
15. To walk on the ocean floor.
16. To become a famous actor (or actress).
17. To live at the North Pole.
18. To find buried treasure.
19. To be a great lover.
20. To be adrift at sea on a raft.

BUILD THE MOOD

This is to help beginning players become flexible in expressing moods and emotions. The performers line up onstage. The play director stands before them and calls out a mood, such as one of those listed below. He then calls out the numbers *one, two,* and *three,* slowly and in order. These numbers indicate the strength of the mood which the players are to express. Number *one* means that they should express it only mildly; number *two* asks them to increase it to a mood of medium strength; on *three* they must express the feeling as strongly as possible.

After several emotions have been expressed in sequence, the director can suddenly shift from one emotion to another and from one strength to another. He might call out, "Humor, *three!*" then ask for, "Surprise, *one!*" This jumping around to various emotions and strengths is the kind of practice which builds an actor's alertness and flexibility.

Before the stunt begins, divide the class into two groups. First, group A goes on stage while group B observes, then vice versa. The observers can gain practical help by watching the onstage players closely.

1. humor
2. surprise
3. doubt
4. delight
5. shock
6. sorrow
7. curiosity
8. timidity
9. reverence
10. boredom
11. dislike
12. confusion
13. cunning
14. pride
15. disappointment
16. innocence
17. dreaminess
18. weariness
19. attention
20. contentment

LOOK AT ME!

Everyone likes to look at himself in the mirror. And everyone likes to look at someone looking at himself!

The stage is set with a large wood or cardboard frame that supposedly contains a mirror. The announcer informs the audience, "A mirror has been placed in the hall of a home and several guests are arriving for dinner. Let's see what happens as the guests come down the hall."

As the announcer exits, the fun begins. One after another, the guests walk down the hall and notice the mirror. Each stops and performs in front of it, then passes offstage at the opposite wing.

Here are some ideas that will give the stunt a comical start:

1. A boy feels and admires his arm muscles. He does a few exercises and takes several strong-man poses. He pats himself on the back with great admiration and struts proudly offstage.

2. A girl enters wearing a hat and carrying a large handbag. She looks doubtfully at her hat and tries to adjust it to a better position on her head. She frowns in disappointment and removes the hat. One by one she takes several other hats from her handbag and tries them on. She sighs in disappointment, replaces her original hat and exits.

3. A boy enters and notices the mirror. He comes close, peers intently at it for a moment, then leaps back and throws up his hands in horror at what he sees. He snaps his fingers as he gets an idea, then pulls a monster-mask from his pocket and puts it on. He again looks into the mirror, nods his head and rubs his hands in satisfaction, and happily walks away.

4. A girl enters wearing a rose on her dress. As she looks in the mirror, she wonders whether it might look better in another place. She holds it up to several places, including her hair, ear, waist and shoulder. She finally places the stem in her clenched teeth, nods in approval exits.

5. A boy enters and notices that his necktie is slightly out of place. But when he tries to straighten it out, it gets even worse. Each attempt to make it look better only makes it look worse. At one time the tie hangs down his back. He finally takes the ends of the tie, holds them out in front, and leads himself offstage.

PANTOMIME MARCH

This march takes place without any of the marchers moving far from the spot. As the directions are given by the leader, the marchers move their legs up and down, and turn as directed, but they never go more than a few feet away.

Short and simple routines will be best for younger players, while older ones may work out longer and more complex movements. With a bit of practice this can be an effective stunt. Accompanying music will add to your performance.

Here are a few ideas for marching which will get your group off to a start.

1. March in step
2. High step
3. Left foot only
4. Right foot only
5. Left turn
6. Right turn
7. About face
8. March on every other beat
9. Stand at attention
10. Clap in rhythm
11. Salute audience
12. Alternate marchers turn right, salute
13. Other alternate marchers turn left, face partner, salute
14. Swing arms
15. March in little circles
16. March in one-step squares
17. Dip knees every third step
18. Alternate marchers circle partners
19. Single line facing audience
20. Exit holding salute to audience

PANTOMIME PARADE

Players enter and exit, one after another, while pantomiming persons and animals which might be seen in or around a parade. Peppy music can be played in the background. An announcer can name the character as the actor reaches the middle of the stage. Here are suggested entries in your pantomime parade:

1. parade marshal
2. drum major, majorette
3. musicians
4. horses
5. trick dog and master
6. clowns, comics
7. dancers
8. policeman
9. popcorn and peanut salesmen
10. balloon salesmen
11. animal mascots and masters
12. local heroes and leading citizens
13. soldiers, sailors, airmen
14. Boy Scouts, Girl Scouts
15. sign carriers
16. elves, goblins, ghosts
17. athletes
18. cowboys
19. Indians
20. dragons
21. stunt marchers
22. beauty queens
23. organ grinder and monkey
24. magician
25. folks with exhibits and displays

MECHANICAL MARCHERS

This is an idea which younger children will enjoy. March about like mechanical dolls and toy soldiers, with short stiff steps and making sharp body movements and turns. Keep your faces solemn and expressionless.

This will be more effective if performed in rhythm with march music.

DREAMY DANCERS

Anyone who can perform this stunt with a straight face will be very successful. A player dances onstage while whispering sweet sentiments to his or her partner. This doesn't sound so funny until you notice that the partner is a broom! Boy and girl performers alternate in coming onstage while waltzing and whispering in pantomime to the broom sweetheart. A performer can continue his act as long as he can make it amusing. Use all your pantomime skill to make a great show of gallantry and affection.

MUSICAL MOODS

Select a phonograph record (preferably a symphony) which includes several changes of mood and pace. Work out movements that will express these various moods. For example:

1. *Opening mood:* sit or lie about while reading, studying, quietly chatting.

2. *Awakening mood:* stand, stretch, look about for something active to do.

3. *Lively mood:* race about, play tag, laugh, shout.

4. *Restful mood:* grow tired, rub eyes, stretch, again lie down.

5. *Majestic mood:* march about in step, exit.

For other types of music, other actions are appropriate. After doing obvious, concrete motions to express the moods of the music, try doing rhythmic and symbolic movements to express the same moods. (See the Dance suggestions in Section 1, pp. 13–14.)

MUSICAL PANTOMIMES

Here is a fairly simple musical routine. Each actor goes through the motions of playing a musical instrument, while the others try to guess what it is. Some will be easy, while others may be moderately difficult. For group practice, the director can lead the players in pantomiming together.

See how many instruments you know.

1. saxophone	16. flute
2. cello	17. bugle
3. oboe	18. ukelele
4. bass drum	19. clarinet
5. banjo	20. bells
6. tuba	21. cornet
7. bagpipes	22. harp
8. guitar	23. violin
9. fife	24. xylophone
10. cymbals	25. piccolo
11. trumpet	26. accordion
12. snare drum	27. bassoon
13. organ	28. castanets
14. trombone	29. piano
15. French horn	30. bass viol

LIVING SONGS

A narrator reads aloud the words of a well-known song while two or more pantomimists in turn act out the song as a whole. Music can accompany the words and actions to give a more lively performance. For more humor and interest, try contrasting your actions with the meaning of the words. The listed songs and ballads are especially suitable for this stunt.

1. For He's a Jolly Good Fellow	8. Sailing
2. My Bonnie	9. The Old Oaken Bucket
3. When Johnny Comes Marching Home	10. Oh! Susanna
4. Good-By, My Lover, Good-By	11. Row, Row, Row Your Boat
5. Home, Sweet Home	12. Good Night, Ladies
6. Jeannie with the Light Brown Hair	13. Home on the Range
7. Tramp! Tramp! Tramp!	14. Oh, My Darling Clementine
	15. Pop! Goes the Weasel

ALL KINDS OF SONGS

A player pantomimes the act of singing a certain type of song. He does everything he can to express the nature and the mood of his song. While the stage properties may be real or imaginary, keep them imaginary if possible. The type of song may be announced beforehand or at the end of the act to the viewers, or they may try to guess it. Here are some suggestions that will lead you on to other kinds of songs.

1. Patriotic song.
2. Love song.
3. Indian song.
4. Sad song.
5. Cowboy song.
6. Operatic song.
7. Comic song.
8. Sea song.
9. Lullaby.
10. Christmas song.
11. Military song.
12. Sacred song.
13. Hawaiian song.
14. Winter song.
15. Spanish song.

THE SURPRISING SINGER

In this stunt one player pantomimes the act of singing while another person (or record) does the actual singing. The pantomime actor stands in front of a screen while the singer (or phonograph) remains hidden behind it. Find other ways than the few suggested below to build entertaining acts from this basic idea.

1. The hidden singer (or record player) suddenly changes the speed of the song, to the embarrassment and confusion of the pantomimist.

2. Several hidden singers take turns in singing, thus making it appear as if the pantomimist is capable of changing voices.

3. An actress stands before the audience, but an actor's voice comes from behind the screen.

4. The pantomimist bends low as the voice goes down and stretches on tiptoe as the pitch rises.

5. Several voices combine to make it appear as if the pantomimist is harmonizing with himself.

ALL SORTS OF SOUNDS

Another stunt with sounds is to go through the pantomimed act of producing a noise. Examples: for *tinkle* you can pretend to tap a spoon against a drinking glass, for *drip* you can turn off a faucet and cup your hand to hear the remaining drops, for *flutter* you can raise a flag and then listen to its motions in the wind.

1. tinkle	16. ring
2. drip	17. knock
3. flutter	18. zoom
4. pound	19. crash
5. slide	20. break
6. clap	21. tap
7. rip	22. scrape
8. scratch	23. crackle
9. boom	24. cut
10. crack	25. rub
11. shuffle	26. bounce
12. skid	27. pop
13. slam	28. squeak
14. shatter	29. roll
15. chop	30. blast

ADD THE SOUND

A player performs (and keeps performing) a pantomime action that would normally make a sound of some kind. As the viewers guess the act they imitate the sound that would normally go with it. The performer nods when the viewers have made the right sound. He can wave them on if they are close in guessing, or shake his head sadly when they are not. It is not too easy to imitate some of the sounds (such as that of shaking a rug), but this adds extra gaiety to the game.

1. groaning
2. firing a rifle
3. laughing
4. swimming
5. singing
6. shaking a rug
7. typing
8. tearing paper
9. hammering
10. popping a balloon
11. sawing
12. sneezing
13. cracking peanuts
14. gulping
15. pouring water
16. humming
17. filing metal
18. snoring
19. whispering
20. exploding dynamite

SCREAMS

This is a surprise act for the performers as well as the audience. Each time it has been performed properly it has caused everyone concerned to explode with laughter. A clever sound effects crew will help put it over with a bang.

The announcer tells the performers that they are about to discover a savage lion in the living room. Of course, anyone who comes upon the savage king of beasts is bound to scream. But, the announcer continues, the scream must be done in pantomime. No actual sounds should be uttered. The player must open his mouth and throw up his arms as if to scream, but—and here's the surprise—the actual sounds will be supplied half the time by a crew handling the sound effects!

One by one each player comes onstage, walks a few steps, opens an imaginary door and pretends to see the savage lion. Then he must pantomime the act of screaming wildly.

When he pretends to scream, the sound crew may or may not add the sound effect. Or, instead of a scream they may use all sorts of peculiar sounds. Here are examples: blow a whistle, crash pans together several times, pop a paper bag filled with air, rip a newspaper, ring a bell, play briefly and sharply on a musical instrument. The sound crew can also use their own voices by shrieking and howling, or even giggling.

Correct timing is important. At the instant that the player pantomimes his scream, the sound should be added, if there is going to be a sound. Alternately, if there is no sound, and the audience and player have just about given up expecting, then the sound crew may come through. Surprise all the time is what you are after.

VOICE SOUNDS

A performer pantomimes the act of making a vocal sound by making facial expressions and body movements which indicate it. The other players try to identify the sound he is making. After each player has performed, the leader may make suggestions for improvement. In this way you will build up your vocabulary of movement.

1. sigh	16. whisper
2. sneeze	17. gurgle
3. whistle	18. snore
4. choke	19. hum
5. shriek	20. snarl
6. growl	21. sniff
7. shout	22. chuckle
8. laugh	23. cry
9. breathe	24. groan
10. sing	25. pant
11. cough	26. gasp
12. smack	27. giggle
13. gulp	28. snort
14. swallow	29. bark
15. blow	30. sputter

LAUGH ACT

The actor who performs this pantomime has but one thing to do
—to laugh silently in as many ways as he can. The performer
comes on stage, faces the audience, and takes a piece of paper
from his pocket on which a joke is supposed to be written. He
reads the joke—and starts laughing at it! A clever actor can make
the audience howl with delight by going through hilarious actions
himself. Build up the laugh from a chuckle to a belly laugh and
finish by collapsing from merriment, rolling on the floor, kicking
your legs, drying your eyes or wringing out your handkerchief.
The champion performer is one whose audience laughs more than
he does!

SCIENTIFIC SPEECHES

A player selects one of the sciences listed below. He then
pantomimes a speech on the subject. The audience tries to guess
the particular science. A player pantomiming the science of
botany might act as if he were planting and pruning bushes,
while the chemist could pretend to mix and test a formula.

1. botany
2. chemistry
3. astronomy
4. geology
5. medicine
6. zoology
7. archaeology
8. engineering
9. agriculture
10. oceanography

DESCRIPTIONS

In this pantomime game, a player is to describe a famous person from history or fiction by his distinguishing characteristic. The viewers first try to guess the symbol of the pantomime (such as *tallness*) and then try to name the famous person who matches the description (such as *tall Abraham Lincoln*). Viewers may supply the name of any famous person who matches the description, not necessarily the example supplied below.

The group may use these examples for thinking up their own descriptions.

1. A tall man. (Abraham Lincoln)
2. A soldier. (George Washington)
3. A sleep man. (Rip Van Winkle)
4. An orator. (Patrick Henry)
5. A small man. (Napoleon)
6. A writer. (William Shakespeare)
7. A detective. (Sherlock Holmes)
8. A worried man. (Jonah)
9. A king. (King Arthur)
10. A strong man. (Samson)

BUILD IT

Pantomime the building of the listed items. A bit of thinking, and you will build a clever act out of this. A player can make his act clear by showing the kinds of materials used, by pantomime shape and size, and by showing uses. Also, what problems might you run into as you build these items?

1. clay vase
2. doghouse
3. kite
4. picture frame
5. wooden fence
6. bookcase
7. dress
8. paper glider
9. weather vane
10. necklace
11. brick wall
12. comic mask
13. mailbox
14. belt
15. fishing pole

STRANGE SPEECHES

A player pantomimes the act of giving a rousing speech. The more bounce, enthusiasm and energy he puts into his act the better!

A performer should be given a brief spoken introduction, such as, "And here is Jerry Wilson who will speak on the topic, *How to Fly a Kite in a Closet.*" A prize might be awarded to the best—that is, to the most enthusiastic—performer. Players may think up their own topics or may select a listed one.

1. How to Fly a Kite in a Closet
2. My Cold Trip to the North Pole
3. What I Think About Spaghetti
4. How to Stand on Your Head
5. Famous Cowboys of the West
6. Washing Dishes Can Be Fun
7. How to Blow Soap Bubbles
8. Why I Like to Climb Trees
9. Build Your Own Airplane
10. Strange Facts about Alligators
11. How to Make a Cabbage Salad
12. What Happened on My Last Birthday
13. The Funniest Story I Ever Heard
14. Keep an Elephant for a Pet
15. How to Carry Peanut Butter in Your Pocket

OCCUPATIONS

It would be a good idea to read aloud the listed occupations and permit each player to select the one he prefers. The more an occupation appeals to a player the more likely he is to succeed with it.

After everyone has given a solo pantomime, the leader may combine various players who can then work out a simple pantomime skit. Example: (a) The *airplane pilot* lands his craft in the field of the *farmer*. (b) The *farmer* telephones the *automobile mechanic* who repairs the plane. (c) The *mailman* enters and requests a ride from the *pilot*. (d) The *mailman* and the *pilot* take off together as the *farmer* and *automobile mechanic* wave goodbye.

1. fireman	31. airplane pilot
2. dressmaker	32. painter
3. truck driver	33. florist
4. automobile mechanic	34. cook
5. jeweler	35. scientist
6. teacher	36. soldier
7. farmer	37. sailor
8. telephone operator	38. surveyor
9. hairdresser	39. printer
10. lawyer	40. tailor
11. carpenter	41. train engineer
12. plumber	42. usher
13. artist	43. photographer
14. judge	44. editor
15. banker	45. dancer
16. musician	46. magician
17. doctor	47. weatherman
18. librarian	48. maid
19. typist	49. tourist guide
20. gardener	50. druggist
21. nurse	51. miner
22. bus driver	52. candy maker
23. barber	53. auctioneer
24. mailman	54. roofer
25. butcher	55. actor
26. saleslady	56. songwriter
27. electrician	57. ticket seller
28. grocery checker	58. fashion model
29. waiter	59. shoemaker
30. postal clerk	60. athletic coach

SILLY SIGHTS

Everyone thinks up a silly sight which he might have seen, such as those listed below. One after another the performers act them out, while the others try to guess what they are. The audience keeps guessing as the act is performed, while the actor nods either *yes* or *no* to the guesses.

1. A laughing rabbit
2. A motorcycle with six wheels
3. A cat that walks backward
4. A green sun
5. A swimming camel
6. A red dollar bill
7. A crying ostrich
8. A talking scarecrow
9. A book that can be eaten
10. A man as tall as a tree
11. A flying dog
12. A square football
13. A dancing spoon
14. A cloud in a closet
15. A walking pencil
16. A whale in a goldfish bowl
17. A rowboat on the desert
18. A horse only five inches tall
19. A purple pig
20. A railroad track made of sugar

BUY IT!

A player pantomimes the act of buying something. With a little thought, you can build a funny act by testing the product, dropping it, losing it, and so on. The player who buys perfume could grow more and more rapturous with it, sniff it, apply it to her elbows, drink it, pour it on her head, and so on.

Players should be allowed at least a few minutes to work out their acts. They can then be announced—for example, "Let's watch Miss Lucy Parker as she buys a bottle of perfume." Here are some items that will be interesting to purchase:

1. typewriter
2. tall lamp
3. gasoline-powered lawn-mower
4. bicycle
5. trombone
6. television set
7. derby hat
8. alarm clock
9. dictionary
10. oil painting
11. small automobile
12. long gloves
13. umbrella or parasol
14. toothbrush
15. automobile tire
16. portable sewing machine
17. set of dishes
18. diamond necklace
19. tank-type vacuum cleaner
20. evening gown
21. house paint
22. bouquet (corsage)
23. bathroom scale
24. riding boots
25. perfume
26. roller skates
27. basketball
28. fishing pole
29. earrings
30. garden hose

WHAT GAME AM I PLAYING?

Each player is assigned a game or sport. He reveals it by acting it out in pantomime. The following games will serve as suggestions.

1. golf
2. skating
3. soccer
4. long-distance run
5. tennis
6. high jump
7. basketball
8. croquet
9. water ski
10. football
11. broad jump
12. baseball
13. bowling
14. archery
15. badminton
16. handball
17. hurdle race
18. sprint
19. volley ball
20. speedboat race
21. ice hockey
22. javelin throw
23. skiing
24. table tennis
25. pole vault
26. discus throw
27. weight lifting
28. shot-put
29. dart throw
30. dodge ball

CHALLENGES

Here is a stunt which helps actors to think quickly. Four or five volunteers sit on the stage. Members of the audience think up a pantomime act and challenge a volunteer to perform it. The challengers should not be too difficult. A volunteer might be asked to imitate an animal or to show how a policeman directs traffic. The audience may call for a single performer or for several actors to perform at once.

GOOD TIMING ACT

This stunt will help you to estimate the length of time you are taking for your performance which will later keep you from running too long or too short. Here's how it goes: A player goes onstage to perform any kind of pantomime he likes within a time limit. The objective is for each player to plan his act so that it concludes just within the permitted length of time.

The period of time might be:
1. ten seconds
2. thirty seconds
3. one minute
4. two minutes

When a player has concluded his act the play director (armed with a watch with a second hand) informs him of the time he took so that next time the actor can shorten or lengthen his on-stage appearance.

It is important for you to build your awareness of the all-important factor of time, so that your act will not drag but will become more pointed.

CORRECTIONS

This is an idea which, if used with good judgment, can improve pantomime performances. After an actor or actress has gone through a pantomime, the leader asks any two observers to comment upon the act. The observers should only make comments that will help the performer to improve himself, not just give a general opinion, such as, "The act was good, but it could have been better." A comment like "I would have taken off my shoes to give the idea that I was swimming" is more constructive. Performers, too, should be ready to give and take this kind of criticism. That is what builds topnotch actors and actresses.

PEAK PERFORMANCE

This dramatic stunt will prove an important point about the art of acting—that it is largely the performer who makes a scene as good as it is. Even a mediocre scene will become interesting when the actor spices it with his skill and personality.

Select a pantomime scene from this section that calls for a single actor. Choose one that takes no more than 30 or 40 seconds to complete. Next, have everyone in the group take turns acting it out while the others observe. Every actor and actress will perform a bit differently, and the differences will be what make the same scene interesting.

The leader or director can point out the best features of various players. This helps everyone to become aware of a peak performance when they see one. This does not mean that one player should try to copy another, but rather learn the little differences between a mediocre act and a topnotch one. Every actor will turn in a better performance by discovering what *is* better.

Section 3

Pantomime Skits

In this section you will find not only skits but also suggestions for creating your own skits. Also, refer back to Section 1 for more hints on how to prepare and present pantomime skits. The rules of pantomime apply to all the skits here, and no lines need to be memorized, but some rehearsal will be necessary for top performance. The narrator (when a narrator is called for) can read his lines.

The following chart of stage positions will help you more clearly to direct the performance of others or to find your own stage positions. Use this guide whenever you need to establish or change a position on stage. All positions are given from the viewpoint of the actor as he faces the audience. In olden days, the back part of the stage was higher than the front, and the stage was pitched toward the audience. This may help you to remember the difference between *up* stage and *down* stage. *Down* stage is next to the audience.

(Audience here)

Left wing	Down stage left	Down stage center	Down stage right	Right wing
	Center stage left	Center stage	Center stage right	
	Up stage right	Up stage center	Up stage left	

(Back of stage here)

78

Add sound effects wherever possible. Have an offstage sound man accompany the act with sounds such as bells, crashes, slammed doors, etc. The offstage sound should occur at exactly the same moment as the onstage action. A bit of practice will help your sound man create effects that are just right.

In some cases it is a good idea to give your skit a musical background. The music should harmonize with the mood of the onstage action; for instance, light, tinkly music should accompany a merry scene. The music should not play so loudly that it takes away the attention of the audience from the performers. A record player or a pianist will serve nicely.

If you have no real stage or if your stage does not have a curtain, the players may show that their act has ended merely by bowing and exiting.

While you do not want to use only the obvious movements, gestures, and facial expressions that a situation calls for, remember that your audience is at a distance and so you must exaggerate everything you do. If you smile, make it a *wide* smile, if you are gay, show that you are *very* gay. Make every mood clearly mean what it is supposed to mean.

When one group of players is leading the action, the other players should more or less remain inactive. The audience can usually follow only one action at a time, so do not divide their attention.

Do not look directly at the viewers. When glancing in their direction, keep your eyes on a level slightly above their heads.

Watch your timing. Do not proceed with a second movement before the first movement is complete. Let each action tell its full story. Do not come onstage too early or too late. Do not permit an actor to interrupt the scene of another actor. Correct timing can be worked out during rehearsals.

When working out your skit, try to put yourself in the place of the audience. Ask yourself such questions as, "If I were out there, could I clearly see everything? . . . Would I know exactly what is supposed to be happening? . . . Could I improve things by moving a bit faster or perhaps a bit slower?" By answering your own questions you will surely build a popular skit. Use the ideas given in this section for acting out your skit, but use your own imagination also to better your art.

Put everything you have into your performance, but remain relaxed about it. When the curtain goes down, try to find out just how and where you can sharpen your next performance. Practicing and learning from experience will help you become a smooth and appreciated actor or actress.

SOLO SKITS

Here are a number of pantomime skits to be acted out by one person. The title of an act should be announced by the teacher or leader.

The Wrist Watch

1. Walk across stage, casually glance at your imaginary wrist watch, suddenly halt and stare at watch as if it has stopped.

2. Hold watch to ear, listen, shake head, wind watch, again listen and shake head.

3. Gently shake wrist, listen to watch, frown and shake head.

4. Gently tap watch with fingers, listen, shake head.

5. Sigh, shrug, take imaginary watch off wrist, again shrug as you hold it out, drop it on ground, jump on it several times.

6. Wave goodbye to watch, walk away a few steps, suddenly halt, curiously cup hand to ear as if you think you hear the watch ticking.

7. Return to watch, pick it up, curiously hold it to ear, jerk back and stare at watch with pleased amazement, nod, quickly fasten watch on wrist, joyously hold up wrist, staring at watch as you walk off.

Setting the Table

1. Enter carrying imaginary tablecloth, shake it out, spread it over table, smooth out wrinkles.
2. Pick up a pile of imaginary dishes, set them in various positions on the table.
3. Step back and study arrangements, shake head in displeasure, change positions of the dishes.
4. Repeat action of step 3 two more times.
5. Sigh in disappointment, gather up plates and pile them high in cradle of left arm.
6. Stiffly stand in back of table (facing audience), close eyes and carefully sail the dishes one at a time onto the table.
7. Open eyes, look at arrangement, grin with joy, nod, brush off hands, triumphantly exit.

Dizzy Dinners

For this pantomime real props will give greater fun. The player goes through the motions of mixing an odd dish for dinner. The principal idea is for the pantomimist to drop all sorts of strange and funny items into a mixing bowl. Here are some suggestions:

1. Peel a potato, add the peels, throw potato over shoulder.
2. Take catsup bottle, unscrew cap, shake catsup into bowl, taste mixture, decide more catsup is needed, repeat action with two or three more bottles.
3. Grab a handful of the mixture, lick it, happily nod, pour in the contents of a small box, shrug, add box also.
4. Pick up newspaper, turn pages, briefly read, tear paper into shreds, let them flutter into bowl.

81

5. Look around for something else to add, notice button on coat, jerk it off, chop it up, add to bowl.

6. Crack several eggs over bowl, also toss shells into it.

7. Look around for something else to add, sweep floor, pour sweepings into bowl.

8. Pick up sugar bowl, taste sugar, smile at its sweetness, add several handfuls of sugar, taste mixture, painfully choke and fall.

The Phonograph Record

1. Enter, take two or three records from shop display, examine them.

2. Search carefully for one record in particular.

3. Find your special record, set it on player, turn switch, set needle on record, listen with pleasure with hand cupped to ear.

4. Remove record, start to carry it to clerk, slip, fall, break record.

5. Look sadly down at broken pieces.

6. Take one piece at a time, carefully place them on phonograph, shove pieces with both palms as if pushing pieces into their original round shape.

7. Again place needle on pieces, listen with hand cupped to ear.

8. Nod in pleasant surprise as the record again plays.

9. One at a time, stuff pieces into pocket or bag.

10. Take money from wallet, pay clerk and happily exit.

Grandma Crosses the Street

1. As an elderly but spry lady, stand at the curb (a low box) with handbag tightly clutched.

2. Timidly turn head back and forth as you watch for an opportunity to cross the busy street.

3. Cautiously step off curb, start to cross, show alarm at approaching car, race back to curb, wag reproving finger after car.

4. Hold palm high for traffic to stop, try to cross, leap back to curb just in time.

5. Cautiously peer both ways, nod as you think you see an opening, quickly tiptoe into street a few steps, jerk about in confusion as cars whiz past, struggle back to curb, breathe heavily.

6. Sigh deeply in despair, hold finger to side of head and gaze slightly upward as if in deep thought, brighten and nod as you get a good idea.

7. Take a banana from handbag, slowly and clearly peel it, quickly eat the fruit, hold peel high to look at it, toss it so that it falls in the street about a foot from the curb.

8. Take a deep breath, deliberately step on peel, slip and slide forward as if the peel has enabled you to dodge the traffic, end up across the street.

9. Grin triumphantly, pick up peel, drop it in handbag, happily walk off.

The Golfer

1. Enter as golfer with imaginary golf club, search for ball, see it, walk to it.

2. Carefully study ball, walk over to hole which is about five yards away.

3. Take putting position, putt ball, watch it miss, shake head, frown.

4. Walk to ball, take aim, again miss, scowl.

5. Walk to ball, very carefully study, putt ball, hold hand to head in disappointment as you again miss.

6. Again walk to ball, carefully study, frown, look up and shake head, suddenly see something on other side of stage, throw club away, walk to other side of stage.

7. Pick up the gardener's shovel which you saw, smile, walk back to ball, dig a hole directly in front of ball, knock ball into hole with shovel, smile in satisfaction.

8. Take ball from hole, kiss it, notice shovel in hand, kiss it, sling shovel over shoulder, walk off with a gay step.

The Fisherman

1. Enter with imaginary fishing pole, sit on chair, prepare to fish.

2. Cast line into water, lean forward and peer at line as you eagerly await a bite.

3. Lean back as you get a mild tug on the line, reel in a fish with little effort, hold hands apart to indicate that the fish is at least a yard long, set fish down, again cast line.

4. Wait for a moment, get another mild tug, reel in the fish without any strain, again hold hands apart to indicate you have a fish about a yard long, set it down, again cast line.

5. Wait a moment, suddenly jerk backward as you get a violent tug on line, twist and squirm as you desperately reel in the powerful fish, take deep sigh as you land it.

6. Stare in amazement as you hold up fish, take it from line and hold hands apart to indicate that it is only two inches long.

7. Shake head in amazement as you stare at fish, give it an underhand toss and throw it back into water, point to water and flex muscles to indicate that it was certainly a powerful little fish, scoop up other fish, exit.

The High Jumper

1. As a high jumper, crouch as you prepare to jump.

2. Run and try to leap over crossbar, knock it off, look down at it, snap fingers in disappointment, replace crossbar on its standards.

3. Repeat actions of step 2 two more times while showing your disappointment in varied ways, such as by groaning and sighing.

4. After third miss, suddenly get bright idea, walk a few steps away from high jump pit, pick up hammer and nails, return to pit, drive nails into crossbar so that it cannot fall off its standards.

5. Crouch, run, leap over crossbar, look back, shake hands above head in triumph, exit.

The Juggler

1. Hold up two fingers to indicate that you will first juggle just two balls.

2. Pick up imaginary balls, pretend to juggle them.

3. Hold up three fingers to indicate that you will next juggle three balls.

4. Pick up a third ball, juggle with a bit more difficulty.

5. Hold up five fingers to show that you will now juggle a total of five balls.

6. Juggle the five balls with a bit more difficulty than before.

7. Proudly hold up ten fingers.

8. Awkwardly gather several more balls into your hands and arms.

9. Drop a few of them, pick them up.

10. Take a deep sigh as if this is your one great effort.

11. Juggle with frantic and wild movements, such as leaping on to side to catch a falling ball and scooping a fallen ball from the floor.

12. Suddenly crouch, holding hands to top of head as if you are afraid the balls are crashing down upon you.

13. Look fearfully upward to see if there are any more coming down.

14. Rise, sadly hold up two fingers, pick up two balls and exit while juggling them.

The Strong Man

1. As a strong man, enter with arms flexed and a powerful walk, face audience and bow.

2. Display arm muscles one at a time, bend down and grasp imaginary bar-bell with trembling arms, lift to overhead, lower it, bow.

3. Flex and display muscles of right arm, bend down and try to lift bar-bell with right arm, strain and drop it after lifting it only a few inches.

4. Look determined, briefly exercise right arm, bend down, again fail to lift bar-bell more than a few inches, scowl.

5. Shake head in disappointment, cup hand to mouth and pretend to call toward wing. (At this point an offstage assistant slides a small box onstage.)

6. Pick up box, hold it high so that audience can see its label which reads VITAMINS.

7. Scoop several handfuls of imaginary vitamins into mouth, swallow pills, set box down, flex muscles.

8. Stand over bar-bell, rub hands on trousers as if preparing for a great effort, bend down and succeed—after a mighty struggle—in lifting the bar-bell over head, lower it.

9. Take a step forward, bow to audience, try to casually scoop up vitamin box with one hand, amazingly find that it is too heavy, just barely lift box with both hands, struggle offstage with it.

The Colonel

1. As an army colonel reviewing marching troops, stand on a low platform (real, if possible) while at military attention.

2. Let head and eyes slowly move from your left to your right, then quickly turn to left again and once more slowly observe various imaginary groups as they march past.

3. Briskly salute two or three times.

4. Suddenly glare down at a particular soldier, step down to him, point finger at him, shake head in disapproval.

5. Indicate displeasure at the soldier's posture, march droopily in a small circle (with head bowed and arms flopping) to indicate that this is *not* the way to march.

6. Hold up finger before soldier to indicate that you will now show him the *right* way to march, then stiffly march in a small circle with chin held high and arms properly swinging, wag a finger at soldier and return to platform.

7. Watch parade for a moment, then quickly and briefly repeat action of steps 4, 5, and 6 with a second soldier, return to platform.

8. Move head and eyes from left to right with a broad movement and let head linger at right, looking into distance so as to indicate that the parade is over, stiffly turn body to right and salute departing soldiers, wave goodbye.

9. Mop brow with handkerchief, return handkerchief to pocket, deeply sigh, step down and march off to left in the same droopy manner which you warned the soldiers against.

The Texas Cowboy

1. Enter as cowboy with coiled length of rope in hand.

2. Sight object about ten yards away, uncoil rope as you eagerly look at object.

3. Form a lasso, whirl rope overhead, toss rope, miss catching the object, let eyes follow fallen rope to ground, shake head in disappointment.

4. Pull rope back to you with both hands, again attempt to lasso object, again miss, again frown and tug rope back.

5. Carefully sight object, look very determined as you again whirl and toss.

6. Triumphantly cry out (in silent pantomime) as you catch object.

7. Tug object toward you with strained effort.

8. Clasp hands over head in satisfaction, forgetting that rope is still in your hand, feel sharp jerk, get pulled off stage with animal tugging you away.

Birthday Surprises

The aim of this pantomime skit is for a player to show all sorts of reactions and emotions at receiving a birthday present. He starts off by eagerly opening the package. The package is a real one which has been previously filled with the present by the performer. For convenience, the package should consist of a box which is already open at the top, although the performer pretends to unwrap and open it.

After opening the package he lifts the present from the box and goes into an act which includes a broad variety of exaggerated reactions such as joy, shock, bewilderment, amazement, gratitude, etc.

To build a comedy show, additional actors and actresses can come onstage one after another, look at the present and go through a series of emotions, too.

Here are twenty "presents" with suggestions for pantomime.

1. A shoe (wonder at the single shoe, take off own shoes, put on shoe, limp offstage)

2. A dog collar and leash (hold them out, pretend to call a dog from several directions, shrug as no dog appears, place collar around own neck and lead self off by leash)

3. A comic drawing (peer at it from several angles, laugh lightly, increase laughter until you are hysterically roaring, show picture to audience. NOTE: the picture can be of any comical nature, perhaps a scrawled drawing of the actor with his name beneath it)

4. A tattered, oversized jacket (hold it up in admiration, put it on, brush it off, proudly strut around)

5. A small rug (scratch head and wonder what to do with it, lay it on floor, walk down its length, turn around and pick it up, again lay it in front of you, again walk its length, continue to do this until you have walked offstage)

6. A pillow (lie down, set pillow under head, adjust its position several times, stretch, peacefully sleep)

7. A whiskbroom (go through fancy and funny motions while brushing yourself off—such as brushing your sleeve with dramatic sweeps and brushing off the soles of your shoes, also your elbows and ears)

8. A rope (test it by tugging on it, tie yourself up, happily skip around the stage for a moment or two, skip offstage)

9. A book (read while expressing a wide variety of emotions at the story, grow more excited as you turn pages, close book and sigh with emotional exhaustion)

10. A pencil or some other commonplace and inexpensive object (throw up arms in rapture as you peer into box, lift pencil, hold it up in deep admiration, hug it to chest while swaying in breathless joy)

11. A cube of wrapped butter (unwrap end of cube, take a slice of bread from pocket, rub butter over it, hungrily take a bite or two)

12. A jar labeled GLUE (dip fingers into imaginary glue, frown at your sticky fingers, rub them off on hip, find that your fingers are stuck to hip, try to pull them off with other hand)

13. An unshelled peanut (eagerly open a large box, throw inner wrappings aside, reach excitedly inside, pull out and hold up the peanut, look shocked, shrug, shell and eat peanut)

14. A balloon (playfully toss balloon into air, kick and swat it around, chase it offstage)

15. A small can labeled OIL (grin, pretend to oil your joints, such as elbows, knees, ankles, freely move joints to indicate that they now bend much easier)

16. A glass of water (gaze doubtfully at it as if wondering what to do with it, take a sip, wash your hands, pull a flower from your pocket and place it in glass, exit while sniffing flower)

17. A monster mask (put it on, stalk about stage while imitating a monster by clawing, creeping, grabbing, pretend to chase someone offstage)

18. A tube of toothpaste (nod in appreciation, take toothbrush from pocket, pretend to squeeze toothpaste onto toothbrush, vigorously pretend to brush teeth as you exit)

19. A dish of candy (eat a piece, react with pleasure at its delicious taste, eat another, suddenly become aware of viewers, pass dish down to them)

20. A large feather (playfully tickle your toes, chuckle, tickle your ear and laugh, quickly tickle yourself all over while silently roaring with merriment, exit while tickling and laughing)

HOLIDAY PANTOMIMES

A player selects and acts out one of the listed holidays and special days. Try to combine the obvious ideas which the holiday suggests with some less-known information about it.

1. Hallowe'en
2. Columbus Day
3. Mother's Day
4. Father's Day
5. Washington's Birthday
6. Veteran's Day
7. Thanksgiving
8. Lincoln's Birthday
9. Valentine's Day
10. May Day
11. St. Patrick's Day
12. Easter
13. April Fool's Day
14. Christmas
15. Independence Day

PAIRED SKITS

Pairs of players act out these pantomime skits, which may range in length from a few seconds to three or four minutes. Performers should take as much time as possible to work out their skit. Each act is announced. The first one, for example, would be introduced:

"In this skit, we see a frantic barber as he tries to cut the hair of a wriggling boy."

1. Barber cuts hair of wriggling boy
2. Doctor and patient
3. Mailman and lady-of-the-house
4. Grocery clerk and customer
5. Cowboy tries to rope wild horse
6. Carpenter and his assistant
7. Taxi driver and passenger
8. Dancer and awkward partner
9. Swimming instructor and student
10. Pedestrian asks directions of policeman
11. Sprinter and track coach
12. Lion tamer and ferocious lion
13. Mother teaches her daughter to cook
14. Pianist and singer
15. Bank teller and customer
16. Lady tries to escape angry bee
17. Tight-rope walker and spectator
18. Baseball pitcher and catcher
19. Boss dictates letter to secretary
20. Father tries to soothe crying baby
21. Driving teacher and student driver
22. Fisherman tries to catch cautious fish
23. Play director shows student how to act
24. Man tries to teach dog to shake hands

DIRECTIONS

This pantomime act can bring chuckles and giggles from the audience. All it takes is a clever performance!

Each player finds a partner. They work the act out together. One of them plays the role of a lost pedestrian who asks for directions from the other, a local resident. This situation offers endless opportunities for pantomime comedy at its best.

The act begins as the lost pedestrian approaches the local resident and asks him (in pantomime, of course) for directions for reaching a certain place. He can ask his questions by making gestures or by pointing to an address on an imaginary letter. Also, he can show how helpless he is by shrugging his shoulders and by frowning.

The local resident then replies by pantomiming some fantastic instructions. He can indicate left and right turns; he can get down and crawl to indicate that this is what the other man must do; he can make swimming motions as if there is a lake which must be crossed. The whole idea is to make the directions as strange and as comical as possible.

Of course, the lost pedestrian goes into some reactions to the directions. He can droop in dismay. He can scratch his head. He can start off as if following the directions and then come back in utter confusion for more instructions.

The act concludes as the lost pedestrian finally staggers offstage into one of the wings, while the local resident strolls happily off into the opposite wing.

In turn, each couple presents their version of the act.

TELEPHONE CHUCKLES

The group separates into couples. Each couple works out a pantomime skit centered about a telephone conversation. This skit may run from one to five minutes.

Players should try to build a simple story with a beginning, a middle, and an amusing conclusion. For instance, the plot might be that player A tries to get player B to speak louder on the phone. Player A indicates this by straining his ear at the receiver and by motioning upward. Player B then speaks louder and louder until—at the finish—he bellows so loud that he knocks his partner off his chair.

Partners may sit at tables or simply stand on opposite sides of the stage. The skit begins when one of the partners dials the phone and the other cups a hand to his ear and lifts the receiver.

Here are a few typical ideas:

1. Player A talks so long and so monotonously that player B drops his head and dozes.

2. Both talk excitedly and with sweeping gestures at the same time.

3. Player A wants to show player B something in a book, so player A holds an open book before the mouthpiece and points to the pages without speaking. Player B then nods as if seeing the pages.

4. Both open lunches and munch while conversing. They fumble awkwardly as they try to hold the phone while unwrapping a sandwich or opening a bottle. Player A speaks into a sandwich as if it were the mouthpiece; player B holds an apple to his ear as if it were the receiver.

5. Player A holds up a sheet of music and gaily sings, player B smacks his ear in pain and holds the receiver as far away from his ear as possible, then draws receiver close once more, sways and smiles as he decides the singing is melodious after all.

6. Player A talks on and on without a single break, so player B yawns and rips pages off a calendar every few seconds.

7. Player A assumes a mischievous grin, tells player B to hold the line a moment, picks up a cat which he permits to meow into the phone. Player B reacts with bewilderment at the change in player A's "voice." (The cat can be real or imaginary. An imaginary cat can be indicated by gently picking it up from the floor with both hands and stroking it.)

8. Players chat for a while, rush off hurriedly and briefly to work—such as sweeping the floor—then rush back to phones. This can be repeated two or three times.

MIRROR STUNT

With a bit of practice this idea can be developed into a highly entertaining act. Two players harmonize their pantomime movements so as to give the appearance of *one* player looking at his reflection in a full-length mirror. This means that both players comb their hair or brush their teeth in unison, just as if one player performed these movements in front of a mirror.

Here are notes and suggestions for building a superior performance.

1. Players face each other, sideways to the audience.

2. The two players should be approximately the same height and dress alike.

3. Practice a single movement until it is harmonious, then go on to the next one.

4. Practice all movements in slow motion at first, then speed up slightly. It is best if all movements are done with only moderate speed.

5. Choose broad, sweeping movements that can be clearly seen by the audience.

6. Keep feet planted in one place except when making definite foot movements.

7. Do not smile or laugh. (This makes it even funnier!)

8. Some typically amusing movements are: (a) Lean forward and touch noses as if peering closely into mirror. (b) Gaze in fond admiration by passing hand over hair and tilting head in a dramatic pose. (c) Players push palms together and rotate arms as if polishing the mirror. (d) Twist face into comical expressions. (e) Smile broadly.

9. The act may be given a comical ending by doing the following: Player A waves goodbye but player B beckons "Come here." Player A then beckons "Come here" as player B waves goodbye. They briefly stare in surprise at each other, shrug, face audience, bow in unison, exit.

WAITER!

Few situations offer such a fine opportunity for a pantomime comedy skit as that of a waiter serving a diner—or a group of diners. Several groups can use the listed suggestions here, and not necessarily in the same order. They can then work out their acts and present them one after another. Make no mistake, they will all be different—and more hilarious than they look in print!

1. The diner cannot catch the waiter's attention.
2. The waiter spills imaginary foods and drinks on the diner.
3. The diner changes his order several times.
4. The waiter eats the diner's food.
5. The diner goes to sleep while waiting.
6. The waiter brings the wrong orders.
7. The diner helps himself to trays intended for another table.
8. The waiter hungrily watches the diner eat.
9. The diner chokes on the poor quality of food.
10. The waiter carries the food in his pocket.
11. The waiter sits with feet on table while taking the diner's order.
12. The diner complains of poor service.
13. The diner gets on hands and knees to plead for service.
14. The waiter drops dishes just as he is about to serve.

15. The waiter whisks up dishes just after the diner barely tastes them.

16. The diner chokes on hot food and hastily gulps water.

17. The waiter seasons the diner's food by pouring huge amounts of salt and pepper on it.

18. The waiter clears the table by tossing dishes over his shoulder.

19. The diner gets so hungry he takes off his necktie, sets it on plate, salts it, pretends to cut and eat it.

20. The waiter passes several times while holding fingers in ears so as not to hear diner's frantic calls.

21. The waiter pours water from pitcher into glass, drinks it himself.

22. The waiter, who has been sweeping the floor, brushes off diner with broom.

23. The diner finds he is without money to pay.

24. The waiter holds out hand for his tip and the diner pours water into waiter's palm.

25. The diner attempts to show the waiter how to serve and ends up sadly serving the waiter a full dinner.

THE MECHANICAL MAN

The cast consists of two performers. One of them acts the pantomime role of the mechanical man, while the other player is his employer who gives the orders. The scene is a home. The action takes place as the employer tries to get the not-so-bright mechanical man to perform simple tasks around the house, such as dusting the furniture and cleaning the windows.

The pantomime begins as the employer pretends to call his servant. The robot enters the room by walking stiffly and with short and jerky steps. His arms swing with tight and precise movements; his face has a frozen expression.

The employer then tries to put his employee to work by pantomiming what he wants done. He pretends to sweep the floor, but the machine-man kneels down and sweeps with his hands. The performers can repeat this once or twice.

The employer pantomimes washing dishes and the mechanical man nods stiffly. He turns and stamps slowly offstage. A moment later a loud crash is heard. As the employer stares in shock, the mechanical man enters with bits of broken dishes (from cardboard plates) in his hands.

Let your machine-man continue in a series of funny actions like these for five or six minutes.

SALESMAN!

Here is another situation which can be built into a funny skit. The idea is for the male customer to be trapped in a clothing store where he is the unwilling target of an eager salesman or group of salespeople. With some old clothes as props, this skit becomes more realistic.

1. The customer innocently strolls along the sidewalk when the crouching salesman grabs him and pulls him into store.

2. The salesman locks the door after the customer.

3. The customer protests but the salesman distracts him by pointing out the fine clothes on display.

4. The salesman shakes his head in solemn disapproval of the customer's hat, coat, and tie, and removes them from customer.

5. The salesman forces all sorts of odd and ill-fitting clothes upon the customer.

6. The salesman is so pleased with one of the tattered coats which the customer rejects that he takes off his own coat and puts on the tattered one.

7. The customer tries to escape by crawling on hands and knees, but is caught and gently led back.

8. The customer weeps and pleads to be set free.

9. The salesman measures the customer in several peculiar ways, such as measuring the distance between his left ear and his right shoulder.

10. The customer selects a hat and sets it on his head, but the salesman shakes his head and turns the hat upside down on the customer's head.

11. The salesman removes customer's coat, slowly and deliberately tears it into shreds.

12. The salesman takes off customer's shoes, nods in apprecia-

tion at them, removes his own shoes, replaces them with the customer's shoes.

13. The customer races for locked door, beats against it.

14. The salesman tries to cheer up the customer by peeling a banana and offering it to him.

15. The salesman takes a hat from box, throws away hat, places box on customer's head.

16. The customer gives up trying to resist, invites the salesman to sell him clothing.

17. The salesman finds that a coat is too narrow in the shoulders for the customer so he holds the customer's shoulders together, forces the coat on him.

18. The salesman displays exaggerated pride and admiration as he views the customer's appearance.

19. The salesman brings out several cans of paint, labeled with various colors, and brushes all over the customer's clothes. (Imaginary paint, of course.)

20. The salesman enthusiastically congratulates the customer by shaking his hand and slapping his back.

21. The salesman proudly escorts customer to mirror, customer looks at self in shock, salesman hastily leads him away from mirror.

22. The customer agrees with the salesman that he looks better (even though he doesn't).

23. The customer pays for clothing but the salesman holds out his hand for more and more.

24. The salesman grandly escorts the now-proud customer to the door, unlocks it.

25. The salesman and customer shake hands and the customer proudly exits wearing his tattered clothing.

THE EXPERTS

This "outdoor" scene opens with two seated performers opposite each other, playing a game of checkers. Their backs are to the wings.

As they silently study the checker board, a passer-by enters while reading a newspaper. As he approaches the players he glances over and sees the game, so he stops to watch. Just as player A is about to make a move, the passer-by shakes his head in solemn disapproval and grabs player A's hand, preventing the move. The passer-by then motions for player A to stand aside for a moment. As player A does so, the passer-by sits down, studies the board for a moment, then makes a non-jumping move. Nodding in satisfaction, the passer-by stands and permits player A to return to the chair.

The passer-by remains to watch the game. Player B then makes his move, a non-jumping one.

The above actions are repeated two or three more times as other passers-by stop and make the moves for player A. After each passer-by has finished his move he stays to watch the game. Player B makes a non-jumping move after each passer-by has moved.

Finally, the last passer-by makes his move and stands up to watch. Players A and B silently study the board for a moment, then player B slowly and solemnly makes six long jumps all over the board.

Player A stares at the board in silent shock for a moment, then looks up with a fierce expression at the passers-by. The passers-by look dismayed. Player A suddenly leaps up, scatters the board and checkers, and chases the passers-by offstage.

TENNIS MATCH

Two or four players can take part in this pantomime version of a tennis match.

The performers stand facing each other with their backs to the wings. An imaginary net runs down the center of the stage from upstage to downstage. The tennis balls and rackets are imaginary.

The main idea to remember as the ball goes back and forth is to exaggerate everything. When a player leaps to hit the ball he should leap wildly; when he swings at the ball he should swing with smashing swiftness. The facial expressions should also be exaggerated. This means that when a player is pleased with himself he pantomimes a broad laugh; when he is disappointed with his game his whole face and body sag.

Many amusing actions can be included, such as falling down, striking the ball with the knee, and swinging the racket with both hands as if it were a baseball bat.

The players can make the ball seem very real by keeping their eyes on its imaginary flight back and forth. They should also watch the timing of the ball and not strike too soon. That is, they should allow for the time a ball would normally take in traveling back and forth. During this time, they can be reacting to it and racing after it.

When there are two players on each side, the teammates should alternate in returning the ball.

MEN OF MARS

Here is a nonsense pantomime that calls for a wild imagination—the more vivid the better! An announcer tells the audience that a spaceship has just returned from the planet Mars, full of people who have been studying the Martians. The announcer says that the Martian people have some odd ways of walking down the street, which the actors and actresses will demonstrate.

One by one the performers move across the stage in all sorts of peculiar ways. Here are five suggestions:

1. Cross by shuffling both feet which are set inside cardboard grocery cartons.

2. Cross by pausing every fourth step to blow a whistle while hopping up and down in place.

3. Cross while holding a pillow against the head as if sleeping.

4. Cross while sweeping the floor with the wrong end of a broom.

5. Cross while staring intently at a single large flower which is held by both hands in front of the face.

NEWSPAPER DRAMATICS

This idea is good for a large number of performers. A small group of players or one single performer can pantomime each act.

Clip several news stories from the paper and give one to each group of players, or each individual. After reading the story they must act it out in pantomime and the others must try to guess what the story is about.

The pantomime act should not try to cover all the details of the story; only the central idea need be acted out. For instance, if the story concerns a railroad engine that spilled off its track, the story should be simplified to cover just that single point.

The players may repeat their pantomime once or twice. If the audience cannot guess within a reasonable time, tell them and go on to the next act.

THE PERSONALITY MACHINE

In the center of the stage a screen is set up to resemble a large box. It need not be a complete box, but should look like one from the front and sides. It is labeled THE PERSONALITY-CHANGING MACHINE.

As the show starts, the host enters, bows to the audience, gestures to the machine, walks over to it, and turns several levers (which can be imaginary handles attached to the screen). As the levers are turned, an assistant behind the screen makes all sorts of strange noises in imitation of loud and clumsy machinery. He can rattle tin cans, beat on a drum, and so on. After a few seconds the host again turns the levers as if turning off the machine.

The host greets the first performer, who now walks onstage. The actor represents a man who wants to change his personality. He is a miserable person, shabby in dress and manner. He pantomimes his desire to enter the machine. With a great show of confidence the host places the actor behind the screen, turns the levers, and waits expectantly as the machine noisily operates. A few seconds later he turns it off and watches to see what has happened. To his shock, the actor runs out in an apelike manner, wearing an ape's mask. The actor dances happily around for a moment, takes a banana from his pocket, and scoots offstage. The host sighs, shrugs, and waits for the next actor to enter.

The second actor enters as a weakling and exits from the machine as a strong man. An actress can come onstage as a poor washerwoman and change into a wealthy society lady. And so on. The possibilities are endless.

All the necessary costumes for changing an actor's appearance can be kept behind the screen.

BACKWARD PEOPLE

Be sure that you explain this one to the audience before the play begins!

Things go backward!

The idea is to build a pantomime act in which the actors and actresses perform a number of things in reverse of the usual way. For instance, instead of shaking hands when meeting, the players wave goodbye.

As many players as desired can take part in the pantomime. Some can remain onstage during the whole performance, while others can enter and exit. The scene can take place in any location that offers opportunities for people to move around, such as a home, a schoolroom or a business office.

The best way to build a number of amusing backward actions is to think of a usual movement, then see if it is one that can be reversed. Try these ideas:

1. A player enters without a raincoat or an overcoat, finds one and wears it while working at a desk.

2. The players walk backward.

3. A performer opens a box containing a hat, throws the hat aside and wears the box on his head.

4. A couple dance briefly, back to back and holding hands.

5. A boy dives into the water. Then he takes off shoes and socks.

6. A girl comes into the room, opens her umbrella and holds it over her head. Then she closes it and goes out.

7. A player pours water from a drinking glass into a pitcher and drinks from the pitcher.

8. A player clears an imaginary dinner table, then sits down and eats.

PANTOMIME ORCHESTRA

This musical stunt can provide comedy relief during a serious program or it can contribute extra amusement to a humorous show.

As few as three or as many as twenty players take the roles of musicians. However, they are rather unusual musicians, as they play on all sorts of strange instruments, such as a ruler (for a guitar), a kettle (for a drum), and a cardboard tube (for a trumpet).

An offstage phonograph record can play lively melodies as the musicians perform in pantomime. Colorful costumes worn by the actors will add to the gaiety.

THE DANCERS

The idea of this stunt is for the girls to try to teach the boys to dance. It isn't easy! The scene opens with several boys and girls seated around the stage. Various girls coax different boys out into the center of the stage and try to teach them a few steps. The boys are reluctant and awkward, but they try. The girls are in despair over teaching the boys to dance but they patiently work at it.

This situation is good for dozens of hilarious happenings. Just get your actors and actresses into action. An endless stream of audience-tickling ideas will come along. Here are a few:

1. A girl glides smoothly around the room to illustrate graceful movement to the boys. When two or three boys try it, they are as graceful as elephants.

2. While teaching a clumsy boy, a girl gets her feet stepped on several times. She finally orders him to remove his shoes, which he does.

3. A girl shows a boy how to break away from her and spin lightly backward. When the boy tries it, he spins on and on until he crashes offstage. Sound effects are timed to his offstage crash.

4. Two girls illustrate a movement in which they walk alongside each other for three steps forward, then take one step sideways. They go through the movement twice, while the boys watch. But when the boys try it, they end up by taking the side step toward each other, bumping.

5. As a girl is teaching a boy, he pulls out a bag of potato chips and starts to munch. When she silently glares at him, he grins and stuffs the bag inside his shirt.

SLOW-MOTION PANTOMIME

There is something especially entertaining about a pantomime that is performed in slow-motion. It may be difficult sometimes for the players to keep from laughing during the act, but that is all part of the fun. Two or more performers can take roles.

Select an act that offers plenty of opportunity for physical movements. It should consist of a scene that is familiar to the audience, such as playing tennis or checking out groceries at the market or perhaps a classroom activity.

Once the act has been more or less worked out, the performers should rehearse it at normal speed to get acquainted with the basic movements. The players then repeat the pantomime more and more slowly, until they have it in slow-motion.

There are two special ways to make a slow-motion pantomime as amusing as possible. First, choose funny physical movements such as these two examples: *a.* A golfer spins slowly around several times after giving the ball a terrific whack; he spins again and sinks to the ground in exhaustion. *b.* A waiter tries desperately to balance several imaginary dishes in his hand; as they spill, he desperately grabs the air, trying to catch them before they smash on the floor.

The other important thing is to build the expression on your face slowly. Whenever something happens, build up your facial expression a little at a time until it is quite exaggerated. For instance, the waiter would grow more and more terrified as he grabs at his imaginary dishes.

Keep your slow-motion pantomime short and punchy.

THE WINNERS

The scene opens with everyone onstage. The master of ceremonies steps forward to announce the stunt. He informs the audience that some pantomime champions are about to go into action. In other words, the audience is about to enjoy some prize-winning comedies.

Several brief pantomime acts are then presented. They can be original, or you can use material from other pages of this book. They can be solo acts or acts with several players taking part. When an act finishes, the players return to their chairs to allow the next act to go on.

The announcer makes an act clear by describing briefly what is about to happen.

Try these prize-winning pantomimes:

1. Two or three players act out sudden changes in the weather. They start the act by standing onstage and chatting in pantomime. They then act out sudden heat, then a cold and windy day, rain, fog, and other extreme weather conditions. They show the changes by their gestures, by protecting themselves from rain, and so on.

2. An actor plays the role of an artist, while an actress serves as his model. The model strikes unbecoming odd poses which bring protests from the artist. He paints with wild sweeps and swings. After a few moments the artist holds up the finished painting for the audience to see. It is a simple sketch such as one drawn by a small child.

3. A shoe salesman tries to serve several customers at once. He gets everything all mixed up. He tries to fit a woman with heavy boots, he places a shoebox on the foot of a man, and so on.

4. A golfing instructor, using imaginary clubs and balls, shows several players how to drive a golf ball. After illustrating the movements two or three times, he allows each to take a turn. One player hits the ball so hard that he spins around and falls down. Another swings five or six times before hitting it. A third hits his own foot, and so on.

5. Several customers enter a jewelry shop, one at a time. The jeweler displays some "new fashions" in jewelry, such as necklaces made of vines, bracelets made of rope, and large cardboard rings. The jeweler tries to convince the customers how attractive they look with the jewelry. They are doubtful, but exit wearing the jewels.

WILD DREAMS

The announcer comes onstage to greet the audience, "Good evening. I wonder how many of you have ever dreamed that you were someone else? I ask that question because you are about to see some people who did. Perhaps I had better explain. Some people—whom you may know—had wild dreams last night, and dreamed they were entirely different. They have kindly agreed to show you what they looked like in their wild dreams. Wow! I suggest that you hold on tightly to your chairs; it's going to be wild."

The announcer exits. The players now cross the stage, one at a time. Each is dressed in an odd or comical costume which represents themselves in their wild dreams. (Costumes from other acts are fine for this purpose. Also, good costumes can be put together quickly by using old clothing.)

Here are five good characters that will spark off other ideas for your parade of wild dreamers:

1. A boy hops onstage in the costume of a bird. He imitates a bird by darting and flying around. Just before leaving the stage he turns to the audience to shrug and sigh.

2. A girl enters as a cowboy. She crosses while drawing her (toy) pistol and twirling a rope. She constantly drops the pistol and gets tangled in the rope.

3. An actor crosses as a clown. He leaps about, waves to the audience, does a comical dance. He waves goodbye to the audience as he dances offstage.

4. A girl imitates a singer. She gestures wildly and expresses herself dramatically. She bows deeply and exits.

5. An actor or actress enters as a juggler. Several paper plates are juggled, but they fly off in every direction. As the juggler walks offstage, he kicks some of the fallen plates along.

IN THE ARMY

The audience is informed that the next act is a pantomime at an army camp. A squad of newly enlisted soldiers is being taught the rules of army life. Their instructor is an experienced sergeant who tries to teach them—and tries and tries and tries. The soldiers—both boys and girls can take part—are clumsy, without meaning to be. The pantomime can have marching and saluting, as these examples show:

1. The soldiers march around in different directions, all of them wrong. They turn left when they should turn right, half of them march offstage, while the other half marches in a circle, they bump into each other, and so on.

2. When the sergeant instructs them in a proper salute, they get all mixed up. One recruit salutes with his left hand, another painfully bangs his nose. A third soldier reaches high over his head and tries to find his forehead. He finally reaches up with the left hand to bring his right hand down.

3. The sergeant commands the squad to halt, but one dazed soldier keeps marching around all alone. The sergeant places his hands on hips and glares at the careless marcher. The soldier finally wakes up and scrambles frantically back into line.

TELEVISION TRICKS

The announcer informs the audience: "This scene takes place in the lobby of a large hotel where there is a television set with a program going. Several guests of the hotel are about to enter the lobby to watch the program. Let us watch the guests as they watch the set."

One by one the guests walk in to sit before the television screen. Each reacts in an entirely different way to what is seen. But whatever emotion an actor displays, he exaggerates it. He performs for a few moments and exits.

Prepare this act by having each actor and actress select a single kind of emotion. He or she then concentrates on—and wildly exaggerates—the feeling. Some good emotional reactions are *excitement, fear, surprise, happiness, anger, love, horror, peacefulness, tension, sorrow, merriment.*

Start with these examples:

1. An actor displays great tension by crouching stiffly, by pulling a towel from his pocket and wringing it into knots. At the same time he stares intently at the program.

2. An actress weeps and wails in deep sorrow at what she sees. She pleads toward the screen, she holds her head in her hands

and does everything else that indicates tremendous, but silly, sorrow.

3. An actor bursts out with uncontrollable laughter. He lies on the floor and kicks his feet in the air, he rocks with merriment and so on. Every time he takes a fresh peek at the screen, his laughter breaks out with fresh force.

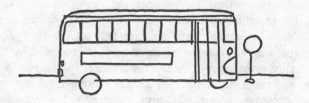

THE BUS

The purpose of this is to build a pantomime play around a bus, its driver and passengers. This is a familiar situation which the players can develop into an entertaining pantomime running for 15 to 20 minutes. It is excellent for large groups, inasmuch as an endless number of passengers can enter and exit.

The play director first gets the actors and actresses together to work out a series of incidents and happenings aboard the bus. The incidents are then acted out one after another to form the total pantomime play. Listed below are fifteen basic situations which can be easily developed into funny and surprising scenes. Players can think of others.

The stage is set with rows of chairs representing bus seats, with a different type of chair at the front representing the driver's seat. Have two rows of chairs with an aisle between them. The play director should make sure that the chairs are so arranged that the audience can see the actions clearly. A good arrangement is to slant the chairs from upstage left to downstage right.

1. A lady passenger fumbles so awkwardly in her handbag for her fare that she spills packages all over the defenseless driver.

2. Three passengers scramble for a single seat. They end up trying to share it.

3. At one stop, all of the passengers get off at the rear door and immediately re-enter from the front. They do this casually, as if it were the normal thing to do.

4. The weary driver tries to explain directions to a lady passenger who just does not seem to understand.

5. Passengers bounce up and down as the bus hits a bumpy road. Some of them bounce across the aisle to exchange seats.

6. A beggar enters, pantomimes the fact that he has no money. He entertains the passengers with a brief dance, passes his hat for a collection, pays his fare and sits down.

7. A passenger insists on telling the driver how to drive. The driver finally gives up by placing the shocked passenger in the driver's seat while he, the driver, relaxes among the passengers.

8. A passenger enters with arms outstretched as if walking in his sleep. He pays his fare, walks to a seat and sleeps. After several other scenes have been performed by other players he rises and exits, still walking in his sleep.

9. The driver pulls to a halt, opens his lunch box, casually eats. An impatient passenger angrily protests while pointing to his watch. The driver offers him a slice of cake which is so delicious the passenger forgets all about the time.

10. An actor in the costume and mask of a monkey boards the bus to cause all sorts of confusion. He tries to sit in the lap of a frightened lady or chases someone out of the rear door.

11. A pair of players dressed as swordsmen enter while dueling (with imaginary swords). They halt long enough to pay their fares casually, then resume dueling down the aisle and out of the rear door.

12. A small child insists on offering his lollipop to the driver. When the driver frantically refuses, the child continues to insist by rubbing the imaginary lollipop into the driver's face and hair.

13. The bus driver makes wide turns and sudden halts. The passengers sway or fall forward or perform other movements according to the driver's actions.

14. The first man in line at a bus stop is crowded onto the bus by those behind him. He is further crowded down the aisle and out of the rear door.

15. A lady standing in the aisle uses every trick possible to get the attention of a seated man (in hopes he will prove gallant), but he carefully avoids taking the hint.

BIBLE PANTOMIMES

A player acts out an activity which reveals the name of a biblical character. A player taking the part of Adam could go through the motions of gardening, while a girl portraying Esther could play the role of a queen.

Various groups from the Bible can be dramatized, also, such as Noah and his three sons, and Daniel and the prison guards.

SUPER SALE

Scene: A clothing store. A variety of old coats, hats, boots and other articles of clothing are on counters and hooks or racks. A large sign reads SUPER CLOTHING SALE.

1. The store salesman enters, flicks dust off the sign, looks at his watch. He rubs his hands together in eager anticipation of a busy day. He walks to edge of stage, pantomimes opening the door, and is immediately pushed backward by a throng of customers.

2. The customers rush about, scattering the clothing. They take their purchases to the salesman, toss him money, and exit.

113

3. One at a time, several customers enter. The salesman pressures them into trying on all sorts of odd and ill-fitting clothes. They unhappily exit, wearing the floppy clothes.

4. Two women enter, one after the other. They inspect the clothes for a moment, but fail to find what they want. Each notices the clothing of the other. They exchange a few items, shake hands and exit. The salesman shakes his head sadly.

5. A customer enters wearing ill-fitting clothes. The salesman shakes his head to indicate dismay over the customer's appearance. The salesman sells the customer a new set of clothes that fit even worse than his original set. As the salesman beams happily, the customer proudly exits.

6. A customer finds nothing of interest in the displayed clothes, but takes interest in the coat and tie worn by the salesman. Without asking permission, the customer removes the stunned salesman's coat and tie, pays him for them, and exits. The salesman is too astonished to protest.

7. The salesman exits, returns with an armful of clothing which he tosses onto the floor. The customers rush over and go through the pile. Clothing flies in all directions.

8. The salesman takes his lunch from a paper bag and begins to eat. A customer walks over, takes a sandwich from the bag, casually eats it as he continues to inspect the clothes. The astonished salesman shakes his head as he looks into his empty lunch bag.

9. As all the customers leave, the salesman happily counts his money. He suddenly notices his own poorly fitting clothes. He selects other clothing that fits even worse, and exits cheerfully counting his money.

STAGECOACH STOP

Scene: A stagecoach stop on the prairie. A prominent sign reads STAGECOACH STATION. The station agent is dozing, his hat over his eyes.

1. Several Indians rush in from the right and do a war dance. One of them calls the attention of the others to the *stagecoach*

part of the sign. All gesture to the right, whooping. The station agent, ignored by the Indians, dozes peacefully on.

2. Some cowboys rush in from the left, peer to the right and fire their (imaginary) pistols after the Indians. The cowboys exit at left.

3. The Indians return from the right with several passengers from the stagecoach as prisoners. They perform a war dance around them.

4. The cowboys rush in to battle the Indians. After a few seconds the Indians run off to the right. The cowboys escort the rescued prisoners offstage left.

5. The station agent stretches sleepily, slowly rises, and lazily looks around. He strolls to each wing in turn, looks out, shrugs, stretches, returns to his chair and goes back to sleep. The curtain falls.

CAKE BAKE!

Scene: A large kitchen. Several tables are set with baking ingredients and cooking utensils. A large box labeled OVEN is in a prominent place. A sign on one of the tables reads CAKE BAKE CONTEST.

1. Everyone gaily enters. One girl takes charge. She gives directions, which the boys have trouble understanding. The girls patiently try to explain to the boys.

2. The girl in charge indicates that this is to be a very large cake for the contest. A tub is set on a center table as a mixing bowl.

3. Everyone works at preparing the cake. They open boxes, pour the contents into the tub, stir it, and so on.

4. The boys do everything wrong. For example, they toss the boxes into the mixing bowl as well as the ingredients. The girls spend half their time undoing the mess.

5. One of the boys dips his finger into the batter, tastes it, goes into a comical act of staggering around in great pain. The other boys laugh, but the girls scold him.

6. The tub is finally set inside the oven. Everyone exits.

7. A moment later the boys stealthily creep back onstage, look slyly around, and pull out the tub as if going after the cake.

8. The girls rush in, catch the boys at the cake and scold them. The boys take the scolding with grins.

9. The mixing bowl is taken from the oven and placed on a table. A girl lifts out several pieces of (imaginary) cake and passes them around. Everyone reacts in disappointment at the taste. As some of the girls weep, the boys comfort them.

10. A man wearing a large badge reading *Fudge* enters and tastes the cake. For a moment his face is expressionless. Then, he smiles broadly and pins a huge ribbon reading *First Prize* on the girl in charge. Everyone exits, happily munching cake.

THE PICNIC

Scene: Outdoors. A picnic background is set with a few shrubs and flower pots.

1. A group gaily enters with picnic baskets and blankets. They set everything out and prepare to eat.

2. Suddenly there is an imaginary rainstorm. The players scramble around in an attempt to hold a blanket above the food. They sigh with relief as the rain ends.

3. They begin to eat. One player suddenly scratches, then a second and a third, as if ants have attacked. Everyone leaps about, scratching and yelling. As the ants go away, the players sit in a circle around the food and again start to eat.

4. A bear (a simple cardboard mask and a sign "Bear" on his back will serve) walks up, curiously looks over the shoulders of the players. They do not notice him. The bear taps a player on the shoulder and mutters something. Without looking up, the player hands the bear an egg.

5. The bear nods in thanks, walks away nibbling the egg. He suddenly stops, comes back and asks for salt, gets it, and walks away, still unnoticed by the busy players.

6. The bear comes back, sits down on a blanket and eats. The players notice the bear and run offstage. One timidly returns, pauses a moment, then slowly walks over to tap the bear on the shoulder. Without turning around the bear hands

the player some food. Two other players enter, tap the bear, also receive food.

7. The other players return, one by one. Finding the bear to be a jolly animal, they all join together to dance in a circle.

SOUR NOTES

Scene: An orchestra, with as few or as many musicians as desired. Some of the instruments can be real, while others can be made of cardboard, or they can be imaginary, as indicated in the script.

1. The conductor raps for attention and conducts the orchestra in a short selection.

2. As the orchestra plays, the conductor cups a hand to his ear and frowns to indicate that someone is playing sour notes.

3. The conductor wanders from musician to musician, trying to find the sour notes. Finding the off-key musician, he grabs the (imaginary) instrument and breaks it in half.

4. One of the musicians steps to the front and does a silly dance while playing his instrument. The conductor stares in astonishment for a moment, then chases the dancer offstage.

5. To the conductor's surprise, a musician eats a sandwich while continuing to play the piano with his other hand. The conductor glares, walks on over, scolds the musician, then covers him with a sheet. On second thought, the conductor turns back, reaches beneath the sheet for the sandwich, eats it eagerly.

6. The conductor leads the musicians in single file around the stage, while the music continues. They return to their chairs.

7. The conductor again hears some sour notes. He locates the off-key musician, jumps up and down on his instrument and returns it.

8. The conductor leads the orchestra in a fast piece. Everyone makes wild and exaggerated movements.

9. The music ends. The conductor and musicians bow and exit.

SKITS OF FAMOUS EVENTS

Players pantomime famous events of history. You can announce the event beforehand or the viewers may be allowed to guess what event is taking place.

Offstage music may be played in keeping with the mood of the action; for example, a patriotic theme may accompany Washington and his soldiers as they march offstage.

A complete show may be presented by assigning skits to several groups or classes. Costumes will help in setting the right atmosphere.

Basic movements for each event are supplied. The leader may wish to add extra touches wherever they will add to the effectiveness of the skit.

118

Washington at Valley Forge

1. Cold and tattered soldiers are sitting and lying on the ground.
2. Women enter to feed, clothe, and bandage them.
3. Washington enters, looks about in concern.
4. A few of the healthier soldiers struggle to their feet to salute him.
5. Washington passes from soldier to soldier, patting each and speaking words of comfort.
6. A dispatch rider races in, hands a message to Washington.
7. Washington peers offstage as if observing enemy troop movements.
8. Washington becomes alert, signals to a bugler who steps forward.
9. As the bugle sounds the soldiers struggle to their feet, grab their rifles.
10. Soldiers form a marching column.
11. The flag is advanced to the front of the column.
12. Washington gestures outward to indicate that they will march forward to victory.
13. Washington places himself at head of troops.
14. With heads held high, the soldiers follow Washington offstage.

Daniel in the Lion's Den

1. Daniel prays with eyes closed, head uplifted.
2. At opposite side of stage, several lions pace and growl.
3. Soldiers enter, scoff at Daniel, seize him.
4. Soldiers roughly escort unresisting Daniel to cage.
5. Soldiers lock cage, scoff at Daniel, exit.
6. Lions snarl and claw as they approach Daniel.
7. Daniel calmly prays.
8. Lions gradually grow less fierce, retreat somewhat.
9. Soldiers re-enter while laughing and scoffing.
10. Soldiers express amazement at unharmed Daniel.
11. They unlock cage, motion for Daniel to leave.
12. Daniel calmly walks across the stage, exits.
13. Soldiers exchange baffled glances.
14. They cross stage while quietly talking, exit.

California Gold Discovery

1. Three or four miners dig for gold.
2. One finds a large nugget, holds it high, shouts.
3. Others excitedly crowd about him while shouting and gesturing.
4. Several more miners rush onstage to see nugget.
5. All dig furiously on various parts of stage.
6. More miners rush in to join them.
7. Two or three miners also find large nuggets, hold them up.
8. Some miners race off with nuggets, others continue to dig.

Building of the Panama Canal

1. Surveyors enter, survey the land.
2. Workers enter to dig, shovel, haul earth.
3. Foreman enters, makes gestures to indicate the course of the canal.
4. Foreman instructs and encourages various workers.
5. Workers labor on either side of partially completed canal.
6. Two or three distinguished-looking men (government officials) enter and look about in approval.
7. Workers halt; players stand on either side of finished canal.
8. All turn toward wing and eagerly watch.
9. A large paper boat (carried by players who walk in back of it) sails across stage as if through canal.
10. All players cheer and congratulate each other as ship sails across stage.
11. All players happily follow ship offstage.

Lincoln's Gettysburg Address

1. A crowd enters and gathers about a platform.
2. A few soldiers march in, form a guard about the platform.
3. Several government officials enter, take chairs on platform.
4. Lincoln solemnly enters, is saluted by an army officer.
5. Lincoln is greeted by government officials.
6. He sits in center of platform.
7. A speaker pantomimes an introduction of Lincoln.
8. Lincoln stands before audience as if preparing to speak.
9. As Lincoln silently gazes over audience—without pantomime of any kind—an offstage voice recites his Gettysburg Address.
10. Lincoln steps back, is again greeted by officials.
11. Lincoln is escorted offstage by soldiers and officials.

First Flight of the Wright Brothers

1. The Wright Brothers work on their airplane.
2. They make arm movements to each other which indicate flight.
3. They again work on airplane, discuss various parts.
4. Curious neighbors enter to watch.
5. The onlookers talk among themselves, make motions which indicate flight.
6. The Wright Brothers shake hands, look skyward.
7. One of brothers pantomimes the act of piloting; he flies offstage.
8. Other brother races off after the airplane, exits.

9. Neighbors look upward and offstage in amazement as they watch the flight.

10. Brothers return onstage.

11. Neighbors crowd around to congratulate Wright Brothers.

The Ride of Paul Revere

1. Several citizens pretend to sleep.

2. Paul Revere rides in with shouts and gestures.

3. The citizens rise, look about in surprise and alarm.

4. Paul Revere knocks on door after door.

5. Citizens open windows, peer out.

6. Paul Revere makes motions which indicate that the British are coming.

7. Citizens quickly dress, dash into street.

8. Paul Revere rides offstage.

The Pony Express

1. Pony Express rider waits at relay station.

2. Another rider gallops in.

3. Mail pouch is quickly transferred from one to another.

4. The new rider gallops about stage as the other rider exits.

5. Indians ride onstage and stealthily creep in ambush around rider.

6. Indians attack rider but he eludes them.

7. Indians give up, exit.

8. Pony Express rider gallops about and finally rides offstage.

David's Battle with Goliath

1. Goliath (a tall player) struts onstage.
2. Several frightened players fearfully enter.
3. Goliath roars and threateningly steps toward them.
4. Players cringe, retreat.
5. Goliath proudly stands in place with arms folded and legs set apart.
6. David (a short player) enters.
7. The crowd looks hopefully toward David.
8. David picks up a stone (imaginary) as Goliath laughs.
9. David slings stone, Goliath falls.
10. David races to fallen Goliath, stands over him.
11. David walks back to his friends who cheer him.
12. David exits surrounded by his friends.

Columbus' Discovery of America

1. A crewman stands at ship's wheel and turns it.
2. Columbus enters, stands with arms behind back while gazing seaward.
3. His crew approaches as he continues to gaze.
4. The crew surrounds him, angrily arguing.
5. Columbus solemnly shakes his head, gestures seaward.

6. The crew grumbles, draws back from Columbus.

7. A crew member separates himself from the others, walks to rail, peers through telescope.

8. He shouts, points outward, calls the attention of the others.

9. All except Columbus race to rail, peer outward, cheer.

10. A crew member joyously escorts Columbus to rail.

11. Columbus peers at land through telescope, gratefully nods.

12. Part of crew congratulates Columbus.

13. Another part of crew happily gazes toward land.

14. Third part of crew hoists more sail and excitedly works about ship.

The Pilgrims' First Thanksgiving

1. Pilgrims enter with food, set outdoor table.

2. A Pilgrim rushes in, indicates that friendly Indians are approaching.

3. Pilgrims welcome several Indians.

4. Pilgrims and Indians chat as dinner is further prepared.

5. Pilgrims escort Indians to table; all sit.

6. All bow heads as standing Pilgrim leads in brief prayer.

7. Dinner and conversation is enjoyed by all.

8. All rise.

9. Pilgrims and Indians exchange greetings of friendship.

10. Pilgrims wave goodbye as Indians leave.

11. Pilgrims happily clear table and exit.

The Boston Tea Party

1. Players enter from several directions, gather in stage center.

2. They huddle, glance furtively about, quietly talk.

3. They disguise themselves as Indians.

4. They row to a ship on opposite side of stage.

5. They climb ship's deck.

6. They rush about, toss boxes into sea.

7. They row back to shore.

8. They remove disguises, go separate ways.

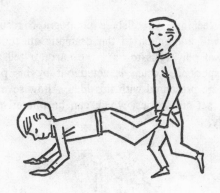

TABLEAU

A tableau is a dramatic scene which is both silent and motionless. Two or preferably more players pose in an interesting tableau for a few seconds. If the stage has no curtain, a pair of assistants can raise and lower a sheet in front of the performers.

A tableau is very simple to stage. It can be built around a famous historical scene or it can portray a great moment in the life of a well-known person. A tableau can be humorous and it might be surprising. It is a good idea to plan some ten different tableaux to be presented one after another, if you are planning a big party or a stage presentation.

ACT-OUT STORIES

Two players perform this stunt together. One of them takes the part of the narrator, while the other is the actor. As they stand side by side onstage, the narrator tells (or reads) any kind of story, perhaps a children's classic such as "Jack and the Beanstalk" or a familiar poem which has lots of action. The narrator pauses every so often during the story to permit the player to act out an incident in pantomime.

The story then resumes until the next good place for the player to demonstrate the narrator's lines. The actor can make any kind of movement which illustrates the story, such as leaping about, putting on a pained expression, and performing specific acts such as climbing or sleeping. An offstage phonograph record playing suitable music will add much to the dramatic effect.

Another way of playing is to have the narrator tell a funny or embarrassing experience which is acted out by his partner. An entire show can be presented with this idea. Allow several couples time to prepare act-out stories, which can be offered at intervals during the party.

DARING SAILORMEN

(A narrator reads the verses aloud while the players act according to the instructions. All the actions are performed quickly and briefly.)

One daring sailorman sailed the ocean blue . . . (a player marches onstage, faces audience, steers ship) Along came a friend of his . . . (second player enters, they exchange greetings, stand alongside each other) And so there were two!

Two daring sailormen sailed the stormy sea . . . (both steer at wheel while holding tight and swaying) They called and called for extra help . . . (as they call with cupped hands a third player joins them) And so there were three!

Three daring sailormen stepped upon the shore . . . (players step forward, march in place) And when the three stepped back again . . . (as the three step back to original positions a fourth player joins them) The three had turned to four!

Four daring sailormen did a fancy dive . . . (they make diving motions) They looked so fine and fancy . . . (fifth player enters, looks in admiration, joins them) That soon there were five!

Five daring sailormen fished with crooked sticks . . . (they pretend to fish) Their dinner was so tasty . . . (as they pretend to eat a sixth player joins them) Very soon there were six!

Six daring sailormen opened up a door . . . (they face wing and pretend to open doors) In jumped another friend . . . (seventh player jumps in) So there was one more!

Seven daring sailormen all began to skate . . . (all pretend to skate) It looked so much like lots of fun . . . (eighth player skates onstage) That their number came to eight!

Eight daring sailormen all stood in a line . . . (they line up at attention) And before they knew it . . . (ninth player quickly enters to join end of line) The line had stretched to nine!

Nine daring sailormen wondered where they'd been . . . (they shade eyes with palms and gaze outward) Someone came to tell them . . . (tenth player enters, gestures outward) And that made ten!

Ten daring sailormen all went swimming for fun . . . (all make swimming movements) And so they swam and swam and swam . . . (they swim offstage) Until at last there were none!

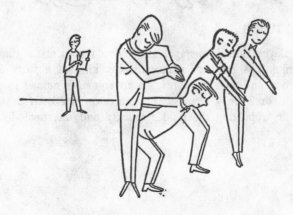

IN THE JUNGLE

Several players stand onstage. Each one represents a different
jungle animal. A narrator makes up any kind of a story about
a jungle boy and wild creatures. As an animal is named its actor
imitates it for 3 or 4 seconds. The narrator can keep the stage
jumping by repeating the names quickly and unexpectedly.

THE MAN WHO DIDN'T LIKE RAIN

Characters

Narrator
The Man Who Didn't Like Rain
Farmer
Fish
Schoolchildren (two or more)
Weatherman
Robin

Setting: Outdoors. A chair is set upstage center.

NARRATOR (enters, stands near wing): Ladies and gentlemen . . . there was once a man who didn't like rain. He liked trees and rivers and flowers and lakes, but he just *didn't* like rain. He didn't like showers or drizzles or downpours . . . (sadly shake head) He didn't even like pitters and patters. As you can see . . . (gesture to wing as Man enters) he just didn't like rain of any kind. (Man enters with a large sign reading DOWN WITH RAIN! He scowls at sky, glumly takes position alongside Narrator.)

NARRATOR: He didn't like rain because it got him wet all over . . . (Man angrily brushes raindrops from face and shoulders) and because it made him slip when he walked . . . (Man slips about a few steps) and because he couldn't go out to water his garden. (Man sways imaginary garden hose while scowling skyward.)

NARRATOR: So the man who didn't like rain spent most of his time just sitting around. (Man sits on chair with sign propped on knees. He gestures skyward for the rain to go away.)

NARRATOR: One day as he sat in the rain, he saw a happy farmer gathering some fruits and vegetables. (Farmer enters with basket, sets it down, smiles at raining sky, digs potatoes and picks fruit, exits with heavy basket.)

NARRATOR: He also saw a gay little fish swimming in the big, big river. The river was getting even bigger and bigger because of the heavy rain. (Fish enters with swimming motions, swims gaily about, swims offstage.)

129

NARRATOR: And then he saw some youngsters having lots of fun playing in the rain. (Children briskly enter to perform various fun-in-the-rain stunts, such as cupping hands to catch rain, hopping over puddles, splashing water on each other.) One little boy thought it was a good time to get clean! (A boy stands stage center, pulls towel and soap from pocket, scrubs himself—without disrobing! Children exit.)

NARRATOR: Then he saw that hard-working fellow, the weatherman! (Weatherman solemnly enters with upraised umbrella, halts at stage center, faces audience. Three times he holds out a palm, wipes wet hand on his coat, nods, unfolds and reveals to audience a large sheet of paper which reads, RAIN PREDICTED. He solemnly exits.)

NARRATOR: And finally the man who didn't like rain saw a thirsty little robin who needed a drink of rain water. (Robin flies in, hops about, goes through the motions of drinking from a pool, hops offstage.)

NARRATOR: All these things caused the man who didn't like rain to *think* . . . (Man thinks by peering curiously at sky) and *think* . . . (Man stands, thinks harder) and *think!* (Man thinks very hard by pacing the floor with head bowed and hands clasped at back.) He began to think that rain might be pretty good after all. He thought of all the good things it gave to the world. Like vegetables . . . (Farmer enters, freezes in digging position) and rivers . . . (Fish enters, holds swimming pose) and playtime . . . (Children rush in, freeze in play positions) and

130

weather reports . . . (Weatherman enters, holds outstretched palm) and water to drink . . . (Robin flits in, holds drinking pose.)

NARRATOR: All of a sudden, the man who didn't like rain started really to *like* rain. He smiled at the sky . . . (Man smiles upward) and smiled even more. (Man broadens smile) He even laughed! (Man laughs, joyously throws arms skyward.)

NARRATOR (excitedly): So he went out and had fun in the rain just like everyone else!

(Man races in turn to each of the others, briefly acts out their frozen positions, races to his sign DOWN WITH RAIN, holds it up to audience with one hand while wildly gesturing skyward for the rain to come down. As he finishes, the others exit while acting out their roles—for example, the Farmer walks off while picking fruit. The Man gaily skips offstage while happily holding high his sign.)

NARRATOR: And that is how the man who once said (frown) down with rain, finally said (smile) *down with rain!* (bow and exit).

THE TAKE-TURNERS

Characters

Narrator
Mr. Melody, a pianist
Do ⎫
Re ⎪
Mi ⎪
Fa ⎬ Musical Notes
Sol ⎪
La ⎪
Ti ⎪
Do ⎭

Setting: The Musical Notes are lined up facing audience. A chair is set in front of them. A few items which indicate a musical theme, such as instruments or sheet music, may be set in the background.

NARRATOR: Ladies and gentlemen, we would like you to see—

and hear—an exciting story. The story is about eight young musical notes who lived inside a piano. (Gesture to Notes who briefly and awkwardly jump up and down in unison.) Their names are Do, Re, Mi, Fa, Sol, La, Ti, and Do. As you can see, the Notes are all played at the same time—they had not as yet learned how to take turns playing. (Notes again jump in unison.) Our story is also about Mr. Melody, a world-famous pianist. (Gesture to Mr. Melody who enters, bows to audience, sits in chair facing Notes.)

NARRATOR: One day Mr. Melody sat down to play a lovely piece of music. (Mr. Melody pretends to play by striking an imaginary keyboard. As the Musical Notes awkwardly jump up and down, more or less in unison, an actual offstage pianist plays a few notes in disharmony.)

NARRATOR (dismayed): What is this? What has happened? This isn't a lovely song. (to Mr. Melody) Mr. Melody, please try again. (Mr. Melody again plays with the same discordant result.)

NARRATOR (to audience): Perhaps Mr. Melody has not shown the musical notes how to take turns. (to Mr. Melody) Mr. Melody, did you notice that all the notes played at the same time? Perhaps you should show them how to take turns. Once they know how to be *take-turners* I am sure we will have a lovely song. (Mr. Melody nods. As he taps each note, one at a time and going upscale, the notes jump up in turn. The offstage pianist taps notes accordingly. The action is then repeated downscale.)

NARRATOR (pleased): Now that they are *take-turners* I am sure we will have a lovely song. Try again, Mr. Melody. (Mr. Melody plays a slow piece as the notes jump up and down. Note: they jump in any order and not in unison, much as actual notes might move. The result is a melody.)

NARRATOR (brightly): And that is just about the end of our story. The *take-turners* have learned how to make a merry melody by taking turns. So they play (music plays as Notes happily jump in rapid movements) and play . . . and play. (as music ends, all bow and exit.)

132

THE CHILDREN WHO FOUND NEW FRIENDS

Characters

Narrator
Western Children (as many as desired)
Indian Children (about equal in number to
Western Children)

Setting: Outdoors during days of early West. A few bushes, buckets and similar items will help to indicate the period. A river, which splits the stage from upstage to downstage, is indicated by lengths of rippled rope set a few feet apart.

NARRATOR: Many years ago some pioneer children journeyed to the West with their parents. One morning they ran from their covered wagons to play in the wide, lazy river. (Western Children rush in from the right, play between the right wing and their side of the river bank. They recognize the river by wading near the shore, drinking, splashing water on each other.)

NARRATOR: On that very same morning a band of Indian Children came down from the hills to play in the wide, lazy river. (Indian Children enter from left, also play about.)

NARRATOR: The Western Children heard some strange noises coming from the other side of the river, so they stopped to listen. (Western Children halt, listen with hands cupped to ears.)

NARRATOR: And so did the Indian Children. (Indian Children also halt, listen.)

NARRATOR: One little Western boy waded to the middle of the river to take a look. (Western boy wades to center of river, peers by raising palm to brow, throws up arms in fright, rushes back in

133

alarm, tells others of Indians. The Western Children excitedly peer and chatter with each other while gesturing across the river.)

NARRATOR: And a little Indian boy decided to see who was making all the noise on the other side of his river. (Indian boy duplicates action of Western boy. The Indian Children also talk it over excitedly.)

NARRATOR: The Western Children were so frightened by the Indian Children that they ran off! (Western Children rush offstage.) And the Indian Children were so frightened of the Western Children that they also scooted away! (Indian Children run offstage.)

NARRATOR: Now this was a very sad thing. None of the children could enjoy the wide, lazy river any more. It's too bad they were so scared of each other! (sadly close book, shake head.) So I guess that is the end of the story . . . (happily uplift head as a Western girl timidly enters, speak hopefully.) Wait a minute . . . looks like there's more to the story . . . let's see what happens . . . (The Western girl cautiously peers across the river, slowly wades to its center, waves at the hiding Indian Children. An Indian girl timidly enters, pauses, waves back, wades to center of river where the girls stand opposite each other. They shyly look each other over, touch each other's hair, finally smile and pat each other in a gesture of friendship. Both turn, gesture for the others to come. Two more children from each camp enter and repeat the gestures of friendship and welcome. All six now turn and enthusiastically wave to the rest who rush out to meet and mingle. Western Children pair off with Indian Children and they play together.)

NARRATOR: And that is *really* the end of the story . . . a very happy ending, don't you think? (All bow and exit.)

THE HAPPY HIKERS

Characters

Narrator
Happy Hikers (as many as desired)
Setting: Bare stage. The Happy Hikers stand in various stage positions, facing audience.

NARRATOR (gesturing to Hikers): Ladies and gentlemen, meet our happy hikers! (Hikers smile, wave to audience, hike in place. Note: all movements are in place.) Let's watch their adventures as they hike through the woods and over the mountains. There they go! (Hikers increase pace slightly.)

NARRATOR (as he looks at Hikers): Looks like they're climbing a steep hill! (Hikers bend backward as if climbing.) They're on top! What a lovely view! (Hikers look around in appreciation.) Now watch them get down! (Hikers slip and slide as if plunging downhill.) They must be out of breath! (Hikers hold hands on chests, breathe heavily.)

NARRATOR: Now they're passing through a meadow. (Hikers walk, then halt. Narrator peers closely at Hikers.) What do they see? A rabbit! (Hikers swiftly glance from left to right.) And a meadow lark! (Hikers quickly glance from ground to sky.) And a bumblebee! (Hikers jerk heads and eyes about. Narrator cries out a warning.) Watch out for the bumblebee! (Hikers run swiftly in place, waving arms as if battling off bumblebee.)

NARRATOR: As I said, they are *happy* hikers, happy because of the beautiful mountains they see . . . (Hikers happily shield eyes with palms and peer.) And because of all that clean, fresh air they breathe . . . (Hikers happily breathe while expanding their chests.) And especially because they got away from that buzzing bumblebee! (Hikers smile and nod, turn heads slightly to rear, wave goodbye to the bumblebee.)

NARRATOR: Looks like they are tired from all that hiking. (Hikers slow down, walk droopily. Narrator excitedly waves outward as he peers ahead.) There's just what they need—a cool, refreshing drink from the river. (to Hikers) Can you make it to the river, Happy Hikers? (Hikers nod, pick up speed, kneel down at river, drink, scoop water over their faces.)

NARRATOR: Ah! How refreshing! On your way, Happy Hikers! (Hikers rise. Narrator speaks to them with caution.) Try to jump all the way across that river—keep those little tootsies dry! (Hikers jump but look down in dismay as they shake their wet feet. Narrator speaks sympathetically.) Don't feel too bad about not making it—after all, that river was more than a block wide. At least you have cool toes.

NARRATOR (as he looks ahead): Look what's in front of them—a fork in the road. Hope they take the right road. (Hikers turn somewhat to left.) No, they took the *left* road. Well, maybe the *left* road is the *right* road . . . (Narrator is confused by his own speech.) I mean . . . maybe the *right* one is the *wrong* one and the *left* one is the *right* one . . . (Narrator shakes head.) Maybe we'd better just see what happens . . . (Hikers turn in circles as they march in place; some turn in left circles, some in right circles. The Narrator is distressed.) They're lost! I guess the *right* road was the *left* road after all . . . hmmm, I'd better not start that again. (Narrator sighs in relief as Hikers again march straight ahead.) Looks like all is right . . . I mean, all is *well.*

NARRATOR: I wonder when they will stop for lunch? (Hikers suddenly stop, keep heads and eyes straight ahead, reach into pockets, bring imaginary bits of food to lips, munch briefly, take handkerchiefs from pockets, quickly pat lips, replace handkerchiefs, resume marching. Note: this action should be done in unison or with as much unison as possible. The Narrator shakes his head in surprise.) Guess they weren't very hungry.

NARRATOR: Look! A lovely lake. (to audience) I wonder if they will hike around it or swim across? Let's see . . . (Hikers sit on floor as if getting into rowboats, make rowing motions. The Narrator smiles, shrugs.) I guess that's better than trying to *hike* across. (Hikers stand, resume marching.)

NARRATOR (peers at trail): Look at that crooked trail ahead! Nothing but twists and turns! (Hikers twist and turn in various directions as they march. Note: this need not be done in unison; players twist about individually. After a few seconds they resume their forward march. Narrator sighs.) I'm glad that's over—I was getting dizzy.

NARRATOR: Looks like they have come to the end of the trail. I wonder what their final destination is? (Narrator speaks to Hikers.) Say, Happy Hikers, wait a minute. (Hikers halt.) Now that you have reached the end of your hike, what are you going to do next? (Hikers grin broadly, march with a higher and livelier step than before. The Narrator staggers as if fainting, painfully holds his head.) You mean that the next thing you are going to do is to *march some more?* (Hikers vigorously nod their heads. The Narrator apologetically speaks to audience.) I'm sorry folks, but I just can't keep up with them any longer. Goodbye. (Narrator waves to Hikers.) And a happy hike to you, Happy Hikers. (Narrator weakly exits at right. The Hikers face left, march off while keeping heads and eyes turned offstage, wave farewell.)

HOW MUSIC MADE EVERYONE HAPPY

Characters

The Very Lonely Man
The Very Nice Children (as many as desired)
Setting: A single chair is set at left stage, a number of others chairs are set in semicircle at right stage. Note: Actual music may be added to the skit if desired. If an offstage piano or other instrument is employed, it may be played in unison with the children's pantomimes.

NARRATOR (enters, stands near left wing): There was once a very lonely man. (Man feebly enters from left, sits.) Next door was a school. (Children enter from right, sit.) The very lonely man was very sad because he had no one to play music for him. He wished and wished for someone to play. (Man sadly nods.) And the very nice children were very sad because they had no one for whom they could play their music. They wished and wished for someone to hear their music. (Children sadly nod in unison.)

NARRATOR: One day the very lonely man said to himself, *I will open my window. Maybe someone will send music into my home.* So he opened his window. (Man opens window at stage center, returns to chair.) And on that very same day the very nice children said, *We will open a school window. Maybe someone will listen to our music.* So one of the boys opened a school window. (Boy opens window at stage center.)

NARRATOR: So the very lonely man listened. (Man cups hand at ear toward window.) And the very nice children played . . . first the trombone . . . (trombonist pantomimes) then the violinist . . . (violinist pantomimes) then the kettle drums . . . (drummer pantomimes.) Then *all* the musicians played! (All pantomime various instruments.)

NARRATOR: So the very lonely man was not sad or lonely any more. (Man briskly beats time and sways to the music.) And the very nice children were not sad any more. (Children smile, play spiritedly.) The happy man kept his window open from that day on. And so did the very nice children. (All bow and exit.)

Section 4

Charades

What are charades? The basic idea is for someone to act out in pantomime a word (or a series of words) which an audience tries to guess.

Suppose that the charade actor chooses to act out the word *highway*. Since this is one word containing two syllables the actor would first show one finger to the viewers (indicating one word) and then two fingers (indicating two syllables). When the audience shows it understands, he then holds up one finger to indicate that he will now act out the first syllable of his secret word.

His syllable is revealed through pantomime actions, such as gestures and motions. He answers "yes" or "no" to guesses from the audience by nodding or shaking his head. No words are ever spoken by him, nor do his lips form words; everything is acted out in silence. His syllable of *high* could be acted out in a number of ways; for instance, he could hold his palm at a high level, or raise his palm higher and higher, or just point upwards.

Once the viewers have guessed the syllable, *high*, it is possible that they will call out the complete word, but if they do not the actor goes on to the second syllable, *way*. This might not be easy to act out. One method of revealing it would be for the actor to cup his hand to his ear, to let the audience know that he will not act out the exact syllable but something that *sounds like* the syllable. The actor could then pretend to shovel *hay* into a wagon. If viewers catch on to *hay* they call it out and the performer nods his head. It probably will not be long before the rhyme *way* is guessed. The audience now has the complete word *highway*.

If a performer finds it difficult to act out the first syllable of a word, he can hold up two fingers at the right moment to indicate that he will act out the second syllable first. Likewise, the third syllable of a long word can be pantomimed first. The actor can then go back to the first syllable if it becomes necessary.

The audience has to be informed beforehand if the charade is a sentence or phrase of several words. So at the very beginning of a performance the actor's held-up fingers indicate either a single word or the number of words in his sentence.

Signals can be used. For instance, if one of the words in a sentence is a short word, such as *and, the, or,* the actor holds his thumb and forefinger in the air about an inch apart, indicating a small word.

Charades may be played with teams or with individual contestants. For team play, divide the group into equal numbers of actors and actresses, with one player acting as timekeeper. One at a time the players of team A act out their words while the other members of their team try to guess them. Players of team B then go onstage and try to guess what one of their team acts out. At the end of the contest the timekeeper announces the winning team, that is, the one which finishes in the least amount of time.

With small groups (fewer than 6) it is best to have each player perform individually. The player acts out one or more charade words while all the others try to guess.

If the game leader chooses to do so, he can set a reasonable time limit in which a player must reveal his word. With younger and inexperienced players it would be best to allow as much time as necessary.

In this section you will find three different kinds of charade material:

1. Easy charades for those who are learning the game.

2. Varieties of game ideas which add spice to the basic game of charades.

3. Lists of interesting and educational topics which can be used by both beginning and advanced players.

All ready? All right. Let's play charades!

FIRST CHARADES

Here is an excellent starting game for actors of charades and also for those trying to guess for the first time. The performer acts out only the first syllable of his word. For example, with the word *for*mation he could act out the sound of *for*. As soon as the spectators guess this first part, they then go on to guess words which begin with this sound until they find the correct one. Then the next performer acts out the next word. Give each performer his word on a slip of paper.

The viewers will find it fairly easy to play their part in the game, once they understand what they must do. Beginning actors and actresses will gain confidence from this first game as they see how easy it is to act with a minimum of effort. It won't be long before they can act out complete words with confidence and skill.

1. *for*mation
2. *king*dom
3. *art*icle
4. *ti*ger
5. *doll*ar
6. *add*ress
7. *sales*man
8. *skip*per
9. *mist*er
10. *arm*y
11. *too*th
12. *bow*ling
13. *rock*et
14. *star*fish
15. *wind*ow
16. *catt*le
17. *tea*cher
18. *pan*cake
19. *batt*ery
20. *chair*man

A B C CHARADES

Each player is assigned a different letter of the alphabet. He is allowed one minute in which to act out as many objects as possible which begin with his letter. The performer having the letter *A* might act out *apple, arm, automobile, ape, airplane.* When the viewers guess an object the performer scores a point. The player with the most points at the end of the game wins. If desired, a shorter or longer performance period may be set.

THREE-LETTER CHARADES

This is played somewhat as the above game, except that players try to act out as many objects as possible which are spelled with three letters. A player might try *cat, ice, cup, rug, hoe.*

After a number of three-letter words, you might try four-letter or five-letter words.

COLOR CHARADES

A player is assigned one of the listed colors. He reveals his color for the audience to guess by acting out an object or two which is associated with the color. For *purple* he could act out *plum* or *eggplant.* The color *silver* could be associated with a *dime* or a *cloud.*

1. purple	8. blue
2. silver	9. orange
3. red	10. black
4. gray	11. gold
5. pink	12. scarlet
6. white	13. brown
7. yellow	14. green

CHANCE CHARADES

This one will help actors and actresses to think and act quickly while onstage. A player goes onstage where an assistant holds an open book before him. (It can be any page of any book.) The player closes his eyes and jabs a finger onto the page. He then acts out whatever word his finger lands upon. He takes three turns at poking and acting. Some of the words will be easy and others will be difficult, but all will help the player to become a better performer.

DOG NAMES

Here is a charade with a humorous twist. A player acts out the name of his dog. However, his dog does not have a common-place name such as Fido or Rover, but the strangest name possible. He might be called Bonechew or Barkerboy or Catchase. It is up to the audience to discover the unusual name.

INITIAL ACTS

Here is an interesting way to build short charade acts. Players build their secret words by using the initials in their first and last names. A player named Betty Lewis, for example, could use her initials of *B* and *L* to work out *beautiful lake* or *bouncy lions*. For the second time around the players could use their middle initials also. A performer named Charles Frank Dennis, for instance, could act out *cake for dessert*.

ADD-A-LETTER CHARADES

The pantomimist acts out a word, such as *tree*, which the viewers must guess. Once they have the sound of *tree*, they must add a single letter of the alphabet to reveal the secret word, while the actor tries to help them with gestures. In the case of *tree*, the proper letter to be added is T, thus making the secret word of *treat*. The sound (not the spelling) of the acted-out word, plus the sound of an added letter, completes the secret word.

1. treat (*tree* plus *T*)
2. single (*sing* plus *L*)
3. droop (*drew* plus *P*)
4. sticky (*stick* plus *E*)
5. tense (*ten* plus *S*)
6. ready (*red* plus *E*)
7. goat (*go* plus *T*)
8. short (*shore* plus *T*)
9. toot (*two* plus *T*)
10. slate (*sleigh* plus *T*)
11. yellow (*yell* plus *O*)
12. load (*low* plus *D*)
13. soak (*sew* plus *K*)
14. shine (*shy* plus *N*)
15. squawk (*squaw* plus *K*)
16. great (*gray* plus *T*)
17. hair (*hay* plus *R*)
18. arrow (*air* plus *O*)
19. cattle (*cat* plus *L*)
20. change (*chain* plus *G*)
21. slide (*sly* plus *D*)
22. cellar (*sell* plus *R*)
23. grope (*grow* plus *P*)
24. frenzy (*friend* plus *Z*)
25. pine (*pie* plus *N*)
26. hurry (*her* plus *E*)
27. hide (*high* plus *D*)
28. slipper (*slip* plus *R*)
29. spice (*spy* plus *S*)
30. storm (*store* plus *M*)

TAKE-AWAY CHARADES

This game usually moves along at a fast pace. Performers act out the listed one-syllable words, but the secret word for the audience to discover is obtained by taking away the first letter. Example: The performer acts out the word *cloud* and the viewers take away the letter *c* to end up with the secret word *loud*.

1. hear—ear
2. fall—all
3. ground—round
4. hair—air
5. star—tar
6. crow—row
7. bread—read
8. speak—peak
9. feast—east
10. farm—arm
11. feel—eel
12. broom—room
13. wink—ink
14. table—able
15. sport—port
16. trip—rip
17. steam—team
18. spill—pill
19. box—ox
20. wheel—heel
21. plate—late
22. flight—light
23. reach—each
24. sour—our
25. tape—ape
26. cup—up
27. bright—right
28. glove—love
29. flip—lip
30. flag—lag

CHARADE CONTEST

Two performers occupy the stage at the same time for a charade contest. The game leader swiftly calls out a number to each. The numbers should range between three and six. For instance, the leader might call out "Five!" to one player and "Three!" to the other one. Each player must think of a word containing the number of assigned letters, and immediately act out that word. The players compete simultaneously for the attention of the audience. A point is scored by the one whose word is guessed first by the viewers. Whoever first scores three points wins the contest. Another two contestants then take the stage.

BEGIN-END LETTERS

The listed words give the viewers an opportunity for fast answers. They are told that the secret word being acted out starts and ends with the same letter.

1. rooster
2. museum
3. label
4. treatment
5. clinic
6. eclipse
7. register
8. tonight
9. hurrah
10. lawful
11. classic
12. depend
13. elegance
14. target
15. overdo
16. level
17. triumphant
18. willow
19. napkin
20. refrigerator
21. typist
22. defend
23. cubic
24. nation
25. experience
26. regular
27. cosmetic
28. laurel
29. discard
30. maximum
31. glaring
32. northern
33. recover
34. elude
35. telecast
36. radar
37. tumult
38. liberal
39. yearly
40. transparent

HA!

Each performer in turn acts out one of the listed words, all of which begin with *ha*. Give each performer his word (or words) on a slip of paper before starting. The audience should be informed beforehand that all the words to be acted out begin with these letters. This makes it easier for both actors and viewers —and supplies a *ha* or two for all!

1. hammer	16. harbor
2. handshake	17. hard
3. hat	18. hand
4. hack	19. halo
5. hail	20. handle
6. hair	21. hay
7. half	22. handsome
8. hawk	23. ham
9. haunt	24. halt
10. haul	25. handcuff
11. handball	26. hairpin
12. harvest	27. hammock
13. happy	28. halfback
14. harness	29. hasten
15. harmony	30. handkerchief

NAME CHARADES

This one is fun for both beginners and experts. Below are lists of names of boys and girls which are especially good for charade play. The idea is to act out the sound of the first part of the name. This supplies the audience with a clue for guessing the complete name. The viewers should be informed in advance that they will be given only the first part of a name and that they must take it from there.

Girls	Boys
1. Lois (low)	1. Richard (rich)
2. Julia (jewel)	2. Gilbert (gill)
3. Lydia (lid)	3. John (jaw)
4. Mildred (mill)	4. Dennis (den)
5. Phyllis (fill)	5. Walter (wall)
6. Peggy (peg)	6. Woodrow (wood)
7. Patricia (pat)	7. Tony (toe)
8. Jane (jay)	8. Michael (my)
9. Doris (door)	9. Raymond (ray)
10. Grace (gray)	10. Donald (dawn)
11. Barbara (bar)	11. Orville (ore)
12. Sharon (share)	12. Cecil (see)
13. Gladys (glad)	13. Keith (key)
14. Sylvia (sill)	14. Lionel (lion)
15. Rose (row)	15. Chester (chest)
16. Sandra (sand)	16. David (day)
17. Harriet (hair)	17. Warren (war)
18. Joyce (joy)	18. Carl (car)
19. Irene (eye)	19. Eugene (you)
20. Hazel (hay)	20. Stuart (stew)

PARTNER CHARADES

This is played in the usual way except that each syllable in the secret word (or each word in the secret sentence) is acted out by a different player. Thus the three-syllable word *volcano* would be acted out by three partners, while the proverb *Better late than never* would need four players. As soon as one part of the word or sentence is guessed, the next member of the partnership takes over.

This can be played as a contest by assigning different words having an equal number of syllables to two teams. A timekeeper keeps track and at the end of each round announces which team completed its word in the shorter time, and awards them a point. The first team to score five points wins the contest.

THE SOUND OF T

Players take turns in acting out the listed words. Even though the viewers are informed that all the words end with the sound of *t* they may have to do some extra thinking in order to come up with the right answers.

1. activity
2. celebrity
3. curiosity
4. hilarity
5. timidity
6. university
7. intensity
8. liberty
9. oddity
10. personality
11. mighty
12. captivity
13. poverty
14. piety
15. electricity
16. beauty
17. serenity
18. royalty
19. perplexity
20. thrifty
21. authority
22. deputy
23. stability
24. property
25. ability
26. velocity
27. popularity
28. immensity
29. rapidity
30. prosperity

QUESTION AND ANSWER CHARADES

Two performers occupy the stage together. One of them asks a simple question (such as "What time is it?") which the other answers (by looking at his watch and holding up two fingers, for example). Both the question and the answer must be given in pantomime, of course; no words are spoken. Each player asks and answers just one or two questions, after which another couple takes the stage.

The viewers follow the performances by calling out as they get the questions and answers. This is a good charade with which to start off a large party.

KING CHARADES

Players act out these words which end in *king*. Viewers try to guess which kind of king is on the throne, or rather on the stage.

1. waking	21. soaking
2. parking	22. stacking
3. shrieking	23. shaking
4. thinking	24. ducking
5. breaking	25. stroking
6. joking	26. blocking
7. hiking	27. clicking
8. packing	28. hacking
9. working	29. wrecking
10. talking	30. kicking
11. cooking	31. quacking
12. sneaking	32. blinking
13. backing	33. basking
14. choking	34. licking
15. raking	35. thanking
16. locking	36. tracking
17. poking	37. sticking
18. peeking	38. tacking
19. honking	39. sinking
20. smacking	40. striking

NICKNAME CHARADES

Each player is given a comical nickname which he or she acts out for the others to guess. Try these examples:

1. Prince Charming
2. Twinkletoes
3. Angel Face
4. Big Hero
5. Muscles
6. Lover Boy
7. Princess Fair
8. Happy Farmer
9. Jumping Jack
10. Dragonfire
11. Beauty Queen
12. The Brain
13. Magnificent One
14. Champ
15. Personality Plus

TRIPLE CHARADES

This is a slightly more difficult game than the preceding ones. Three charade actors perform at the same time, each acting out a different word. However, the audience knows their words are all of one syllable and rhyme, like *leap, weep, peep.* The spectators try to guess any or all of the three as soon as possible. As soon as the viewers guess a word, its performer retires from the stage, while the others continue to act. Here is enough material for twenty rounds.

1. sing, sling, cling
2. knock, talk, walk
3. sigh, fly, pie
4. cake, ache, break

5. fall, haul, call
6. hum, drum, gum
7. swift, lift, gift
8. freeze, breeze, sneeze
9. east, feast, beast
10. strain, chain, cane
11. drink, blink, sink
12. girl, curl, pearl
13. fig, pig, twig
14. shine, nine, pine
15. tree, bee, sea
16. hat, bat, mat
17. boy, joy, toy
18. joke, oak, yoke
19. hay, clay, jay
20. giggle, wriggle, jiggle
   (tell the audience word has two syllables)

PERFORMING POET CHARADES

Players are allowed enough time to make up their own simple two-line poems. The verses are then acted out for the audience to guess. A poem can be on any subject the player prefers and can be just as sensible or nonsensical as he likes. Below is a pair of examples:

I like summer and I like fall,
But I like ice cream best of all.

Oranges, apples, lemons and limes,
It may not make sense but at least it rhymes.

RHYMING WORD CHARADES

Each player in turn is assigned one of the secret words listed below. Before the performer begins, the audience is told that the word suggested by the pantomimed action rhymes with the secret word. The idea is to guess both words. For instance, if the pantomimist pretends to saw a piece of wood the viewers would first have to guess the word *saw*. The players in the audience may shout as many guesses as they can as rapidly as they can. When a guesser shouts the word *saw,* the pantomimist nods to indicate that he has found the right word. The viewers now try to guess the secret word which rhymes with *saw,* which might be *law*.

This stunt is especially good for team play. Members of each team are each assigned a secret word. One at a time, they perform while their team guesses. The team that guesses the secret words in the shortest time is the winner. Here are some secret words with suggestions for pantomiming them.

1. cake (pretend to *shake* hands)
2. gold (shiver as if *cold*)
3. ball (hold hand at *tall* level)
4. leap (pretend to *sleep*)
5. ring (pretend to *sing*)
6. cook (pretend to read *book*)
7. sound (*pound* fist)
8. out (cup hands, *shout*)
9. blue (hold up *two* fingers)
10. sink (*blink* your eyes or pretend to *drink*)
11. drop (*hop* around)
12. match (*scratch* arm)
13. green (*lean* to one side)
14. toe (pretend to *row* boat)
15. ice (pretend to *slice* bread)
16. chair (pat *hair*)
17. burn (*turn* around in circle)
18. fine (pretend to *shine* shoes)
19. bush (*push* away)
20. calm (point to *palm*)
21. chance (*dance* about)
22. please (tightly *squeeze* arm)

23. ripe (pretend to *type*)
24. snow (pretend to *sew*)
25. haste (pretend to *taste*)

HINK-PINK CHARADES

Each player is assigned to act out for the audience to guess two single words which complete a little but not necessarily sensible rhyme. (More difficult would be "Hinky-Pinky" Charades—two rhyming words of two syllables each. Advanced players could try that. Then go on to "Hinkety-Pinkety!")

1. long song
2. small ball
3. pull wool
4. flat hat
5. my pie
6. keep sheep
7. hurl pearl
8. slow throw
9. fly high
10. red head
11. sweet wheat
12. warm storm
13. crush mush
14. I spy
15. shun sun
16. whole bowl
17. stop mop
18. see bee
19. grip lip
20. jump stump
21. munch lunch
22. scrub tub
23. love dove
24. sad lad
25. bake cake
26. blue shoe
27. clean screen
28. big fig
29. spill pill
30. house mouse
31. float boat
32. brown clown
33. sock clock
34. one gun
35. tug rug
36. throw snow
37. drink ink
38. chew stew
39. sour flower
40. toss sauce

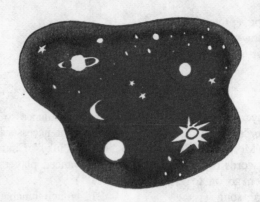

CHARADE NUMBERS

The idea of this game is for player to act out a word which is connected with a number. The viewers silently guess the word from which they guess aloud the number. For example, if the actor portrayed the word *alphabet* the audience would guess number 26—the number of letters in the alphabet. In this list of usable words and numbers, the charade words are in italics.

1. 7 days in a *week*.
2. 4 *seasons*.
3. 3 corners to a *triangle*.
4. 60 seconds to a *minute*.
5. 10 *fingers* on hands.
6. 24 hours to a *day*.
7. 31 days in *March*.
8. 9 *planets*.
9. 2 *ears* on a person's head.
10. 12 months in a *year*.

OPPOSITE ACTIONS

This is a tricky game of charades. The idea is for a performer to reveal his secret word by acting out its exact opposite meaning. For instance, for the secret word of *tall*, the player would act out the word *short*. Once the audience guesses the word *short*, it must keep guessing until it gets *tall*. The performer must not nod his head when and if the audience guesses the word acted out (*short* in this instance). The viewers are to keep guessing until they finally guess the exact secret word.

154

The charade performer acts out a word and the viewers call out, not the word acted, but that word spelled backwards. The audience must not call out the word, only the reversed word.

For example, if the performer acts out the word *nap*, a viewer would first discover that it is *nap*, then reverse its spelling and call out the secret word *pan*. Here are enough backward charades for 20 periods of play.

1. ton—not
2. peek—keep
3. tap—pat
4. deer—reed
5. nab—ban
6. trap—part
7. won—now
8. pool—loop
9. dial—laid
10. pin—nip
11. gulp—plug
12. yam—may
13. net—ten
14. no—on
15. war—raw
16. lap—pal
17. pit—tip
18. saw—was
19. nod—don
20. step—pets

THINK OF A QUESTION CHARADES

Here is a quiz contest with an unusual twist. The charade performer acts out one of the words supplied in the list below. Once someone in the audience guesses the word he must raise his hand, keep the answer secret, but ask a *question* that demands the same answer. For instance, if the secret word turns out to be *diamond* the guesser would ask the question, "What precious stone is mined in South Africa?" As another example, for the word *Paris* the question could be, "What city is the capital of France?"

The player who first indicates that he has guessed the secret word is allowed a few seconds to think up a question. If he succeeds he scores a point for his team. If his question reveals the wrong answer, and he has guessed an incorrect word, the charade simply continues. The game ends when one team has scored fifteen points. Here are enough charade words for several games.

1. diamond		30. pearl
2. Paris		31. forest
3. whale		32. cream
4. pepper		33. palace
5. Sweden		34. Tokyo
6. clock		35. cotton
7. river		36. squirrel
8. beaver		37. ocean
9. Delaware		38. letter
10. prince		39. Christmas
11. mountain		40. waterfall
12. treasure		41. igloo
13. bouquet		42. carpenter
14. tomato		43. root
15. salmon		44. detective
16. valley		45. Wednesday
17. Canada		46. bay
18. soldier		47. army
19. doctor		48. robin
20. collie		49. butterfly
21. village		50. fence
22. tunnel		51. book
23. snowstorm		52. carrot
24. Japan		53. rancher
25. cave		54. August
26. library		55. picture
27. college		56. pillow
28. Panama		57. meadow
29. tiger		58. wheel

59. volcano	80. candle
60. school	81. celery
61. Mexico	82. leopard
62. dinosaur	83. carnation
63. statue	84. Monday
64. zebra	85. sergeant
65. London	86. nutmeg
66. walnut	87. highway
67. farmer	88. pumpkin
68. mayor	89. fountain
69. bridge	90. Mars
70. comet	91. gorilla
71. rainbow	92. telegram
72. pineapple	93. bakery
73. Hawaii	94. iceberg
74. eagle	95. Boston
75. cloud	96. giant
76. pony	97. senator
77. coffee	98. medal
78. Australia	99. Indiana
79. emerald	100. blossom

SYNONYM CHARADES

The pantomimists (either individuals taking turns or teams alternating), keeping the list secret, act out the listed words for an audience (or for the other team) to guess. When someone in the audience (or a member of the guessing team) thinks he knows the word being acted out, he must call out two words, synonyms (words meaning more or less the same thing) which should correspond to those on this list. However, it's best not to be too exact in the requirements, as there are many words meaning the same thing. For example, the list calls for *quick* and *fast,* but *rapid* and *speedy* would be just as acceptable. If the guess is wrong, the pantomimist continues until he hears two correct words. Then the game continues with the next synonyms.

1. quick and fast
2. laugh and chuckle
3. strong and mighty
4. look and see
5. mystery and puzzle
6. drop and spill
7. fasten and tie
8. listen and hear
9. sleep and slumber
10. tune and melody
11. small and tiny
12. far and distant
13. shy and timid
14. brace and courageous
15. shout and yell
16. calm and peaceful
17. rich and wealthy
18. wise and intelligent
19. groan and moan
20. breeze and wind
21. beautiful and attractive
22. gay and merry
23. sad and gloomy
24. disappear and vanish
25. late and tardy
26. price and cost
27. dinner and supper
28. love and affection
29. hard and solid
30. heavy and weighty
31. work and effort
32. grab and grasp
33. honest and truthful
34. easy and simple
35. take and receive
36. throw and toss
37. run and sprint
38. keep and save
39. stone and rock
40. valuable and precious
41. want and desire
42. trip and journey
43. repair and mend
44. thin and slim
45. friend and chum
46. woman and lady
47. thought and idea
48. begin and start
49. new and fresh
50. talk and speak
51. shake and shiver
52. city and town
53. large and giant
54. empty and vacant
55. choose and select
56. umpire and referee
57. street and avenue
58. meadow and field
59. gift and present
60. game and sport

ANTONYM CHARADES

This is played just like the preceding game, except that the guessers try to think of the word being acted out and another that means the opposite.

1. open and close
2. north and south
3. agree and oppose
4. confident and afraid
5. believe and doubt
6. continue and cease
7. active and still
8. bright and dull
9. fancy and plain
10. freedom and slavery
11. gentle and rough
12. silence and noise
13. happy and sorrowful
14. gain and loss
15. famous and unknown
16. hit and miss
17. proud and humble
18. dangerous and safe
19. scarce and abundant
20. few and many
21. over and under
22. different and same
23. deep and shallow
24. accept and reject
25. collect and scatter
26. crooked and straight
27. melt and freeze
28. top and bottom
29. equal and uneven
30. separate and join
31. dry and wet
32. interesting and boring
33. serious and funny
34. wrong and right
35. all and none
36. cloudy and clear
37. stand and sit
38. mountain and valley
39. winter and summer
40. follow and lead
41. in and out
42. perfect and faulty
43. thrifty and wasteful
44. strange and ordinary
45. ready and unprepared
46. sweet and sour
47. build and destroy
48. tight and loose
49. on and off
50. backward and forward
51. left and right
52. best and worst
53. true and false
54. inhale and exhale
55. float and sink
56. often and seldom
57. nothing and something
58. most and least
59. ask and answer
60. increase and decrease

GO-TOGETHER WORDS

Each player in turn acts out a word which is commonly matched with another word, such as *salt* which is usually associated with *pepper*. The audience must guess the go-together words.

1. salt and pepper
2. up and down
3. hammer and nail
4. wash and dry
5. read and write
6. sun and moon
7. ham and eggs
8. day and night
9. soap and water
10. work and play
11. cup and saucer
12. fast and slow
13. enter and exit
14. bow and arrow
15. long and short
16. dog and cat
17. bread and butter
18. lock and key
19. bat and ball
20. east and west
21. black and white
22. knife and fork
23. hook and line
24. pail and shovel
25. pen and pencil
26. nut and bolt
27. shoes and socks
28. see and hear
29. arms and legs
30. land and sea
31. king and queen
32. aim and fire
33. first and last
34. give and take
35. stop and go
36. eat and drink
37. win and lose
38. yes and no
39. rich and poor
40. add and subtract
41. heel and toe
42. bride and groom
43. buy and sell
44. boy and girl
45. thick and thin
46. high and low
47. push and pull
48. teacher and student
49. hat and coat
50. brush and comb

ANAGRAM CHARADES

An anagram is a word built by rearranging the letters of another word. For this charade the exact letters in the first word are used to build the second word. For instance, from the word *swing* the anagram of *wings* could be built.

To begin, a player acts out the first word, and when this is guessed by one of the viewers, he (or his team) must rearrange its letters to find a word which contains the same letters. The first viewer (or team) to do this is awarded a point for himself (or for his team). If a blackboard is handy the game director can write out the first word (once it is guessed) so as to make it easier for viewers to rearrange it letters.

The first word in each of the following sets is the one to be acted out. The second word suggests an anagram answer, although in some cases there are several answers possible.

1. lamp (palm)	16. leap (peal)
2. pear (reap)	17. grin (ring)
3. stop (post)	18. plum (lump)
4. read (dare)	19. tide (diet)
5. stew (west)	20. drop (prod)
6. eat (tea)	21. shoe (hose)
7. north (thorn)	22. golf (flog)
8. petal (plate)	23. steam (meats)
9. rope (pore)	24. wolf (flow)
10. sword (words)	25. smile (miles)
11. taste (state)	26. snap (naps)
12. throw (worth)	27. stub (tubs)
13. stab (bats)	28. owl (low)
14. race (care)	29. heart (earth)
15. blow (bowl)	30. march (charm)

WORD-BUILDING CHARADES

This game is also an anagram one, and is best for contests between teams. Before the game begins, a scorekeeper is appointed. One performer then acts out any short word, like *time* or *rain*. The moment a member of the other team guesses the secret word he shouts it out. If he has guessed correctly his team is allowed a few seconds to rearrange the letters to form as many other words of two or more letters as they can. For example, from *time* they might get *tie* and *me* and *met*. The team scores a point for each word they are able to build from the letters in two minutes. The game continues until one team scores a total of twenty points.

161

WORDS WITH SIMILAR SOUNDS

Here is an opportunity for two pantomimists to perform side by side at the same time. Each acts out one of the paired words. Both words sound the same, although they have different spellings and different meanings. As soon as the viewers guess one of the words they will quickly find the other. It will be interesting to see which performer helps the audience the most.

1. beat, beet	21. pear, pair
2. cot, caught	22. one, won
3. tea, tee	23. cent, scent
4. blue, blew	24. horse, hoarse
5. meat, meet	25. write, right
6. sun, son	26. plane, plain
7. hair, hare	27. tide, tied
8. Sunday, sundae	28. ball, bawl
9. sew, sow	29. pail, pale
10. four, fore	30. rap, wrap
11. rode, road	31. waist, waste
12. see, sea	32. heal, heel
13. eight, ate	33. him, hymn
14. brake, break	34. toe, tow
15. clothes, close	35. beach, beech
16. soar, sore	36. wait, weight
17. hour, our	37. pain, pane
18. I, eye	38. stake, steak
19. knight, night	39. buy, by
20. sale, sail	40. board, bored

CHARADES ON SPECIAL SUBJECTS

Thinking up charades is often more difficult than acting them out. Here are handy lists of special topics to consult when you are stumped for an idea. The charade maker should indicate the category by gestures before acting. For instance, with *Precious Stones and Gems,* you might indicate a pendant on a necklace or a ring on your finger, until the audience guesses that the category is "jewel." Then each word should be split into syllables if the whole word is too difficult for the audience to guess. Take "opal" —split into an exclamation "oh" and a friend "pal."

Precious Stones and Gems

1. emerald
2. opal
3. diamond
4. sapphire
5. agate
6. amethyst
7. onyx
8. ruby
9. pearl
10. topaz
11. garnet
12. turquoise

Musical Instruments

1. clarinet
2. trombone
3. drum
4. harp
5. violin
6. flute
7. trumpet
8. piccolo
9. piano
10. tuba
11. organ
12. saxophone

Birds

1. oriole
2. swallow
3. bluebird
4. owl
5. eagle
6. wren
7. parakeet
8. sparrow
9. turkey
10. hawk
11. penguin
12. dove
13. cardinal
14. lark
15. duck
16. canary
17. robin
18. parrot
19. blackbird
20. chicken
21. raven
22. ostrich
23. goose
24. crow
25. mockingbird
26. sea gull
27. pheasant
28. pigeon
29. woodpecker
30. hummingbird
31. quail
32. swan
33. goldfinch
34. chickadee
35. stork
36. nightingale
37. thrush
38. crane
39. falcon
40. albatross

Fish

1. mackerel
2. bass
3. perch
4. salmon
5. sailfish
6. barracuda
7. trout
8. sardine
9. cod
10. shark
11. tuna
12. swordfish

Vegetables

1. carrot
2. spinach
3. celery
4. beet
5. lettuce
6. squash
7. artichoke
8. onion
9. potato
10. turnip
11. radish
12. garlic
13. corn
14. parsnip
15. cabbage
16. bean
17. tomato
18. pumpkin
19. peas
20. broccoli
21. asparagus
22. cauliflower
23. parsley
24. cucumber
25. pepper
26. eggplant
27. yam
28. horse-radish
29. rhubarb
30. okra

Fruits

1. peach
2. cherry
3. pineapple
4. apple
5. grape
6. watermelon
7. plum
8. orange
9. apricot
10. lime
11. pear
12. banana
13. fig
14. cantaloupe
15. grapefruit
16. pomegranate
17. date
18. lemon
19. persimmon
20. quince
21. nectarine
22. prune
23. crab apple
24. tangerine

Berries and Nuts

1. loganberry
2. almond
3. filbert
4. blueberry
5. coconut
6. strawberry
7. cashew
8. blackberry
9. cranberry
10. pecan
11. gooseberry
12. peanut
13. raspberry
14. mulberry
15. walnut
16. Brazil nut

Flowers

1. tulip
2. poppy
3. zinnia
4. carnation
5. lily
6. iris
7. rose
8. pansy
9. snapdragon
10. orchid
11. petunia
12. violet
13. lilac
14. daisy
15. chrysanthemum
16. hibiscus
17. cosmos
18. geranium
19. sunflower
20. daffodil

Trees

1. maple
2. cypress
3. oak
4. birch
5. willow
6. redwood
7. hemlock
8. fir
9. beech
10. cottonwood
11. elm
12. ash
13. cedar
14. palm
15. sycamore
16. pine
17. spruce
18. balsam
19. poplar
20. magnolia

Planets

1. Venus
2. Neptune
3. Mars
4. Earth
5. Jupiter
6. Mercury
7. Pluto
8. Saturn
9. Uranus

Famous Characters of the Bible

1. Samson
2. Ruth
3. Paul
4. Moses
5. Adam
6. Solomon
7. Esther
8. Abraham
9. Peter
10. Joshua
11. Cain
12. Rebekah
13. John
14. Elijah
15. Eve
16. Isaac
17. Noah
18. Andrew
19. Samuel
20. Joseph
21. Jonah
22. Sarah
23. David
24. James
25. Jacob
26. Benjamin
27. Lot
28. Aaron
29. Mary
30. Abel
31. Esau
32. Salome
33. Matthew
34. Gideon
35. Luke
36. Jonathan
37. Goliath
38. Rachel
39. Mark
40. Delilah
41. Daniel
42. Naomi
43. Jeremiah
44. Saul
45. Hannah
46. Leah
47. Isaiah
48. Ishmael
49. Nicodemus
50. Stephen

Foreign Countries

1. Brazil
2. Australia
3. Turkey
4. India
5. Panama
6. Holland
7. Japan
8. Portugal
9. Russia
10. Peru
11. China
12. Belgium
13. Sweden
14. Mexico
15. Spain
16. Denmark
17. Egypt
18. Norway
19. Pakistan
20. Chile
21. Italy
22. Greece
23. France
24. Argentina

FAMILIAR SIMILES

Here are fifty phrases which are similes. All of them are familiar to us and can be used for a rousing game of charades. As an actor pretends to flip pancakes the audience will catch on that the saying is *As flat as a pancake.*

1. As busy as a bee.
2. As red as a rose.
3. As quick as a wink.
4. As easy as pie.
5. As curious as a cat.
6. As pretty as a picture.
7. As fresh as a daisy.
8. As strong as an ox.
9. As slow as molasses.
10. As fit as a fiddle.
11. As hard as a rock.
12. As flat as a pancake.
13. As light as a feather.
14. As smooth as silk.
15. As stubborn as a mule.
16. As white as snow.
17. As tight as a drum.
18. As happy as a lark.

19. As dry as a bone.
20. As fast as lightning.
21. As slippery as an eel.
22. As good as gold.
23. As old as Methuselah.
24. As blind as a bat.
25. As pale as a ghost.
26. As snug as a bug in a rug.
27. As quiet as a mouse.
28. As clear as mud.
29. As swift as the wind.
30. As mad as a wet hen.
31. As black as coal.
32. As sharp as a tack.
33. As peaceful as a dove.
34. As hungry as a horse.
35. As green as grass.
36. As clean as a hound's tooth.
37. As stiff as a board.
38. As smart as a whip.
39. As silly as a goose.
40. As weak as a kitten.
41. As blue as the sky.
42. As fat as a pig.
43. As sticky as glue.
44. As sly as a fox.
45. As proud as a peacock.
46. As solid as an oak.
47. As neat as a pin.
48. As wise as an owl.
49. As cool as a cucumber.
50. As straight as an arrow.

FORTY FAVORITE PROVERBS

Proverbs are always welcome guests at a charade party. The following selections are especially good for act-out fun.

1. Birds of a feather flock together.
2. He who laughs last laughs best.

3. Nothing ventured, nothing gained.
4. A word to the wise is sufficient.
5. We learn to do by doing.
6. Let sleeping dogs lie.
7. Half a loaf is better than none.
8. All things come to him who waits.
9. Haste makes waste.
10. Where there's smoke there's fire.
11. Every cloud has a silver lining.
12. Easy come, easy go.
13. A miss is as good as a mile.
14. It is never too late to learn.
15. Seeing is believing.
16. Don't count your chickens before they're hatched.
17. Actions speak louder than words.
18. Too many cooks spoil the broth.
19. A new broom sweeps clean.
20. Business before pleasure.
21. Better safe than sorry.
22. Two heads are better than one.
23. A bird in the hand is worth two in the bush.
24. Practice makes perfect.
25. A stitch in time saves nine.
26. Heaven helps those who help themselves.
27. Don't cry over spilt milk.
28. Absence makes the heart grow fonder.
29. Better late than never.
30. Paddle your own canoe.
31. Turn-about is fair play.
32. You can't have your cake and eat it too.
33. A rolling stone gathers no moss.
34. If at first you don't succeed, try, try again.
35. Practice what you preach.
36. Out of sight, out of mind.
37. A barking dog never bites.
38. A friend in need is a friend indeed.
39. A watched pot never boils.
40. A penny saved is a penny earned.

EVERYDAY EXPRESSION CHARADES

Here are 100 familiar phrases to be acted out by charade actors and actresses. The viewers can start guessing as soon as they think they know the phrase; they need not wait until the performer is finished. In fact, the sooner they identify the phrase the higher compliment they pay to the actor's skill.

1. On top of the world.
2. Now or never.
3. Rainy day.
4. Loud and clear.
5. Just as well.
6. Change of mind.
7. Sure cure.
8. Hope for the best.
9. All tied up.
10. Better than ever.
11. More or less.
12. Peace on earth.
13. Lost and found.
14. Fair and square.
15. Talk of the town.
16. April showers.
17. Rise and shine.
18. Good as gold.
19. Flying high.
20. Hope springs eternal.
21. Watch and wait.
22. Wishful thinking.
23. Lend a hand.
24. On the dotted line.
25. Debt of honor.
26. Holding the bag.
27. Above average.
28. On time.
29. A friend in need.
30. Yours sincerely.
31. Take it easy.
32. Hard hitting.
33. Out of breath.
34. Opportunity knocks.
35. Take a chance.
36. Great day.
37. All worn out.
38. In a daze
39. Hang your hat.
40. Bring home the bacon.
41. Make the grade.
42. Good news.
43. Just a minute.
44. No hard feelings.
45. Short and sweet.
46. Down to business.
47. Tender embrace.
48. Figure it out.
49. Wheel of fortune.
50. Maybe so.
51. Think it over.
52. Best of all.
53. Pardon me.
54. Take my word for it.
55. In and out.
56. Steady nerves.
57. Weather report.
58. Wedding bells.
59. Make up your mind.
60. Down payment.
61. Comedy of errors.
62. Out of control.
63. Do your best.
64. Get the point.
65. Come and go.
66. Make a bargain.

67. Calm down.
68. Miles per hour.
69. First things first.
70. Make yourself at home.
71. Welcome mat.
72. Best wishes.
73. Thanks a million.
74. For sale.
75. Home run.
76. Down and out.
77. Forgive and forget.
78. Live it up.
79. No doubt about it.
80. Fair play.
81. Peace of mind.
82. Good morning.
83. Bright and early.
84. Best man.
85. Fill the bill.
86. Holiday spirit.
87. Set an example.
88. Once and for all.
89. Free sample.
90. A word to the wise.
91. Smooth sailing.
92. To tell the truth.
93. Safe and sound.
94. One step at a time.
95. Dreams come true.
96. Ready to go.
97. Out of this world.
98. On the spot.
99. Speed up.
100. Happy ending.

RIDDLE CHARADES

Each pantomimist acts out a riddle. The audience must first identify the riddle itself, then try to figure out its answer. If no one knows the answer, the performer acts it out for them to guess.

1. What is the best thing to put into a pie? (Your teeth)
2. Which month has twenty-eight days? (All of them)
3. Where is the Danube River? (Between two banks)
4. How would you write your name on the ocean floor? (Write it first on a rock)
5. What is in the middle of India? (The letter *d*)
6. How does a barber cut hair? (Off)
7. How can you make salt taste better? (Shake it over a steak)
8. What makes a horse run? (Its legs)
9. How can you spell Mississippi backwards? (Turn your back and spell it)
10. Where can you find happiness? (In the dictionary)
11. When do camels have eight legs? (When there are two of them)

12. Why are newspapers like ghosts? (Because they appear in sheets)
13. How can you make time fly? (Throw your watch out of the window)
14. What word is always pronounced wrong? (Wrong)
15. Where is the North Pole at four o'clock in the morning? (In the same place)

WHO AM I?

Half the players leave the room. They then return, one at a time, as fully disguised as possible. (A typical disguise might be an oversized coat, plus a paper bag—cut with eye-holes—over the head.) The actor performs any kind of a pantomime which will reveal his real identity. For instance, a boy who is known to have a paper route might pretend to deliver papers; a girl who plays a musical instrument might imitate a musician. The clues should not be too easy.

When all the members of one group have been idenitfied, they become the guessers of the other group.

WHERE?

The game leader divides the performers into two groups. Each player in group A thinks of a brief question starting with *where*, such as those given in the list below. Each player in group B thinks of a short answer which states a location. Next, a player from group A and one from group B go onstage. There will be some funny and unusual results as one acts out the question and then the other acts out the answer he has prepared. Here are fifteen typical performances.

1. Where do you live? (In a cave)
2. Where do monkeys sleep? (In my kitchen)
3. Where can I make money? (At the North Pole)
4. Where is your hat? (At a barber shop)
5. Where is coal mined? (On the front porch)
6. Where can I find happiness? (In my pocket)
7. Where do you sell fish? (At school)
8. Where are my shoes? (In the sink)
9. Where are you popular? (In Southern Japan)
10. Where do you have dinner? (At the glue factory)
11. Where should I spend my vacation? (In the garage)
12. Where is my lost dog? (On the table)
13. Where can I grow potatoes? (Twenty miles south)
14. Where will I go to college? (On the roof)
15. Where do you buy candy? (On the ocean floor)

TOMORROW'S TASK

Players take turns in revealing in pantomime something which they are going to do tomorrow. The audience should be told in advance that each task is described in just two words and that both words start with the same letter.

1. sell sardines
2. repair roof
3. bake biscuits
4. sew socks
5. chase chipmunks
6. taste turnips
7. polish piano
8. wash windows
9. dig diamonds
10. catch crocodiles
11. sharpen scissors
12. grow garlic
13. collect cash
14. fry fish
15. make masks
16. play piccolo
17. cook cabbage
18. tame tigers
19. find food
20. peel potatoes
21. clean closet
22. press pants
23. buy bananas
24. ride rhinoceros
25. pick peaches
26. feed foxes
27. carry coal
28. borrow book
29. sail sea
30. watch walruses

DIRECT CHARADES

The charade actor thinks of some action which he wants the viewers to perform. His whole charade-sentence then tells them exactly what they must do. As soon as the viewers guess the charade-sentence, they must perform the action. The following suggestions will get the game off to a good start.

1. Clap your hands five times.
2. Imitate a monkey.
3. Shake hands with three friends.
4. Go to sleep.
5. Count aloud from ten back to one.
6. Walk stiff-legged in a circle.
7. Touch your right elbow to your right heel.
8. Compliment the person next to you.
9. Sing out loud.
10. Take off and replace your shoes.

MILLION DOLLAR CHARADES

What would you say if you were offered a million dollars? Everyone playing this game has an opportunity to act out in pantomime what he would reply if someone walked up and offered to give him a million dollars. The other players try to guess what the pantomimist is saying. Performers should try to be as funny and clever as possible. You may act out the listed replies, or you may think up your own.

1. I think I'm going to faint.
2. Just stuff it in my pocket.
3. Thank you; call again.
4. I must be dreaming.
5. I'll spend it all on candy.
6. Please repeat that.
7. That's a funny joke.
8. That's the best offer I've had this week.
9. Quit your kidding.
10. Sorry, I'm not interested.
11. I wouldn't know what to do with it.
12. I'm speechless.
13. I'll think it over.
14. Give it to someone else.
15. I already have a million dollars.

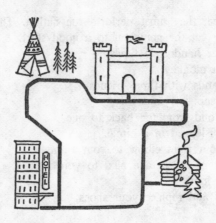

WHERE DO YOU LIVE?

This is a quick charade and a good icebreaker for a party.

The game leader asks each player to select a number from one to twelve. Whatever number he selects is the one he acts out as his dwelling place.

1. mansion
2. wigwam
3. hut
4. cottage
5. tent
6. lodge

7. castle
8. house
9. hotel
10. cabin
11. shack
12. barracks

MIXED MEAL CHARADES

Each player secretly thinks of a single item of food. The food can be anything at all, just as long as it represents something to eat. The game leader then announces that he would like to have a snack consisting of two different treats—so he sends any two players onstage to act out the foods for him to eat. There are likely to be some odd and painful combinations as the various couples act out such suggestions as ice cream and catsup, or mayonnaise and peanuts.

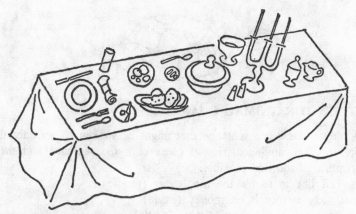

SET THE TABLE CHARADE

This one is good for team play. Two (or three) groups of equal number gather in secret huddle to think of words related to the dinner table. Such items could be *plate, bowl, potato, sauce*—anything at all connected with dinner. Each player takes a single dinner item to act out. Team A then acts out its words (one player at a time) as rapidly as possible, while Team B tries to guess, and one of the players keeps time. After that, Team A tries to guess the charades of Team B. (With three teams, A acts for B, B for C, and C for A.) The winner is the acting team which "sets the table" in the shortest time.

177

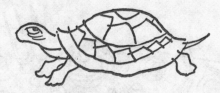

GUESS THE ANIMAL CHARADES

A player acts out a sentence that might be spoken by an animal or bird. The audience tries to guess both the sentence and the creature as soon as possible.

1. I like to nibble the top leaves (giraffe)
2. My picture is on money (eagle)
3. People say I move slowly (turtle)
4. Listen to me talk (parrot)
5. My big bill holds lots of fish (pelican)
6. Here comes that toreador (bull)
7. Watch my spout (whale)
8. I am a sly one (fox)
9. My arms are built for swinging (monkey)
10. I am a symbol of peace (dove)
11. Farmers try to scare me (crow)
12. I am also called a mountain lion (cougar)
13. Your coat may come from me (sheep)
14. I am large, white, and graceful (swan)
15. I live within sight of the pyramids (camel)

178

WONDERS OF AMERICA CHARADE

Act out the charades of these famous places and historical sites, then see if the viewers can identify the state or area where it is located.

1. Mount Rushmore (South Dakota)
2. Crater Lake (Oregon)
3. Yellowstone National Park (Wyoming)
4. West Point (New York)
5. Petrified Forest (Arizona)
6. Lake Superior (several states)
7. Mount McKinley (Alaska)
8. Washington National Monument (Washington, D.C.)
9. Pike's Peak (Colorado)
10. Everglades (Florida)
11. Harvard University (Massachusetts)
12. Colorado River (several states)
13. Fort Sumter (South Carolina)
14. Meteor Crater (Arizona)
15. Yosemite National Park (California)
16. Statue of Liberty (New York)
17. Lake Erie (several states)
18. Puget Sound (Washington)
19. Annapolis (Maryland)
20. Great Salt Lake (Utah)
21. White House (Washington, D.C.)
22. Plymouth Rock (Massachusetts)
23. Black Hills (South Dakota)
24. Carlsbad Caverns (New Mexico)
25. Lake Michigan (several states)
26. Yale University (Connecticut)
27. Niagara Falls (New York, Canada)
28. Lincoln Memorial (Washington, D.C.)
29. Gettysburg National Military Park (Pennsylvania)
30. Alamo (San Antonio, Texas)
31. Hoover Dam (Arizona, Nevada)
32. Bunker Hill (Massachusetts)
33. Little Big Horn (Montana)
34. Golden Gate Bridge (San Francisco, California)
35. Fort McHenry (Maryland)

36. Valley Forge State Park (Pennsylvania)
37. Mount Vernon (Virginia)
38. Mammoth Cave (Kentucky)
39. Rio Grande River (several states)
40. Rocky Mountains (several states)

WHICH WAY?

This charade is turned into a lively contest by dividing the audience into two teams. The charade actor may reveal any two states (some are listed below) which are supposedly involved in his traveling. The first viewer to identify correctly not just the states but the direction he is traveling on this imaginary trip from the center of one state to the center of the other scores a point for his team. However, if a wrong answer is given the team loses a point. Only four directions are used: north, south, east, or west.

The team with the greater number of points wins the game. Various performers can take turns in acting out the states.

1. From Idaho to Oregon (west)
2. From Wisconsin to Illinois (south)
3. From Alabama to Tennessee (north)
4. From Maryland to Pennsylvania (north)
5. From Vermont to New Hampshire (east)
6. From Montana to North Dakota (east)
7. From Ohio to Indiana (west)
8. From Oklahoma to Texas (south)
9. From Iowa to Minnesota (north)
10. From Utah to Colorado (east)
11. From Nebraska to Wyoming (west)
12. From New York to Pennsylvania (south)
13. From California to Nevada (east)
14. From North Carolina to Virginia (north)
15. From Louisiana to Arkansas (north)
16. From Michigan to Indiana (south)
17. From Rhode Island to Connecticut (west)
18. From Kansas to Missouri (east)
19. From Florida to Georgia (north)
20. From New Mexico to Texas (east)

180

21. From Washington to Oregon (south)
22. From Arizona to Utah (north)
23. From Pennsylvania to Ohio (west)
24. From South Dakota to Nebraska (south)
25. From Kentucky to Indiana (north)

If there is a dispute about the direction, consult an atlas.

NAME THE STATE

The performer acts out a word or sound which forms only a part of the name of one of the 20 states listed below. The audience must guess the state from the acted-out portion.

1. Florida (floor)
2. Oklahoma (home)
3. Pennsylvania (pen)
4. Rhode Island (road)
5. Utah (you)
6. Delaware (wear)
7. Mississippi (sip)
8. Ohio (high)
9. Indiana (Indian)
10. Oregon (ore)
11. Maryland (merry)
12. North Dakota (coat)
13. California (four)
14. Nebraska (ask)
15. Washington (wash)
16. Connecticut (connect)
17. Colorado (call)
18. Missouri (miss)
19. Montana (tan)
20. Tennessee (ten)

MAJOR U.S. CITIES CHARADES

Players take turns in acting out the names of some larger cities. The player who guesses a city should try to name the state in which it is located.

1. Racine		31. Harrisburg
2. Seattle		32. Fresno
3. Grand Rapids		33. Wheeling
4. Raleigh		34. Hartford
5. Amarillo		35. Toledo
6. Spokane		36. South Bend
7. Peoria		37. Pueblo
8. Akron		38. Erie
9. Sacramento		39. Tulsa
10. Detroit		40. Roanoke
11. Trenton		41. Lansing
12. Milwaukee		42. Shreveport
13. Altoona		43. Atlantic City
14. Saginaw		44. Tacoma
15. Brockton		45. Duluth
16. Madison		46. Beaumont
17. Charlotte		47. New Orleans
18. Topeka		48. Flint
19. Knoxville		49. Scranton
20. Savannah		50. Davenport
21. Cincinnati		51. Lancaster
22. Sioux City		52. Macon
23. Ogden		53. Montgomery
24. Atlanta		54. Waterbury
25. Galveston		55. Cleveland
26. Lincoln		56. Jacksonville
27. Albuquerque		57. Syracuse
28. Evansville		58. Reading
29. Buffalo		59. Kenosha
30. San Diego		60. Terre Haute

ISLAND VISIT CHARADES

The charade actors take their viewers to various islands of the world. The audience tries to guess the names of the places they are visiting.

1. Borneo
2. Sicily
3. Hawaii
4. Okinawa
5. Ireland
6. Easter
7. Formosa
8. Tahiti
9. Puerto Rico
10. Vancouver
11. Philippines
12. Crete
13. Java
14. Trinidad
15. Manhattan
16. Jamaica
17. Iceland
18. Japan
19. Cuba
20. Madagascar

AROUND THE WORLD CHARADES

A speedy performance will help to win this charade contest. Each player is allowed an equal amount of time on stage, to be used to act out the names of as many foreign places as possible. The player can act out the names of countries, cities, rivers, and other geographic places. The performer who reveals the greatest number of names within the time limit is crowned the champion world traveler.

STRANGE SEA CREATURES CHARADES

Have the charade actors use the listed names of creatures from
the sea. Here are twelve of them:

1. jellyfish
2. sponge
3. oyster
4. shrimp
5. eel
6. sting ray
7. starfish
8. lobster
9. clam
10. mussel
11. sea horse
12. octopus

FACTS ABOUT FOLKS

Before playing this game the leader collects one interesting secret
fact about everyone in the room. He then says something like
"And here is something interesting about Tommy Carter." An
assigned player then acts out the secret fact, while the rest of
the players try to guess what the secret is. Here are typical facts
which might be used.

1. He was born in Nebraska.
2. She has three older brothers.
3. His favorite sport is swimming.
4. Her middle name is Belle.
5. His hobby is photography.

WHAT'S IN THE NEWS?

A few players pretend to read a newspaper heading, then together act out for the rest of the players or audience the event which they have "read." The audience need only guess the general nature of the headline. Players may select their own topics or use the following headings:
1. Students Honored at Graduation
2. Voters Flock to Polls
3. Rocket Fired Toward Moon
4. Relay Team Sets Track Record
5. Storm Hits City
6. Fireworks Displayed on Independence Day
7. Bathers Crowd Cool Beaches
8. Wedding Plans Revealed
9. General Reviews Troops
10. Hikers Explore Desert

OCEANS AND SEAS CHARADES

For a geographic charade, use these names of oceans, seas and gulfs of the world.

1. Pacific	11. North
2. Caribbean	12. Persian
3. Black	13. Mexico
4. Indian	14. Caspian
5. Bering	15. Arabian
6. Atlantic	16. Coral
7. Baltic	17. Aegean
8. Irish	18. South China
9. Arctic	19. Adriatic
10. Mediterranean	20. Tasman

EXPLORERS CHARADES

Everyone who has enjoyed a class in history or geography will recognize the names of these early explorers of the western hemisphere. The performer acts out a last name only. Once it is guessed the charade actor can inform the audience of the full name.

1. Pizarro (Francisco)
2. Ponce de León (Juan)
3. Frémont (John C.)
4. Magellan (Ferdinand)
5. Drake (Francis)
6. de Balboa (Vasco Nuñez)
7. Cortez (Hernando)
8. Lewis (Meriwether)
9. Joliet (Louis)
10. Raleigh (Sir Walter)
11. Hudson (Henry)
12. de Soto (Hernando)

FAMOUS AMERICAN CHARADES

Each player is given the name of a noted American to act out. For Henry Wadsworth Longfellow, for example, a player could

186

act out *hen,* then *long* or *low.* One or more syllables can be acted out at a time. With a name like Longfellow, you might choose to act out the whole name at once. Here are twelve suitable names for starting the game:

1. Robert Fulton
2. Andrew Jackson
3. Ralph Waldo Emerson
4. David Crockett
5. Julia Ward Howe
6. George Washington Carver
7. Richard E. Byrd
8. James Russell Lowell
9. Mark Twain
10. Francis Scott Key
11. Luther Burbank
12. Alexander Graham Bell

BIG RIVER CHARADES

Here are the names of ten famous rivers. See if your audience can guess both the river and the country or continent where it is located.

1. Ganges (India)
2. Danube (Europe)
3. Yellow (China)
4. Rhine (Europe)
5. Congo (Africa)
6. Amazon (Brazil)
7. Nile (Egypt)
8. Volga (Russia)
9. Jordan (Asia)
10. Euphrates (Asia)

SUCCESS CHARADES

The game leader asks each player in turn to call out a different number from one to sixty. The number the player calls is matched with the list below. The performer is then secretly assigned to act out the trait which follows that number. The game leader might announce an act like this: "Next, let's see what Norman Rogers is going to use for making a success of his life."

1. courage	31. sympathy
2. alertness	32. efficiency
3. cooperation	33. decisiveness
4. accuracy	34. consistency
5. persistence	35. thoroughness
6. friendliness	36. optimism
7. patience	37. imagination
8. bravery	38. eagerness
9. enthusiasm	39. sincerity
10. confidence	40. truthfulness
11. resolution	41. humility
12. foresight	42. effort
13. energy	43. watchfulness
14. courtesy	44. affection
15. valor	45. helpfulness
16. discretion	46. appreciation
17. kindness	47. reliability
18. responsibility	48. firmness
19. cheerfulness	49. sociability
20. consideration	50. preparation
21. determination	51. politeness
22. peacefulness	52. endurance
23. moderation	53. vigor
24. earnestness	54. stamina
25. simplicity	55. integrity
26. promptness	56. loyalty
27. initiative	57. fairness
28. tenderness	58. application
29. generosity	59. pleasantness
30. concentration	60. resourcefulness

AMERICAN PRESIDENTS CHARADES

Here is a list of some of the Presidents of the United States. The audience should be able to guess them after the charade performer acts out the italicized name only. The performer may tell the audience if he is acting out the first (middle) or last name.

1. *Grover* Cleveland
2. Andrew *Jackson*
3. *John Quincy* Adams
4. *Ulysses* S. Grant
5. *Woodrow* Wilson
6. James *Buchanan*
7. *Thomas* Jefferson
8. *Abraham* Lincoln
9. *Dwight* D. Eisenhower
10. *Calvin* Coolidge
11. James *Madison*
12. *Theodore* Roosevelt
13. *Zachary* Taylor
14. *Benjamin* Harrison
15. James *Monroe*
16. Andrew *Johnson*
17. *Harry* S. Truman
18. James A. *Garfield*
19. John *Tyler*
20. *Franklin* Pierce

INDIAN CHARADES

Have the players go on the warpath in acting out the names of these Indian tribes. They are among the most famous in American history.

1. Apache
2. Mohican
3. Osage
4. Comanche
5. Omaha
6. Sioux
7. Navaho
8. Cherokee
9. Dakota
10. Crow
11. Mohawk
12. Choctaw
13. Iroquois
14. Arapaho
15. Cheyenne

FAMOUS FICTIONAL CHARACTERS CHARADES

Here are thirty noted names from the pages of fiction and legend. Let a player act out one or more of them.

1. William Tell
2. Snow White
3. Aladdin
4. Robinson Crusoe
5. Simple Simon
6. Robin Hood
7. King Arthur
8. Count of Monte Cristo
9. Romeo
10. King Midas
11. Cinderella
12. Sir Lancelot
13. Oliver Twist
14. Rip van Winkle
15. Village Blacksmith
16. Alice in Wonderland
17. Don Quixote
18. Tiny Tim
19. Jo March
20. Sir Galahad
21. Paul Bunyan
22. Friday
23. Old Mother Hubbard
24. Pied Piper
25. Sherlock Holmes
26. Little Boy Blue
27. Juliet
28. Tom Sawyer
29. David Copperfield
30. Red Riding Hood

MYTHOLOGICAL CHARADES

The thirty names listed here are from the pages of mythology. First, the performer acts out the assigned name until the audience guesses it. Then the spectators try to identify the name briefly, either from previous knowledge or from clues given by the performer. If they are unable to do so, the charade actor can inform them.

1. Diana (goddess of the woods or hunt)
2. Neptune (god of the sea)
3. Ajax (a huge warrior)
4. Adonis (a handsome youth)
5. Circe (a sorceress)
6. Thor (the god of thunder)
7. Fortune (goddess of fortune)
8. Jupiter (king of the gods)
9. Mercury (fleet-footed messenger of the gods)
10. Daphne (a nymph)
11. Achilles (a Greek hero)
12. Ceres (goddess of agriculture)
13. Venus (goddess of love)
14. Pegasus (winged horse)
15. Aurora (goddess of the dawn)
16. Minerva (goddess of wisdom)
17. Pandora (opened box, let evils loose)
18. Apollo (god of youth and beauty)
19. Europa (a captured maiden)
20. Athena (goddess of industry and art)
21. Ulysses (a wandering hero)
22. Cupid (god of love)
23. Atlas (god who held world on his shoulders)
24. Centaur (half man, half horse)

25. Flora (goddess of spring flowers)
26. Orpheus (a skilled musician)
27. Pan (pipe-player, the shepherd god)
28. Jason (secured golden fleece)
29. Juno (goddess of marriage)
30. Hercules (strong-man and popular hero)

SHAKESPEARE CHARADES

Some of the plays by William Shakespeare are familiar to everyone. Find out how quickly an audience can guess the names of twenty of them.

1. Macbeth
2. Julius Caesar
3. A Midsummer Night's Dream
4. The Comedy of Errors
5. Romeo and Juliet
6. Love's Labour's Lost
7. The Winter's Tale
8. Antony and Cleopatra
9. Othello
10. The Merchant of Venice
11. Measure for Measure
12. The Taming of the Shrew
13. Twelfth Night
14. Much Ado About Nothing
15. Hamlet
16. The Merry Wives of Windsor
17. King Lear
18. As You Like It
19. The Tempest
20. All's Well That Ends Well

ANCIENT AUTHOR CHARADES

Here are the names of ten ancient authors whose writings and speeches still carry considerable influence in the world today. Inasmuch as we hear about them quite often, you might have one charade-maker act out all their names for the audience to guess.

1. Socrates
2. Homer
3. Cicero
4. Aristotle
5. Plato
6. Sophocles
7. Horace
8. Plutarch
9. Ovid
10. Archimedes

CLASSICAL COMPOSERS CHARADES

Here are the names of twenty of the greatest classical composers of all time. Because we all enjoy their music, it is a good idea to renew acquaintance with them. Have the performer act out the last names only; see if the audience can supply their last *and* first names.

1. Schubert (Franz)
2. Rachmaninoff (Sergei)
3. Handel (George Frederick)
4. Massenet (Jules)
5. Bach (Johann Sebastian)
6. Chopin (Frederic)
7. Wagner (Richard)
8. Verdi (Giuseppe)
9. Tchaikovsky (Peter)
10. Beethoven (Ludwig van)

11. Puccini (Giacomo)
12. Brahms (Johannes)
13. Berlioz (Hector)
14. Schumann (Robert)
15. Bizet (Georges)
16. Haydn (Franz Joseph)
17. Mendelssohn (Felix)
18. Sibelius (Jan)
19. Liszt (Franz)
20. Mozart (Wolfgang Amadeus)

FAMOUS INVENTION CHARADES

Below are listed the names of forty great inventions, products or scientific discoveries. All of them have changed the course of history and affected everyone on earth. Some are ancient while others are fairly recent. The actors are to perform pantomimes which reveal the inventions. An act continues until the invention is guessed by the audience.

1. thermometer	21. undersea cable
2. electric motor	22. elevator
3. life preserver	23. microscope
4. ink	24. adding machine
5. pendulum	25. searchlight
6. cellophane	26. fountain pen
7. steel	27. pneumatic tire
8. clock	28. X-ray
9. cash register	29. jet plane
10. nylon	30. fingerprinting
11. gasoline engine	31. lightning rod
12. paper	32. drinking glass
13. safety match	33. printing press
14. bicycle	34. safe
15. harvester	35. telescope
16. linotype machine	36. television
17. refrigerator	37. vacuum cleaner
18. locomotive	38. sewing machine
19. barbed wire	39. camera
20. storage battery	40. safety pin

WHO SAID IT?

Each player secretly thinks of a noted man or woman. The famous person may be real or a noted character from fiction. The player also thinks of a short (preferably humorous) sentence which the same character might have spoken. In turn, each player acts out his sentence (not the name) and the viewers guess the sentence and the person who supposedly said it. They need not guess the exact quotation. Here are a dozen examples which may be used.

1. Benjamin Franklin: *Just let lightning strike my kite!*
2. Ludwig van Beethoven: *I will certainly become famous if I write nine symphonies.*
3. Betsy Ross: *I really like purple, green and yellow flags, but they want red, white and blue.*
4. Luther Burbank: *I'm tired of eating the same old kinds of fruit.*
5. Robin Hood: *Anyone is welcome to Sherwood Forest.*
6. Marco Polo: *I'm off to China in the morning.*
7. William Shakespeare: *I will make Julius Caesar famous.*
8. General Custer: *I think we'll settle here at Little Big Horn.*
9. Hannibal: *I hope those elephants can climb the Alps.*
10. King Arthur: *I really prefer a long one, but this round table will do.*
11. Leonardo da Vinci: *She looks like a girl I once knew: Mona Lisa.*
12. Napoleon: *There must be a million soldiers around Waterloo.*

FORTY FAVORITE SONGS

Titles of songs are excellent for charade play. Here are forty favorites, including patriotic tunes, western ballads, love songs, and many other kinds. In larger groups, it is more fun to form two teams. Although everyone takes part in the guessing, the player who first identifies the complete song title wins one point for his team. Ten points win a game. The listed titles will serve for several contests.

1. Battle Hymn of the Republic
2. Love's Old Sweet Song
3. Dixie

197

4. The Blue Bell of Scotland
5. Londonderry Air
6. The Lost Chord
7. My Old Kentucky Home, Good Night
8. Grandfather's Clock
9. America, the Beautiful
10. In the Gloaming
11. Silent Night, Holy Night
12. Tenting on the Old Camp Ground
13. Home, Sweet Home
14. 'Tis the Last Rose of Summer
15. Maryland! My Maryland!
16. Listen to the Mocking Bird
17. Jingle Bells
18. Annie Laurie
19. Lead, Kindly Light
20. Juanita
21. Red River Valley
22. Sweet Genevieve
23. Auld Lang Syne
24. Believe Me if All Those Endearing Young Charms
25. Cradle Song
26. Kathleen Mavourneen
27. Silver Threads Among the Gold
28. Marching Through Georgia
29. La Paloma
30. Sweet and Low
31. Flow Gently, Sweet Afton
32. Beautiful Dreamer
33. Columbia, the Gem of the Ocean
34. Yankee Doodle
35. Turkey in the Straw
36. Santa Lucia
37. Rose of Tralee
38. Deck the Halls
39. Loch Lomond
40. I'll Take You Home Again, Kathleen

Section 5

Humorous Monologues

The young man or young woman will find many good things in a monologue—an opportunity for discovering and developing dramatic talent, an excellent means for self-expression and an open door for fully entering into social activities. The performer develops self-confidence, poise, and leadership qualities.

Besides all this, it's fun! You and your audiences will enjoy and appreciate the entertainment to be found in a monologue. It is a delightfully refreshing experience to see a "live" dramatic performance.

Anyone can perform the monologues in this section—but the more practice and experience you have and the better acquainted you are with the principles in Section 1, the better your presentation will be. Monologues have long been a favorite type of dramatic entertainment, because they provide hilarity at the party, in the club, camp, and schoolroom, and at social gatherings of all kinds and descriptions. They also provide a practical and wholesome outlet for pent-up dramatic abilities or unsuspected talents. Monologues may be presented individually or a festival of monologues might be staged with a group of volunteers performing on the same stage.

This section starts with easy material for those who have had little or no experience with this lively form of dramatic art. The following ideas and suggestions are specifically listed to make *your* performance easy—and funny!

Selecting Your Material

You have a wide choice of pieces in this section. Go through and select one that appeals to you in particular. Choose one that you can handle with ease. Get familiar with its feeling by reading it several times. Before long you will begin to picture yourself in the role.

Some of the monologues are suitable for performers of either sex. In some the character's name only needs to be changed to fit.

Setting

In most monologues, no particular background is needed. Of course a few background properties will help to establish a gay mood. In the monologue, *Look, George,* an art gallery could be indicated by hanging a few pictures; in *Complaint Desk,* the performer could sit behind a desk labeled as such. Enough room should be provided to allow the freedom of movement that the monologue requires.

You don't need a stage, but a raised platform is a help. If you have no platform, clear a fairly wide space in front of you and let your audience sit in a half-circle around you.

Atmosphere can also be created by having background music. A phonograph could be operated by a friend, or a live musician could play gay tunes, sad refrains, and other types of music in keeping with the mood of the monologue. The instrument or musician should play offstage or off to one side. Of course the speaker should always be clearly heard above the music.

Your Introduction

A guest may introduce you to the audience—"Let me now present Mr. Eddie Greenhorn, who will tell us of the origins of many of our famous proverbs"—or, you may simply introduce yourself.

Your Performance

Remember, your audience is probably relaxed and in a *mood to laugh.* Take advantage of this and even the tiniest joke or gesture—or even a mistake!—may bring howls of mirth. Laughter is your main object! Enter briskly, take immediate command of the situation, speak boldly and confidently. Never give a hint of apology in word or expression. Forget who you are—*imagine that you are actually the character you are portraying.*

Make believe you're talking to someone in the back row. Your voice need be no louder than that. If guests are informally seated about you, speak to the tops of their heads. Don't look anyone directly in the eye. Speak clearly, make your gestures so that they are easily understood. Stay in full view of the audience and, when possible, keep your face or profile toward them.

Exaggeration may be necessary if you are playing to a large audience. Remember that distance dims eyesight.

Most of the monologues in this book are also suitable for simple reading aloud to an audience. Lots of chuckles can be produced by assuming the role just as if you were delivering it from memory. In this case you can explain the character and situation to the listeners. Hold the book to one side, so it is not between you and your audience. Look at it when you need to, not continuously. Look up from the book as you supply the gestures. The piece should be read with all the usual gestures and inflections. You might wish to deliver your first monologues by the reading method. As you gain experience and familiarity with dramatics, you'll want to perform from memory more and more often.

Your first performances are worth their weight in experience. Analyze them, try to make the funny spots even funnier. Go over the weak sections to see how they might be improved. Don't hesitate to ask a few friends how they think the piece could be made funnier.

Let the audience enjoy a full laugh at a funny line. Do not proceed to the next line until you are certain they will hear it. If a laugh fails to come when you expect it, calmly proceed as if you really didn't expect laughter. You may also hear laughter when you least expect it; if so, pause. As you grow more familiar with audience reactions you will be able to judge your timing more accurately.

KISS ME GOOD NIGHT!

Character: A young man.

I was seeing my girl friend home the other night . . . wanted to ask her for a goodnight kiss, but couldn't get up nerve . . . *Well, good night,* I whispered. *Good night,* she whispered. (shout)

Good night! her father shouted from an upstairs window. *Could I have a goodnight kiss?* I asked her father. *It's all right with me,* he replied, *but my daughter's much prettier.*

Please, Ruthie, I pleaded, *Just one little smack?* After she gave me the smack I asked, *How come you used the palm of your hand? . . . I just love rosy cheeks,* she said.

You know, I said, *any other girl would just die for a kiss from me . . . I don't feel so healthy about it myself,* she said.

May I see you again? I asked. *Well,* she said, *I'll be at the corner of Fifth and Broadway* (name local streets) *at three in the morning . . . How come so early?* I asked. *I hear you're always late,* she said.

One kiss would send me to the moon, I whispered. *Go ahead, Ruthie,* her mother called, *but make sure he goes.*

I'll never come back! I said . . . *You promise but always do,* she said.

May I take you to the football game? I said. *Throw in a bag of popcorn and you've got a deal!* shouted her little brother. *Let the two of us be very reasonable about this,* I said. *Let's all six of us be reasonable,* said little sister.

I'll join the army! I threatened. *Forward . . . march!* she said.

Florence always gives me a good-night kiss, I proudly said. *What?* she exclaimed in astonishment, *Florence, the beauty contest winner? . . . No,* I said, *I don't think my mother ever won a beauty contest.*

Look, I said, *do you know that I'm the handsomest boy in town? . . . I know,* she said, *that's why I'm moving.*

Well, good night, mother, I said (wave while looking upward), *And good night, father* (wave in another upward direction), *And good night, little brother and sister* (wave low), *And good night, Fido* (pretend to pat dog). *Well! Don't you want a goodnight kiss?* she said. (shrug) *No,* I said, *my evening is complete just in meeting that lovely family of yours . . . Be sure to call again,* she said. *Oh, I will,* I said, *it's been lots of fun!* (bow and exit)

MY FIRST FOOTBALL GAME

Character: Teen-age girl.

Shall I tell you about the very first football game I ever saw? Of course I didn't see it very well because Harry couldn't afford very good seats. In fact the seats we got were so far back we found it better to sit on a very sturdy branch that grew over the edge of the stadium . . . And even this was crowded. I was constantly moving over to make room for others up there: Six crows and three redheaded woodpeckers.

I must admit that Harry did everything possible for my comfort. We had popcorn, peanuts, hot dogs, ice cream bars. Best of all, Harry promised to pay me back the very next day . . .

Harry taught me the idea of the game. A man has to carry the football from one end of the field to the other. Isn't that a perfectly silly thing to make a *game* out of? . . . But there they were—full grown men running, falling, kicking all over the place just to have the ball for a few seconds . . . Why, they could have saved their money so *each* player had one.

My biggest confusion came when I tried to tell *our* team from the enemy team. Harry said that our team was the one with the football. But pretty soon the other team had the ball and I was all confused again.

One time I looked down and there was a player carrying a bass drum instead of a football. I asked Harry about it and he said it was the half. Well, it certainly looked like a *whole drum* to me . . . Then it was the musicians' turn to play. Of course they didn't play football . . . they played *music* . . . I guess someone had kicked the football over the fence because all the players were gone quite a while looking for it. But pretty soon they found it and the players came whooping back again.

Harry explained to me about the men with the striped shirts. They seemed to be afraid of the football and just stood off to one side and played their own little game—whistle blowing. Every time a player fell down with the ball these funny little men blew their whistles like mad and made crazy little motions with their arms. Harry said it was all part of the game.

I finally got the game figured out. I think it goes this way. Each player has a number on his back. If player number 67 catches the ball his team scores 67 points; while if player number 88 catches the ball his team scores 88 points. Somehow this doesn't seem fair to players with little numbers like 12 and 15, does it? . . . It was an exciting game all the way. The final score was five thousand, nine hundred and thirty-five to zero.

THE BOY FRIEND

Character: A fluttery girl describing her boy friend.

(Enter oddly dressed, giggle throughout) Hello, folks . . . (shyly) I'd like to tell you about *Norman* . . . Norman is my boy friend. I call him my boy friend because he's my friend . . . but especially because he's a *boy.*

Norman thinks I'm very beautiful. Just yesterday I heard a girl whisper, *What in the world does he see in her?* (shrug in superiority) Another girl once whispered, *Isn't it amazing the way he goes for her?* (smile) I hate to say it, but I think they're jealous.

On the way to the party last night, he said I'd be the prettiest girl in the room . . . if I got there before everyone else. So I ran real fast!

I think the dear boy tried to propose last night. He got down on his knees, looked up into my beautiful blue eyes and whispered, *I want you* . . . When I asked him to go on he said, "I want you . . . to lend me five dollars." . . . (shrug) Guess he lost his nerve.

Last week when he came to take me to the concert he was very late. "The concert was over an hour ago," I said. "I know," he replied, "it's cheaper to sit here and listen to you." So for the rest of the evening I *talked* and he *applauded.* When I asked him why he clapped so much he said he was overjoyed at the money he'd saved. Don't you think he has a nice sense of *thrift?* (smile)

Last night he brought me an interesting bouquet of pansies and roses and lilies . . . which was very coincidental because the flowers in our front yard are also pansies and roses and lilies . . .

that is, the flowers we *had* in our front yard. I'll say one thing about Norman . . . (shake head) No, I'd better not.

Oh, yes, Norman can also *sing*. One evening he stood beneath my window and sang me an old Spanish love song. My dad poked his head out the window and shouted something in Spanish . . . Norman dropped his guitar and ran all the way home. When I asked Dad what he said he told me he told Norman to drop his guitar and run home. Isn't it lucky that Norman understands Spanish? Especially the way my dad speaks it.

(Dreamily) Norman always knows just the right thing to say. When I'm sad he says, "Cheer up." When I'm discouraged he says, "Smile." When I'm broke he says, "Goodbye." (frown)

(Gesture) Anyway, that's the way Norman *is*, . . . isn't it wonderful? (doubtfully) Of course if any of *you* girls want him I don't think I'd put up much of a struggle. (bow and exit)

ROMANTIC FACTS FOR MEN

Character: A young man.

(Enter with this book) Good evening, young lovers everywhere! I have a few vital loving statistics for you.

(Read from book) *Every year five thousand American boys propose marriage on their knees.* (look up) And let me tell you, American girls accept before the boys have a chance to get off their knees.

(Read) *A dozen red roses is a sign of love.* (sadly look up) And an empty wallet, unless you happen to own a rose garden.

(Read) *During leap year a girl may ask for a boy's hand in marriage.* (look up) She may only get his foot, however, as he leaps away. (laugh at own joke)

(Read) *Lovers discover romance when they walk in the moonlight.* (sadly) My girl and I walked five hours only to discover we didn't like each other.

Here's an unusual statistic. (read) *A boy is usually taller than his girl unless she is unusually tall in which case the usually taller boy is usually shorter than the unusually tall girl in which case he should stand on a box.* (smiling sweetly) I do hope everyone was paying attention.

(Read) *Girls whose names start with the letter M make excellent wives.* (look eagerly, hopefully over audience) Anyone out there named *Mildred? . . . Margie? . . . Marilyn? . . .* (desperately) Personally, I'll settle for *any* letter.

(Read) *She will like it if you bring her candy.* (look up) *My* girl didn't like it . . . I brought her candy home. (grin)

(Read seriously) *Your girl likes to be called a pet name.* (look up, puzzled) Then how come mine doesn't like *Fido?*

(Read) *Women are attracted by many things—most of them in the shape of men.* (look up, beam happily)

(Read) *Girls like boys with a sense of humor.* (look up, grin) I must have a good sense of humor because my girl friend starts laughing when I show up. (close book, bow, exit)

ROMANTIC FACTS FOR WOMEN

Character: A young woman. (Note: For extra fun, deliver this monologue immediately after the preceding one entitled *Romantic Facts for Men.*)

(Enter with this book) Good evening, lovers everywhere! I want to read you some statistics that are confusing, but which I will try to straighten out for you.

(Read from book) *The American girl has an average of one and one-half dates per month.* (look up, puzzled) How does a girl have half a date? (read) *The average American boy has an average of two and one-quarter dates per month.* (look up, frown) That means he has ¾ of a date by himself!

(Read from book) *A boy usually proposes after the sixth date.* (look up, scowl) Eddie proposed to me after the sixth date. He proposed that he stop coming!

(Read from book) *June is the most romantic month of all.* (look up, shrug) Oh, I don't know . . . my dad chased nine boys home last month.

(Read from book) *Men with short hair make the best husbands . . .* (look up, grin) I guess that's what Delilah figured with Samson!

(Read) *The wise young-lady will call her boy friend hand-*

some. (look up, speak in complaint) Every time I call Eddie *handsome* he looks around to see who I'm talking to.

(Read) *Niagara Falls is a great place for a honeymoon.* (look up, disgusted) My Eddie suggested we save money by sitting on the front lawn and watching the sprinkler.

(Read) *Men named Charley usually become rich.* (eagerly wave over the audience) Charley, I may be convinced to give up Eddie. (Note: If desired, substitute a local name for Charley.)

(Read) *The average American man prefers food to romance.* (angrily look up) I know . . . my boy friend can sit for hours mooning over a cherry pie.

(Read) *You will go far by showing an interest in your man's activities.* (sourly look up) Last week I went far . . . three hundred miles to watch him enlist in the army.

(Read) *Men prefer wives who can cook, sew, wash, sweep, and scrub.* (look up, then look back for place) Did it say *wives* or *slaves?*

(Read) *Statistics indicate that most men want to get married.* (look up) Forget the statistics—let's see some *proof!* (close book, bow, exit)

OUR NATIONAL SPORTS

Character: An athlete (male or female).

I would like to give you a brief yet fascinating history of how some of our national sports were started.

Baseball was created as a result of a number of confusing circumstances. It was first called Faceball and consisted of Pilgrims throwing pumpkin pies at Indians on Thanksgiving Day . . . When the Indians, in turn, chased the Pilgrims, it was called Chaseball . . . The Pilgrim ladies retaliated by throwing household items at the Indians, after which it was called Vaseball . . . But the Indians and Pilgrims finally got together in peace and decided to rename the sport. They called it Baseball in honor of Robert T. Base, who had held the coats of both teams.

It's hardly worth mentioning, but handball is so named because the ball used for this game is usually shaped like a hand . . . When the ball is shaped like a foot, it is called football.

Swimming is an ancient sport that was first created by a caveman named Wiglag. It isn't well known, but one day Wiglag was walking along the river when his wife suddenly pushed him in. "That's for not buying me a new dinosaur coat," she screamed . . . Poor Wiglag floated on top of the water for hours, waiting to drown. But since he didn't sink, he called to his fellow cavemen in sign language. As he moved his arms about, he found himself moving on top of the water. His experience created such a great interest in water, it wasn't long before mankind learned to swim. And all because of Mrs. Wiglag not having a new dinosaur coat!

The running broad jump was first introduced in America by a man named Springer B. Leap. It seems Mr. Leap came home one day and found a big water puddle between the sidewalk and porch. He did just what you and I would do under the circumstances. He walked around it. Later he invented the running broad jump.

Pole vaulting was invented by an ancient Roman soldier who had overstayed his leave. Taking a long spear he vaulted smack into the second floor of the barracks . . . Unfortunately for him, the general was holding a midnight inspection and the soldier plopped right on top of him. However, the soldier's ingenuity so intrigued the general that he ordered all soldiers henceforth to pole vault into enemy buildings. This was the beginning of aerial warfare.

Tennis was created by a pair of fishermen who had a big fight over a fish net. Each stood on a side of the net and tossed a week-old herring back and forth at each other . . . They decided after a while that since they had to fight they might as well make it interesting. So instead of a herring they tossed codfish balls . . . But codfish balls had a tendency to muss up the face after a particularly accurate toss. So they then used peaches. When they got tired of peach jam, it was just a short step to fuzzy tennis balls.

The indoor game of Chinese Checkers was created in a supermarket. Between checking out groceries, two clerks played a harmless little game with marbles and a board. The Boss came along, saw what they were doing and remarked, "Looks like Chinese to me, you checkers." And so the game was named.

The relay race was created when a squad of Greek soldiers accidentally came upon a live hand grenade. Having nothing else to do, they just ran around and passed it around to each other . . . Today, there is a bronze statue in Greece dedicated to the memory of these four clever soldiers.

The game of Drop the Handkerchief was first started by a woman of ancient Mesopotamia who dropped her handkerchief to catch the attention of a passing shepherd. When the shepherd saw that it was a much better handkerchief than his own he pocketed it and promptly forgot all about the woman.

And finally, the game of water polo was started by the famous Venetian adventurer, Marco Polo. One day Marco was leaning over the side of a ship and looking thoughtfully at the great expanse of blue below him. One of the crew saw him and said in passing, "That's water, Polo." The name has stuck ever since.

If you wish to know the origin of other kinds of sports, just ask Ed Jones . . . (substitute name of prominent local person for Ed Jones) He's a great sport!

THE STAFF OF LIFE

Character: A scholarly lecturer.

(Enter with a tray loaded with slices of bread, set it on table, wave a slice of bread at audience) Good evening, good evening, bread lovers! As you know, bread is called the staff of life. It is also called the *laugh of life* because of its history. I'd like to tell you how mankind developed bread . . . Incidentally, this bread was donated by Tom Morris (substitute name of prominent local person), who just cleaned out his bread box.

(Set down original slice, hold up another) This is *rye* bread . . . once called *sly* bread by foreign spies . . . *cry* bread by spies who got caught . . . *high* bread by mountain climbers . . . *sigh* bread by young lovers with troubles.

(Hold up another slice) The history of this bread is very short . . . it's *short* bread . . . first made in a bakery just two feet long . . . called *port* bread by sailors . . . *court* bread by tennis players. (smile) Am I making you hungry?

(Hold up another slice, talk faster) Here's *wheat* bread . . . called *cheat* bread by folks who only got half a loaf . . . *heat* bread by desert dwellers . . . Tidy folks called it *neat* bread . . . poor people *treat* bread. It was also called *greet* bread . . . instead of shaking hands you exchanged loaves.

(Hold up another slice) *Corn* bread was once called *horn* bread . . . but only by talking cows.

(Hold up another slice, talk faster) *French* bread . . . called *trench* bread by hungry soldiers . . . *bench* bread by second-rate football players.

(Hold up another slice, talk still faster) Of course there's *white* bread . . . called *fight* bread by angry people . . . *flight* bread by the folks at whom they were angry. It was called *night* bread by people who liked midnight snacks . . . *light* bread by people who liked to see what they were eating. Clever boys sliced it very thin, tied it to a string . . . and called it *kite* bread.

(Gesture to tray) I could go on and on, but I see someone out there (shade eyes, peer at audience) with some jam. I'm not sure if it's intended for the bread or for me . . . but I'm taking no

chances. (gesture to tray as you start to leave) Help yourself to
rye bread . . . goodbye bread! (grab a slice, munch it as you exit
quickly)

LITTLE KNOWN FACTS ABOUT BIRDS

Character: A nature lover (male or female).

Cheep-cheep, everyone! My name is Bobwhite B. Birdwatch.
I am here to tell you some little-known facts about birds. Are
you settled comfortably in your nests? Splendid!

The first bird I would like to tell you about is the parrot. The
parrot is noted for his ability to talk. A parrot was once entered
in a contest, reciting the Gettysburg Address, but he was disqualified for editing it . . . Parrots are also famous for their
ability to mimic the bark of a dog. I once wasted seven cans of
dog food before discovering the trick . . . Parrots are usually
found in South America, Asia, and on the shoulders of returning
sailors.

Tree sparrows are so named because they like to perch in
trees. When they perch on the ground they are called Ground
Sparrows. I once watched an active little fellow and found out his
name was Tree-Ground-Tree-Ground-Tree-Ground-Tree-Ground-
Sparrow . . . Bird watchers who favor this bird all have stiff
necks.

The Nightingale is a famous songbird, most often seen on the
covers of love songs. Traditionally, they sing outside ladies' windows on warm summer nights. Most Nightingales are named
Florence.

The Raven is best known for his part in a great poem written
by a bird lover, Edgar Allen Crow . . . I mean Poe . . . Mr.
Poe originally wanted to call it the Meadowlark, but the only
rhyme he could think of was *fleddokark*. So you might say the
Raven is famous because fleddokark doesn't make much sense
. . . Mr. Poe made a mint.

You can always tell a Mourning Dove by his sad, mournful
song. Some Mourning Doves have cheery songs but their mates
hate them for being so happy . . . The Mourning Dove is usually
seen in the morning. When seen in the afternoon he is called an

211

Afternoon Dove . . . If he stays up all night he is called a tired Mourning Dove.

The lovely Skylark has long been an inspiration to poets and songwriters. You have probably read the epic, To a Skylark, which is the tale of a torrid romance between two larks . . . I am presently completing my own little epic entitled, To a Yellow Crested Barn Owl. Let me quote from my little poem:

> Lo, the Yellow Crested Barn Owl,
> Lo, the Yellow Crested Barn Owl,
> Lo, the Yellow Crested Barn Owl.

It's short, but says a good deal, don't you think?

The Duck Hawk is so named because of his ability to duck when pursued by other birds . . . He ducks into alleys, abandoned warehouses and into the living rooms of lady Duck Hawks. Many a lovely romance has been started this way.

The Turtle Dove is often mistaken for a turtle because of its confusing name. There is a movement on foot to change its name to Serpent Dove because it is less confusing to tell a snake from a turtle when it is a bird.

I must now spread my little wings and fly away to lunch. Once again, cheep-cheep! (exit with arms bent, hands flapping as wings)

CALLING ALL COOKS

Character: A cooking expert on television.

Ladies, I am delighted to be able to stand here before you today. I have just eaten one of my own recipes—and that is why I am glad to be *able* to stand before you.

The first thing I would like to discuss is French pastry. I say I would *like* to but I don't know a thing about it. Therefore, we will first take up a recipe for *Spanish* spaghetti. We must be careful how we take up this subject, for it is rather gooey . . . Spanish spaghetti consists of a cup of Spanish chopped onions, three pounds of Spanish olives, and the shredded cape of a defeated matador. The spaghetti itself can be obtained by writing directly to our Spanish ambassador in Madrid . . . or, if you're in a hurry

you can simply use a few strings from an old guitar . . . Mix all ingredients well, toss them out, and go down to Manuel's Spaghetti House.

The next recipe is for date bread. However, this is a special date bread and can only be made on February thirtieth . . . so we will have to discuss pineapple upside-down cake instead. It's a bit difficult to make while standing on your head, so you may cheat a bit and make a pineapple *sideways* cake.

There's nothing like Mother's Molasses Cookies. *Nothing!* I wanted to give you the recipe for this, but Mother wouldn't let me. But I *do* have a secret recipe from Uncle Charlie. Unfortunately, it's a recipe for making ink for dollar bills and the government doesn't like anyone to talk about it.

When roasting a turkey, remember the importance of stuffing! The best way is with a spoon or a fork or a long knife. Of course it's still better if you use bread crumbs . . . it saves the silverware . . . I am sure you'll be interested in knowing how to make a jelly roll. I personally just take my forefinger like this (skid forefinger along table top) and the jelly rolls any place it wants . . .

Ladies, I'd like to mention the new tangy sauces. Your husband will positively *rave* when you serve him a tangy sauce on his favorite meat. What a lovely variety of sauces you can create! Onion sauces, cream sauces, and flying sauces . . . It's always a good idea to serve sauces that suit the personality of your guests.

For example, you could serve blubber sauce to your Eskimo friends and seaweed sauce to sailors . . . Remember, ladies—a *saucy* cook is a *successful* cook!

And now we come to Chicken a la King. For this you will need a very large chicken and a very small king . . . If you can't find a king you can always substitute a prince or a duke. Mix well, sprinkle with a cupful of shredded crown. Of course, if this is to be served at a ladies' luncheon you would make Chicken a la *queen*.

Next, suppose we look into stuffed eggs . . . (think) No, it's not easy to look into stuffed eggs without pulling the whole egg apart . . . Instead, we will look into sandwiches. As everyone knows, sandwiches were first created by the Earl of Sandwich. Wouldn't it be dreadful if he had been the Earl of Eastern Patagonia? . . . An interesting variation in a sandwich is to spread peanut butter and jelly on the *outside* of the bread . . . You can be sure that your friends will stick by you with this . . . And the chicken sandwich! Of course most chickens don't like sandwiches so we'll skip this one.

Finally, I would like to give you my secret recipe for a little delicacy I call a Mystery Cake. Primarily, the mystery is how anyone can eat it. Now I leave you with the favorite expression of that famous French chef, Pierre LaFrance . . . (hold stomach, groan, stagger offstage) Ohhhh . . .

AROUND THE WORLD

Scene: The comedian stands alongside a large map of the world. He uses a stick to point to the various countries.

Ladies and gentlemen, we are about to take a trip around the world. I assure you that it will be unlike any other trip you have taken.

(Point to the United States.) Let's take off from this country which is called . . . (peer puzzledly at map) oh, yes, the United States of America.

Off we go across the sea to England. England has many people, mostly Englishmen. England also has a few Frenchmen, but that has nothing to do with our trip. Japan also has a few Canadians, but that has even less to do with it.

214

(Point to map.) Here you see the tiny country of Switzerland. I should explain that you can't actually see the tiny country of Switzerland; you can see only a piece of paper called a map. We get Swiss cheese from Switzerland. Some people think we get Swiss cheese from a delicatessen. Such people need help.

Let's next leap from Switzerland to Spain. It is really very difficult to leap to Spain. As a matter of fact, only healthy rabbits can do it. Now that we are in Spain we can enjoy the sights—mostly healthy rabbits.

But let us travel on. Here we see the romantic country of Italy. I must again explain that we don't really see the country of Italy—we see only a piece of paper called a map. I make this explanation for a good reason—if friends ask you whether you have seen Italy, you can reply, "No, but I've seen an interesting piece of paper." They are sure to admire your honesty.

Next, I would like to take all of you to Norway. I would like to, but I can't afford it. So let's go on to South America instead. (Point to several South American countries.) As you can see, South America is a very colorful continent. (Name the map colors.) Blue, red, green.

Here is the Amazon River. (Dab handkerchief at Amazon, wring handkerchief out.) It seems to be overflowing. If we were to travel up the Amazon we would find many strange tribes. Why should we find many strange tribes? Personally, I prefer to find money.

So let's say goodbye to South America. It's not that South America is going anywhere—*we* are.

Now we cross the Pacific Ocean. Here is China. Once more I must tell you that it isn't really China. It's just a spot on a map.

But we must call it China. If we didn't call it China we would have to call it a piece of paper. You can see how confusing that would be.

Thank you for traveling along with me. You may now throw money at my feet. (exit)

HOW TO BE SUCCESSFUL

Character: A lecturer (male or female).

Good evening, ladies and gentlemen. Allow me to introduce myself. My name is . . . is . . . (pull out slip of paper, read name) Ah, yes . . . Aubrey Q. Fliptop. No doubt you recognize me as the author of that best-selling book, How to Make Friends with Airedales.

I have been asked to give you a few *pointers* on how to make a success of yourself in the world. My first advice to you is to *think big*. Let me repeat that . . . *thimk* . . . (shake head) *thimk* . . . (give up) Whatever you do . . . aim high!

Secondly, you must put yourself in the place of the other fellow. Take the case of Robert B. Switchouse who was an unsuccessful salesman for twenty years. One day he walked boldly into the office of the president of Associated Gum Wrappers Corporation. He asked the president if he could sit in his chair. The president agreed, so Mr. Switchouse took his place at the desk. He hasn't left that chair since. How come? Bubble gum on the seat.

Another important thing to remember is to *act the part*. If you are a salesman, *look* like a salesman. If you're a bum, *look* like a bum . . . I recall the case of Thomas T. Tigerfang who wanted more than anything else to resign as a professor and be a great lion tamer. He got himself a whip, a chair, and a pistol loaded with blanks. Unfortunately, the part he wanted to play didn't last very long. When he walked into a lion cage, five hungry lions promptly ate him up.

To be successful, you must make people *like* you. Take the experience of Samuel Albert Shiftless. For twenty years Mr. Shiftless was disliked by everyone. Everyone except, of course, his dear wife . . . who *hated* him . . . Then Mr. Shiftless discovered the secret of saying nice things. He paid such little compliments as, "My, but you're pretty . . . what a darling hat . . . I love your new hairdo." Unfortunately, because Mr. Shiftless only learned to say nice things to women, his wife beat him up in a jealous rage.

Finally, here is a golden phrase which I want all of you to remember . . . (try to remember, fumble in pocket, pull out a slip of paper, read from it) Three pounds of hamburger and a box of chili powder . . . (in embarrassment, toss paper aside) Ah, yes, here is the golden phrase—*Keep trying!* No matter how bad the situation, you must *keep trying.* I myself always keep trying.

(Look at watch) Now, if you'll excuse me, I have to go to work. (reach offstage, take broom, sweep stage, speak to audience) The mayor promised that I'll be promoted to head street sweeper if I keep up the good work. (exit, sweeping)

HOW TO IMPROVE YOUR MEMORY

Character: A memory expert.

Tell me, do you forget easily? Do things slip your mind? If so, you'll be glad I came out here to tell you how to sharpen your memory . . .

The first thing to do is . . . (frown, shrug) The *second* thing is to *write it down.* Whenever you want to remember things, just write them down on tiny slips of paper. Then try to remember where you put the slips of paper. (smile brightly)

I've heard of an absent-minded man who wanted to ask his girl to marry him . . . As he walked toward her house he kept repeating, *marry me, marry me, marry me!* . . . By the time he got there he was engaged to sixteen other girls on the street.

My brother can remember everything but his own name. *Why can't you remember your own name?* I asked. Well, he replied, *no one's perfect.*

Just remember that you're never too old to learn. A friend of mine wanted to remember to put on his shoes in the morning . . . At the age of thirty-five he had it down just right.

If you have trouble remembering your birthday, just remember it has to be one of the 365 days of the year . . . which is much better than not knowing at all.

My sister remembered that she wanted to send a present to her boy friend . . . But she never sent it because she also remembered she wanted to forget him.

Speaking of remembering, you'd better remember to forget everything I've said! (exit)

YOUR HAPPY FRIEND

Character: Anyone (male).

(Enter, bow) This is your happy friend, Charley Green! (If desired, use own name) Please notice I did not use that old, worn-out greeting, *hello.* There's a mighty good reason. I'm on a one-man crusade against the word *hello* as an official greeting . . . especially on the telephone. When you say *hello* to someone, what do you really say? *Nothing!* Nothing except *hello.* So since hello is *nothing,* why say it? (shrug) I'm as confused as you.

Anyway, I propose a sparkling new method for opening a phone conversation. (pick up imaginary or toy phone) The idea is simply to greet all calls with the cheery little phrase of (speak into phone with exaggerated cheer) *This is your happy friend!* (to audience) Your friends will wrap themselves around the phone cord with friendly happiness! Now I'm not one to toss around vague theories. I'm going to *prove* the efficacy (smile) —good word?—the efficacy (smile) of my new method. Let's just see how we can fill our lives with joy and gladness with my *This-is-your-happy-friend* technique!

(Gesture to phone) My sixth sense tells me the phone is about to ring . . . (look at phone) Ah! There we go! Now listen carefully . . . (take phone, speak with exaggerated cheer) This is your happy friend, Charley Green! (listen, nod, write on pad as if recording conversation, hang up, hold pad up and pretend to read from it) I-hate-you-happy-friend. (sadly) Such is the life of a pioneer.

(As phone rings, speak cheerfully into it. Note: Vary your cheeriness each time you take phone, making it bold or overly-sentimental or bouncy or impish) This is your happy friend, Charley Green! What's that, young lady? . . . am I *rich* as well as *happy?* No, but I . . . (frown at phone, shrug to audience) She hung up.

(As phone rings) This is your happy friend, Charley Green! (frown) What? . . . I'll be *unhappy* if I don't pay my laundry bill?

(To audience) As I said, this is still in the experimental stage . . . This is your happy friend, Charley Green? I mean, this is your *happy* friend, Charley Green! (listen, nod) Yes, ma'am, I'm very friendly . . . yes, ma'am . . . very, *very* friendly . . . (listen, shake head) No, ma'am, I'm not so friendly that I'll lend you ten bucks! (scowl, hang up)

(Sigh to audience) Anyone else want to try? (as phone rings) This is your happy but discouraged friend, Charley Green! (puzzled) What? You just want to hear me answer the phone? (shrug to audience, speak into phone) Well, all right . . . Hello-hello-hello-hello-hello. (curiously) Why all the *helloes?* (Indignant) How else would I answer the phone? (smile, bow, exit)

SUPPER IN SILENCE

Character: Anyone.

(Enter and stand beside a table set for dinner) Ladies and gentlemen, doctors tell us that we should take our meals in peace and quiet . . . It's good for the system. I have therefore invented a handy-dandy little method for eating in total silence . . . I call it *Silent Speech for Soothing Suppers.* Let me show you how my little sign-system works . . .

(Sit at table, sideways to audience, rapidly spin hand in a small circle as if speaking sign-language to another diner, turn to audience) This means, *Please pass the pepper.* (spin hand in opposite direction) The opposite direction means, *Don't pass the pepper* . . . I have plenty.

(Face table, scratch ear) A scratch on the ear means you want an ear of corn. (scratch shoulder) A scratch on the shoulder means that you have an itch.

When you want a glass of water, make diving motions like this . . . (place palms together, repeatedly dive them forward and downward)

(Wiggle fingers of one hand) This asks the question, *How come you're stirring my soup with your fingers?* (wiggle fingers of both hands) This asks, *Why don't you at least wear gloves?*

(Hold up four fingers) This asks, *Could I have a fourth piece of pie?* (shake angry fist) This asks, *Who are you calling a pig?*

See how *quiet* everything is? Now suppose you want the butter . . . try this form of Silent Speech . . . by spelling out *butter* in the air . . . (quickly trace letters in air) B . . . U . . . T . . . T . . . E . . . R . . . If no one can read your writing just reach for it.

This one is handy-dandy for telling your big brother to stay out of your ice cream . . . (jerk fist downward at head level over adjoining chair) And the same idea for a *bigger* brother . . . (repeat movement at a higher head-level over another chair)

Silent Speech makes dinnertable conversation absolutely unnecessary! Suppose you want to tell someone that it's raining . . . just drip you fingers in a glass of water (do so) and sprinkle it around . . . (shake fingers around) Just watch them race for their umbrellas . . . but watch out they don't race for *you*. (smile) And here's the way to inform them that an earthquake is on the way . . . (jerk table up and down) Marvelous, isn't it? Of course, the conversation may be a bit limited, but you can't have everything.

Here's the way to keep things nice and quiet when you want to show your appreciation for the food . . . (rapidly twirl forefingers around each other) This means you're *pleased* . . . (rapidly twirl hands around each other) This means you're *delighted* . . . (rapidly, awkwardly twirl arms around each other) This just means you're *nervous!*

(Stand, hold up finger) So remember, whatever it is you wish to say . . . say it in silence. Everyone will appreciate the quietness . . . just be careful it's not so quiet that you miss the call to supper! (bow and exit on tiptoe)

FAMOUS WORDS

Character: A lecturer (male or female).

(Enter with book) Ladies and gentlemen, after weeks of intensive research . . . between games at the local ball park . . . I have come up with some little-known sayings of famous people in history. Let me tell you a few I found:

George Washington to Lord Cornwallis: *Give up yet?*

Cleopatra, when bitten by the serpent: *I hope the scar won't show.*

Buffalo Bill: *Did a Buffalo run me down or am I lying here because I'm tired?*

Alexander the Great, just before conquering the world: *What's there to do around here, anyway?*

Columbus, after crossing the Atlantic: *Man, that's some lake!*

Eli Whitney, after inventing the cotton gin: *Just stack the money in the closet.*

Alexander Graham Bell, with his first telephone: *But operator —that's the wrong number!*

Sir Francis Drake, after losing his ship: *The salt water is going to ruin my new uniform.*

Benjamin Franklin, when discovering electricity: *Ouch!*

Daniel Boone: *Someday I'll learn how to shoot this thing!*

Davy Crockett: *I'll bet I get more famous than Daniel Boone.*

Shakespeare, after a hard day's work on his sonnets: *Hope somebody reads this stuff.*

Noah Webster, after completing his dictionary: *Maybe they'll make it into a movie.*

General Custer, at Little Big Horn: *Who invited all those Indians?*

(Look up to audience) And finally, I'll quote these noted gems. (refer again to book)

Henry Wadsworth Longfellow, after writing a very long poem: *Wish someone would invent the typewriter.*

Franz Schubert, reviewing his "Unfinished Symphony": *What happened to those last eight pages?*

Orville and Wilbur Wright at Kitty Hawk: *Ooooops!*

Stephen Foster: *I wonder what comes after do re mi?*

General Grant to General Lee: *I told you so!* (bow and exit)

OUR FAMOUS PROVERBS

Character: A scholarly lecturer (male or female).

I thought perhaps you would be interested in hearing a few facts about the proverbs that we so glibly quote every day. You know, *Experience is the best teacher; Beauty is only skin deep; Don't hold a lighted firecracker between your toes . . .*

One of our most famous proverbs was born when two boys of ancient Greece came upon a bottle of glue in the road. "It's mine!" shouted one. "It's *mine!*" shouted the other. And so was born the proverb, *It takes glue to make a quarrel.*

Another famous proverb first appeared in Spain. An orange grower was crating up his oranges. He piled crate upon crate, crate upon crate until the crates were twenty feet high. A gust of wind suddenly blew the whole works down on his head. And so we have the proverb, *Everything comes to him who crates.*

Another noted proverb was originated in a dog kennel. Their trainer was teaching them to jump over a high fence when a lady

222

came in. "Those dogs can't jump that fence," she insisted. The man quietly replied, *"Let leaping dogs try."*

Speaking of animals, by the way, I just heard what I think is a fairly new proverb. It all started when a road hog was squeezing into the last parking place at the curb. Another motorist drove up and said, "I'll fight you for it." "Don't be silly," said the other. *"A parking hog never fights."*

A famous proverb was first uttered when an Indian mother complained to her husband that she had no washing machine, kitchen stove, or television set. So the poor man went out and invented them. Thus was born the proverb: *Mother is the necessity for inventions.*

One afternoon in ancient Rome another housewife complained to *her* husband that there was no water in the house. He angrily turned on her and shouted, "Remember, woman, *Rome wasn't built on a bay."*

A chicken coop is responsible for another famous proverb. It seems that a hen saw some choice corn beneath a board. The hen tugged and tugged until it got the board out of the way. A watching farmer casually remarked, *"The hen is mightier than the board."*

A famous poet was responsible for one of our best-known proverbs. He wrote poetry all day long but was unable to see it. He sadly remarked, *"Rhyme does not pay."*

Another old proverb originated this way. It seems that William was so much in love with May that he followed her wherever she went. People said, *"Where there's a Will, there's a May."*

One day a small boy tried to rake leaves, but they piled up faster than he could work. He angrily started beating the rake against the sidewalk until it broke. And so was born the saying, *You can't have your rake and beat it, too.*

The last proverb I have began in this manner. A king of a primitive country, who lived in a grass hut, bought a throne from a passing salesman. Since he didn't have any room for it on the floor of his little grass hut, he put the throne in the loft above his one room. One day it came tumbling down on the king and his guests in the midst of dinner. So began the saying, *People who live in grass houses shouldn't stow thrones.*

I'll be back when I gather some more information! (exit)

223

SPACE TALK

Character: A space-travel expert.

(Enter with this book which is covered with a temporary jacket, reading *Space Talk*) Good evening. As you know, we are getting closer and closer to space travel . . . vacationing on Mars, Jupiter, Saturn, etc. It's just as well that we brush up on our space talk . . . never know when you'll find yourself speaking to a Martian. (open book) Let me give you a few phrases the Martians are likely to say to you.

(Read from book) *Og wiggly woo* . . . (look up) This asks, *Did you have a nice trip getting here?*

(Read from book) *Lippy mag sag* . . . (look up) This means, *Why don't you ugly scientists go back and send us some more pretty girls?* (read from book) *Loddy soo top* . . . (look up) This is usually spoken by unmarried ladies of Mars and means, *Why don't you pretty girls go back and send us some more ugly scientists?*

(Read from book) *Wip tabby grip* . . . (look up) This is spoken by Martian real estate agents and means, *For five dollars you can have the whole planet.* (read from book) *Sooey tooey* . . . (look up) *Three dollars more and I'll throw in Jupiter.*

(Read from book) *Ray muggy lop* . . . (look up) This simply means, *ippy tip tag* . . . which means nothing at all.

(Read from book) *Pad paddy pug* . . . (look up) Translation: *Let's have a pie eating contest—you bring the pies.* (shrug) Tricky people, those Martians.

Here's a tough one. (read from book) *Sip noppy kay* . . . (look up) This asks the question, *What's the difference between a touchdown and a butterfly?* (frown, hopelessly shake head)

Here's another question. (read from book) *Labby rik nub* . . . (look up) *Do you have the same television shows we have?*

(Read from book) *Bakky wakky moo* . . . (look up) This is an invitation which means, *Please have dinner with us tonight.* (read from book) *Ikky wikky wug* . . . (look up) This is a P.S. which means, *Please leave your noisy children home.*

(Close book) So whatever you do, brush up on your space talk. You never know when you'll be faced with *og wiggly woo!* (exit)

THE ARTIST

Scene: An artist, wearing a smock and beret, explains a series of pictures. All of them are meaningless and are made up of blobs and streaks. The artist holds them up one at a time.

Good evening. I would like to show you some works of art.

Here we have a very remarkable picture. Any way you look at it, it looks exactly the same. (Hold picture at angle.) Like this. (Hold it at another angle.) And this. (Hold it at third angle.) And this. Yes, any way you look at it.

(Display blank sheet.) This is a picture of an Indian on a horse. The horse has just thrown the Indian over here (point beyond left of picture), while the horse ran over here (point beyond right of picture). So, naturally, we can't see either one.

This one is called *Shredded Paper*. You can only appreciate its true beauty by doing this. (Quickly rip picture into several pieces, toss them aside.) See?

(Hold up a picture with a large hole cut out of its center.) This one gives you a choice. If you don't like the picture, you can look through to something better on the other side.

I want you to take special notice of this one. It is connected with one of the most famous artists of all time, Leonardo da Vinci. It comes from the same town in Italy.

(Hold up mirror.) This is called a mirror picture. In order to see the painting you must look into the mirror. (Look into mirror, nod with smiling approval.) I would judge this to be the handsomest picture I've ever seen.

Here we have one that looks best when you stand at a distance —a distance of five miles.

Finally, I want you to know that all of these paintings are for sale. They cost one thousand dollars apiece. I know that's a horrible price, but after all, they *are* horrible pictures. (exit)

COURTESY AT THE WHEEL

Character: A motorist (male or female).

When I'm driving my car I try to keep one thing in mind—*courtesy.* I *try,* but actually I think about others things like *girls,* (*boys*), *money, week-end vacations* . . . I'm very rude the rest of the time, but *courtesy at the wheel!* . . . Yes, sir, courtesy pays off. I remember the time when two of us came to an intersection at the same time. *I* waited, *he* waited, *I* waited, *he* waited . . . it was midnight before either of us courteous drivers got home!

If there's one thing I can't stand, it's a speeder. I am a self-appointed speeder stopper. The other day I saw a man rushing past me doing ninety. "What are you doing going ninety?" I courteously screamed at him. "What are *you* doing on the railroad tracks?" he screamed back. He was the engineer on the Santa Fe Challenger.

Of course, Sunday drivers are the worst. Last Sunday one joker piled into the rear of my car. I courteously said to him, "Look what you did to my car, you Sunday driver, you!" "My mistake," he admitted, "I usually do this on Thursday."

One morning last month I came across a motorist who was stalled in the middle of the road. "Can I give you a push?" I courteously inquired. "Just down to the nearest gas station," he replied. Three days later we got out of the desert, and reached town.

Of course, courtesy should be combined with humor whenever you meet a traffic cop. I got stopped last night and the cop snarled, "You were doing *eighty,* ran *five* red signals, knocked down *three* light poles! What does *that* add up to?" Quick as a flash I said, "Eighty-eight!" . . . My quick wit pleased him. He even helped store all the tickets he gave me in the car trunk.

Finally, let me tell you of my experience with a road hog. We had quite a race but I finally won. Seems the hog wandered from the farm right onto the road . . . I'll be having roast pork chops for dinner. Trouble is, the farmer got my license number. The pork chops are costing me $50! I smiled as I paid, however.

So, remember, whatever you do when on the road, do it courteously! (bow and exit)

THE TIME OF MY LIFE

Character: Anyone, imitating a small boy or girl.

(Enter with a watch on wrist, speak and act excitedly in the manner of a small child, hold up wrist to show watch) See my watch? I'm learning to tell time! . . . and having the time of my life!

Yesterday I told my dad the time of day, but he wasn't interested . . . in fact he almost threw a pillow at me . . . I think it was because the time was three in the morning.

Last week I asked my mother what time it was, and she said it was time to wash my face. She's always saying that. That's why I got my own watch.

I like to time myself to see how long it takes to walk to school. One time it took me three hours . . . I didn't have the wrong time, I just had the wrong school. (smile)

My dad says there is the right time and the wrong time for everything. It's funny but it's always the right time to do the dishes and the wrong time to play. I'll have to get him a new watch.

Last week my watch went fast . . . that was when it went out the window . . . it slowed down fast when it hit the ground. (smile)

I was two hours late getting home last night. (sadly) When I asked my mother what time it was, she said it was the *last* time I was going out for a while.

(Look at watch) Wouldn't you nice people like to know what time it is? (smile) Time for me to leave! (curtsy or bow and exit)

MY VOCAL CAREER

Character: A singer (male or female).

Did I ever tell you about my vocal career? It all started one morning as I was walking through the woods. I heard a nightingale singing while perched on the back of a cow. I listened and listened until I could imitate the sound perfectly. I now sing exactly like that cow.

227

My career really got started in St. Louis when I was discovered by a talent scout. He heard me singing a romantic Italian song. First thing I knew I was on a fast boat to Italy . . . It was there I first met the great Señor Galoppi of the Milan Opera House. He heard me sing and gave me my first big break. But I was out of the cast in six weeks.

I'll never forget the time I brought down the house in Rome. The neighbors in the apartment upstairs came down to slug me with big rolls of salami . . .

I also write beautiful music. Listen to the opening of this composition, which I call, *Etude in C Flat Major for Trombone and Xylophone.* (Hum a single, short note) . . . As soon as I add the rest of the notes I'll have a big hit.

But back to my vocal career. As you know, voices have various classifications. There are contraltos, tenors, baritones, sopranos and basses. My voice has a classification all its own . . . I am known as a bull-moose soprano.

Probably my biggest success came at the South Dakota Open Air Festival. There were contestants from every state except South Dakota . . . There I was, perched on a huge brown rock in the middle of a prairie. I started to sing. The wheat started to sway . . . Then the earth rumbled and opened up . . . What an earthquake! . . . I wouldn't say that I won first prize. I wouldn't even say that I won second prize. To tell the truth, I was disqualified for using a cheap tin whistle on the high notes.

Another great triumph of mine was on television. I brought out the deeper emotions of millions of viewers. They laughed, cried, and hysterically called the broadcasting station.

I have also made a few records. Maybe you have heard of my recording called, *Come Back to Texas Where the Longhorns Grow and the Little Spanish Señorita Waits Beside the Old Garden Wall in the Pale Moonlight with Sweet Guitars Strumming Down Where the Mississippi Flows* . . . This song could have been a hit except for one thing. (sadly) Everyone hated it.

Like all great careers, mine came to a triumphant end. Ah, how well I remember that lovely spring evening in August. I sang that old favorite, *It's a Long Long Way to Tipperary.* Five Irish cops marched up on that stage and started carrying me home . . . It seems they didn't want to help me home, though . . . they wanted to help send me to Tipperary! (bow and exit)

HOW I CONQUERED WORRY

Character: Anyone.

You can conquer worry too. It just takes a little relaxed effort. Let me tell you how. Take the time I was worried about the mortgage payment on my home. I worried, fretted, made myself perfectly miserable about it. But guess what happened . . . when the payment was due I went to the mailbox expecting to find a final demand for money . . . Instead, I found an apologetic note from the bank saying there had been a mix-up and the money was six months overdue. That did it—it left me nothing to worry about . . . except where to store the furniture when I was put out on the street.

Now take the time I worried about the payments on my car. "Pay up," one letter said, "or you'll be riding the bus." Instead of worrying, I just laughed and laughed about it . . . everyone on the bus thought I was crazy.

One of the best ways to combat worry is to *relax*. Just lie down and forget about it. No matter where you are or what you're doing, lie down and relax. I remember the time I was worried about my golf score, so I lay down on my back right there and relaxed. Would you believe it—when I was snoring, two golfers thought my mouth was the seventeenth hole . . . The doctor who removed the golf balls from my throat said I was the most relaxed person he'd ever seen!

Of course you can always sleep off your worries. Take the time I was worried about the river flooding my house. Instead of fretting, I just put myself to bed and slept it off. I woke up feeling like a million. Then I just took all those catfish out from between the blankets and had them for breakfast!

One of the better methods for conquering worry is to repeat words of strength to yourself. I tried this one time while I was out in the forest. A big bear was charging straight at me, so I repeated to myself, "Courage, courage, courage, courage . . ." As I ran faster and faster it sounded more like "Ouch, ouch, ouch, ouch . . ." Another helpful phrase you can use is, "Tomorrow will be different, tomorrow will be different." I tell you, this works *every time!* Your troubles on *Tuesday* are never the same as your troubles on *Monday* . . .

One of the proven methods to keep from worrying is to keep your mind occupied. If you're worried about being overweight, think how it would be if you were underweight. If you're worried about low grades in math, worry about low grades in social studies. Try to keep this golden rule in mind—*there's always something else to worry about.*

Another good method is to look on the *sunny* side of things. Suppose your morning started off badly, as mine did the other day. As I bounced out of bed, I said to myself, "Suppose you *did* break your leg—so what—you can always hop to work on the other one! Suppose you can't hold a job—the soup's not bad at the Salvation Army." I tell you it *pays* to look on the sunny side.

There are also some things that you should *not* do when worrying. For example, never throw yourself out of the window. I remember one big business executive who tried it . . . he ended up being sued by the city for sidewalk repairs . . . Another executive thought he could solve all his problems by running away to Mexico. What happened . . . ? Indigestion from all that spicy food.

My final word to all you worried folks is—don't tell *me* your troubles, I've got loads of my own! (hastily exit)

HOW?

Character: A book lecturer (male or female).

(Enter with several books and a list) Good evening, ladies and gentlemen. My name is Bookbug Binder. I am editor of the How Publishing Company—not how to publish—how to do things. I would like to read you a list of our latest publications. For you nature students we have a number of new titles . . . (read from list)

How to Make a Butterfly.

How to Play Pool with a Running Brook.

How to Stay Dry While Sitting Beneath a Weeping Willow.

How to Entertain a Leopard.

How to Get Away from a Leopard Who Isn't Entertained.

I'm sure you nature lovers will be delighted with our little list. These books sell for five dollars apiece—two for three dollars . . . We set this odd price just to confuse you. Oh, yes, these nature books are authentically illustrated by a trained seal . . . Our next list is for you folks who love to travel. Listen to these moving titles . . . (read from list)

How to Swim the Pacific Ocean.

How to Make Friends with Sharks.

How to Get to France on a Five-Dollar Bill.

How to Get There on a *Boat*.

How to Go to the North Pole.

How to Keep Your Tootsies from Freezing.

You may obtain these books from our shop any time after dark . . . I say this for your own protection—anyone seeing you buy them might think you a little odd . . . Ah! Our next little list of newly published titles is for you folks who like handicrafts . . . (read from list)

How to Work with Your Hands.

How to Work with Your Feet If You Have Clumsy Hands.

How to Build a Six-Car Garage.

How to Get Six Cars.

How to Build Almost Anything.

How to Tear Down Most of It.

How to Install Your Own Plumbing System.

How to Call for the Nearest Plumber.

All of these books are exactly three hundred pages long, and cost three dollars. If you can't afford more than two dollars' worth we'll gladly tear out one hundred pages.

We also have a new series of new books that are very new. Actually, they're not really new but we call them new to compete with other publishers. Listen to the titles. (read from list)

How to Eat Soup with Your Fingers.

How to Ignore Folks Who Call You a Pig.

How to Be a Perfect Gentleman.

How to Be a Perfect Lady in Case You're Not a Gentleman.

How to Attract Attention at a Party.

How to Get Back Down from the Ceiling.

How to Be Popular.

How to Be Repulsive in Case You'd Rather.

How to Walk with Grace and Dignity.
How to Walk with Jane and Susie.
How to Make People Like You.
How to Stop Twisting Their Arms.
Lastly, we have some splendid *how-to* books. (read from list)
How to Be a Bullfighter.
How to Remove Horns from Your Back.
How to Be Happy Though Miserable.
How to Be Miserable Though Happy.
How to Sing at Midnight.
How to Get Out of Town Fast.

If you want copies of these titles, better get your order in right away . . . they're going like crazy. There's said to be a fuel shortage! (bow and exit)

IT'S A MYSTERY

Character: Anyone.

(Enter with a book, hold it up. Note: You may use this book by covering it with a jacket entitled, *Great Detective Stories*. Pretend to turn pages from time to time as you proceed)

Have you read any good detective stories lately? I've just finished *this* . . . (lower book, shake head) Detectives just aren't what they used to be . . . (wave book) Take *this* detective . . . Let me read you a few of his sharp observations.

(Read from book) *Ah, this robbery looks like the work of a master jewel-thief* . . . (shrug, speak to audience) It turned out to be a neighborhood kid who thought the pearls were marbles.

(Read from book) *I'll never hit bed until I crack this case* . . . (to audience, chuckle) He slept on the floor for fifteen years.

(Read from book) *Tell me, ma'am, who is your worst enemy?* . . . (to audience) So she told him all about her husband.

(Read from book) *I expect to make an arrest within twenty-four hours* . . . (to audience) He arrested his sister for double-parking.

(Read from book) *Have the crime lab clean this coat* . . . (to audience) it was his *own* coat . . . he was saving on laundry bills.

(Read from book) *I must give this case some deep thoughts* . . . (to audience despairingly) He was filling his briefcase with notes!

(Read from book) *It looks like an inside job* . . . (exasperated, to audience) It took place on a Kansas prairie!

(To audience) See what I mean? . . . these are real mysteries. Let's try to solve some more of the detective's statements . . .

(Read from book) *I deduce that the criminal is a professional wrestler* . . . (to audience) It turned out to be a pretzel bender.

(Read from book) *Someone has poisoned my soup!* . . . (to audience) His wife's soup *always* tasted that way.

(Read from book) *Sergeant, arrest the owner of those footprints* . . . (to audience) The sergeant became the first man in history to handcuff a rabbit.

(Read from book) *Confess, you scoundrel!* . . . (to audience) He confessed that he was a scoundrel . . . but denied everything else.

(Read from book) *The criminal is the most beautiful woman in this room!* . . . (grin) Five women immediately confessed.

(Read from book) *Please, ma'am, don't talk that way about your friends* . . . (shrug, to audience) She was trying to tell him who did it.

(Read from book) *I have it!* . . . (to audience) He was fishing for the last olive in the bottle. (exit)

NOT EXACTLY

Character: Someone trying to speak precisely.

Ladies and gentlemen, I was asked to say a few words for this occasion. (gesture aimlessly) I was not exactly asked to say a few words . . . it was more that *I* asked to say a few words . . . which is not really the same thing. On the other hand it's not really the opposite, either. To tell you precisely how it happened, my phone rang last night and it turned out to be a member of the party committee (or other suitable committee name).

I imagine you want me to deliver a monologue! I exclaimed. *Not exactly,* she replied. *Maybe you just want me to recite a poem or two,* I asked. *No, that's not just it,* she said. *Well, how about just a few pleasant words,* I pleaded. *Well, not really,* she stated, *we really want you to do the dishes.*

(Indignantly) You can imagine my indignation at *that! The dishes!* I shouted, *That's like asking Beethoven to play a second fiddle in a high school orchestra. That's a thought,* she replied, *maybe he'll do it if we ask him in a real nice way. Look,* I said, *I know you can't see very well over the telephone but I have such expressive hands.* (wave hands about with exaggerated grace) *Can't you see them expressing great emotion as I deliver a speech? No,* she said, *but I can see them expressing some dirt right off those dishes!* I indignantly replied, *Do you know I can almost talk with my hands? Well, then,* said she, *why don't you tape your mouth sometime and deliver the Gettysburg Address for us?* (smugly) *That would be very handy,* I cleverly retorted. *Perhaps,* she said, *and it would certainly fan up a big breeze. Can I count on you for the dishes?*

(Firmly) *Not quite,* I said, *but if you let me say a few words I'll do the dishes* (smile triumphantly, draw self up in self-satisfaction) So I will now say my few words . . . (look to wing, tilt head in questioning glance, shake head in despair) No? (sigh, as you take apron, speak your last lines as you tie it around waist while walking) Have I enjoyed my few words? . . . (sadly, shaking head) *Not exactly!* (exit)

234

HOW ARE YOU?

Character: Anyone.

How are you, folks? (gesture vaguely) When I ask, *how are you?* I don't really mean *how are you?* . . . it's just my way of saying *hello.* Suppose I really asked *how are you* and you started telling me? I'd hear your troubles, you'd hear mine, and we'd have a very dull conversation.

I think it would be more interesting if I came out here and asked you how *aren't* you? See what possibilities there are? You can tell me you're not six feet tall or that you're not sick or that you're not a midget . . . People *aren't* many things than they *are* . . . which leaves room for lots of lively conversations.

Now that the greetings are over with, I will read to you a haunting Hungarian poem by a wandering gypsy. It is called (look at book) *A Haunting Hungarian Poem by a Wandering Gypsy.* It is also called *A Wandering Hungarian Poem by a Haunting Gypsy* . . . but only by those who don't speak Hungarian. (Laugh at own joke) Anyway, it is indeed a haunting poem. The author wrote all his poems on bedsheets . . . His wife hated him. She left him for a poet who wrote all his verse on pillow cases. (Look up puzzled, shrug)

Now I would like to recite Lord Byron's dreamy love-poem called, *To Marilyn—the Only Girl in the World* . . . which was written about the same time he wrote, *To Josephine—the Only Girl in the World.* Byron was a very confused man. All his life he thought every girl was named Marilyn. Even Josephine. He almost went crazy one day when he met a girl named Louise.

235

Isn't your name Marilyn? He asked Louise. *No, it's Patty Lou,* she replied. They almost went crazy together. Are you confused?

(Turn page, hold up book) Here's a poem called, *A Boy and a Girl in the Moonlight* . . . (turn page) Then, *Two Boys and a Girl in the Moonlight* . . . (turn page) Then, *Why Doesn't One of You Boys Take a Walk?*

(Open book) For my final selection I will read, *The Barbarian and the Barber* . . . by Karl von Clipper. It is a very long poem because the barbarians marched from February 28th to April 1st . . . which left a March of 31 days. (smile at own joke, look hopefully at audience) I'm getting tired so I'll substitute my latest love-lyric entitled, *To Priscilla, Margaret, Linda, Sylvia, Peggy May, and Shirley—the Only Girl in the World.* (pucker lips, tilt head in questioning look at page, snap book shut) It's too confusing . . . are you confused? I'm confused . . . (smile) How aren't you? (bow and exit)

PAY AND BE GAY

Character: Anyone.

(Enter with a batch of papers which represent unpaid bills, mutter as you glance at them, wave bills) Bills are just not what they used to be . . . Now they're written in poetry . . . at least mine are. It's much nicer to get a bill with a few polite little rhymes . . . for example, here's a poetic bill I got from the water company . . . (read from a bill)

> Please, dear sir,
> Your payment make,
> Or you'll be drinking
> From the lake.

(Smile) Almost makes it a pleasure to pay your water bill, doesn't it? Here's one with a pleasant thought . . . (read from a bill)

> We'll give you a day
> Or even a week,
> And then we'll give you
> A poke on the beak.

Isn't that cheerful? Here's a sad one from the music store . . .
(read from a bill)

> Please play on the roof,
> Please play on the floor,
> But please don't play
> On our flute any more.

Listen to this threat . . . (read from a bill)

> Roses are red,
> Violets are blue,
> We're sending our relatives
> To live with you.

Here's what they sent when I got behind in my car payments
(read from a bill)

> We're very sorry
> You ignored our note,
> You'll soon be riding
> To work on a goat.

Here's some poetic advice from my doctor . . . (read from a
bill)

> I made you healthy
> Every day,
> If you pay your bill
> You'll stay that way.

Here's one I got from the school where I took singing lessons
. . . (read from a bill)

> Please send your payments
> In advance,
> Since hearing you sing
> We're moving to France.

(Shrug) Listen to this sly poem from the electric company . . .
(read from a bill)

> Pigeons live
> In the city park,
> *You'll* soon be living
> In the dark.

Here's a strange little message I got from the jewelry store . . .
(read from a bill)

> You've been married ten years—
> A wonderful thing!
> But isn't it time
> You paid for the ring?

(Exclaim) I don't even have a girl friend! (or boy friend)
(Happily nod) There's something about these little bills that
make you *want* to pay . . . Guess it's the lovely way they
rhyme. (shrug, wave bills) Anyway, I'm ready to pay these . . .
except for one little thing . . . the *money*. Guess there's only one
thing left to do . . . I'll write my *own* little poem . . . (take
pencil and pretend to write a poem on a bill, read)

> With these bills
> I have no chance,
> Guess I'll also
> Move to France!

(Happily toss bills in air, exit rapidly)

FORTUNES?

Character: Anyone. Alter slightly if performed by a girl.

(Enter with a bowl containing tiny fortune-telling slips. For
convenience in delivering the monologue, write the various fortunes on the slips and read from them. Walk to stage center,
take a handful of slips, hold them over bowl, drop them back.)

Know what these are? Bits of paper. Know what kind of bits
of paper? *Fortune-telling* bits of paper . . . the kind you get
with Chinese dinners. I've been saving them for years so that I
don't make any mistakes in life. Let me show you how they have
shaped my fortune.

(Take slip, read from it) *Watch out for a red truck when
crossing the street.* (look up) Never did see the truck . . . was
so busy looking that I was hit by a black motorcycle.

(Read from slip) *You will meet a tall beautiful woman* (or
tall, handsome man). (look up) Oddly enough, I *did* . . . she
(or he) sued me for wrecking her (or his) motorcycle.

238

(Read from slip) *You will soon be out of your mess.* (look up, grin) I *was,* as soon as I took off my jacket with the chop suey all over it.

(Read from slip) *A small misfortune will come your way.* (look up, nod) A midget stole my wallet.

(Read from slip) *Beware of a woman* (or *man*) *who has designs on your money.* (look up) This one I didn't pay any attention to. I don't have any money!

(Read from slip) *Keep your good health by keeping your fingers out of my plate.* (look up) This was from the woman at the next table.

(Read from slip) *You are about to take an exciting journey.* (look up) On the way out I fell downstairs.

(Read from slip) *For the last time, keep your hands out of my plate.* (look up, scowl) That selfish woman at the next table.

(Read from slip) *Now is the time to make use of your musical talents.* (look up, shrug) I just happened to have my saxophone ready, but the management didn't agree with the fortune cookie. (Read from slip)

> *Roses are red,*
> *Violets are blue*
> *I'm glad I'm handsome* (*or pretty*)
> *Instead of you.*

(Frown, shrug, crumple and toss slip away)

(Read from slip) *You will be happier if you leave the waiter a dollar tip.* (look up) This writing seemed a bit different than the other fortunes.

(Read from slip) *Look for another job.* (look up, frown) It was signed by my boss.

(Read from slip) *Beware of women* (or *men*) *with shaggy eyebrows.* (look up, grin) I've been afraid of my girl friend (or boy friend) ever since.

And here's the last one. (read from slip) *Your plans will be changed.* (look up, sadly) I had to pay the dinner bill after all.

(Toss fortunes at audience) Here—read the rest and see what happens to you! (exit)

DEAR MR. LOVELETTER

Character: A newspaper columnist (man or woman) who answers questions concerning love and courtship.

(Note: A prominent member of the party should introduce Mr. Loveletter and explain that this expert adviser is here to answer questions he has received from the audience. Mr. Loveletter then enters and sits behind a desk stacked with letters.)

(Mr. Loveletter) Good evening, ladies and gentlemen. I am here to solve your love problems. Shall we proceed to solve?

(Read from a letter) *Dear Mr. Loveletter: A girl in South America writes that she is as graceful as a swan, as gentle as a rabbit and as pretty as a lamb. Do you think I should go to South America?* (look up) I'd suggest you visit a farmyard.

(Read from a letter) *Dear Sir: How can I cure my husband of putting his feet on the table?* (look up) Try putting the *table* on his feet. If this doesn't work, build a table six feet tall.

(Read from a letter) *Dear Love-Expert: My boy friend insists on calling me by the pet name of Snooky. Snooky, Snooky, Snooky—all day long he calls me Snooky. If there's anything I hate it's the name Snooky.* (look up) Signed—*Snooky.* (toss letter aside)

(Read from a letter) *My girl friend owns an oil well but I am very poor. What difference do you think this makes?* (look up) Probably about fifty thousand dollars.

(Read from a letter) *My boy friend insists that I call him Adam because he thinks he is the only man in the world. What can I do about this brazen conceit? . . .* signed—*Eve.* (smile at audience) I certainly get wonderful letters, don't I?

(Read from a letter) *Dear Mr. Loveletter: Can you recommend a good place to meet at least six lonely men? . . .* signed—*At Least Six Lonely Women.* (look up) They are six logical lonely women, at least.

(Read from a letter) *One of my boy friends hasn't called me for six weeks. My question is—how can I keep it this way?* (crumple letter)

(Read from a letter) *My girl friend accuses me of flirting with every girl I meet. What can I do about this untrue accusation? . . .*

240

signed—*Winky*. (look up) I suggest you close your eyes to this untrue and unfair accusation. (laugh at own joke)

(Read from a letter) *My boy friend and I get along fine at dinner except for one thing—he likes a French salad and I like a German. P.S. The German I like is a man named Adolf Glotz.* (frown at letter, set it aside)

(Read from a letter) *Dear Sir: I live on the sixth floor and am attracted by a man who lives on the second. How can I get him to notice me?* (look up) Wait until he comes out of his apartment and slide down the banister. He'll notice you.

(Read from a letter) *The other day I met a charming man who says he is madly in love with me, but I think he cares only for my money. How can I be sure?* (look up) Just send me your money and then see how he feels.

(Read from a letter) *Dear Mr. Loveletter: Whatever gave you the idea you're an expert on love letters?* (rise, shrug) Frankly, I haven't the slightest idea! (bow, exit)

ALL WASHED UP

Character: Anyone, playing the role of a beachcomber.

(Enter barefoot, dressed in rags, wearing a floppy hat. Carry four or five bottles and several slips of paper) I guess you can guess what I am . . . a beachcomber. (set bottles and paper on table) I guess you know what a beachcomber is . . . someone who collects driftwood just for the fun of it but who doesn't find it much fun . . . Actually, it's more fun to collect bottle messages.

Folks used to put messages in bottles because there were no mailboxes in the ocean. It's cheaper to send them by bottle also, as long as you're not fussy about *who* you're sending them to. Here are a few of the more interesting ones I've found.

(Read from slip) *Please tell my wife I'll be late for supper* . . . signed—*Magellan.*

And another . . . (read from slip) *Dear Cleopatra: Unless your payment is immediately received we will be forced to repossess Egypt* . . . signed—*your old enemy, Caesar.*

Here's a desperate little message from a man who was stranded for thirty years on a deserted island . . . (read from slip) *It's not that I'm lonely or sad or discouraged or weary* . . . *it's just that I hate it here.*

Here's a good one . . . (read from slip) *If I don't make it, please tell Queen Isabella I'm sorry* . . . signed—*Christopher Columbus.*

Here's one that's quite old . . . (read from slip) *Dear Adam: Please trim the garden* . . . *angrily yours, Eve.*

How about this one? . . . (read from slip) *Will the finder of this message please break the bottle—I'm inside.* (to audience) He *was,* too.

Here's a poem from a budding author . . . (read from slip)

> *Roses are red,*
> *And so are noses*
> *Especially when*
> *A cold wind blowziz* . . .
>
> signed—*Willie Shakespeare, age five.*

Here's one that touches the heart . . . (read from slip) *Dear Susie: Please meet me on the corner of the Fifth Latitude and Sixth Longitude* . . . signed—*Lonely Sailor.*

This one was found in the middle of the Atlantic Ocean . . . (read from slip) *Ten years ago I floated down a mountain stream that got wider and wider* . . . *how wide can a stream get?* (shake head)

Another note (read from slip) *Situation desperate* . . . *please send an aerial* . . . signed—*Television Lover.*

Here's one of historical importance . . . (read from slip)

Dear Citizens of France: Please send me a fast horse . . . signed
—Napoleon at Waterloo.

This one has a strange message . . . it simply says . . . (read
from slip in crying voice) *Waaaaah!* (to audience) It was found
in a baby bottle.

Well, it's time to get back to the beach and see what else
the waves delivered. (bow and exit)

MEET ME IN THE MOONLIGHT

Character: A song writer.

(Enter with a batch of music sheets) Good evening, lovers of
lovely music. My name is Sam (or Sally) Songstyle. No doubt
you have all heard love songs where the lovers meet in the
moonlight or met under the village tree. They always seem to be
meeting in either place . . . for a little variety I'd like to suggest
some other places.

Let me read some of the titles of my new songs and you will
see how much more interesting they are then ordinary old moonlight . . . (pretend to read from various sheets)

Meet Me Down by All Those Oil Wells You Own.

*Meet Me Again in Your Garden But I Won't Again Spend the
Evening Pulling Weeds.*

*Meet Me Down by the Old Oak Tree But First Tell Me the
Difference Between an Oak Tree and a Willow So That We
Won't Get Mixed Up.*

*Meet Me at the River Bank But Better Yet Meet Me at the
Bank Where You Have Your Money.*

*Meet Me Where We Usually Meet But the Trouble Is I Can't
Remember Meeting You Before.*

*Meet Me Down by the Lake But Don't Embarrass Me Again
by Bringing Your Toy Boats.*

*Meet Me at the Café at Seven O'clock Where We Will Have
an Expensive Dinner If I Can Sell My Car by Six O'clock.*

*Meet Me Tomorrow Unless Irene Happens to Phone in Which
Case Meet Me the Day After Tomorrow.* (Note: If performed
by a girl, use *Donald* instead of *Irene*.)

Meet Me Down by My Canoe But Be Sure You Can Swim Because I'm a Clumsy Paddler.

Meet Me on Pay Day and Naturally I Mean Yours.

(Lower sheets, smile) Can you stand any more?

Meet Me Where It Is Cool and Breezy But This Time Not On the Kitchen Floor While You Swing the Refrigerator Door Back and Forth.

Meet Me at the Entrance of the Most Expensive Café in Town But Don't Be Surprised if I'm at the Exit.

Meet Me Tonight and I Will Let You Know If I Want to Meet You Again Tomorrow Night.

Meet Me at Six O'clock But If I Am Not There by Seven It's Because I Met Someone Else at Five.

Meet Me Where We Met the Last Time But How Come It's Always the Kitchen Piled High With Dishes?

Meet Me Again With My Name on Your Lips But Please Remember That My Name is Not Eddie or Richard or Tommy Which You Called Me the Last Three Times. (Note: If performed by a girl, use *Linda, Helen, Sylvia,* instead of *Eddie, Richard, Tommy.*)

Meet Me Where We Can Be Alone, So Leave Your Five Brothers and Six Sisters at Home.

(Lower sheets, smile) Isn't it wonderful? I have one final song which I would like to give to any girl (boy) who would like to meet me . . . (read from sheet)

Meet Me Any Place You Like Just as Long as You Like Telling Me How Handsome (Pretty) I Am! (bow and exit)

MONOLOGUE MATERIAL

You can use these jokes for several short monologues or for one long humorous one. Start your act with the first happening, then follow quickly with as many as you like.

Last week, while strolling in the countryside, I ran into something interesting. I met a very clever farmer. Do you know what he was doing? He was crossing his bees with lightning bugs so that they could gather honey at night.

I used to be twins, you know. My mother has a picture of me when I was two.

244

I slept in a country cabin last night. The bed was too short, but I added two more feet when I got in.

Do you have trouble getting places on time? I'm usually late. It's all caused by that silly alarm clock—it always goes off while I'm asleep.

I hear some of you fellows are going into the army. I was in uniform for a while. It was all right, except for one thing. I didn't like all that marching and drilling between meals.

Did I tell you about my girl friend? Her name is Marjorie. She's different from all the other girls I know. She's *really* different—she's the only girl who will go out with me.

Speaking of girls, I've been told that blondes are more pleasant than brunettes or redheads. I don't know about that. My girl has been all three and there's no difference.

The other night I sat in a comedy movie behind a man who must have weighed at least three hundred pounds. I complained to him that I couldn't see the comedy. He told me to keep my eye on him and laugh when he did.

Speaking of weight, I've just invented something great for people who want to reduce. It's a chocolate bar with a lettuce filling.

You know what dinner is, don't you? That's when children sit down to continue eating.

I didn't know what to do with myself the other day, so I went down to the corner market—bought three corners.

When I came home I saw a new kind of western on television. It had a stagecoach with no wheels. What holds it up? The bandits.

You know, around town I'm considered a fancy dresser. I have a suit for every day of the year—the one I'm wearing.

I was late for work again. The boss asked me whether I knew what time they started. I told him no. They're always at work when I get there.

I'll say one thing for my boss—he's completely fair. He's grouchy to everyone.

How many of you people can keep a secret? I can always keep a secret. The trouble is, I keep telling people who can't.

I ran an advertisement in the paper last week. I asked to hear from people who could bring some light and warmth into my life. I've had two replies—from the gas and electric companies.

Did I tell you about my small apartment? Small! Why, it's so small my dog has to wag his tail up and down.

The people in the apartment upstairs were sure noisy last night. They kept banging on the floor. But it didn't bother me—I was practicing all night on my drums.

The other night we had to call in a baby sitter for my little sister. You know what a baby sitter is—a girl you hire to watch your television set.

I have a new girl friend, and the other day I asked her to sew a button on my coat. The next day she phoned to tell me that she had lost the button, but that it was all right. When I asked her what she meant, she told me that she had sewed up the buttonhole.

My girl friend causes me to break things—like fives and tens.

The other night I asked my girl to marry me. She said we couldn't get married until I had saved five thousand dollars. I told her I had exactly eight dollars and ten cents. She said that was close enough.

See these shoes of mine? They're so tight they hurt. Someone told me that I have them on the wrong feet, but how could that be? These are the only feet I have!

I went fishing the other day and had such great luck that I wanted to remember the exact spot—so I put a cross mark on the boat . . . but I'm worried. The next time I may not get the same boat.

Did I tell you about my brother? He's on a reducing diet. He's doing fine. In fact, last week he disappeared completely.

246

I can always tell an intelligent man when I meet one. He agrees with my ideas.

They say that a boy and a girl with opposite characteristics make a good match. So I'm looking for a girl with money.

Last week my phone rang at three in the morning. It was the wrong number, so the caller apologized for waking me up. I told him it was all right—I had to get up anyway to answer the phone.

Before I came up here, someone asked me a question. He wanted to know how long I've been working at the grocery market. I told him I've been working ever since the boss threatened to fire me.

The other day I stopped at the snack shop for a glass of lemonade. I put eight lumps of sugar into it. The waitress watched me for a minute, then asked why I didn't stir the sugar. I told her that I didn't like sweet lemonade.

My girl friend got upset with me last night. I asked why she had a bandage on her forehead. She told me that bandage was her new hat!

I used to work for an advertising company. My boss told me that a good advertisement repeats the same message over and over and over. So I went in and asked for a raise, a raise, a raise, a raise.

I've just discovered a way to keep cool without using electricity. You stand before a disconnected fan and spin yourself around.

The other night my shoulders got cold because my blanket was too short. I fixed it all right. I cut a strip from the bottom and sewed it on the top.

Speaking of bedtime, I sleep pretty well at night. But I just twist and turn all morning and afternoon.

I went down to the clothing store to buy a new robe. The clerk said I'd look good in something long and flowing. So I jumped into the river.

Well, I have to go and clean up my room. I wouldn't say it's messy—it's just that when the phone rings I can't find it!

247

HOW TO DO ANYTHING

The fun comes when you get all mixed up! For example, suppose you intend to teach your audience how to build a kite. As you do so, you accidentally thrust your hand through the paper, making a jagged hole. Next, you drop all your kite sticks. Finally, you get all tangled up in the sticky paper. Just get yourself confused as much as you can.

Prepare your act by selecting some simple activity, such as one of those supplied below. Think of a number of funny things that could happen. When you practice, set the items you need in front of you on a table, such as kite sticks and paper. This will help you to think.

Add remarks as you go along. Whenever something goes wrong, say "Oops," or "Maybe we'd better try another way." Then go ahead once more.

Start with the following examples:

How to Cook a Pancake

1. Pour imaginary pancake batter and try to stop it as it runs onto floor.

2. Flip imaginary pancake and let it fall on your head.

3. Flip furiously as if you have a dozen pancakes in the air at once.

4. Flip a pancake high, look up and remark that it's stuck to the ceiling.

5. Flip pancakes and race around with a real plate trying to catch them.

248

How to Wrap a Present

1. Try to cram the gift into a box that is too small.
2. Accidentally rip the wrapping paper several times.
3. Drop the box, shake it to see whether the present is broken.
4. Get your fingers caught in the knots.
5. Discover, finally, that you have left the present out of the wrapped package.

How to Make a Dress

1. Hold up several pieces of ragged material to your audience, ask them whether they've ever seen anything like it.
2. *Rip* the material, then remark that *cutting* would be best.
3. Hold the pieces over your shoulder and around your waist to show how they look when worn.
4. Pin a few pieces together and ask the audience whether it looks like a dress as yet.
5. Remark that maybe you had better show them how to make a dress for a scarecrow.

How to Arrange the Furniture

1. Announce that you will show the audience how to arrange light pieces of furniture.

2. Set everything in odd arrangements, such as a lamp on a chair.

3. Grow tired, doze for a moment on a chair.

4. Get foot stuck in wastebasket.

5. End up with furniture in original positions.

How to Shine Your Shoes

1. Get several pairs of shoes mixed up and try to find pairs.

2. Try to put on a shoe that is too small.

3. Accidentally use something other than shoe polish, such as paste.

4. As you talk to audience, absently shine your socks.

5. Walk around in unmatched shoes.

How to Play Checkers

1. Play the roles of both players by jumping back and forth to either side of the checkerboard.

2. Spill the board and checkers once or twice. Pick them up and start over.

3. Jump seven or eight checkers at a time.

4. Explain that the game takes intense concentration; then set your nose against the board.

5. Talk with your imaginary opponent, changing places each time.

How to Dress Neatly

1. Display several kinds of odd and ragged clothes.
2. Try to wear several coats and sweaters at one time.
3. Walk awkwardly around when modeling the clothes.
4. Place a cereal box on your head and announce it is the new fashion in hats.
5. Exit wearing the worst possible combination of clothes.

Section 6
Situation Monologues

Think about the character you are going to portray before you begin. How will he or she *act* as well as speak? Remember to keep *whom* you are speaking to firmly in mind, in order to make the situation realistic for both you and the audience.

DEAR JUDY

Character: Small boy writing his first love note.

Let's see, how should I start it? *Dear Judy* . . . no, I'd better make it more loving . . . *Dear dear Judy* . . . I don't want to sound *too* mushy—I wonder if she'll like *My dear pretty loving honey-pie* . . . Let's see, maybe I can write a little poem . . . *Dear Judy* . . .

> Your hair is red,
> Your eyes are blue,
> I'd like to give
> My pet frog to you! . . .

No, that doesn't sound so good. I need something sweet and romantic, like a real poet. I know . . .

> If I were a bird,
> I would make a *wish*,
> I would wish that you
> Were a flying *fish!* . . .

That doesn't seem to be what I want to say either. Maybe I'd just better say nice things like, "I think of you all day long . . . except when I'm thinking of Barbara, Marilyn, or Carolyn" . . .

252

Maybe I'd better phone her . . . That's it, I'll quote her a love poem on the phone . . . (dial phone) Hello, Judy, I have a little poem for you . . . listen . . .

> For you I long,
> For you I pine,
> How come your feet
> Are bigger than mine?

Isn't that sweet, Judy? What's that, you're *not* Judy? . . . You're her beautiful sister? Well, look, Joyce, will you just tell Judy I called? Why not? You *like* my poetry? You want to hear *more?* Well, since you *ask* . . .

> Joyce or Judy?
> Judy or Joyce?
> If you'll both come over
> I'll make my choice!

(Hang up, grin, and exit)

WALKING WITH WILMA

Character: **A young man.**

I'll never forget those happy days when Wilma and I went walking together. Oh, we made a lovely couple as we strolled along—one of us with a cane and the other with a pretty new hat . . . How Wilma could strut with that cane! . . . I was always careful to observe the courtesies with Wilma. I always gently took her arm when crossing the street . . . If I didn't, she would rather roughly twist my elbow . . . I always permitted her to enter the taxicab first. Sometimes the driver would take off before I got in—when I was lucky.

On rainy days Wilma brought along her usual rain equipment —raincoat, boots, toy boats for sailing along the gutter . . . She almost always beat the kids in those boat races. What a romantic couple strolled beneath her umbrella—Wilma and her St. Bernard.

We would always stop for lunch at some quiet little restaurant. Of course it wasn't quiet after Wilma got there. She had the curious habit of thumping on the table in order to attract the waiter. One time she attracted six waiters and the police . . . And then Wilma would give the waiter her order. This made it easy on me because I could just sit and listen for the next thirty minutes . . .

Very soon after lunch Wilma would look coyly at me and ask a question. "Eddie, dear," she would say, "isn't it time for *dinner?*" Well, when dinner was over, we'd continue walking. We'd walk where Wilma wanted—down to the bank to see if I had any money left . . . If you have the impression that Wilma was expensive, I want to assure you of one thing—she *was* . . . Once when I told her I was down to my last dollar, do you know what she said? "Let's split it—ninety and ten."

One time when I had money we came to a hot-dog stand. I courteously asked Wilma if she wanted something. She *did*. I was never sorry we purchased that hot-dog stand.

As I said, I'll never forget those happy days when I went walking with Wilma. But I've sure *tried!*

FREDDIE PROPOSES

Character: A boy proposing to a girl.

(Dial phone) Hello, Freddie? . . . this is Linda . . . (flustered) I mean, hello, Linda? . . . this is Freddie . . . How are you, Linda?

(Nervously loosen collar) Say, Linda, there's something I'd like to ask you . . . yes . . . I'd like to ask you if . . . if . . . (frown in defeat) Do you remember what I told you last night about a cute little vine-covered cottage? (hopefully pleased) You do? What did that suggest to you? (frown) That someone had better get busy and trim those vines? No, Linda, that's not the point . . . what I'm trying to say is . . . is . . . wouldn't you like to move into a cottage covered with vines? I see, you'd rather move into one covered with a roof . . .

(Sigh) Listen, Linda, can't you hear the beautiful chimes of church bells? Why not? Oh, a couple of boys are screaming outside your window . . . no, *imagine* the chimes, Linda! How about rice? Can you see rice being thrown all over the place? (delighted) You can? Because a box of rice just fell off your kitchen shelf? (sigh)

(Coyly) You remember what Tom and Shirley did at the church last week? (shake head) No, no, I mean after they slipped on the ice. You know, they stood side by side and looked at each other. (frown) No, they weren't trying to see who was the taller of the two! (taking a deep breath) Tell me, Linda, what kind of a husband do you want? (repeat her words) *Tall . . . handsome . . . blue eyes . . . dark hair . . . charming . . . clever . . . wealthy . . .* (look at audience, sigh, shrug, almost hang up, suddenly speak pathetically into phone) How about *short . . . ugly . . . red* (or your color) *hair . . . clumsy . . . dull . . . poor?*

Please, Linda, I don't want to go through life lonely and wretched and miserable and sad. You know we'd be happy together. We have so many things in common . . . like debts and unpaid bills . . . (business-like) Linda, dear, after we're married I promise to shower you with diamonds and emeralds and pearls and rubies. No, I haven't got them yet but I'm terrific with a pick and shovel. (coyly) Can't you just see us tripping through life together? (scowl) Well, we'll just be careful *not* to trip each other! (delighted) What, dear? You'd like something to go on your finger? (sadly) All right, dear. I'm coming with a Band-Aid. (put phone down, shrug helplessly to audience, exit)

PARTY NIGHT

Character: Girl on telephone.

Hello . . . Randy? This is Carol. You know, Carol Wallace, the girl you winked at in the hall? Oh, you wink at *everyone* in the hall? . . . I'm the girl who offered to carry your books home from school . . . I know it was unusual but I wanted you to think I was an unusual girl. How did I get your number? Well, I knew your last name was Morris, and that your dad was a doctor, and that he had an office on West Street—so I just put two and two together and asked Millie for it . . . You don't think me bold for calling, do you? Oh, you think I have very good taste in boys. (gushy) Oh, Randy, you say the nicest things about yourself!

I want you to know that I admired the way you hit that home run the other day. You *didn't* hit a home run—it was Sammy Sharp? . . . Do you have *Sammy's* number handy? No, I mean, what I called for was to talk about *you* and *me*. Oh, you'd rather just talk about *you* . . . Well, all right, let's see . . . tell me, do you have a girl friend? (thrilled) *No?* (disappointed) Oh, girl *friends*.

Look, Randy, do you have anyone to take to the party tonight? (coy, cute) You know—someone soft and cuddly to sit at your side? . . . (disappointed) Oh, you do have someone . . . your *pet rabbit?* . . . But wouldn't it be nice to have a *girl?* . . . *Why?* (flustered) I don't know exactly why . . .

I want you to know that I've been secretly admiring you for months. What's that, you've only been at school for two weeks? . . . (muse to self) Then who *was* that big hunk of man? . . . Anyway, all I know is that all the girls at school talk about you. They say you're big, strong, handsome, kind, generous, sweet . . . huh? Oh, *curly-haired,* too. I guess you must get all kinds of scented notes from pretty girls . . . oh, pretty notes from scented girls.

You want me to describe myself? Well, I'm five feet nine inches tall . . . (frown) That's too short? Well, I'm sitting down . . . I'm a blonde in the morning, a brunette at noon, and a redheat at night . . . How do I *do* it? Oh, I just *love* all those bottles. I'm an all-American girl all right—red cheeks, white skin, blue eyes. I'm as dainty as a deer, as graceful as a swan, and as pretty as a peacock. (angry) No, they *don't* miss me at the zoo!

(Plead) Please, Randy, say that you'll take me to the party. (sad) Oh, Randy . . . tell me Randy, have you given your heart to someone else? No, it just stays inside your chest and beats loyally away?

What kind of a car have you got? *Really?* But can this horse of yours carry *both* of us? . . . I don't believe you have a horse at all. What's that—bring along a sack of hay?

Maybe I'd better give you my address in case you decide to take me tonight. It's fifteen-fifteen Silverplate Drive. The house with the hand-carved fence around it. Just tell the guard at the driveway that you're a friend and drive on up past the swimming pool to the front porch. One of the butlers will announce you.

You won't meet Dad because he's in Europe lending money to some government. Mother is in South America buying up the entire coffee crop. Randy, are you there? . . . (look offstage, happily walk toward wing) Oh, there you are, Randy. (exit)

A BOX OF CHOCOLATES

Characters: A girl who has just received a box of chocolates from her boy friend.

(Sit on couch with a box of chocolates in lap) Oh, Larry, what a lovely surprise . . . *chocolates!* (eagerly open box, offer it to Larry) Have one? . . . (glance back and forth from Larry to box and back to Larry as if he is taking several, scowl) I said *one.*

(Eagerly, as you peer into box) Here's a chocolate-cherry . . . I wonder how it tastes? . . . (frown, look from box to Larry, silently stare for a moment) How *was* it?

(Shyly flutter eyelids) Larry . . . am I as sweet as candy? What? . . . you'll let me know when it's all gone? (delighted, unsuspecting, as you extend box) Oh, Larry! (suddenly frown in suspicion, jerk box back, speak in annoyance) Larry, I just can't

257

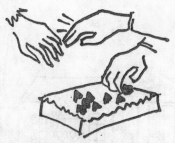

see how you can eat so much . . . what? . . . just keep my eyes open?

(Surprised, peer into box, take out a flower) How come a flower instead of a chocolate? (pleased) Because I'm as sweet as a flower? (shyly delighted) Oh, Larry . . . (puzzled) But what happened to the chocolate? (nod) It was sweet, too?

(Take a slip of paper from box) What's this? . . . (read from slip) *ten dollars* . . . oh, the sales-slip . . . Oh, Larry, you shouldn't have done it . . . What? . . . you *didn't?* . . . you just put it in to impress me? (sigh) You're so *different* from most boys. Do you know that you're the first boy to give me such a *big* box? . . . (shrug) Of course the other boxes held more *candy*.

What's that? . . . you have *another* surprise for me? (pleased) Just close my eyes? . . . all right. (close eyes, smile happily, expectantly) Ready? (open eyes, look briefly about, look down at box, frown) What happened to the top layer? . . . that's the *surprise?*

(Run finger over box as if searching) I wonder if there's a caramel? . . . I simply love caramels . . . (look at Larry in surprise) Why are you digging in your pocket? . . . Oh, you saved them just for me. (take one from him and eat it)

(Shyly lower head) Larry . . . it would be so nice if you would recite a little poem to go with the candy . . . you know, a *love* poem . . . (dreamily listen as he quotes) Larry . . . how lovely! Let me repeat it . . . (repeat his poem)

> Oh, give me your heart,
> As sweet as the dawn,
> And give me some candy
> Before it's all gone!

(Romantically) Every time I take a chocolate I think how nice you are . . . what? . . . let *you* do the *taking* and *me* the *thinking?* . . . (gently reproving) Larry, you're *teasing* . . . what? . . . just *hungry?*

(Search box) I mustn't have *too* much . . . bad for the waist-line. (puzzled at his remark) What do you mean, it's *good* for your waistline? . . . Oh, it *must* be good the way it's growing.

(Peer into box) Larry, did you make this candy with your own clever little hands? You *did?* (frown as you take a necktie from the box, hold it up) Well, you left your necktie in the fudge. What's that . . . you'd like the box for a souvenir? (look around) All right, I'll find a dish . . . what? . . . you'll take the candy as a souvenir also?

(Shyly, romantically) Someday I hope you'll give me a little, tiny box (hold fingers two inches apart) with something round and sparkling in it . . . (indignantly) No, *not a shiny rock!* What would I do with a rock? (frown, nod at Larry) I think I know . . . (hold empty box upside down, frown and exit)

A CALL TO A BRIDE

Character: Husband phoning bride.

Hello . . . Susie? This is Wally. Wally *who?* Wally Lee, the man you married last week . . . What's that, dear, you're afraid to be *alone* in the house? But what about the *goldfish?* Oh, I guess they are hard to have a conversation with . . . Look, dear, try to find something to do. Maybe you can wash some of my dirty shirts . . . You gave them to the Salvation Army . . . Dear, why do you think I bought you that new washing machine? (incredulous) You thought it was a new kind of television set! Those mistakes can happen, dear.

Have any visitors today? A salesman? I hope you didn't let him talk you into buying anything foolish. (dismayed) *What's foolish about a gold-plated bird-bath?* . . . No, it's all right, dear, as long as you love birds that much. No, I'm not angry. (rising anger) I assure you I am *not* angry . . . after all, it's not *everyone* who can afford a gold-plated bird-bath. (shout angrily) I tell you, *I'm not angry!*

Have any phone calls? One? I mean *besides* me!

You have something sweet to tell me? (coy) Go ahead, dear, tell me something sweet. What? You ate a whole pie all by yourself? . . . Well, that *is* kind of sweet. (coy) What's that, dear? You want to whisper three little words to me? Go ahead . . . what? (disappointed) *Your tummy hurts.*

Look, dear. Tomorrow night I'm bringing the boss home for dinner. Think you can cook something special? You can? Fine! *How do you boil cabbage!* . . . Look, sweetie, maybe you'd better open a few cans for dinner. No, you throw the *cans* away. You'll find the food inside . . . That's right. By the way, the boss is a great one for baked pork chops. Think you can get some? No, you can't buy them baked. You get them raw at the store and bake them at home. Yes, in the oven.

Do you love me, dear? You did this morning but now you don't know? Oh . . . your mother phoned. What did she say? She called me a beast, an ape, a fiend . . . She must *like* me better. Last time she called me four names.

(Coy) I want to tell you something, honey pie. You know, what I used to say and you'd always reply, *I do, too.* It's something very tender. You know. No, it's *not, "I want a hamburger."*

Look, sweetie, I have to get back to work. What are you going to do the rest of the day? Start the baked pork chops? What's that, you can use the *stove in the living room?* But, dear, there's no stove in the living room. (startled) Smoke and flames are coming from there! Look, dear, run and turn in a fire alarm. I'll be right home! (exit running)

HOUSEWORK FOR HUBBY

Character: Husband, reluctantly doing housework.

(Enter scowling, carrying and dragging household cleaning items such as a broom, mop, dust rags. Drag yourself to stage center, hold arms straight out at sides, briefly pause and noisily drop everything. Note: Try to drop everything as close as possible to a chair where you will sit later. Sigh deeply as you shout toward wing)

Yes, dear, I'm hard at work . . . Can't you hear me? (grin, groan, rub back) Oh, my poor, overworked back . . . (continue

260

to bang for a moment, nod, briskly rub hands together in self-satisfaction, settle comfortably in chair, stretch out legs, doze for a moment)

(Look up as wife calls, answer her) What's that, dear? . . . *pick up the papers?* Okay . . . (lazily reach over, pick up a newspaper, shout) Okay . . . it's picked up! (drop paper, resume dozing)

(Look up as she calls) Yes, dear, I'll rearrange the flowers. (remain seated, reach over to flower vase on nearby table, carelessly turn flowers upside down in vase, happily shout) You ought to see them now! (lazily stretch, cup hand to ear as she again calls) What, dear? . . . *dust the floor?* (remain seated, pick up dust mop, frown as you look from end to end, shrug, drop mop, pull handkerchief from pocket, lazily flick it over floor three or four times, cheerfully shout) Gusty-wusty, all gone dusty!

(Lazily stretch, call) Dear, may I rest a few minutes? Thank you. (your next stretch is interrupted by her call) What? *Wash the windows?* (scowl) But you said I could rest a few minutes. (nod) Oh, your few minutes is much shorter than mine . . . (shrug) But darling, the windows are already clean . . . what? . . . *you'll come in and make them dirty for me?* (scowl) Very thoughtful of you.

(Doze, snore, awake) What's that, dear? . . . *who's snoring?* That's a TV program called, *Sleep Your Troubles Away.* (angrily) Okay, I'll switch to, *Work Your Troubles Away.* (listen as she again calls) What? . . . *sweep the cobwebs off the ceiling?* (protesting) But dear, think of all the trouble those spiders went to . . . (remain seated, take broom) Okay, okay . . . I'm sweeping . . . (lazily pass broom overhead as if sweeping ceiling, suddenly stare intently at ceiling, lower broom while staring, peer at ceiling from several angles, shout) Dearest, how come we have a picture of the sun on the ceiling? It *is* the sun? (angrily) Okay, I'll fix that hole in the roof.

(Lazily gesture, call) Okay . . . all done . . . ready for inspection. (stand as she enters) Well, how do you like it? (amazed at her reply) *Just fine?* (stare in disbelief as you glance around, nod as she speaks) Oh, you like *informal living* . . . (pleased) Funny thing, so do *I!* (bow and exit)

THE LETTER

Character: Husband who forgot to mail wife's letter.

(Husband, cheerfully returning home, removing hat, greeting wife) Hello, dear . . . (pat her cheek) Such a pretty little pink cheek! (tilt head in inquiry) What's that, dear? . . . *Did I remember to mail your letter?* (smile, again pat her cheek) Did I remember to mail your letter! (laugh) Don't I *always* mail your letters? Why, the first thing this morning I took it from my pocket like this . . . (take letter from pocket) walked over to the mail-box . . . (take a few brisk steps) opened the slot . . . (pretend to lift mail-box slot) and dropped it in just like this! (drop letter, in mounting horror stare at it on floor, look sheepishly back and forth from floor to wife, grin in embarrassment, pick up letter, brush it off with palm, read its address aloud) *Mary Wilson, Philadelphia, Pennsylvania.*

(Speak pleadingly to wife as you try to smooth things over) Look, dear, I *meant* to mail it . . . It was just that I met some of the boys . . . (flustered) I mean the bus was late . . . (quickly correct yourself) I know, I know, I don't ride the bus . . . (wave letter) Look, what's so important about a little old letter? What is it, anyway? . . . just some paper and ink . . . and what's paper and ink? (shrug) Practically *nothing. Anyone* can own paper and ink . . . even *poor* people. Look, I'll show you how important it is . . . (cheerfully rip letter to shreds, let bits trickle through fingers) See! What have you got? Even *less* paper and ink. Little bits of nothing at all!

(Briskly rub hands together, pat wife's cheek) Now, darling, what's for dinner? (pat both her cheeks with both hands) You kitchen-genius you! (tilt head in inquiry) What's that, dear? What about the letter? (gesture broadly) Forget it, dear, I'll write you another. What's that? . . . (in growing horror) *You enclosed five dollars? . . . for Mary's children?* (groan, get on hands and knees, pick up bits, look sadly up) Go get the paste, dear . . . maybe I can have it together by the time the mailman calls.

TEXAS ROUNDUP

Character: Husband, giving directions to wife (or wife giving directions to husband) as he (or she) hangs picture on the wall.

(Enter holding hands apart as if carrying a picture. Speak to imaginary wife as you admire picture) Look, dear, at the lovely picture I just bought . . . It's called *Texas Roundup* . . . See the cowboy chasing the stampeding cattle? (tilt head as if listening to her comment) What's that, dear? . . . *why* is he chasing them? (baffled as to how to explain) Well . . . because he gets *paid* for it . . . What? . . . Why pay anyone to go around chasing cattle? (frown, quickly change the subject by extending picture) Here, you hang it while I give directions . . . (drop hands as if she took picture, step back, hold up palms, look at wall as if ready to give directions. Note: Throughout the monologue, make suitable gestures as you speak)

(Tilt head and arms as if picture is set at a severe slant) No, try again . . . (tilt head and arms in opposite direction) No, still not right . . . (twist head and body so that you are looking at picture with head upside down, shake head) No . . . the cowboy's riding on his head instead of his horse.

That's it . . . a little to the left . . . a little more . . . more . . . more . . . more . . . (shake head in annoyance as you look far to one side) You went *too* far . . . come out of the kitchen!

There . . . hold it a minute while I take a look . . . (peer at picture, grin, nod, answer wife's question) What's that? . . . No, the position's no good—I was just thinking how interesting it would be if the *cattle* were chasing the *cowboy* . . . (seriously,

263

shrug, gesture) Let's put it in the light so we can see every detail
. . . (gesture) to the left . . . (pleased) There! . . . It's so clear
I can see a bull's horns . . . (frown as you peer closely, shake
head) My mistake—those are your hands . . . (quickly gesture)
Get them off the poor bull's head.

(Listen, as wife speaks) What's that, dear? . . . we should
hang it outdoors so the cowboy will feel at home? (smile) Very
clever.

(Hold up hands) That seems about right . . . (step forward)
Hold it while I drive the nail . . . (step to wall, pretend to drive
nail with a single blow, look quizzically at wife) Was that *you*
or the *cow* that yelled *ouch?* (return to original position)

(Gesture, then frown as you peer closely) What happened to
the *Texas Roundup?* . . . all I see is a dry desert. (nod)
Oh, I'm looking at the back of the picture . . . well, let's get
back to the roundup. (gesture downward) Bring it lower . . .
lower . . . lower . . . (shake head) *Too* low . . . the cattle
are lying down. (sharply gesture upward, smile) *Now* they're
running.

By the way, do you know what I paid for all those stampeding
cattle? Just fifty dollars. What? . . . You wish I'd just bought a
few pounds of steak?

(Look high on the wall) No, that's too high, . . . the cowboy
will get dizzy from the height . . . (gesture) lower . . . lower
. . . lower . . . hang it just above your head . . . (shake head)
No, I don't mean *above your head,* exactly, I mean *above your
head on the wall* . . . (annoyed, quickly speak) No, don't put
your *head on the wall* . . . (exasperated) Look, all I meant was
to hang it on the wall at a height just above your head.

(Pleased, shout) That's it! . . . Quick, drive the nail! (peer
as she drives it, frown, shake head) No, dear, the nail goes above
the picture, not through the cowboy's boot . . . He has enough
trouble with those cattle.

(Gesture) To the left . . . toward the window . . . more . . .
more toward the window . . . that's it . . . (push both hands
forward, speak emphatically) Push it against the wall . . . There!
. . . (puzzled, stare) Where'd the picture go? . . . (startled)
Out the window? (sigh deeply) Oh, well . . . at least it's outdoors where the cowboy will feel at home. (bow, exit)

EXPLANATIONS

Character: Wife, explaining driving mishap to husband.

(Cheerfully enter with shopping items, set them down, sigh in relief) Whew! What a shopping spree! (see husband in chair, wave) Hi, Wally, have a good nap? Fine! What, dear? . . . *did I put the car away?* (nod, as you remove hat) Yes, I ran it into the garage . . . (tilt head, think) Come to think of it, I didn't exactly run it into the *garage* . . . What I mean is, the garage was sort of over *here* (hold out left palm) and so was *I.* (swiftly swing right palm over to left palm, smack them together) Both in the same place. (cheerfully) Wasn't that a funny coincidence? . . . *what?* . . . *how big a funny hole did I make?* . . . *Which* hole are you talking about? (shake head) Oh, no, it wasn't much bigger than this . . . (hold up fingers to indicate hole the size of a saucer, shrug nonchalantly) But with all the rest of the glass in the windshield it shouldn't matter much. (think, nod) Of course the hole in the garage was slightly larger . . . *how much larger?* . . . (tilt head, think) Well, let's say the garage now has *two* entrances . . . it's more convenient, I think.

(Surprised, as you stare at him while moving head up and down) Wally, why are you jumping up and down? . . . you did your *exercises* this *morning.* (doubtfully) Are you *nervous?* (shake head) *Jittery?* (shake head) *Restless?* (shake head) *Mad?* (nod) Calm down, dear, we can always get a new side on the house . . . (nod) Yes, I scraped the side of the bedroom before I hit the garage . . . sort of a practice try . . .

(Suddenly remember) Oh, I almost forgot! I also ran into your boss! (look down at floor, shout) Wally stop rolling on the floor! . . . I ran into him on the *sidewalk* . . . (vigorously shake head) no, no, the *car* wasn't on the sidewalk—*I* was on the sidewalk, just walking along. Anyway, the boss told me to tell you that you are now the general manager of the entire factory. (pretend to hug him) Darling, you're a success! We're rich! We can run into garages every day! (smile) Darling, you look so happy! (suddenly frown) But how in the world did I ever hit that garage? . . . well, Wally, I've been trying long enough! (bow and exit)

LOOK, GEORGE

Character: Wife leading husband through art gallery.

Please, George, try to show a little dignity as we go through the art gallery. Just act like *I* do and you'll be all right . . . George, stop screaming at the top of your voice that you have nothing to wear! . . . Come along and let this rich culture penetrate the innermost recesses of your soul . . . how should *I* know what it means? . . . I read it over the entrance.

Ah, here we are . . . look at that picture called "A Hot Day in August" . . . doesn't it make you fairly perspire? . . . And isn't that a realistic painting of a fire extinguisher? It *is* a fire extinguisher? . . . Oh, George, feast your eyes on that one . . . it's called "A Bit of Fruit." On the wall, George! Not those orange peelings on the floor.

George, will you stop looking at every pretty girl who goes by and look at the art? What do you mean, there's more than one kind of art? Why do you embarrass me everywhere we go? You promise *not* to embarrass me at the ball game? . . . Oh George! Please, drink in this beauty around us, *drink* the loveliness of creative art, drink the enchantment of these . . . I'm sorry, George, I didn't mean to make you thirsty . . .

(Peer closely) My, but that's a realistic-looking picture of a door . . . it's called "Exit" . . . oh, it *is* the exit . . . Oh there's a masterpiece by Sir Stanley Squirrelhead who painted nothing but wildlife. He painted foxes, bears, raccoons . . . just think, George, if you could paint like this you'd have everyone talking about you . . . oh, you wouldn't like to hear what they were saying?

George, please stop looking at every pretty girl who walks by . . . (weary) All right, just look at those who *stand still* . . .

(Excited) Oh, George, here's the modern art section. I really don't expect *you* to understand modern art, it takes a deep and soulful understanding of the hidden meanings of life . . . I just read that in the guide booklet . . . You see, George, every little movement has a meaning . . . what's that, you *do* understand that every movement has a meaning? (shout) George, why are you waving to that pretty girl? Please pay attention to the movement on the paintings . . . You see, George, in modern art you must stand back, study the picture, close your eyes, and meditate. You'll *try* it? Fine . . . That's it, stand back . . . close your eyes . . . meditate . . . (pause, then snap fingers) That's long enough, George! George, *wake up!*

Well, now, here is something that even *you* can appreciate. Look at this one called "The Baseball Game." See that player sliding into first base? It's home plate? Oh! . . . Well, the umpire is calling him out . . . (startled) George, why are you shaking your fist? Oh, you think he was safe by a mile!

George, don't stand so close. I told you that art must be appreciated from a distance. That's it, farther back . . . farther . . . farther . . . (look around) George, where are you . . . ? (look around with realization he is gone, sob) *George!* (exit looking for him)

THE SHOPPER

Character: A lady at a grocery store.

(Wheel grocery cart around market as you shop. Note: A baby carriage may be used as the cart by attaching a sign to its side reading, *Bill's Market*)

(Speak to self) Let's see . . . for tamale pie I need olives, chili powder, corn meal . . . (think) Hmmm . . . (see clerk) Oh, there's the clerk. (call to clerk) Young man, what do you put into tamale pie? Your *teeth?* Very funny!

(Wander) I wonder what Walter would like for dinner . . . Hmmm . . . I'll phone . . . (step to phone, dial) Hello . . . is this Walter? What would you like for dinner? *Steak . . . potatoes . . . custard pie . . .* Got it! What? You'll be home early? . . . Will the boss let you off? Oh, this *is* the boss. Well, what time will Walter be home for dinner? *As soon as he invites you?* But Mr. Smith, our table only seats *two* . . . What? . . . *you'll keep Walter overtime?* Oh, dear . . . (hang up)

(Speak to clerk) Young man, what's the difference between green and red cabbage? (impatiently) Besides the color! Oh . . . *one grows underground and one on top.* Which grows underground? *Who can see underground?* Well, maybe some gophers could inform us . . .

(As you see a friend) Oh, hello, Mary . . . I'm so confused . . . the boss is coming for dinner. What do you suggest? That *Walter finds another job?* Oh, Mary, you know how *handy* I am in the kitchen. Could you tell me your secret recipe for cherry pie? (eagerly listen with hand cupped to ear, frown) But all you said was *buzz-buzz-buzz* . . . (nod) *That's so it'll still be a secret?* Okay, I won't buzz a word. What's that? . . . *pork chops are on sale for ten cents a pound?* (excited as you start to leave) I'll rush right over . . . (halt) What? (disappointed) All gone? . . . but *you'll let me have them for fifty cents a pound?* What are you, a pork tycoon? . . .

(To self) I get so tired of the same old thing for dinner . . . (to clerk) Young man, could you suggest something *different* to serve at dinner? *You?* (shrug) Okay, you can sit next to the boss. By the way, do you have frozen peas? Just frozen *knees?* Well, you just climb right out of that freezer.

(Wander) I know! I'll bake macaroni and cheese! (to clerk) Young man, tell me, what goes into macaroni and cheese? (astonished) *Cherries?* (nod) Oh, you got Mary's secret recipe. Young man, if you were my husband, what would you like for dinner? What? . . . *if you were my husband you'd have no appetite at all?* (eagerly) You mean you'd be so filled with *love* you wouldn't need food? (delighted) What a lovely thing for you to say . . . (frown) How old is this lettuce? *You're not sure, but you're planning a birthday party?* Is that a joke? *No, but the lettuce is?* (look around)

(Speak to clerk) Young man, where are the cake mixes? . . . *Section five?* . . . where's section five? . . . *Just after section four?* But where is section four? (gesture as you repeat his directions) *Three blocks south, turn left, one mile east, pass the crossroads and there I am* . . . (amazed) But that's the way to the next town! (frown) *That's the whole idea?* (angrily) Young man, do you like your job as a grocery clerk? What? . . . *you're not a clerk?* . . . *just another confused shopper?* (embarrassed) Oh, I'm *sorry* . . . (quickly exit, wheeling cart)

WAITING FOR GRANDMA

Character: A young mother with her three small children, Ellen, Billy, and Ralph, who call on Grandma.

(Enter by walking with closed hands down at sides as if leading your children. Note: Whenever you speak to the children, look downward, since they are small; speak quickly and somewhat sharply.)
Here we are, children . . . Grandma's house. I'm leaving you with Grandma while I go shopping and I want you to behave . . . Ralph, stop that! I want you to be nice . . . Ellen, stop shoving Billy . . . Billy, please don't do that . . . (pretend to open door) All right, go on in . . . stop that screaming!

(Look around room, call) Grandma, we're here! (glance around) Wonder where she is? . . . No, Billy, Grandma's not in the backyard climbing trees . . . (sit on chair) No, Ellen, neither is she out making mud pies. Ralph, stop bouncing up and down on that chair . . . No, you can't bounce on Billy *instead*. (hold up finger) Now remember, be sure to give Grandma a great big kiss . . . (frown) *Why?* Why because *everyone* kisses Grandma . . . No, Ellen, *not even the milkman*.

(Impatiently glance at watch) Wonder where she could be? No. I will *not* look in those trees . . . Why would Grandma climb a tree? . . . *So she could slide down?* (sigh) I think it will be all right if you run into the kitchen for some cookies . . . Go ahead . . . Take just one or two . . . (shake head) No, not just one or two *pockets full*. Ellen, will you stop banging that table? What? . . . It's *Ralph?* But Ralph's in the *kitchen* . . . (nod) Oh, I'm hearing his *echoes*.

(Glance at watch, walk to window on opposite side of room, call out) Mrs. Miller, is my mother there? No, but you're expecting her any minute? How come? (frown) You think she *saw us coming?* (sigh, return to chair)
I want everyone to sit down for a moment . . . No, no, *not on top of each other!* There, that's better. Now remember, try to be nice and quiet. What's that, Billy? . . . *you'll try but you don't think you'll make it?* At least you're honest. Now I want to give you some *don'ts* . . . no, not *doughnuts* . . . some *don'ts* . . . *Don't* spill the goldfish bowl, *don't* fight over the TV set,

269

don't scream and yell. What's that Ellen? . . . *What else is there in life?* (sigh to self) Poor Grandma, what am I getting her into?

Children, let's play a little game . . . you have a game, Ellen? . . . what's it called? *Toss Cookie Crumbs on the Floor?* Ellen, please act like a little lady. What's the difference between a little lady and a little terror? (touch hair) *Gray hairs,* dear. Billy, stop cramming that cookie down your throat . . . (sigh, shake head) No, I can't think of a better place for it . . . Go ahead.

Billy, where's your left shoe? On your *right foot?* Where's your right shoe? On Ralph's *left foot?* . . . never mind. Ellen, stop switching your shoes . . . it's not a *game.*

(Glance at watch) I'll be late if she doesn't . . . Ellen, where are you going? After *Billy?* Where's Billy going? After *Ralph?* Where's Ralph going? After *you?* (shout) Stop all that *going!*

(Glance around) I wonder where? . . . (stand, tilt chair, look under it, shake head, walk to a door, knock) Grandma, are you in there? (step back, see Grandma, who enters) Grandma, where have you been? *Taking a nap?* . . . *You'll need strength for the rest of the morning?* (sigh, nod) I understand perfectly.

(Turn to children) Children, here's Grandma . . . (look around) Now where did *they* go? (look upward to wall, shout) Stop climbing that wall! Children, here's Grandma . . . see how fresh and strong she looks? . . . Please try to keep her that way. (to Grandma) Grandma, tell them what a quiet little child *I* was . . . (think, shake head) On second thought, you'd better *not.* (wave to children) Goodbye, dears, I'll be back at noon . . . (turn to Grandma) And don't worry, Grandma, if the very worst happens I'll buy you a new house! (exit)

PEP TALK

Character: Coach to football team between halves.

All right, men, huddle up! . . . Never in my thirty years of coaching have I seen a more miserable, ragged, sorry, sloppy, excuse for football. Football players! I could train seals to play a better game!

(Step from player to player as you name them) You, Gallagher! You call yourself a right tackle. I have a grandmother who can go uphill in her wheelchair faster than you hit that line.

270

And *you,* Lindquist. You know what you are? You're a disgrace. A total, complete disgrace. A disgrace to the name of your father, a disgrace to the name of your school, a disgrace to the name of football. It's even a disgrace to call you a disgrace.

Pentwhistle, why did you stop running with the ball to wave to someone in the crowd? . . . You were waving to your girl? Ah, what a touching little gesture of affection. You touch me deeply. But pray tell me, Mister Pentwhistle, *why did you have to wave with the ball?* . . . So she could see you had it? (sweetly) You didn't have it very long, did you?

Mister Robert B. Batwig, I believe. You might say I am dying of curiosity, Mr. Batwig. You did something out there that I have never seen before and I hope I never see again. Tell me, sir, *why did you carry the ball to the one-inch line and then stop?* . . . . (pause as if listening) A splendid answer, Mr. Batwig—you figured since you had run that far that an inch or two more or less made little difference. How logical!

Ah, there, Redblack! Why did you shift to the left when the rest of the team shifted to the right? (shout) *You didn't want to be a copycat!*

Wampwell, how come you're always whispering in the ear of the enemy tackle? *You're telling him our next play?* . . . But *why?* . . . *What do you mean, he dared you?*

Tell me, Clapnip, how come you missed *five straight passes* in a row? You missed Smith's, Morgan's, Wilson's, Parker's and Morton's . . . before you finally caught one from Leeversham. How come you caught only Leeversham's? (despairingly) I see, you're mad at the others . . .

Allenby, how come you stopped to tie your shoelace *before* you punted the football? (shout) *Your mother says that neatness is more important than anything?*

(Tenderly, affectionately) And now we have come to you, Snorkle. You were positively brilliant. Never have I seen a finer exhibition of masterful dodging, superb blocking, clever passing. You were easily the most outstanding player on that field. Let me shake your hand, son. Next time, Snorkle, my boy, *would you mind running the right way?*

(Again brisk) Okay, men, back on the field for the second half. We only have them sixty-eight to nothing so get out there and let's see you do better!

SCHOOL DAZE

Character: Teacher (male or female) to class.

Good morning, children. Are we ready for our test? No, Billy, I didn't say *our* test because I'm taking it, too . . . *I* already know the answers . . . No, it's not cheating for me to know the answers, Billy.

Martha, can you tell me why Washington crossed the Delaware? . . . Yes, it's true it was too long to go around. Jimmy, why did Alexander the Great die so young? . . . No, it wasn't that he wanted to make history easier. (sigh) . . . Susie, where is Norway? . . . He went out for a walk? . . . I said *Norway,* not *Norman!* Alice, can you repeat the alphabet backward? . . . No, I don't mean while facing the rear of the room . . . Harry, why do bees keep honey in their mouths? . . . Because they don't have jars? Oh, my.

Stanley, if I had a dozen apples and gave you one, what would you say? . . . *Selfish?* . . . That's not quite the answer I had in mind. Morton, can you spell *gorilla?* B-I-G A-P-E? I see, it spells easier and means the same thing . . . Eddie, how long did it take for Magellan to sail around the world? . . . Very funny, he didn't check in and out with you . . . Leonard, where was Napoleon defeated? . . . On page fifty-three of our history book? No, no, I'll give you a hint—Water . . . Water . . . Water . . . no, Mary, *I'm not thirsty!*

Walter, what small creature lives in a corner and is in constant fear of life? Besides your *father!* . . . Pauline, can you name three presidents? Billy Jones, Sammy Smith, Eddie Green? . . . I didn't mean presidents of the Student Organization.

Did all of you memorize one of Shakespeare's poems as I asked? Mildred . . . ? Fine! Will you recite your choice for us? . . . (pause as if listening, smile) A very lovely bit of verse; let's see if I can remember what you quoted:

> I'd like to be a zephyr,
> I'd like to be a breeze,
> But best of all I'd like to be
> A piece of moldy cheese!

But, Mildred, you know that wasn't written by Shakespeare,

the great English poet. Oh, it was written by Sammy Shakespeare who runs the corner grocery store.

Now, children I have some questions that are answered by *numbers*. Are you ready? Well, I'm afraid we'll have to go ahead anyway. Here's the first.

How many miles did Paul Revere gallop during his famous journey? Why do you say *none*? His *horse* did all the galloping? . . . Here's a difficult one. Marie, can you name the nine planets? Go ahead . . . lettuce, carrots, potatoes, spinach . . . Marie, I said *planets,* not plants.

Let's try just one more. Jeff, how many times can bees sting you? Once, because after one sting you don't fool around with them again. I see.

(Look at watch, sigh) Well, children, your answers could have been worse, but I'm not sure *how.* I'll give you one final question—would you all like a recess? (hold ears) Finally, a direct answer.

LINCOLN'S MIDDLE NAME

Character: A student (male or female).

(Enter with pad and pencil, pretend to write as you speak aloud) Let's see, how shall I start this essay on Abraham Lincoln? This ought to be easy. (think) Hmmm, . . . he was born in Kentucky, he built log cabins, he was the . . . he lived in . . . he tried to . . . (shake head) Hmmm, guess I don't know as much as I thought . . . I know, I'll ask Wally Carter . . .

(Dial imaginary or toy phone) Hello, Wally? Say, Wally, what do you know about Abraham Lincoln? (frown at phone) What class is he in? So long, Wally . . .

(Dial phone) Is this Susie? Hi! Say, Susie, what do you know about Abraham Lincoln? (pleased) *Everything?* Good! Go ahead. (write) Our sixteenth president . . . also served in Congress . . . was Civil War president . . . What's that, Susie? You're trying to think of his middle name? That's funny, I've never thought about Lincoln's middle name. Thanks anyway, maybe I can get it from Eddie . . . Goodbye.

(Dial phone) Hello, Eddie? Say, Eddie, can you tell me Abraham Lincoln's middle name? You can't? Why not? Oh, you've got a mouthful of taffy . . . okay, so long.

(Dial phone) Dotty? How are you? Say, Dot, do you know the middle name of our sixteenth president? What's that—you don't even know his first name? For your information, it's Abraham . . . *What's his last name?* (sigh) Skip it, Dotty.

(Dial phone) Say, Bill, do you know Abraham Lincoln's middle name? You do? Tell me! (frown at phone) *Marion?* What makes you think it's Marion? (shout) *Just a wild guess?* Thank you, goodbye!

(Pace floor, think deeply) I've just *got* to get his middle name before I go on with this essay. I'll try Mildred. She may know . . . she lives on Lincoln Avenue . . . (dial phone) . . . Hi, Millie, this is Bobby . . . do you know Lincoln's middle name? You do, but you want me to guess? Let's see . . . William? . . . Kenneth? . . . Thomas? . . . I give up, Mildred. *Marion?* (angrily replace phone) Wish she'd stay away from Bill.

There's just one thing left to do. I'll phone the principal, Mr. Baxter. He's sure to know. (dial phone) Hello, Mr. Baxter? This is Bobby Jones . . . you know, the boy who's in your office quite a bit . . . that's right. Say, Mr. Baxter, would you please tell me Abraham Lincoln's middle name? (surprised) You can't? Are you sure you can't? Why not? Oh, he doesn't have a middle name! Well, now my essay will be a bit shorter, but thank you, Mr. Baxter.

(Look at pad) At the rate I'm gathering information about Abraham Lincoln, he'll be a year older by the time I have this essay done! (bow and exit)

LARRY'S LESSON

Character: A big sister (or brother) trying to get little brother to practice his piano lessons.

(Briskly enter, look around, call) Larry . . . time for your piano lesson . . . (search about, frown) Larry, you come out here . . . (shake head, mutter) That little brother of mine . . . (quickly search behind chairs and table, lift tablecloth and peer suspiciously under it)

(Then see the imaginary Larry behind a chair) Ah, there you are! Give me that ear . . . (pretend to lead him by ear to piano. Note: The piano may be real or imaginary, but set him in a real chair) Go ahead and play something . . . (shake head) No, not *marbles*.

(Pretend to set music before him) Here, play this little piece called *Lively Leap Frogs* . . . (scream) Eeeeek! Put those frogs back in your pocket!

(Pretend to set another piece before him) Here, try this one . . . Go ahead . . . (look away, tilt head as if listening, sway hand back and forth in rhythm, nod in pleasure) Say, that's very lovely . . . is it something from Beethoven? (frown) What? . . . *it's something from the record player?* (look at him in annoyance) Well, you just shut it off and get back to the piano.

(Plead) Please, Larry, *practice* . . . go ahead . . . (again listen as he plays, suddenly frown, look at him) What's the name of *that* piece? . . . *The March of the Elephants?* (groan) Sounds like real ones are walking on the keys!

(Bend over at his side) Touch the keys lightly . . . very *lightly* . . . like *this* . . . (lightly strike keys) See? Come down very, very lightly. (stand erect, look away) Now you try it. See if you can touch them so lightly I can barely hear them . . . (look away, listen, suddenly frown) How come I didn't hear them at all? (sigh, nod) Oh, you missed the keys altogether . . . (shake head) No, it won't help to paint a target on middle C.

(Look in shock) How come you're playing with your *elbows?* (listen to his remark) *Two elbows are simpler than ten fingers?* Who knows? Maybe you'll develop a new technique.

(Desperately trying to encourage him) Larry, don't you want to become the world's greatest pianist. (frown) *What's a pianist?* A pianist is a piano player. *Why didn't I say so?* (exasperated) Larry, for the last time, will you *please practice?* (frown) *Okay, if it's for the last time?* (groan)

Larry, what did Mrs. Smith say the last time she gave you a lesson? (frown) *Goodbye forever?* (nod in understanding) So *that's* why she moved away . . . (nod as you exit) Hmmm, maybe I need a trip myself. (turn to Larry) Just keep practicing, and I think I'll get moving! (exit)

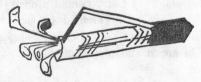

GOLF LESSON

Character: A golf instructor giving lessons to a beginner.

(Enter with a golf club, speak to imaginary student) Good morning, sir (or madam) . . . ready to learn the great game of golf? Fine! The first thing to learn is the *language* of golf . . . You see, golf has a language all its own . . . (tilt head as if listening, frown) What? . . . it must be the Mexican language? . . . why do you say that? . . . (nod) Oh, because of the *Golf of Mexico* . . . that's *gulf,* sir, *gulf.* (shake head)

(Hold up club) This is called a *club* . . . for clubbing the ball . . . (shake head) No, not like *this* . . . (beat club up and down) but with a gentle *sweeping* motion . . . like *this* . . . (gracefully swing club three times) Sweep . . . sweep . . . sweep . . . (frown at student) Yes, it's like keeping things clean. (shake head again)

(Gesture down fairway) Now there are eighteen holes out there . . . (tilt head) *Why don't they fill them up before someone trips?* (annoyed) Look, the whole idea of the game is to get the ball into the hole . . . (grin) The *hole* is the *whole* idea . . . (chuckle at own joke) Ha, ha . . . (frown) Okay, so it's not funny.

(Take driving position) Now watch as I *drive* . . . (frown) What? . . . *where's my car?* . . . (impatiently) I mean *swing* . . . (frown) What? . . . *where's my rope?* (sigh) Please, sir, just watch as I hit the ball. (swing, watch flight of ball) Pretty good shot, I must say!

(Stand, gesture to student) Okay . . . you try it. First of all, look down the fairway . . . that's it, get a good look . . . (briefly pause, frown) Why are you still looking? I see. You like the looks of that handsome man (or beautiful woman) down there. Come, come, back to golf.

Okay . . . swing . . . *go!* (indicate that the ball goes straight

276

up by slowly raising head until you are looking straight up, then lower head halfway, suddenly yell and leap aside to dodge ball, shout angrily to student) What do you call *that?* . . . (nod) Oh, a hole-in-*fun!* (plead) Please don't be so *funny* . . . it's hard on the head.

Go ahead, try again . . . set the club next to the ball . . . (scowl, drag hand over face) No, no, put the club in *back* of the ball . . . (sigh) That's right . . . now start swinging . . . swinging . . . swinging . . . (angrily shout) The *club,* not your *hips!* (sigh) Start all over . . . go ahead . . . that's it . . . *swing!* . . . there it goes! (follow ball with shaded eyes, frown) Did you see where it went? (frown) You *heard* where it went? . . . Someone yelled *ouch?* (shake head) No, you don't get extra points for hitting someone.

Try again . . . go ahead. (shake head) Wait . . . you're digging a hole . . . (shake head) Still digging . . . (tilt head) What? . . . *you're digging your own hole—you don't like those little ones?* (groan, hold head) Okay, okay . . . (scowl, fold arms, slowly lower head and eyes as if student is sinking into a deep hole, walk over, get on knees, cup hands, shout down) Are you there? (stand, extend hand pull student back up) Up you go! What's that? . . . *you struck oil?* (nod) It's a good thing . . . this lesson will cost you a fortune.

(Stand aside) Come, sir, keep trying . . . (stare at ground) How come you're using *eighteen* balls? (nod) *One for each hole* . . . (sigh) Never thought of that. (swing your club) Swing smoothly . . . and lift the ball . . . lift the ball (angrily shout) Not with your hands! (again swing) Like this . . . (shout) That's it! . . . (shade eyes, follow flight of ball, nod) Not bad, considering you used the wrong end of the club.

(With exhausted patience) Look, sir, let's get this over with . . . No, it's not that I'm tired. It's just that people are *watching.* (gesture) Go ahead, just hit the ball *anywhere* . . . That's it . . . *swing!* (follow flight of ball with shaded eyes, shout in amazement) You did it! . . . a hole-in-one! (tilt head) What's that? . . . You're surprised, too? How come? Oh, you aimed at the clubhouse. (wearily shrug) Well, if that's your system, stick with it. As a matter of fact . . . (step forward, place ball on ground, peer about with shaded eyes) Where is that clubhouse? (bow and exit)

ROLLER COASTER

Character: A young man on a roller coaster with his girl. A prominently displayed sign reads: *Roller Coaster.*

(Enter with crooked arm, as if your girl is holding it. Speak to her as you approach two chairs—which face audience—and which represent the roller coaster) Here we are, Doris—the roller coaster! (speak confidently) Now don't be frightened, dear, I'll hold you tight . . . just relax. (as you assist her into chair) There you are . . . (sit down, put arm around her) Don't be frightened . . . (as roller coaster starts) Here we go! (jerk about somewhat, hold onto bar in front with other hand, tilt head to answer her question) What's that? . . . *is it dangerous?* (boastfully laugh) Dangerous? . . . ha ha . . . not so long as big old *me* is holding little old *you!*

(Jerk more violently as roller coaster gathers speed, look upward) Look up there . . . we're on our way to the top! (continue to jerk as you lean back to indicate climb; look somewhat fearfully down at side) Wow! It's a long way down . . . (look anxiously to top, peer almost straight up) I can't even see the top . . . all those clouds . . . (fearfully) Oh . . . Doris . . . do you mind if I hold on with *both* hands? . . . I don't want anyone to think I'm showing off . . . (remove arm from Doris, tightly clutch bar with both hands, tightly close eyes, speak in trembling voice) Are we . . . are we . . . near the top? What . . . we've hardly *started?*

(Lean even farther back, open eyes, tilt head to Doris) What's that? . . . *am I scared?* (indignantly) *Scared? Me?* Of course not . . . my eyes are closed because I'm so *relaxed.* (continue to shake and lean farther back) What's that? . . . *wouldn't I like to hold on to you?* . . . How about *you* holding on to *me?*

(Lean forward to level position as roller coaster hits top, open eyes, scream) The *top!* . . . We're on the *top!* (groan, stare in wide-eyed horror, lean forward as roller coaster starts down) Here we go! Yiiiii! (jerk violently about, desperately clutch bar as the roller coaster plunges about) Hang on, Doris! Hang on to *me!* (After a few seconds of desperate jerking, sit in level position, stop jerking, stare straight forward as if in a daze with hands still clutching bars, sigh deeply, mutter) What's that? . . .

it's all over? . . . we're back? (let hands fall limply to side, sway, almost faint, look up to Doris who is already out of seat, raise your arm as she assists you getting out) Yes, take my arm . . . (weakly climb out) Thanks . . . (stagger somewhat) What's that? . . . *Let's take another ride?* (nod) Okay, let's take another ride . . . (gesture toward exit) I think the merry-go-round would be safer for you . . . (weakly wander offstage)

LEFT TURN

Character: Driving instructor (male or female) to female pupil.

That's right, ma'am, just relax . . . we'll have you driving this car in no time . . . now, the first thing to do is sit in the driver's seat of this dual control car. Nothing can go wrong . . . no, no, don't sit on me . . . wait till I move over . . . that's right. All right, the next thing to do is turn the motor over . . . no, no . . . just press this little button. That's it. Now gently let the car ease forward . . . (jerk violently, shout) I said *gently!* Well, we're on the way. Remember, if you want to stop, just gently apply your brakes . . . no, a tree will *not* do just as well. Watch out for that truck over there. *Why?* Well, maybe he's a new driver . . .

Let me show you proper signals. Straight out for a left turn . . . that's right . . . (shout) One arm, not two! . . . Up for right and down for stop, that's right. No, ma'am, you may *not* just wave wildly and let them take their choice . . . No, we have no signal for waving to a good-looking man in the next car. You are going ten miles an hour—speed up a little . . . no, ma'am, *sixty* is not a *little*. Now slow down—a little at a time . . . (jerk forward)

Be careful, we're coming to a tunnel. Don't worry, there *is* an opening there. Careful, now . . . (shout) Please, lady, *open your eyes!* Here we are, in the tunnel. Don't be frightened, there are rarely any bears in here. Nothing to frighten you . . .

The next thing to learn is how to go around corners. See that corner coming up? I want you to make a right turn. Turn the wheel . . . (shout) no, the *other way!* . . . That's right. Now, make a turn here and watch out for that hardware store . . .

279

Careful . . . Well, that's wasn't *too* bad but we'll have to return those rakes and shovels that got caught in the bumper.

See that white line in the middle of the road? Be sure you stay on this side of it. I know there are cars on the other side . . . but if you look very closely, you'll see that they're *going the other way.* Yes, when we come back *you* can have that side—it's all fair and square . . . Just keep thinking to yourself, *my* side, *his* side, *my* side, *his* side.

Remember to keep your eyes open for traffic signs. See those over there . . . thirty mile limit . . . slow, curve ahead . . . railroad crossing . . . see if you can read a few . . . Joe's Hot Dogs . . . Eggs For Sale . . . well, that's the *general* idea . . . And be extra careful for animals that might dart across the road . . . you know, dogs, cats, rabbits . . . no, it's not likely that you'll see an alligator . . .

Do you think you can drive back to town without help? You can? Fine! Just a minute while I put on this blindfold . . . *Why?* Oh, I just think I'll feel better that way.

COMPLAINT DESK

Character: Employee (male or female) at complaint desk of department store.

Good morning, sir, can I help you? A clerk in the sporting goods section was rude to you? What did he do? . . . He showed you how to use a pair of boxing gloves? What was rude about *that?* Oh, he knocked you out in the first round? . . . I'm *so* sorry. I'll see that his boxing license is revoked. In the meanwhile, I recommend the dark glasses section for those black eyes.

Yes, madam, do you have complaint? Your husand is a good-for-nothing? I'm sorry, madam, but we only replace merchandise bought in this store. You met him here? Sorry . . . Yes, sir, what can I do for you? You want to complain about the gopher poison you bought? . . . What's that, the gophers actually *like* it? . . . They follow you around and plead for more? . . . I don't believe it! (pull away) Please, put that gopher away!

Yes, madam, I understand—the baby shoes you bought don't

fit your baby. How old is the child? *Twenty-three?* . . . Oh, you bought them twenty years ago. We certainly appreciate your patronage all these years.

Hello, sir . . . You want to buy a collar for your dog? I'm sorry, but we don't sell dog collars. We just have *goat* collars, *monkey* collars, *raccoon* collars, and *camel* collars . . . No dog collars . . . What's that, you'll settle for a dog leash? But why do you want one just three inches long? Oh, you're very close to your dog and you want to stay that way . . . You also want some dog biscuits? Well, try our bakery department—everything they bake tastes like dog biscuits.

Yes, madam, you say our prices are outrageously high on jelly beans? *Twenty dollars per jelly bean?* Madam! You were at the jewelry counter! Stop munching those pearls!

What is your complaint, sir? . . . You can't find the book department? (Scratch head) Well, the book department is where the furniture department used to be, the furniture department is where the hardware used to be, the hardware is where the food used to be . . . Why don't you read a magazine until we get things straightened out?

What's that, sir, you've lost your wife? Have you tried women's dresses? Women's hats? Women's shoes? You haven't looked in any of those places? Why not? . . . Oh, you're liable to *find* her.

Yes, madam, you can get birdseed in our pet department . . . Yes, for all kinds of birds . . . No, planting a package won't give you a bird garden . . . But, if you plan to have seagulls be sure to give them plenty of water.

What's that, you bought a pair of snowshoes and it hasn't snowed once all winter? Sir, the guarantee on the snowshoes does not mean that we guarantee it will snow!

(Cheerfully) Sorry, everyone. Time for my lunch. Come back this afternoon and by all means don't forget to bring your complaints with you! (bow and exit)

SIZE, PLEASE

Character: Woman buying a pair of shoes.

I'd like to buy some shoes . . . How many? . . . One pair would be fine. Do you think you have anything in my size? A couple of *shoe boxes* might fit? Very funny . . . Now, what I really want is a pair of red shoes with black trim . . . (think) Or, was it *orange* shoes with *lavender* trim? Dear me, I can never remember what I want . . . (excited) I got it! I want a pound of beef liver and some onions . . . oh, no, that's another store . . . Maybe you'd better measure me for size . . . (shout) What are you doing with that yardstick? . . . I assure you, sir, I have *very tiny feet!*

I'm tired of high-heel shoes that make the same old sound . . . *clickity clack, clickity clack* . . . don't you have some that go *bumpity bump?* I like to be *different.* You do have something that's different? How do they go? I see, *slosh slosh*—but they can only be worn in the shower.

Young man . . . you don't mind if I call you *young man,* do you? After all, I don't know you well enough to call you by name . . . What? that pleases you immensely. Maybe you could show me some beach sandals. I simply *adore* beach sandals. No, I'm not going to the beach—I just like to set them on the table and think of a winter vacation in Florida.

How about that pair of low-heels over there? Yes, try them on. No, no, on *me!* . . . They are *not* too small for me . . . is it necessary for you to groan like that? . . . Well, I wish you wouldn't make it so obvious by bracing yourself against the wall . . . Are they on? My, but that left foot feels tight . . . Let me stand up . . . better take my arm, I feel like I'm standing on rocks . . . Easy, now, see if I can walk to the mirror. (stare) Heavens, I'm wearing *your* shoes . . . oh, please step aside. (pleased)

There! My, but I make a pretty picture. Look! They're splitting at the seams! . . . Poor quality to split so soon! How *dare* you say they're five sizes too small! . . . Four sizes, perhaps, but not *five* . . . Well, you'd better take them off. All right, I'll wait until you can get some help . . . Easy, now . . . oof! Heavens, you've ruined my feet.

Young man, I'm going to report you to the manager. What is your name? Bill Foote? What's the manager's name? Phil Foote? What's the owner's name? *Daddy* Foote? Well, I'll give you one more chance.

Tell me, do you have shoes that will make me four inches taller? Oh, only *two* inches taller. Well, sell me two pairs then —no that won't work.

How about showing me some open-toes? No, I'm not asking you to show me your tootsies! . . . Can you get me the latest fashion from Paris? You *can?* (baffled) Where are you going? To buy a ticket to France? Young man, you are very impertinent to me. Wrap up my purchases and I'll be on my way. I haven't bought anything yet? . . . I don't doubt it, with the kind of service I've been getting! Goodbye. (exit)

FLIGHT FIFTEEN

Character: A busy executive on an airplane flight.

(Set stage with four chairs, one pair in back of the other so as to represent two rows of airplane seats.)

(Enter briskly with briefcase, speak to imaginary stewardess) This is Flight Fifteen, isn't it, miss? Thank you. (find way down aisle to seat at window, sit down, eagerly open briefcase, pull out batch of papers as you mutter to self) Just enough time to read these contracts before the big conference . . . (eagerly read, make pencil notes, suddenly look to lady passenger in next seat who speaks to you) What's that, ma'am? You'd like my seat next to the window? Yes, of course . . . (fumble awkwardly with batch of papers, drop some on floor, pick them up, finally shift seats, speak kindly to lady) Yes, ma'am, I understand . . . that's all right . . . yes . . . yes . . . lots of people like to look out of airplane windows . . . (shake head as she persists in gratitude) No, no, thank you . . . I don't eat peanut butter sandwiches . . . No, that's all right, glad to let you have the window for nothing.

(Resume paper work, lean over as lady again speaks) What's that, ma'am? Do I know what town we just passed? (look over and down) I believe it's Greenwood . . . yes, ma'am . . . Greenwood . . . delightful, isn't it? (in annoyance, resume work, again look at lady) What's that? *Orangeville?* (puzzled) *Orangeville?* (nod in understanding) Oh, you think it was Orangeville instead of Greenwood . . . (nod) Yes, I believe you are right . . . yes. (resume work, scowl as lady again speaks) Yes, ma'am? It was *Greenwood,* after all? No oranges there, but you saw a lot of green wood lying around? Yes, ma'am. (in annoyance as the lady persists) Please, ma'am, I'm working on . . . (gesture to papers) I'm trying to . . . (shake head) No, ma'am, I don't think the pilot will go back for you to make sure . . . No . . . you see, most people in airplanes don't care whether it's Greenwood or Orangeville . . . No . . . They think about other things, like business things, for example . . . You'd be surprised the things people think about on airplane trips . . . (sigh deeply at your little speech, resume work)

(Again look at lady somewhat wearily) What? It's Orangeville now? Orangeville has a little red church on the corner? I see. (Nod head)

(Frown at lady) Yes, ma'am! (Brightly) You'd like to change seats again? Why? . . . Because you can't tell one town from another? There are no signs on them? . . . I know. They don't even paint the states different colors . . . like they do on maps. Okay, we'll change. (awkwardly change seats, spill papers, resume work, read aloud) This agreement is effective as of April tenth . . . (as your thoughts drift) April tenth . . . (look out window, look at lady, look out window, look at lady in inquiring manner) We're passing over the mountains, ma'am . . . (peer closely at lady) Oh, sorry, ma'am . . . you're taking a nap . . . (pretend to adjust her coat around her shoulders) Your coat . . .

(Try to resume work, mutter as you shake head) This contract is effective as of a little red church in the middle of the green woods . . . (doze off to sleep)

LOOK HERE, BOSS

Character: Employee (male) asking the boss for a raise. Can be altered slightly for female.

(Hesitant) Uh, nice of you to see me, Mr. Prop . . . I . . . uh . . . would like to ask you about something . . . something to do with wages . . . What's that, Mr. Prop—do I think I'm *overpaid* . . . ? Well, I was sort of thinking the *opposite* . . . oh, you also want to talk to me about my work? I hope its satisfactory, sir . . . You say I ruined six refrigerators last week? Yes, sir, I'll admit that, but at least it was an improvement over the two weeks when I ruined *sixteen* . . .

I also took time out on the job to get a haircut . . . ? Well, I figured since the hair *grew* on the job I should get it *cut* on the job . . . Huh? I was two hours late this morning? Yes, but I made it up by *leaving* two hours early . . . I think we're off on the wrong track, Mr. Prop.

I want to talk about my wages. Suppose we say five dollars more starting next week? . . . What? Ten dollars *less* starting right *now?* But, sir, I have a wife and ten children who have to eat . . . It's a careless habit they've gotten into. Maybe I can cut my wife to one meal a day . . . The children can always go into the street and beg from strangers . . .

(Somewhat bolder) Now, look here, Mr. Prop, do you know how long I've worked for you? . . . Too long? . . . Do you know what I am, Mr. Prop? . . . your slave, that's what I am, your *slave* . . . (tearful) Sir, I've worked for you for ten years, and do you know that in all that time you haven't said even one kind sentence to me? No, I don't think that's particularly kind . . . *Please, dear employee, go home!*

Mr. Prop, why don't you put yourself in my place for a while . . . Just take a good look, Mr. Prop . . . You see before you a poor, dejected, miserable, unhappy creature . . . huh? . . . I left out *worthless?* . . . Do you remember that day ten years ago when I first started to work for you? I was a simple, innocent, unassuming boy of sixteen . . . (shout) All right, so I *was* a simple, innocent, *stupid* boy. But look how I've grown with the store . . . huh? I've grown around the middle? . . . Mr. Prop, I appeal to your sense of fair play, your sense of honor, your sense of sportsmanship . . . What? you don't have any sense at all or you wouldn't have hired me in the first place? . . .

Do you realize, sir, that I am responsible for a hundred per cent rise in the last two years? . . . Oh, the rise was in expenses? . . . Well, do you realize that I have personally increased efficiency around here? . . . You admit that every day that I'm away things really hum? . . . Another thing—have you noticed how everyone is happy when I'm around? . . . Mr. Prop, I don't think they're laughing *at* me!

(Bold) Mr. Prop, I'm going to come right out with it. I'm going to speak just four little words . . . *I want a raise!* Understand, Mr. Prop? . . . *I want a raise!* (happy) You will give me a raise? Oh, Mr. Prop . . . (sadly) . . . You'll let me work on the top floor instead of in the bargain basement?

CALLING ALL SPIES

Character: Army officer on telephone.

Hello, operator, I want Army Intelligence . . . Hello, Army Intelligence? What? *The Naval Supply Depot?* . . . Operator, I want Army Intelligence . . . hello . . . is this . . . ? No, I do *not* want the submarine base at San Diego . . . Operator, please, Army Intelligence . . . hello, hello, is this the . . . (frown) Who wants the Twenty-Third Pursuit Squadron! . . . Operator, could you please . . . (think slyly) Operator, could I speak to Senor Antonio Moreno in Rio de Janeiro . . . (pause, then happily) Hello Army Intelligence! Thank you!

Hello, who is this speaking? *Operator G-Three?* Who else is around there? F-Eight, J-Six, O-Five and Eddie Smith? . . . Better check that Eddie Smith—sounds like a phony name . . . I'd like to speak to B-4, please. What do you mean, *before* what? . . . I want *Operator B-4.* What's that, he's going under an assumed name? Oh, 4-B. All right, let me talk to him . . .

Hello, 4-B? This Colonel Greep . . . I want a full report from you. How big is the enemy's fleet? Size 12, double A? . . . Look, I said *fleet,* not *feet* . . . How many *ships* does the admiral have? Not *hips, ships!* . . . Did you find out how many guns he has? Great, let me write it down . . . five *guns* and six *daughters* . . .

How good are their flyers? They fly just like eagles? How is that possible? Oh, they *are eagles* . . . How many submarines do they have? One hundred and three? But we sank one hundred of them yesterday! Oh, I see, all but three were ours . . . Remind me to send a note to the camouflage department.

Now, then, I want you to contact a female spy known as Little Mary. She's six feet tall and weighs three hundred pounds . . . She's called Little Mary because her sister is *twice* that big . . . I want you to contact Little Mary and give her the following secret message. (quote) *Please return my medals, I know all about you and that Lieutenant* . . . Also please take a letter to Lieutenant Albert Morrison. (quote) *Dear former Captain Morrison: How does it feel to be booted downstairs? Yours privately—Colonel Greep.*

Are you there, 4-B? I want you to sneak into the enemy lines and bring back a prisoner. You already have? Fine! What's his name? *Her* name is now *Mrs.* B-4? . . . What did I tell you about marrying on the job? Well, maybe a wife *would* be useful in your work—she can wash and iron your secret messages.

Speaking of secret messages, the next time you send a secret message don't hide it in my pancake batter. Three more bites and we would have lost the war . . . Another thing, I don't mind your hiding them in the refrigerator but please keep your grimy hands off the baked ham.

Here's your next assignment and I want you to follow orders very carefully. You are to make a time bomb that will go off at exactly three o'clock. (look at watch) It is now five minutes to three . . . I want you to plant this bomb in the apple orchard down the street. No, there are no troops there but I thought a little apple sauce would go well for dinner . . . Exactly three o'clock. Go ahead, I'll wait . . . (hum idly) Ta, ta, ta, ta . . . Hello, hello, are you there, 4-B? What do you mean—BOOM? (reflectively) Hmmm, guess that wasn't you.

(Frantically into phone) Hello, 4-B, hello, hello, hello . . . (sadly hang up, again dial) Hello, is this the Spy Replacement Center? I'd like to have a good operator sent up at once. I can have my choice of S-Nine, C-Seven, or Lulubelle Jones? Send up Lulubelle Jones, she sounds like a pretty smart number . . . What happened to 4-B? I'm afraid he had a bit of trouble with an assignment . . . If he ever shows up tell him I've been transferred to the infantry . . . tell him anything . . . just don't tell him where I live . . . thanks.

BUT, DOCTOR

Character: Doctor to patient.

Hello, Mrs. Treep . . . what's that, you have shooting pains? Any idea what caused them? Oh, your husband's shotgun . . . (amazed) But that's fantastic, how could he mistake you for a wild duck? *You were flying around the house in a wild rage?* . . .

You also see squares before your eyes? That's odd, most people see spots . . . oh, you like to be different . . . Are you getting enough sleep, Mrs. Treep? *Thirty-six* hours per day? . . . Oh, you sleep *faster* than most people . . . How much do you weigh? Five hundred and sixty pounds? But how much when you're *not* carrying the piano?

Mrs. Treep, would you please say *Ah?* Say it again in a higher voice . . . again in a lower voice . . . again, in a higher voice . . . no, nothing, I just wanted a little music . . . How is your appetite? I mean how mucy do you eat in a week? Two roasts of beef . . . a leg of lamb . . . five dozen eggs . . . nine pounds of spaghetti . . . twelve loaves of bread . . . you eat that in a *week?* I see—that's not for a week—it's *daily!*

Did you take that bottle of pills I gave you? *Why* was it hard going down? Well, try taking them *out* of the bottle! . . . What's that, you have an earache . . . from listening to a screaming voice all day long? Why don't you tell your husband to keep quiet? Oh, it's *your* voice . . .

What's that, Mrs. Treep? You hear bells every afternoon at three? Well, you'll be all right . . . just wait till the ice cream man turns the corner.

You also have hiccups? Try holding your breath and counting. You *did?* For how long? Well, try going *over* a million next time . . . You're overly tired at night after a simple day of washing, ironing, scrubbing? Well, you'll just have to give up tunnel digging on the night shift . . .

You dream heavily after eating sauerkraut and you're going

to eat it again tonight? But *why?* Oh, you dream that your husband is rich and handsome and you like it better that way . . .

I recommend that you go to the country for a rest. Oh, *any* country . . . you know, France, Japan, Australia . . . goodbye . . . (bow and exit)

Section 7

Two-Character Monologues

Monologues may call for double roles. There is extra humor as you make swift changes from one character to another. These changes can be effected in a number of ways, such as switching from a male to a female hat, by speaking in a low voice as a boy and a high voice as a girl, or by simply shifting physical positions back and forth.

Many audiences find something especially funny about a boy taking a girl's role and vice versa. If you keep your natural voice while acting an opposite-sex role, this sometimes adds to the humor, sometimes detracts. Choose a monologue that *you* can get the most humor and feeling out of.

Most of the double-role pieces may be turned into skits with two players taking part. It would be an excellent idea to present several two-man skits during an evening's entertainment.

VALENTINES

Character: Small shy boy trying to get up nerve to give a Valentine to his small girl friend (double role).

(Boy, on left, sits stiffly, staring straight forward) Hello . . . Mary . . .
(Girl, on right, sits shyly, staring straight forward) Hello . . . Jimmy . . .
(Boy) Mary . . . hello.
(Girl) Jimmy . . . hello.
(Boy) Mary . . .
(Girl) Yes . . . ?
(Boy) Know what day it is?
(Girl) Tuesday.

(Boy) But it's a *special* day.

(Girl) I know—I always wash my hair on Tuesday.

(Boy) I mean . . . it's *Valentine's Day*.

(Girl, giggling) Oh . . .

(Boy) I've got something for you . . .

(Girl) Another pet frog?

(Boy) Something *sweet*.

(Girl, beaming) *Candy?*

(Boy) Something made of paper.

(Girl, frowning) *Paper* candy?

(Boy) Something you get in the mail.

(Girl, frowning) A *bill?*

(Boy) Something with *pictures* . . .

(Girl, brightly) A comic book!

(Boy) It has a picture of a *heart*.

(Girl, frowning) A doctor's chart?

(Boy) I'll give you a hint . . . what did I give you *last* Valentine's Day?

(Girl) Three grasshoppers and a snail.

(Boy, nervous) Hello . . . Mary . . .

(Girl) Hello . . . Jimmy.

(Boy, gulping) Mary . . .

(Girl) Yes? . . .

(Boy, bold) Will you be my . . .

(Girl) Yes? . . .

(Boy) Will you be my . . .

(Girl, eager) Yes? . . .

(Boy, slump, sigh, speak rapidly) Will you be my partner in a game of hopscotch?

(Girl) Jimmy . . .

(Boy) Yes? . . .

(Girl) What's that in your hand?

(Boy, trembling) My . . . my . . . hand? Which hand?

(Girl) The hand with something in it.

(Boy) That's . . . that's . . . (blurt it) just my fingers.

(Girl) I mean something white and trembly . . .

(Boy, miserable) It's *still* my fingers . . .

(Girl, reach in back, withdraw Valentine, read it) Jimmy . . .

(Boy) Yes? . . .

(Girl) I have something for you, too.

(Boy) You have? . . .

(Girl) Something you *like*.

(Boy, excited) A guinea pig!

(Girl, coy) No, something for Valentine's Day!

(Boy, smiling) You mean? . . .

(Girl, facing Boy, hold out Valentine) A Valentine!

(Boy, takes Valentine, looking straight out) Mary . . .

(Girl, hopeful) Yes? . . .

(Boy) I have something to say to you . . .

(Girl, more hopeful) Yes?

(Boy, again miserable, slumping) Hello . . . Mary . . . (bow and exit)

HOOK AND BAIT

Character: Boy teaching girl to fish (double role). Shift quickly from left to right for each character.

(Boy, on left, speaking guardedly) Well, here we are by the sea. You sure you want to learn to fish, Jennie?

(Girl, on right, in innocent high voice) Is it anything like knitting, Harold?

(Boy, muttering fiercely) *Knitting!* Here, take your pole! (pass pole)

(Girl, taking it, delighted) Oh, it *is* like knitting. But isn't this needle too long?

(Boy) *Needle!* Look, Jennie, don't you know what a pole is for?

(Girl, innocent) For poking the fish as they swim by?

(Boy, groaning) Only if your aim is good. Now, look, you hold the pole like *this* . . . (illustrate) . . . over the water.

(Girl, baffled) *Over* the water? (brightly) I know—for *flying* fish!

(Boy) That's right. Now take the hook in your hand.

(Girl) Where's the hook?

(Boy) At the end of the line.

(Girl, puzzled) *Which* end? Oh, I have it. (Shake hook loose from finger)

(Boy, groaning) Now put some bait on the hook.

(Girl) Like *this?*

(Boy, trying hard to be patient) That's fine, but why use the cheese sandwich from our lunch? Use the bait in the can.

(Girl) There! It's on the hook. (sympathetic) What should I do next?

(Boy, brightly) You could go *home* . . . No, next thing is to cast your hook into the water. Go ahead . . . (alarmed) Why did you cut the line? (groan) No, that's not the way to cast the hook *deeper.* Let me fix it . . . (do so) Okay, toss out the bait . . . (shout) Not the whole can! . . . just the bait on your line . . . That's right. There! At last we're fishing.

(Girl) Harold, shouldn't we have on a steel helmet or something?

(Boy, baffled) A steel helmet! *Why?*

(Girl, innocent) In case we tangle with a swordfish.

(Boy, weary, resigned) No, dear, I'll just file off its sword. Look, Jennie, do you know what it means if your pole jumps up and down?

(Girl, brightly) That there's a fish at the end!

(Boy, pleased) That's right!

(Girl, excited) Harold, look, the end of my pole is bobbing!

(Boy) It means nothing, dear.

(Girl) Why not?

(Boy) *You're shaking the other end!*

Time passes.

(Boy, sighing) Darn, I haven't had a bite yet.

(Girl) Hungry? Have a bite of cheese sandwich.

(Boy) I mean a bite on my hook . . . Looks like there isn't a fish in the whole ocean.

(Girl, sympathetic) Oh, dear, what will happen to all the fishing industries?

(Boy, shrugging) Why should we worry?

(Girl, brightly) I know what size pole we'd use for a sardine!

(Boy) What?

(Girl) A toothpick! (laugh at own joke)

(Boy, depressed) Bad luck, today . . . not a nibble.

(Girl, casual) Harold, I have a nibble.

(Boy, disinterested, glumly stare out) A nibble? Well, pull it in.

(Girl, casual) I've got it, Harold.

(Boy, still glum) Okay . . .

(Girl, still casual) Harold, there's a fish on the end . . .

(Boy, still glum) A fish? Okay . . . (wake up) A fish! (look to right, shout) Jennie, you've done it . . . you caught a sword-fish! (horrified) Jennie, what are you doing? . . . don't throw it back! Jennie! (watch fish swim away, turn in despair to girl) Why did you toss it back?

(Girl, indignant) Did you think I wanted to take the last fish alive?

A DRIVE IN THE COUNTRY

Character: Steve and Linda, an engaged (or married) couple on a drive (double role).

(As Steve, sit on left side of chair, pretend to drive by holding hands up on steering wheel, glance happily about at scenery) Lovely day for a drive in the country . . . nothing like the great outdoors!

(As Linda, sit on right side of chair, snuggle close, speak dreamily) Stevie . . . darling . . . tell me that you love me.

(Steve, happily driving) I love you, dear . . . very, very much, Linda, dear.

(Linda) Dear . . . tell me . . . *why* do you love me?

(Steve, gesture vaguely) Oh . . . (glance at her) I think because of your funny-bunny little nose.

(Linda, thrilled) My funny little nose? (coyly) Oh, Stevie . . . (think with expression for a moment, suddenly frown, touch nose) Dear, do I really have a *funny*-bunny nose?

(Steve, explaining) No, no, darling . . . I don't mean a *funny* nose . . . you know . . . (gesture) just a funny-bunny nose.

(Linda, nod) Oh . . . (snuggle) Why else do you love me?

(Steve, think, glance at her, come up with compliment) Be-cause of your cute little winky-blinky eyes.

(Linda, thrilled) Winky-blinky eyes! How sweet! (suddenly frown) Darling, what do you *mean* by winky-blinky eyes?

(Steve, try to explain) Sweetheart, when I say winky-blinky eyes I mean . . . (pucker lips, shrug) Winky-blinky is nice I thinky. (chuckle at your cleverness)

(Linda, snuggle) Say something else nice about me.

(Steve, smile, glance at her) Well, I just adore those (wiggle forefinger at her ear) pretty pink ears.

(Linda, thrilled, sigh) Oh, sweetheart . . . (think, frown) Do you mean I have *Pink* ears?

(Steve, hastily) Darling, please . . . please . . . I mean they are soft and cuddly. You know, soft and cuddly like a little bunny. (as Linda is unconvinced) Darling, let me make it clear to you . . . sweetheart . . . darling . . . You see, I love you because . . . because . . . of your funny little nose and your winky-blinky eyes and your pretty pink ears. All together you make one wonderful girl.

(Linda, pout suspiciously, pull away) All together, the description makes one a rabbit! I can see you down at the office . . . (imitate his voice) *Hey, fellows . . . Look at this picture . . . my girl's the third rabbit on the right!*

(Steve, try hard to be calm) Darling . . . let's start all over . . . okay? . . . I'll stop the car . . . (pretend to pull brake, turn off ignition) There! (pat her) Now darling, just pretend we're starting our quiet little drive in the country . . . a fresh start in life . . . Okay? Okay, here we go . . . (loosen brake, turn on ignition, turn steering wheel, assume a forced cheeriness as you look at roadside, gesture outward) Look dear, the countryside . . . look at the pretty little pink rabbits? . . . (groan at your blunder, drag a hand over your face)

(Linda, look up finally, speak martyr-like, philosophically) Darling, it's all right . . . You think I look like a rabbit . . . Life has its burdens . . . I'll try hard not to mind . . . (grimly) I'll try very, *very* hard . . . after all . . . (sarcastically) There may not be many girls who look like rabbits . . .

(Steve, finally give up, explode) All right . . . (gesture wildly) all right . . . you look like a rabbit . . . a big, floppy-eared carrot-munching hippity-hoppity rabbit. But once and for all . . . (shout) I love you . . . *I love you, my little rabbit* . . . You're a rabbit and I love you . . . (assume pained expression at the whole unhappy mess, drive for a moment or two, see a rabbit ahead at side of road, gesture outward) Look, rabbit, a darling . . . (groan, quickly correct yourself) I mean, *look, darling, a rabbit* . . . look . . . just what we were fighting (correct yourself) *talking* about . . . isn't it cute?

(Linda, lower handkerchief, nod as you look at rabbit) Cute!

(Steve, again stop car) I'll see if I can . . . (get out of car, off of chair, reach down) Here, little rabbit, little bunny . . . (pick up rabbit) Friendly little fellow . . . (hold rabbit out for her to see as you pat it) See, darling . . . a funny-bunny nose and winky-blinky eyes and pretty pink ears? . . . so soft and cuddly . . . *Darling,* isn't it *darling?*

(Linda, weakening) Am I as soft and cuddly as *that?*

(Steve, pleased that you are winning her) Especially those cute little bunny-like ears.

(Linda, sigh with pleasure) Oh, Stevie, you say the *nicest* things . . .

(Steve, anxious to encourage her pleasure) See how nice it is to be compared with a cuddly bunny? . . . (tickle her chin) you *funny-cuddly-bunny.*

(Linda, sigh happily) Oh, Stevie . . . Stevie, why don't you think I'm as graceful as a swan?

(Steve, frightened) Dearest . . . darling . . . to me you are like a cuddly little rabbit.

(Linda, tense) And I'm not like a gracefully gliding swan? . . .

(Steve, clap hand to forehead) Yes, dear, you're like a swan *and* a rabbit . . . white and pink . . . and graceful and hoppity . . . and soft and cuddly . . . and feathery . . . and . . .

(Speak while exiting, return and bow)

YOU LOOK LOVELY, DEAR

Character: Wife, trying to select a new hat while husband looks painfully on (double role). Prominently displayed sign reads, *Helen's Hat Shop.*

(Wife, in ecstasy, as she stands by table set with hats and other items mentioned in monologue) Oh, what darling hats! (remove own hat, put on shop hat) How does it look, dear?

(Husband) You look lovely, dear. (Note: If performed by a single player, indicate role of husband by standing in a different spot and by speaking in a lower voice)

(Wife, remove hat, frown) No, it won't go with my dress. (try another, frown) No, it won't go with my shoes. (try another, frown) No, it won't go with my umbrella. (try another, beam) Ah! Here's one! What do you think, dear?

(Husband) I love it, dear.

(Wife) See the pretty pink lace?

(Husband) I love it, dear.

(Quickly stare at price tag, frown) I hate it, dear.

(Wife, place a mixing bowl on head) What an interesting style!

(Husband, groan, nod) Just the thing for kitchen wear.

(Wife, try another) Please, darling, give me your honest opinion.

(Husband, sourly) You *really* want my honest opinion?

(Wife) Yes.

(Husband, scowl) You look *awful.*

(Wife, hurt) Next time keep your opinions to yourself! (take from table a tiny bit of paper, just large enough for the audience to see) My, what a tiny, *tiny* hat! (place it on head) It looks as small as a postage stamp!

(Husband, peer at paper, take envelope from pocket, take paper and press it on envelope, scowl) That's because it *is.*

(Wife) My, my, the larger the hat the more expensive. (take a small hat) Five dollars. (take medium hat) Ten dollars. (take large hat) Fifteen dollars.

(Husband, withdraw envelope, try to rip off stamp) How about going back to the three-cent one?

(Wife, plead, as you hold up hat) Please, darling, tell me that you like it.

(Husband, shrug) I like it.

(Wife) Are you *sure?*

(Husband, emphatic) I *like* it.

(Wife) Absolutely certain?

(Husband, shout) *I like it!*

(Wife, sadly eye hat) That's too bad.

(Husband, puzzled) Why?

(Wife, hat down) *I* don't like it. (look helplessly around) Darling, if you were me, which one would you take?

(Husband) If I were you, darling, I'd take the most beautiful hat in the store.

(Wife, delighted) You *would?* (eagerly look over hats) But which one *is* the most beautiful?

297

(Husband, hand her her own, original hat) *This* one, dear.

(Wife, baffled) But that's the one I came in with!

(Husband, gallantly, smiling sweetly) I know, dear, and that's why it's the most beautiful of all! Any little hat that has crowned your lovely head is *always* the most beautiful!

(Wife, in ecstasy) Darling, you say the sweetest things! (put on own hat) It *is* lovely isn't it? (take his arm) Come, dear!

(Husband smiles triumphantly at audience as he exits)

PERFUMES

Character: A flighty lady at a perfume counter and the clerk (double role). The clerk may be either male or female.

(Breezily enter as oddly dressed lady, step up to a counter with a sign reading *Perfume* and assorted perfume bottles. Speak to clerk) Good afternoon . . . do you have something that will make attractive little old me even *more* attractive?

(Clerk, frown as you look her over) Give me the names of the things you wish to attract.

(Lady, romantically hold hand over heart) Well, there's *Tommy* and *William* and *Louie* . . . *any* name as long as it belongs to a *man*. What's this called?

(Clerk) *An Evening on the Desert* . . . fifty dollars an ounce.

(Lady) Don't you have something cheaper?

(Clerk, touch bottle) Here's *An Afternoon on a Fish Boat* . . . ten cents a bottle.

(Lady, hold up large bottle) What's this large bottle?

(Clerk) Ah! . . . one of our most effective items . . . it's called *Mantrap*.

(Lady, clap hands) *Mantrap!* How wonderful! What's in it?

(Clerk, happily) A small metal trap.

(Lady) *Please* . . . I want something that will make men *miss* me.

(Clerk, hand her a ticket) This will make them miss you.

(Lady, puzzled) What is it?

(Clerk, smile) A one-way ticket to Africa.

(Lady, sigh in exasperation, hold up a large bottle with a fuse at the top) This is a funny one . . . what's it called?

298

(Clerk, enthusiastically) Ah! You'll go over with a bang with that . . . it's called *Love's Explosion.*

(Lady, brightly, eagerly) How does it work?

(Clerk, touch fuse) You just light this little fuse and *boom*— love explodes all over the place.

(Lady, shake head, look at bottles) Do you have something that will make men *fight* over me?

(Clerk, nod, hand her a bottle) This will make them fight like crazy over you.

(Lady, peer at bottle) What's in it?

(Clerk, smile) Ten thousand dollars!

(Lady, impatient) *Please!* Just give me a perfume that will make men *stare* at me.

(Clerk, shrug, hand her a bottle) Stares coming up!

(Lady, hopefully) How will this make men stare at me?

(Clerk, shrug) In five minutes you turn *green.*

(Lady, scowl, look at bottles, hold up one) What's this one? . . . (peer at label) called *Love at Your Elbows?* Does that mean I'll have love at my elbows all the time?

(Clerk, emphatically) Absolutely! They'll be wild about your elbows.

(Lady) Well . . . suppose I just sample *all* of them . . . (quickly and wildly shake several bottles on head, arms, feet) There! What do you say to *that?*

(Clerk, stare at her while holding head in shock) Wow!

(Lady, happily) I *knew* I'd impress you. (turn to audience, wave) See you later, ladies and gentlemen . . . (brightly) especially you *gentlemen!* (breezily exit)

FOOT IN THE DOOR

Character: Fast-talking salesman at the door (double role).

(Salesman, breezily knocking) Ah, good morning, Miss! Could I interest you in some pots and pans, a little ant poison, a bucket of apples, tickets to the County Fair? . . .

(Housewife, slamming door) No!

(Salesman, knocking again) Sorry, Lady, I didn't catch that last word. How about some chili sauce, shoe polish, a gallon of green paint, a few baby bottles? . . .

299

(Housewife, slamming door) No!

(Salesman, knocking) Did you say *snow!* I just happen to have a bucket of fresh snow with me . . .

(Housewife, slamming door) *Please!*

(Salesman, knocking) Did you say *keys?* I have all sorts of keys with me—garage, basement, doghouse . . .

(Housewife, slamming door viciously) Get out!

(Salesman, holding foot) Ouch!

(Housewife, sympathetic) I'm sorry, did I close the door on your foot?

(Salesman, not hearing, again hop, and knock)

(Housewife, grim) Young man . . .

(Salesman, still knocking) Yes? . . .

(Housewife) *You're knocking on my nose!*

(Salesman, briskly) Oh, excuse me, young lady, I represent the Footinthedoor Company. Do you know that we have a reputation for never taking our foot from the door?

(Housewife, sarcastically) How wonderful! . . .

(Salesman) Our top salesman has been stuck in the same door for fourteen weeks. A Saint Bernard brings him soup and crackers twice a day.

(Housewife) All very interesting, but I'm busy making a cake. Good day . . .

(Salesman, pleading) Please, lady, I have ten hungry children at home.

(Housewife) How come they're not in school?

(Salesman) They were expelled for eating the teacher's flowers.

(Housewife, relenting) In that case show me your sample case. Do you have anything that will make a good chocolate cake?

(Salesman) Yes, my *wife,* but I won't sell her. How about some Spanish stew?

(Housewife, amazed) You have Spanish stew in your sample case?

(Salesman, pointing to sample case) No, but I have a small Spaniard in there who can whip it up in no time.

(Housewife) Please, young man, I have work to do. Couldn't you come back tomorrow?

(Salesman) Why tomorrow?

300

(Housewife, grim) I'm thinking of putting a few bear traps on the porch!

(Salesman, puzzled) Bare traps? . . . you'd better cover them up if you expect to catch anything.

(Housewife) Sir, you are a *nuisance*.

(Salesman, happy) Really?

(Housewife, puzzled) What makes you so happy when I call you a *nuisance?*

(Salesman, happy) The lady next door called me much worse.

(Housewife) I'll give you exactly three to remove your foot from the door. *One!*

(Salesman) Wait!

(Housewife) *Two!*

(Salesman) Please!

(Housewife) *Three!* (slam door)

(Salesman, holding foot) Ouch!

(Housewife, repentant) Oh, I'm sorry . . .

(Salesman, groan in pain) Ohhhhhhhh . . . I'll get fired . . . no paycheck . . . no food . . . my poor wife . . . my starving little babies . . . ohhhhhhhh . . .

(Housewife, sympathetic) My poor, poor man, I'm *so* sorry I hurt you. Tell you what, I'll buy whatever you have left in your sample case . . . How's that?

(Salesman, wipe eyes, stiffling sobs) You . . . really . . . mean . . . it? . . .

(Housewife) Of course I do! Now, what do you have?

(Salesman, sudden briskness, loud as before) How about some pots and pans, some ant poison, a bucket of apples, tickets to the County Fair? . . . (bow and exit)

HELP WANTED

Character: A young man (or woman) applying for a job and a personnel manager (double role).

(Young Man, enter with a briefcase or a paper sack filled with assorted papers) Good morning, sir, I'd like to apply for the job of assistant clerk.

301

(Personnel Manager, behind desk. Note: If performed by one player, quickly shift back and forth) Ah, yes, young man! Do you have your birth certificate?

(Young Man, fumble in briefcase) I was born *somewhere* in here . . . (find paper) Here you are.

(Personnel Manager) And your high school diploma?

(Young Man, sadly) All I have is a *low* school diploma . . . I was at the foot of the class.

(Personnel Manager, sigh) Skip it. As you know, young man (gesture to sign), we manufacture secret weapons. So you must have at least fifteen character references.

(Young Man, shrug) I've only got *two*.

(Personnel Manager) How come just *two*?

(Young Man, grin) Nobody likes me but momma and poppa.

(Personnel Manager, sigh) Oh, well, none of us is perfect. (hold out hand) Give me your doctor's certificate, your fingerprints and your clearance from the F.B.I.

(Young Man, fumble in briefcase, bring out a carrot, a spoon and a jar of glue) Will you settle for a carrot, a spoon and a jar of glue?

(Personnel Manager, throw up arms) Never mind! Just give me your photograph.

(Young Man, hand him a photograph) Here you are.

(Personnel Manager, scowl) Wait a minute, this is a picture of *Abraham Lincoln!*

(Young Man, shrug) He must have had his taken at the same time.

(Personnel Manager, hold head in dismay, wag finger at Young Man) Remember—we manufacture secret weapons so you *must* be able to keep a secret. (point to floor) What would you say if I told you there was buried treasure beneath your feet?

(Young Man, cup hands, eagerly yell toward audience) Someone get a pick and shovel!

(Personnel Manager) Hmmm . . . (hand Young Man an envelope) What would you do if I told you this envelope contained a secret love letter?

(Young Man, grin, eagerly rip open envelope, read) *Dear Mary* . . . (grin, stare, gasp) Wow! Whooo! Wheee!

(Personnel Manager) Young man, after carefully considering

all your qualifications, I am afraid we cannot hire you as an assistant clerk.

(Young Man) Is the position of *president* open?

(Personnel Manager, smile, nod) *Indeed it is.* With you as president no one would ever believe we could manufacture secret weapons. One look at you and they'd think we're bankrupt! (put arm around Young Man, lead him away) Come, young man, let me show you to the president's office. (exit)

THE GIRL WHO DID VERY, VERY WELL

Character: Narrator, Jenny Lou and the Big Boss. This piece is arranged for presentation by one player; however, with minor changes it may be given by two performers, one playing both the Narrator and the Big Boss, and the other player taking the part of Jenny Lou. Jenny Lou's role is all pantomime. Use suitable voices for each character.

(Stand behind a short table while facing audience. Quickly shift from one end of the table to the other for each change of character.)

(Narrator) *There once lived a very, very pretty girl whose name was Jenny Lou.*

(Jenny Lou, smile coyly, flutter eyelids. Note: If both roles are played by a single performer, Jenny Lou's role may be emphasized by putting on and taking off a woman's hat each time.)

(Narrator) *One day pretty Jenny Lou decided to become a Success in the Big World of Television. So she put on her prettiest new hat* . . . (pantomime putting on hat) *And daintily walked down to the big television studio to see the Big Boss.*

(Jenny Lou, walk with exaggerated daintiness for a few steps)

(Narrator) *Said dainty and pretty Jenny Lou to the Big Boss behind the big desk* . . . Good afternoon, Big Boss of the World of Television. I wish to become a Success in the Big World of Television.

(Jenny Lou, make wide gestures with both arms to indicate bigness)

(Narrator) But Jenny Lou, *replied the Big Boss,* you are much too pretty to become a Success in the Big World of Television. Wouldn't you like to become a Success by marrying me? *But Jenny Lou sweetly shook her pretty head.*

(Jenny Lou, shake head)

(Narrator) Well, then, *said the Big Boss,* to become a Success in the Big World of Television you must be able to do something very very well. Can you do something very very well? . . . Oh, yes, *quickly replied Jenny Lou,* I can type the typewriter very very well . . . Ah! *exclaimed the Big Boss,* please show me how you type the typewriter very very well. *So she showed him . . .*

(Jenny Lou, pretend to type, awkwardly with forefingers only, but with a certain speed and rhythm)

(Narrator) My, my, *said the Big Boss,* you type the typewriter very very well in a very different manner from most girls who type the typewriter very very well. Tell me, Jenny Lou, can you do anything else very very well? . . . Oh, yes, *replied Jenny Lou . . .*

(Jenny Lou, eagerly nod)

(Narrator) I can play the piano very very well, *she said . . .* How exciting! *shouted the Big Boss.* Please show me how you play the piano very very well. *So she showed him . . .*

(Jenny Lou, pretend to play piano in exact manner as with previous typing)

(Narrator) Dear, dear me, *exclaimed the Big Boss,* you play the piano very very well in a very different way from most girls who play the piano very very well. Tell me, Jenny Lou, don't you think you would be a bigger Success in the Big World of Television just by marrying me?

(Jenny Lou, a little more doubtful this time, place finger alongside cheek as you consider, finally shake head in doubt, turn and start to leave)

(Narrator) Wait! *the Big Boss suddenly called.*

(Jenny Lou, halt with stride in mid-air)

(Narrator) Come back!

(Jenny Lou, lower mid-air stride, turn, return)

(Narrator) Perhaps there is something you can do very very well after all, *said the Big Boss.* Will you please type very very well for me once more?

304

(Jenny Lou, type as before)

(Narrator) And will you kindly play very very well for me once more?

(Jenny Lou, play as before)

(Narrator) *The Big Boss heaved a great sigh* (sigh deeply) *and explained,* Jenny Lou, I am the Big Boss of that famous television series known as the Happy Horse. But, *said the Big Boss as he unhappily shook his head* (unhappily shake head) our Happy Horse is not doing very well. As a matter of fact, he is a rather unhappy horse. He has severe domestic problems, and being a horse he cannot go to a psychiatrist. So when he gallops over the western plains he sounds like a very unhappy horse—which is not too happy for the story . . .

But what has your unhappy Happy Horse to do with me? *cheerfully inquired Jenny Lou.*

(Jenny Lou, tilt head in inquiry)

(Narrator) Jenny Lou, *replied the Big Boss* (business-like) Dear Jenny Lou, will you please type at the typewriter very very well so that you sound like a happy horse?

(Jenny Lou, tap as before on table, though making it definitely sound like the rhythmic hoofbeats of a galloping horse)

(Narrator) Ah! *the Big Boss happily exclaimed.* And will you also please play at the piano very very well so that you sound like a happy horse?

(Jenny Lou, repeat rhythmic hoofbeats)

(Narrator) Jenny Lou! *the Big Boss gratefully exclaimed.* You will be a Success in the Big World of Television. You sound exactly like a happy horse!

(Jenny Lou, clasp hands behind back, modestly lower eyelids, shyly swing leg about)

(Narrator) I am very grateful to you, Jenny Lou, *the Big Boss gratefully said,* Your happy hoofbeats will make my unhappy horse happy and you will make my sponsors happy and you will make my brother-in-law who borrows money from me happy.

(Jenny Lou, repeat happy hoofbeats)

(Narrator, sadly) But, *the Big Boss sadly added,* it will not make me happy.

(Jenny Lou, give the Big Boss a puzzled look)

(Narrator) You see, Jenny Lou, I am a very lonely man. My

Happy Horse does not make me happy, it only makes me money.

(Jenny Lou, give the Big Boss a sympathetic look)

(Narrator) *Said Jenny Lou to the unhappy Big Boss,* Is there anything else I can do very very well that will make you a happy Big Boss?

Well, *he replied,* I would be as happy as my Happy Horse if you will . . . (shyly) if you will marry me.

(Jenny Lou, sigh, dramatically and cheerfully hold hand over heart)

(Narrator) Why, Big Boss, *she exclaimed,* I can marry you very very well indeed! . . . *And so the Big Boss was very happy.* (smile broadly) *And Jenny Lou was very happy . . .*

(Jenny Lou, happily point to wedding ring finger, smile broadly)

(Narrator) *And the Happy Horse was very happy!*

(Jenny Lou, repeat rhythmic hoofbeats. Bow and exit)

LUNCH AT PIERRE'S

Character: Mr. Burke, the boss, and Lucy Miller, his secretary (double role).

(Mr. Burke, worriedly pace office as you try to figure out the details of a business paper in your hand) Let's see . . . if we promise to start construction on August 5th (shake head) better make it the 10th . . . (set paper on desk, briefly scribble, look around in annoyance) Where's that secretary of mine? . . . (look up as Lucy enters) Hurry, Miss Miller . . . is he out there?

(Lucy, puzzled) Is *who* out there, Mr. Burke?

(Mr. Burke, nervously) The man who may give us a fifty-thousand-dollar building contract, that's who! Mr. Samuel B. Stanton of the Acme Company.

(Lucy, unimpressed) Sounds like a big man . . . (shrug, hold hand at low level) and he's probably a *little* big. (giggle)

(Mr. Burke, frown) Very funny, Miss Miller. (shove the paper at her) He'll be here in a few minutes . . . and we *must* have this contract ready for him to sign. (sit at desk) Read me the first paragraph.

(Lucy, sit on chair at side of desk, pretend to read) *You promised to take me to lunch.*

(Mr. Burke, briskly rub hands) *You promised to take me to lunch?* . . . (impatiently, as you realize her words) Look, Miss Miller, we've got a fifty-thousand-dollar contract at stake and you talk of food. Who can think of food at a time like this?

(Lucy, grin, nod, point to self) I can.

(Mr. Burke, more gently) We'll go to lunch *tomorrow*. (wave hand) Read the second paragraph.

(Lucy, pretend to read, speak with firmness and finality) *You promised.*

(Mr. Burke, baffled) We promised *what?*

(Lucy) Not *we* . . . *you.* (take from pocket a paper the same size and color as the business paper) Look, Mr. Burke, today's menu from Pierre's . . . They're featuring lobster salad and you promised . . .

(Mr. Burke, rise, lean close to Lucy with a strained effort at self-control) I *know* I *promised.* Well, let me tell you, Miss Miller, that I am a promise-breaker. I am known *all over the world* for breaking promises. In college I was nicknamed Old Promise-Breaker Burke. I *like* to break my secretary's heart by canceling my promise to take her to lunch. (throw up arms in despair) Fifty thousand dollars and all you can think of is Pierre's!

(Lucy, lightly weep, dab eyes with handkerchief) I'm sorry, Mr. Burke . . . I was overcome.

(Mr. Burke, tenderly) Miss Miller . . . (affectionately) *Lucy* . . . I promise to buy you a dozen lobster salads if you go along with me just this once. (as Lucy sniffs, recovers) That's my girl . . . (business-like, as you glance at watch) He ought to be here by now . . . quickly, read that third paragraph . . .

(Lucy, read) *Construction on the new school auditorium will begin on August 10th with two fresh lobsters and a cup of mayonnaise* . . . (glance in alarm at Mr. Burke, quickly tear up one of the papers) Goodbye, little lobster . . . (place torn pieces on edge of table)

(Mr. Burke, as you hear door in outer office) He's here! (nervously) Take the contract . . . (hand it to her) and keep him amused while I finish up in here.

(Lucy, exit)

(Note: If performed by one player, the stage is empty for a moment; if performed by two players, Mr. Burke fusses with papers on his desk for a moment)

(Lucy, brightly entering) Mr. Burke, he said he didn't have to see you, just wanted to take the contract. He said he'd send it back later. (dreamily) A dozen lobster salads . . .

(Mr. Burke, puzzled) I don't understand that. (briefly fuss with papers)

(Lucy, take one of the torn pieces from the corner of the desk, gaze longingly at it) Mr. Burke, do you think we can still make it to Pierre's? . . . (stare in dismay at the paper) Oh, dear . . .

(Mr. Burke) What is it, Lucy?

(Lucy, fearfully, as you back away) You know that contract I gave Mr. Stanton?

(Mr. Burke, lighthearted) Yes, what about it?

(Lucy, fearfully back away) It . . . it . . . was the Pierre menu!

(Mr. Burke, stand, freeze in shock as you gesture to paper in Lucy's fingers) That . . . what's that?

(Lucy, sniff, nod, wiggle paper) That's part of the contract . . .

(Mr. Burke, in total shock, close eyes, slam fists against forehead, groan, race offstage)

(Note: For one player, the stage is empty for a moment; if performed by two players, Lucy sadly walks to desk, fingers the torn pieces of the contract)

(Mr. Burke, stomp back on stage, angrily wave hands) Do you know what, Miss Miller? He's *gone?* He'll never sign the contract now. (fiercely, bite every word as you stand very close to Lucy) *Do you know that I'm ruined?*

(Lucy, sob) I'm sorry, Mr. Burke . . . I'm sorry!

(Mr. Burke, angrily stomp about) I'm ruined and you're sorry! Why couldn't *you* be ruined and *me* sorry? (sternly shove page of contract at her) File this, Miss Miller . . . (growl) File this alongside your *last pay check.* And don't worry about your next job . . . I'm sure Pierre can use you as a waitress! (slam fists against forehead)

(Lucy, sadly stare at contract page, walk away, pick up real or imaginary phone as it rings) Good afternoon, Mr. Burke's office. (dramatically wave hand) Pierre's calling?

(Mr. Burke) Ooooooh . . .

(Lucy) Just a moment please. Mr. Stanton! (give phone over)

(Mr. Burke) Hello, Mr. Stanton. We sent you to Pierre's and you're enjoying the *lobster salad?* . . . *Hope I can make it there to discuss the contract?* Certainly I'll bring my secretary along, and we can work there. See you in a few minutes! (Hang up phone, speak affectionately as you extend open arms) Lucy . . . you're a genius . . .

(Lucy, sigh, speak affectionately) No, Mr. Burke . . . just hungry.

(Mr. Burke, offer arm to Lucy) Pierre's for lunch?

(Lucy, take his arm) Pierre's it is! (happily exit)

ARKWOOD TWO-FOUR-TWO-FOUR

Character: Anyone, trying to get a phone connection and the operator (double role).

(Man cheerfully dial phone) Operator, please give me Ark-wood two-four-two-four.

(Operator) Did you say *Hark*wood two-four-two-four?

(Man, patiently) No, ma'am . . . *Ark*wood.

(Operator) *Sark*wood?

(Man, with minor annoyance) No, no . . . *Ark*wood . . . *ark-ark-ark* . . .

(Operator) If you're *choking,* sir, I'll be glad to call a doctor.

(Man, annoyed) *Please!* . . . I'll stop *choking* if you'll stop *joking.* I want Arkwood two-four-two-four.

(Operator) Did you say *Barkwood?* . . . that's a dog-pound.

(Man) Please try and get me *Arkwood* . . . you know *ark.* (try hard to explain) Look, what kept Noah from getting wet?

(Operator, innocently) His *raincoat?*

(Man, shout in exasperation) All I want is Noah's Ark . . . (flustered) I mean *Arkwood.*

(Operator, calmly, efficiently) Sorry, sir, we have no listing for a Mr. Noah Ark. Shall I connect you with the shipyard?

(Man, scowl) Why don't you connect yourself with a fast boat to China. (plead) Look, if you can't get me Arkwood, try *Lark*wood, maybe you'll end up with Arkwood.

(Operator) Did you say *Lark*wood?

(Man, sigh in resignation) Yes, *Lark*wood . . . *lark-lark-lark* . . . like a bird.

(Operator, cheerfully) We *do* have a listing for a Mr. *Eagle* . . . also a Miss *Dove*.

(Man, completely worn out) Anyone—bird, beast or fish— as long as it's not *you*.

(Operator) Here's your number, sir . . . Arkwood two-four-two-four.

(Man, delighted, shout) That's it! That's it! How did you manage?

(Operator, coyly) I just closed my eyes and stabbed at it with my little old finger!

(Man, deeply sigh) Thanks for the fun.

(Operator, eagerly) Please, sir, let me know the next time you want a *Lake*view number. Think of all the fun we can have with *Lake* . . . like *cake* and *steak* and *ache!* (bow and exit)

HOW TO HYPNOTIZE

Character: A teacher of hypnotism and his (or her) student (double role). A prominently displayed sign reads, *School of Hypnotism.*

(Enter as student, greet teacher) Good morning, sir, and hocus pokus to you. I'd like to become a hypnotist.

(Teacher, who is the breezy type) Ah, yes! And why do you wish to be a hypnotist?

(Student, eagerly grin) I wish to have (shout, wildly wave arms) *power over people!*

(Teacher, loudly, confident, hold up finger) When I get through with you the very world will *tremble* at your name! (quietly) By the way, what *is* your name?

(Student) Alphonso Grupp.

(Teacher, scowl) *Alphonso Grupp?* Never mind, we'll change it to Grupp the Great. Now the first thing you must learn is to *act like the master that you are!* I'll show you how! (roll hands before student, speak in a low, slow, persuasive voice as you hypnotize him) Look into my eyes . . . look deeply into my eyes . . . What do you see in my eyes?

(Student, carefully peer into teacher's eyes, shake head) I see little red lines . . . did you have a sleepless night?

(Teacher, impatiently) Come, come, down to business! (again hypnotize student) Sleep . . . sleep . . . sleep . . . your eyes are growing heavy . . . heavy . . . your eyes are very, very *heavy* . . .

(Student, suddenly droop head, but keep eyes open) My eyes are so heavy they weigh down my head!

(Teacher, angrily shout) That's not what I mean! (sigh) I will now show you how to control your subject so that he will obey your every command. (again hypnotize student) Sleep . . . sleep . . . you're going to sleep . . .

(Student, close eyes in sleep, snore) Zzzzz . . . zzzzz . . . zzzzz . . .

(Teacher, briskly, happily rub hands together) You are now in my power . . . you will now lend me fifty dollars . . . lend me fifty dollars . . .

(Student, hypnotized, speak slowly) I . . . don't . . . have . . . fifty . . . dollars . . .

(Teacher, scowl) You will lend me *five* dollars . . . do you hear? . . . you will lend me *five* dollars . . .

(Student) I . . . don't . . . have . . . five . . . dollars . . .

(Teacher, scowl, impatiently snap fingers to wake him up) Wake up! (point to door, scream) And *go!*

(Student, eagerly) Am I ready? Am I a hypnotist?

(Teacher, scowl) No, you're just *broke!*

(Student, happily flex muscles) That's funny . . . I feel like a powerful hypnotist. Let me practice on you . . . by the way, how much do I owe you?

(Teacher, hold out palm) Fifty dollars—*cash!*

(Student, hypnotically rolling hands toward teacher, speaking hypnotically) How . . . much . . . did . . . you . . . say?

(Teacher, eyes closed, hypnotized) I . . . said . . . *five* . . . dollars.

(Student, still rolling hands) How much?

(Teacher) To . . . you . . . my . . . boy . . . free . . . of . . . charge . . .

(Student) Come . . . again? . . .

(Teacher) I'll . . . pay . . . *you* . . . fifty . . . dollars . . .

311

(dig into pocket, hand student money) Here . . . you . . . are . . .

(Student, eagerly count money, snap fingers at teacher) Thank you, sir, you are a most excellent teacher. _EXIT JEN_

(Teacher, now awake, speak proudly as you wave goodbye) Goodbye, young man . . . (to self as you rub hands in self-satisfaction) What a master teacher I am! (suddenly frown, pull out empty pockets) Maybe *too* good a teacher! (Sadly bow, exit shaking head) _BACK CU3 ON SIGN_

THE PROFESSOR AND THE STARS

Character: Professor Blanktop, an unusual astronomer, and his interviewer (double role). If played by a single performer, quickly shift back and forth between two chairs that face each other.

(Interviewer, who holds paper and pencil) Good evening, Professor Blanktop. We feel very fortunate in having this interview with one of the world's greatest astronomers. For our first question, professor, do you think the moon is really inhabited?

(Professor, who is oddly dressed and who speaks just as oddly) *Inhabited?* . . . what do you mean *inhabited?*

(Interviewer) I mean . . . do you think people *live* there?

(Professor) Why didn't you say so? Of course people live on the moon . . . (gesture) I talk with them every night.

(Interviewer, amazed) You talk with moon-people every night? . . . through thousands of miles of space? . . . but how is that possible?

(Professor, smile affably) We talk in loud voices.

(Interviewer, sigh) Professor, tell us, what is the most interesting thing you have ever seen through your telescope?

(Professor, frown in puzzlement) My *what-a-scope?*

(Interviewer, impatiently) Your *telescope . . . telescope!*

(Professor, brightly) Oh, yes, that long thing. (pretend to hold telescope to eye) Well, the most interesting thing I've seen is the new comet named Susanna Smith.

(Interviewer) Oh, you've seen a new comet which you've named after an old girl friend!

(Professor) No, I've seen a new girl friend whom I've named after an old comet named Susanna Smith.

312

(Interviewer) But how come you saw a girl when you were looking up like this? (pretend to hold telescope to eye which is pointed toward sky)

(Professor) Because when I was looking up like this (pretend to look through telescope toward sky) I found it more interesting to look down like this. (lower telescope so that you are looking slightly down as if at street)

(Interviewer) But why did you name your lady friend after a *comet?*

(Professor, sadly) Every time I ask her for a date . . . (zoom palm through air) she zooms away.

(Interviewer, more and more confused) I see. Now then, I understand that you believe that a man on Mars has three ears? . . . isn't that rather strange?

(Professor, shrug) I don't know . . . he has three eyes.

(Interviewer) Professor Blanktop, it is a proven fact that the earth circles the sun, yet I recently heard you say that the sun circles the earth.

(Professor) That is right . . . now what is your question?

(Interviewer) But how can you say that the sun circles the earth?

(Professor, rise) Very simple . . . I can say it like this . . . (hold up finger, speak in monotone) The-sun-circles-the-earth. (sit)

(Interviewer) I see. (desperately) Tell us, professor, in what direction is the planet Jupiter?

(Professor, gesture upward) Up.

(Interviewer, shrug) Most astronomers work at night but I understand you prefer day work. Why is that?

(Professor, cheerfully) Less stars, less work.

(Interviewer) Professor Blanktop, what first got you interested in astronomy?

(Professor) My mother told me to hitch my wagon to a star.

(Interviewer) By that she meant that you should be ambitious, that you should strive for great things?

(Professor, wonderingly) Oh . . . is *that* what she meant?

(Interviewer) Tell us, professor, what is there about the moon that's so romantic? Why do lovers always sit under the moon?

(Professor, with authority) Lovers *have* to sit under the

moon. (gesture to left) Sit over there . . . and you're under
the moon. (gesture to right) Sit over there . . . and you're
under the moon. No matter *where* you sit you're under the
moon. Even *haters* sit under the moon.

(Interviewer, nod wearily) Very logical, professor. Tell us,
how long would it take a rocket ship to reach the planet Mercury?

(Professor, pull out a large sheet of paper and a pencil, briefly
pretend to figure it out, frown as you cross out, again scribble,
smile broadly as you finish) Six years, ten days, five hours, eight
minutes and four seconds.

(Interviewer, in admiration) How did you figure it out so
fast?

(Professor, shrug) I didn't—it was just a guess.

(Interviewer, baffled) But what were you doing with that
pencil and paper?

(Professor, grin, hold up the sheet of paper to reveal a large
drawing of a girl and with the name *Susanna* printed below) I
was sketching Susanna Smith!

(Interviewer, wearily) Professor, can't you talk about anything
but Susanna Smith?

(Professor, nod slowly) Well, there's *Sylvia* Smith.

(Interviewer) Who is *Sylvia* Smith?

(Professor, turn sheet over to reveal another large picture of a
girl with *Sylvia* printed below) Susanna's *sister* . . . she's even
prettier.

(Interviewer, draw a deep breath, shake head) Professor Blanktop, as a final question . . . do you have any advice to give
all those young men out there (gesture toward audience) who
might wish to become astronomers?

(Professor, rise, hold up finger) I have just one thing to tell
them . . .

(Interviewer, rise) And that is? . . .

(Professor, sternly) Don't go peeking around for Susanna
Smith! (walk away, wag finger at audience) Find your own
comets! (exit)

YES, OFFICER!

Character: A lady driver and a policeman (double role).

(As Lady, sit on chair with hands held up as if on steering wheel. As Officer, stand facing chair with pencil and pad in hand. Quickly change positions for change of character)

(Lady, drive while briskly turning steering wheel back and forth)

(Officer, hold hand up to indicate *halt,* shout sternly) Lady!

(Lady, indicate your halt by holding steering wheel motionless, speak in frightened manner) Yes, officer?

(Officer, dip hand up and down and back and forth to indicate the lady's erratic driving, speak sharply in reproving manner) Lady!

(Lady, meekly) Yes, officer.

(Officer, shake head in further reproval, speak kindly) Lady.

(Lady, nod meekly) Yes, officer.

(Officer, business-like, sternly, as you hold up pad and start to write) Lady!

(Lady, frightened) Yes, officer?

(Officer, again go through erratic driving motions to indicate the necessity of your action, shake head reprovingly) Lad-eee.

(Lady, peer at writing, sob) Yes, officer.

(Officer, weakening somewhat, stop writing, unhappily shake head) Lady.

(Lady, sob louder) Yes, officer?

(Officer, make a vain effort at sternness) Lady!

(Lady, wildly sob) Yes, officer?

(Officer, very weak, sympathetically offer your handkerchief) Lady?

(Lady, take handkerchief, dab eyes) Yes, officer.

(Officer, baffled for a moment, suddenly put pad and pencil in pocket, speak sternly) Lady!

(Lady, weepingly look up) Yes, officer?

(Officer, point to lady, make erratic driving motions as if to urge her to admit erratic driving) Lady?

(Lady, nod, admitting her erratic driving) Yes, officer.

(Officer, point to lady, make gently swaying up and down motions as if to suggest her future manner of driving) Lady?

315

(Lady, eagerly, hopefully) Yes, officer!

(Officer, sigh, wave goodbye) Lady.

(Lady, happily, as you gently move steering wheel back and forth to indicate careful driving, exclaim gratefully) Yes, officer!

THE WILD, WILD WEST

Character: Cowboys fighting a duel (double role).

(Gus, hand on holster) I'm going to plug you, Saddlebag Sam.

(Sam, hand on holster) You're going to need plugging after I fill you with holes, Gunsmoke Gus.

(Gus) You coyote.

(Sam) You rattlesnake.

(Gus) You no-good cattle-rustler.

(Sam) You excellent horse thief.

(Gus, taking a step) I'm coming for you, Sam.

(Sam, taking a step) I'm heading for you, Gus.

(Gus) Take a last look at the sunrise, Sam.

(Sam) It happens to be sunset, Gus.

(Gus) Don't tell me I don't know sunrise from sunset, Sam.

(Sam) Don't tell me I don't know sunset from sunrise, Gus.

(Gus) You're going to taste lead, Sam.

(Sam) Too early for dinner, Gus.

(Gus, stepping forward) I'm coming, Sam.

(Sam, stepping forward) Me, too, Gus.

(Gus) You're a copycat, Sam.

(Sam) You're a polecat, Gus.

(Gus) Say your last word, Sam.

(Sam) Speak your last piece, Gus.

(Gus) Never was much for talking, Sam.

(Sâm) Nor me, Gus.

(Gus) Ready, Sam?

(Sam) Ready, Gus.

(Gus, shooting) Bang, Sam.

(Sam, shooting) Bang, Gus.

(Gus) You're a bad shot, Sam.

(Sam) You, too, Gus.

(Gus) Have a glass of buttermilk with me, Sam?

(Sam) Sure thing, Gus.

HOW!

Character: An Indian and a cowboy (double role). Speak quickly.

(Indian, hold palm out in greeting) How!

(Cowboy, baffled) What?

(Indian, shake head) Not *what* . . . (palm out) *How!*

(Cowboy) Why *how?*

(Indian, shake head) Not *why how* . . . just (palm out) *How!*

(Cowboy) Why just *how?*

(Indian, shrug) That's the way I talk.

(Cowboy) When?

(Indian) Now.

(Cowboy, palm out) *Now how?*

(Indian, shake head) Not *now how* . . . (with emphasis as you extend palm three times) *How! How! How!*

(Cowboy, puzzled) *Who?* how! how! how! . . .

(Indian, point to cowboy) *You* how.

(Cowboy, point to self) *Me* how?

(Indian, point to cowboy) Not *me* how . . . *you* how.

(Cowboy) *Where* how?

(Indian) *Here* how, *you* how, *now* how.

(Cowboy, puzzled) *How* do I how?

(Indian, palm out to show him) *How how!*

(Cowboy, palm out) How!

(Indian, exhausted) Next time let's just say hello! (bow and exit)

STAGECOACH

Character: A stagecoach driver and his shotgun guard, Sureshot (double role). Set scene by placing two chairs alongside each other facing audience with a sign tacked to top, reading *Arizona Stagecoach.*

(As driver, sit on chair, turn head and speak to Sureshot) Keep your shotgun handy, Sureshot . . . the hills are swarming with bandits.

(Sureshot, with toy rifle, sit on chair) Right, do the driving, and I'll pick off the robbers.

(Driver, snap reins, shout to horses) Hiiiii! (Note: Throughout rest of monologue, bounce about on chairs, as if riding a rough road)

(Driver, alarmed as you see robber, gesture to left) There's one!

(Sureshot, quickly aim, shoot) Bang! (blow smoke from barrel)

(Driver, gesture to right) There's another!

(Sureshot, aim, shoot) Bang!

(Driver, gesture upward) Up there!

(Sureshot, shoot) Bang!

(Driver, gesture downward) Down there!

(Sureshot, shoot) Bang!

(Driver, gesture outward) Behind that rock!

(Sureshot, shoot) Bang!

(Driver, look happily about) Looks like we got them!

(Sureshot, nod) Yep, but we might have a rough trip back.

(Driver, frown) How come?

(Sureshot, aim rifle) 'Cause every time I aimed . . .

(Driver) Yes? . . .

(Sureshot, sadly) I *missed!* (bow and exit)

BUILD YOUR OWN ACT!

The solo acts you have just read are just to serve as examples—to help you write your own solo show. The whole idea is to make some remarks (preferably funny) about an object or a series of objects. Listed below are fifty familiar items that can be turned into comical programs.

1. empty bottle
2. toy
3. bell
4. box of crackers
5. coat
6. apple
7. letters
8. camera
9. cup
10. length of rope
11. pie
12. ball
13. woman's hat
14. broom
15. dog collar
16. sack of popcorn
17. salt shaker
18. jewelry
19. whistle
20. bar of soap
21. can of paint
22. buttons
23. loaf of bread
24. pencil
25. menu
26. doughnut
27. bottle of perfume
28. pillow
29. mask
30. candy
31. bouquet
32. calendar
33. towel
34. jar of glue
35. shoes
36. sandwich
37. newspaper
38. musical instrument
39. orange
40. flowers
41. cookbook
42. mirror
43. frying pan
44. photographs
45. blanket
46. box of crayons
47. sugar bowl
48. flashlight
49. window shade
50. jar of vitamins

Section 8

Duologues

Rehearse your act several times before you perform until it goes smoothly. Also, more ideas will occur to you on how to improve your act as you rehearse. Substitute your own names for the characters in these skits if you wish.

FUNNY BUSINESS

Scene: Living room, Fred is reading a book. Paul enters.

FRED: Hello, Paul.

PAUL: Hello, Fred.

FRED: Come on in. Shut the door.

PAUL: Why?

FRED: It's cold outside.

PAUL: Will shutting the door make it any warmer outside?

FRED: Look, Paul, we're here to figure out ways to make some money. Do you have any ideas?

PAUL: One or two. But I'm pretty discouraged just now.

FRED: What happened?

PAUL: Last week I sent my picture to a friendship club for lonely people. Today they sent it back with a note that nobody was *that* lonely.

FRED: Cheer up. You'll feel better once you start making some money. Are you in any business just now?

PAUL: In a way. I'm in the food business.

FRED: The selling part?

PAUL: No. The eating part.

FRED: Hmmm. We'll have to do better than that. Maybe we could start a ranch. Do you know anything about cattle?

PAUL: Well, my father once raised a big ox.

FRED: Oh, *you* aren't so big.

PAUL: Wasn't that nice of me to give you that funny line?

FRED: That's real friendship. By the way, did you have a good time last night on your date with Lois?

PAUL: Great time. We spent two dollars.

FRED: Is that all?

PAUL: Well, that's all she had.

FRED: Let's get back to business. You know, I think we'd better make our second million first.

PAUL: Why?

FRED: You know what they say—the first million is the hardest.

PAUL: I hear you put on a comedy show the other night.

FRED: That's right.

PAUL: How did it come off?

FRED: The first night nobody came.

PAUL: What about the second night?

FRED: Business fell off a little.

PAUL: I think I know why, don't you?

FRED: I know why. We'd better get out of here.

PAUL: Fast! (*They exit.*)

HELP WANTED

Scene: Employment office. Fred, the employer, is seated at a desk. Paul, the applicant, enters.

FRED: Ah, good morning, young man! Before we hire you, there are a few questions I'd like to ask. Why don't you start out by telling me a few things about yourself.

PAUL: Well, in the fifth grade I won third place in the hundred-yard dash. Or, was it fifth place in the third grade?

FRED: Uh, young man, I don't mean things like that. Where were you born?

PAUL: I was born in New York but went to school in Chicago.

FRED: Wasn't that a pretty long walk? . . . Well, let's see—what to ask you next. Oh, yes, we like our young men to be on fire with ambition. Take me, for example. A few years ago I made up my mind to become a millionaire.

PAUL: Did you make it?

FRED: No, I found it easier to change my mind. By the way, young man, you were supposed to be here at nine, and here it is ten-thirty. How come you're late?

PAUL: I can explain that, sir. The alarm clock failed me.

FRED: How?

PAUL: Well, there are six at our house but the alarm was set for only five.

FRED: A very reasonable explanation. Now then, you understand that we want a very responsible young man.

PAUL: In that case I'm just perfect. I have often been told that I am responsible—whenever things go wrong.

FRED: Splendid! Next, let's test your good judgment. What would you do with a million dollars?

PAUL: I don't know. Quite frankly, sir, I wasn't expecting that much at the start.

FRED: Hmmm. Maybe we'd better test your alertness. Alertness! That's what we need around here. Let's test your eyes and ears. Can you see that butterfly on the building two blocks away?

PAUL: Yes. It's yellow with black spots.

FRED: Amazing!

PAUL: But my hearing is not so good.

FRED: Why not?

PAUL: I can just barely hear that butterfly flutter its wings.

FRED: Young man, you're hired! Oh, I was just about to have lunch. Will you join me in a bowl of soup?

PAUL: Do you think there's room for both of us? (*They exit.*)

323

COMEDY TEAM

Scene: Fred and Paul enter from opposite wings. They meet at the center of the stage, exchange greetings and go into their act.

FRED: Nice seeing you, Paul. How come you look so gloomy?

PAUL: I've got a problem, Fred. Last night I went to a masquerade party.

FRED: And?

PAUL: Someone told me to take off my mask.

FRED: So?

PAUL: I wasn't wearing one.

FRED: I see. By the way, did I borrow a dollar from you last week?

PAUL: No.

FRED: How careless of me. Well, I'll take care of it now.

PAUL: Not so fast. But speaking of money, I hear you've offered a reward of ten dollars for the return of your dog.

FRED: That's right. Did you find him?

PAUL: No, but I'm going to start looking and I thought you might give me a couple of dollars in advance.

FRED: No, but I might buy that wristwatch of yours. How much do you want for it?

PAUL: Fifty dollars.

FRED: Isn't that pretty expensive?

PAUL: Not for a watch like this. I once tossed it into the Mississippi River and it's still running.

FRED: The watch?

PAUL: No, the river.

FRED: Forget the watch. I hear you fell down on the sidewalk last week.

PAUL: That's right.

FRED: Get hurt?

PAUL: No, I just bounced and bounced.

FRED: You *bounced?*

PAUL: Yes, I had on my new spring suit.

FRED: By the way, I hear you're dating one of the pretty Wilson twins.

PAUL: That's right.

FRED: But how do you tell them apart?

PAUL: Who tries?

FRED: Goodbye.

PAUL: See you later. (*They exit.*)

SATURDAY CHATTER

Scene: Fred is working in his front yard. Paul enters and they greet each other.

PAUL: Hello, Fred. Working hard?

FRED: Yes, but I'm puzzled by something.

PAUL: What?

FRED: Last spring I planted a tree in my back yard but it hasn't given a single apple.

PAUL: That's strange.

FRED: Maybe not. It was a peach tree.

PAUL: Do you think peaches are healthy?

FRED: I've never heard one complain.

PAUL: Speaking of work, I always do my hardest work before breakfast.

FRED: What is your hardest work?

PAUL: Getting up. By the way, what time is it?

FRED: One o'clock.

PAUL: That's funny.

FRED: Why?

PAUL: I've asked the same question all day long and everyone gives me a different answer.

FRED: At least you know that it's Saturday. Let's think of something interesting to do.

PAUL: Why not go swimming?

FRED: Why do you like to swim so much?

PAUL: I hear that it's good for the figure.

FRED: Have you ever had a good look at a duck?

PAUL: Hmmm. Maybe we'd better do something else. You know, I feel like asking Gloria Glamourgal (change to name of school's most popular girl) for a date again.

FRED: Again?

PAUL: Yes. I felt like it once before. Besides, I have to get my car fixed before I go on a date.

FRED: How did you damage your car?

PAUL: I started to cross a bridge.

FRED: And?

PAUL: There wasn't one.

FRED: We'd better quit, Paul.

PAUL: Right, Fred. (*They exit.*)

GIRL TALK

Scene: Lois is seated on a chair, having her hair fixed by Ruth. They talk.

LOIS: How is it coming?

RUTH: It looks fine. Your boy friend will be proud of you tonight. By the way, do you know how to keep your youth?

LOIS: How?

RUTH: Don't introduce him to other girls.

LOIS: Speaking of boys, I saw the handsomest football player at school yesterday. But he was annoying me.

RUTH: Lois! How can you say that? I was right there, and he didn't notice you.

LOIS: I know. That's what annoyed me.

RUTH: I got a book for my boy friend.

LOIS: Well, that sounds like a fair trade.

RUTH: Maybe you should be in a comedy show. Incidentally, what's the difference between a boy and a goat?

LOIS: I don't know.

RUTH: You must have some funny dates. Hold still! I can't fix your hair if you wiggle like that.

LOIS: Speaking of boys, don't you find them changeable?

RUTH: What do you mean?

LOIS: Well, take Fred.

RUTH: No, you take Fred.

LOIS: What's he like?

RUTH: Oh, cake, candy—he likes everything.

LOIS: No, I mean what is his background?

RUTH: His father is a wealthy man.

LOIS: In what way?

RUTH: He owns a newspaper.

LOIS: Oh, we have lots of those around the house.

RUTH: Did you hear that Susie is keeping her engagement a secret?

LOIS: How do you know?

RUTH: She told me.

LOIS: Finished with my hair?

RUTH: All through. I hope you have fun tonight.

LOIS: I'll tell you all about it tomorow. Where can I get hold of you?

RUTH: Not in too many places—I'm very ticklish.

LOIS: Thanks for fixing my hair.

RUTH: Thanks for helping me with this act! (*They exit.*)

BUS STOP

Scene: A bus stop. As Lois waits, Ruth enters.

RUTH: Hello, Lois. Are you taking the bus home?

LOIS: Oh, hello Ruth. What did you ask?

RUTH: *Are* you talking the bus home?

LOIS: No. My dad would just make me take it back.

RUTH: Fun-ny. Speaking of funny things, you should have seen me down at the football stadium yesterday.

LOIS: Why? What were you doing?

RUTH: I was having a great time—yelling and jumping and cheering. But tomorrow it's going to be even more fun.

LOIS: How come?

RUTH: They're having a football game.

LOIS: Hmmmm. By the way, I saw your brother George playing football. Is he the oldest in your family?

RUTH: No. My dad is older than my brother.

LOIS: I mean, is he your oldest brother?

RUTH: Yes. He's the oldest.

LOIS: Who comes after him?

RUTH: All the girls at school.

LOIS: I have a very clever brother. In fact, my brother and I know everything there is to know.

RUTH: Is that right? Well, who was the first President of the United States?

LOIS: That's one of the things my brother knows.

RUTH: Well, I know a few things myself. For example, I can forecast the weather.

LOIS: How?

RUTH: Well, you take some tomatoes and carrots and lettuce. You slice them up and place them in a bowl.

LOIS: What does that give you?

RUTH: A vegetable salad.

LOIS: But what about the weather?

RUTH: You look it up in the newspaper.

LOIS: I have a riddle for you. Ready?

RUTH: Ready.

LOIS: What is gray, has eight legs and a trunk?

RUTH: I give up.

LOIS: Two mice on a vacation.

RUTH: See you in class.

LOIS: Goodbye. (*They exit.*)

SCHOOLWORK

Scene: Living room. Lois is seated on the sofa with various books and papers. Ruth enters carrying her books.

LOIS: Ruth! I'm glad you came over to study with me. Maybe you can give me some help. I have a tough question to ask you.

RUTH: All right. What's the subject? History? Science?

LOIS: Oh, I guess you'd call it science. Anyway, here's the question. What is green, has four corners and lives in a swamp?

RUTH: Hmmm. It's green, has four corners and lives in a swamp? I give up.

LOIS: A square frog! By the way, Ruth, how do you like this picture of me? It was painted by one of the boys at school.

RUTH: Funny, but it doesn't look like you.

LOIS: I know. Joe took so long I had my sister step in and pose for me.

RUTH: That was convenient. Speaking of paintings, I'm something of an artist myself. Would you like me to paint your picture?

LOIS: Would I!

RUTH: Shall I paint you in a pink hat?

LOIS: It won't bother me if you want to wear a hat while you paint. By the way, I didn't know you were smart enough to paint my picture.

RUTH: Oh, I'm pretty clever all right. Take, for instance, what happened yesterday on the bus.

LOIS: What happened?

RUTH: Well, I sat next to a man reading a green book. All at once I knew he was a soldier.

LOIS: How?

RUTH: He was wearing a uniform.

LOIS: You know something, Ruth?

RUTH: What?

LOIS: Before it gets any worse, I think we'd better leave. (*They exit.*)

FRED AND LOIS

Scene: Lois is impatiently pacing around the living room. As she glances at her watch, there is a knock on the door.

LOIS: Come in! Fred! You're late!

FRED: I know. I couldn't help it.

LOIS: You were supposed to pick me up at six, and here it is seven.

FRED: I'm sorry.

LOIS: You *should* be; I was ready ten minutes ago. Well, we might as well sit down for a few minutes.

FRED: Say, Lois, do you like me?

LOIS: Of course I like you.

FRED: How much do you like me?

LOIS: How much help do you want on your homework?

FRED: You're right. I need help desperately.

LOIS: All right. What do you want to know?

FRED: What is an emperor?

LOIS: You should know that. An emperor is a ruler.

FRED: Oh, yes. I carried an emperor to school with me last week.

LOIS: Please! Any more questions?

FRED: Yes. Where are the Rockies?

LOIS: Fred, you've just got to remember where you put things!

FRED: Maybe you're right.

LOIS: You know what I think you need? You need to take command of life. Be brave, be daring, be a tiger!

FRED: Grrrrrrrrr.

LOIS: Something like that.

FRED: You know, I may be a greater man than you think. Didn't you see me in action last night?

LOIS: No. Where?

FRED: Down at the stadium. I spoke to fifty thousand people!

LOIS: Fred! Really? What did you say?

FRED: Peanuts! Popcorn! Ice cream!

LOIS: Fred, before we leave I'd like to ask you something.

FRED: Yes?

LOIS: Do you think I'm beautiful?

330

FRED: Yes.

LOIS: Am I gorgeous and charming?

FRED: Yes.

LOIS: Am I the loveliest girl in the world?

FRED: Yes.

LOIS: Oh, Fred, you say the nicest things! (*They exit.*)

RANCH ROMANCE

Scene: A ranch. Fred, a rancher, is working around as Lois enters.

LOIS: Fred! How are you?

FRED: Lois! At last you've paid a visit to my ranch. How do you like it?

LOIS: Just fine. But don't you get lonely so far away from the big city?

FRED: Oh, no. I have my animals for company. For instance, I have a horse worth five thousand dollars.

LOIS: You're kidding me. How could a horse save that much?

FRED: I also have a pet duck. It always stands with one leg held up.

LOIS: Why does it stand like that?

FRED: Well, if it held up both legs it would fall down.

LOIS: I still think it would be lonely out here.

FRED: No, I don't get lonely. But the other day I did write to a friendship club.

LOIS: Tell me about it.

FRED: Well, I sent in a lock of my hair. I told them to put me in touch with anyone who matches it.

LOIS: What happened?

FRED: So far I've heard from two cocker spaniels and a collie.

LOIS: I imagine it's very beautiful out here in the evening. Fred, do you know it's romantic to walk with a girl in the moonlight?

FRED: No, but if you'll hum a few bars I'll try to sing it.

LOIS: Hmmm. We'd better get back to the ranch. Why don't you tell me more about your animals?

FRED: I have about fifty sheep. Every night I tell them to brush their teeth.

LOIS: Isn't it silly to tell sheep to brush their teeth?

FRED: I guess so, since half of them won't do it.

LOIS: I noticed your dog out there. Is he a good watch dog?

FRED: Excellent! If he hears a noise at night he barks like crazy. There's just one problem.

LOIS: What?

FRED: First I have to wake him up.

LOIS: Why don't you train your animals?

FRED: I have a perfectly trained pig.

LOIS: What do you mean?

FRED: Yesterday I called him up to the window. Then I told him *not* to bring in the mail. And do you know, he *didn't* do it!

LOIS: It's been fun, Fred.

FRED: Come again, Lois. (*They exit.*)

YOUR TREASURE CHEST

Want extra laughs in your show? Add these jokes wherever you need them. Just change the names and the backgrounds in any way that makes them right for your act. There is lots of material here—so have lots of fun!

LOIS: Did you meet your brother at the party?

RUTH: Oh, no—I knew him long before that.

FIRST STRANGER: Haven't I seen your face some place else?

SECOND STRANGER: No, it's always been right up here.

FRED: A funny thing happened last night. It snowed twice as much on my neighbor's yard as mine.

PAUL: That's impossible.

FRED: Maybe it's because my neighbor's yard is twice as big.

CUSTOMER: Are these flower seeds guaranteed to grow?

CLERK: Absolutely. If they don't grow, just bring them back and we'll refund your money.

LOIS: Do you have an open mind?

RUTH: Of course. I always listen with an open mind to ideas I think are pure nonsense.

332

LOIS: I'm sorry to hear that you fell down the stairs.
FRED: Oh, it's all right.
LOIS: All right? It is?
FRED: Yes—I had to come down anyway.

FRED: How come you're so late?
PAUL: Well, you remember you told me to take the Tenth Street bus?
FRED: Yes.
PAUL: Well, I fell asleep after the ninth one went by.

LOIS: What's the date?
RUTH: I don't know.
LOIS: Look at the newspaper.
RUTH: No good. That's yesterday's paper.

PASSENGER: This seems like a long voyage, captain. How far are we from land?
CAPTAIN: Three miles.
PASSENGER: Which way?
CAPTAIN: Straight down.

FRED: How much money do you have?
PAUL: Oh, between forty-nine and fifty dollars.
FRED: That's a lot of money.
PAUL: No—it's just one dollar.

LOIS: Why do you still have that string around your finger?
RUTH: You tied it there so I wouldn't forget to mail your letter.
LOIS: Did you mail it?
RUTH: No, you forgot to give it to me.

MOTHER: Did you divide your three pieces of candy with your friend?
SON: No, I made it easy by eating one first.

SON: Dad, will you buy me a drum?
DAD: No. A drum is too noisy.
SON: I promise to play it only when you're asleep.

333

FRED: Why are you jumping up and down on your garden?
PAUL: I'm raising mashed potatoes.

LOIS: How come you didn't wait to see the second act of the play?
RUTH: I couldn't wait. The program said to took place a year later.

FRED: London has more fog than any city in the world.
LOIS: I've been in a foggier city than London.
FRED: What city was that?
LOIS: It was so foggy I couldn't tell.

FRED: Some day I might be so famous they'll put my face on some money.
PAUL: I'd just like to get my *hands* on some.

LOIS: What did you have for dinner tonight?
RUTH: Three guesses.
LOIS: You must be hungry.

MOTHER: It took lots of strength for you to pull out that big weed.
SON: Yes, the whole world was hanging onto its roots.

LOIS: What are you looking for, Fred?
FRED: A dime I lost on Broadway.
LOIS: If you lost it on Broadway, why are you looking for it here on Main Street?
FRED: There's more light here.

FRED: I learned to dance in one night.
LOIS: I can tell.

FRED: Are there any athletes in your family?
PAUL: My brother has been swimming for five years.
FRED: He must be pretty tired.

LOIS: Is it raining outside?
RUTH: Have you ever seen it raining inside?

PASSENGER: Will you be able to bring this airplane down safely?
PILOT: I haven't ever left an airplane up.

FRED: Paul, I want to be fair about the use of the sled this winter. Let's share it.
PAUL: Fair enough. We'll go fifty-fifty.
FRED: Good. You have it going uphill and I'll have it going down.

STUDENT: Teacher, would you scold me for something I didn't do?
TEACHER: Of course not.
STUDENT: Well, I didn't do my homework.

FRED: You certainly did a bad job of painting this house.
PAUL: Well, you said that it needed painting badly.

FRED: Can you imagine anyone sleeping with his shoes on?
PAUL: Who would do that?
FRED: My horse.

LOIS: Are handsome men always conceited?
FRED: Not always. I'm not.

LOIS: It's fun to lie in bed in the morning and ring a bell for a servant.
RUTH: Do you have a servant?
LOIS: No, but I have a bell.

MOTHER: Did you learn anything in school today?
SON: I guess not. I have to go back tomorrow.

LOIS: Have a cold?
RUTH: No thanks, I already have one.

FRED: I'll have you know I run things around my house.
PAUL: You do?
FRED: Sure—things like the lawn mower and the vacuum cleaner.

335

DINER: I'd like a cheese sandwich without lettuce.
WAITER: Sorry, but we're out of lettuce. Can I give it to you without butter?

VISITOR: Which side of the sheep has the most wool?
FARMER: The outside.

FRED: What is a myth?
PAUL: A female moth?

FRED: Say, Paul, how come you're wearing my raincoat?
PAUL: You wouldn't want me to get your best suit wet, would you?

FRED: Did you have any luck hunting mountain lions?
PAUL: Yes. I didn't meet one.

CARPENTER: You hammer nails like lightning.
HELPER: You mean I'm fast?
CARPENTER: No—you never strike twice in the same place.

FRED: Speaking of girls, I can go out with any girl I please.
PAUL: Then why don't you?
FRED: I don't please any.

FISHERMAN: You've been watching me fish for five hours. Why don't you fish for yourself?
SPECTATOR: I don't have the patience.

FRED: Do you think you're handsome?
PAUL: No, but what's my opinion against thousands of others?

LOIS: Have you any poor relatives?
RUTH: None that I know.
LOIS: Have you any rich relatives?
RUTH: None that know me.

FRED: Did your watch stop when it hit the floor?
PAUL: Did you expect it to go all the way through?

MOTHER: I sent my boy to your shop for two pounds of cookies, but you gave him only one.

GROCER: Have you *weighed* your boy, Madam?

FIRST GOLFER: Well, how do you like my game?

SECOND GOLFER: It's all right, but I still prefer golf.

LOIS: The man I marry must be as bold as a lion, as handsome as a movie star and as charming as a prince.

FRED: How lucky we met.

POLICEMAN: You're driving down a one-way street!

MOTORIST: It's all right. I'm only going one way.

LOIS: Why not come over for dinner tonight?

FRED: Could we make it tomorrow night?

LOIS: Why, yes. What are you doing tonight?

FRED: Your sister invited me over for dinner.

DINER: Looks like rain, doesn't it, waiter?

WAITER: Yes, sir, but I'm sure you'll find it tastes like soup.

FRED: What do you have in that box, Paul?

PAUL: An eagle—to keep the crows out of my cornfield.

FRED: But your cornfield is only imaginary.

PAUL: So is the eagle.

FIRST TOURIST: I was in Switzerland last year.

SECOND TOURIST: How did you like the Swiss Alps?

FIRST TOURIST: Very nice people.

337

FRED: Say, Paul, how come you always sit in the dark with a newspaper?

PAUL It rests my eyes.

FRED: But you can't read the paper in the dark.

PAUL: I know—that's how it rests my eyes.

LOIS: Want to hear something funny? Linda thinks that a football coach has four wheels.

RUTH: Ha! And how many wheels *does* it have?

LOIS: Why do you carry your lunch?

RUTH: Because it can't walk.

FRED: What kind of a dog is that?

PAUL: A police dog.

FRED: He doesn't look like a police dog to me.

PAUL: Of course not.

FRED: What do you mean?

PAUL: He's in plain clothes.

LOIS: Name five things that contain milk.

RUTH: Butter, cheese, ice cream and two cows.

SMALL GIRL: Mother, how long is it to my birthday?

MOTHER: Not very long.

SMALL GIRL: Well, is it time for me to start being good?

MOTHER: Did you give the goldfish fresh water today?

SON: No. They didn't finish the water they got yesterday.

FRED: I heard something this morning that really opened my eyes.

LOIS: What?

FRED: My alarm clock.

FIRST HUNTER: Last night a leopard followed my tracks.

SECOND HUNTER: What happened?

FIRST HUNTER: Well, he seemed to like my tracks so well that I made more of them.

LOIS: Has your little brother learned to talk?

RUTH: Yes. Now we're teaching him to stop.

FRED: Let's go kite-flying.

PAUL: All right, but we'd better take my kite only.

FRED: Why?

PAUL: There's wind enough for only one.

TEACHER: What's the difference between North and South America?

PUPIL: In North America they drink their coffee out of cups; in South America they drink it out of doors.

FRED: How do your friends treat you?

PAUL: Not very often.

FRED: Does your roof leak?

PAUL: Only when it rains.

FRED: Do you know who's in the hospital?

PAUL: No, who?

FRED: Sick people.

VOICE: Hello. Is this the pet shop?

CLERK: Yes, but I can't hear you very well over the phone.

VOICE: Please send me a package of goldfish food.

CLERK: I can hardly hear you. Please speak louder.

VOICE: I want a package of goldfish food.

CLERK: Please speak louder.

VOICE: I can't. I'm a goldfish.

FRED: I never get wet when it rains.
PAUL: How come?
FRED: I stay inside.

FRED: Can I borrow your lawn mower?
PAUL: Sure, as long as you don't take it out of my yard.

FATHER: And that, son, is the story of what your father did during the war.
SON: But, Dad, why did they need all the other soldiers?

LOIS: Last week a tornado hit our house.
RUTH: Hurt it much?
LOIS: Who knows—we haven't found it yet.

FRED: I hear you broke two shovels yesterday. You must work hard.
PAUL: No, but I sure lean hard.

DINER: Do you have any wild duck?
WAITER: No, but you can order a tame one and drive it wild.

LOIS: Why didn't you take a vacation this year?
RUTH: I needed the rest.

FRED: I dreamed I was engaged to the loveliest girl in the world.
LOIS: Did we set the date for the wedding?

BOSS: How many times have you been late this week?
EMPLOYEE: I'm not sure. I thought *you* were keeping count.

FRED: Do you know you can't sell life insurance without a license?
PAUL: I knew I wasn't selling any, but I didn't know why.

DRIVER: When you sold me this car, didn't you guarantee to replace damaged parts?
SALESMAN: That's right.
DRIVER: Well, I want a new garage door.

340

LOIS: Can you understand French?
RUTH: Only when it's written in English.

LOIS: Is it true that a lion won't hurt you if you carry a torch?
FRED: It depends on how fast you carry it.

FRED: Let's test your arithmetic. If you had fifty dollars and I asked you for ten, how many dollars would you have left?
PAUL: Fifty.

LOIS: What's the idea of waking me up?
RUTH: It's time for your sleeping pill.

LOIS: Say, Fred, how come you take your bows before the play begins?
FRED: I want to make sure I still have an audience.

FRED: Do you drink lemonade?
LOIS: What else can you do with it?

FRED: Wasn't that an interesting dream I had last night?
LOIS: How should I know what you dreamed about?
FRED: You *should* know; you were in it.

LOIS: We're having thousands of things to eat for dinner.
RUTH: How can that be?
LOIS: We're having rice.

FRED: Remember how worried you were that I'd eat your lunch by mistake?
PAUL: Yes.
FRED: Well, your worries are over.

JUNIOR: Mother, we're going to make believe we're animals at the zoo and we need your help.
MOTHER: All right. What can I do?
JUNIOR: You can be the kind lady who gives them peanuts and popcorn.

341

LOIS: Why did you buy that dress?
RUTH: Because I couldn't get it free.

FRED: What kind of suit is that?
PAUL: This is a hunting suit.
FRED: You mean you're going hunting?
PAUL: No, I mean my brother is hunting for it.

MOTHER: What are you looking for?
SON: Nothing.
MOTHER: You'll find that in the cookie jar.

LOIS: There's a new baby boy next door.
RUTH: What's his name?
LOIS: I don't know. I can't understand a word he says.

FRED: When you saw me, was I walking up the street or down the street?
PAUL: You were going down.
FRED: Good. I must have *had* my lunch.

TAXI DRIVER: Here you are at home. That will be two dollars and thirty cents.
PASSENGER: But I have only two dollars. Maybe you'd better back up a few blocks.

DINER: Waiter, I'm not a man to complain, but I just can't eat this salad.
WAITER: I'm sorry, sir. I'll call the manager.
DINER: Mr. Manager, I find it impossible to eat this salad.
MANAGER: I'm sorry to hear that, sir. Let me call the chef.
DINER: Chef, I can't eat the salad.
CHEF: What's wrong with it?
DINER: How would I know? I don't have a fork.

LOIS: What are you planting in your garden?
RUTH: Lettuce, tomatoes, celery and beets.
LOIS: Why plant them all together like that?
RUTH: I want a vegetable salad.

GUIDE: I saw some panther tracks about a mile east.
HUNTER: Good. Which way is west?

FRED: What are you doing?
PAUL: I'm hunting for gold.
FRED: But there's no gold around here.
PAUL: If there was, would I have to hunt for it?

FRED: I'm going to be on a television program.
PAUL: What are you going to do?
FRED: I'm going to be a midget.
PAUL: But you're too tall for a midget.
FRED: I'll be the tallest midget in the world.

LOIS: Say, Fred, I hear that you brought a goat up on the
elevator to the fifth floor of city hall.
FRED: That's right, I had to.
LOIS: Why?
FRED: He wouldn't walk up the stairs.

FRED: How come the audience is still applauding your act?
PAUL: I told them I wouldn't go on until it became quiet.

MAN: What! Dinner isn't ready yet? I think I'll go to a
restaurant.
WIFE: Just a minute.
MAN: Will dinner be ready in a minute?
WIFE: No, but I'll go with you to the restaurant.

LOIS: Have you ever noticed how I laugh at Fred's jokes?
RUTH: His jokes must be clever.
LOIS: No, but I am.

FRED: The countryside is very healthy. All the time I was out
there I didn't pay a single doctor bill.
LOIS: I know—the doctor told me.

CUSTOMER: I'd like to try on those shoes in the window.
CLERK: Sorry, sir, but you'll have to try them on in here.

343

LOIS: That's a nice little dog you have there, but his legs are too short.
RUTH: What do you mean *short?* They reach the ground!

LOIS: How much gas do we have left in the car?
RUTH: I don't know.
LOIS: Well, look at the gas gauge.
RUTH: I did, but I don't know whether it means half full or half empty.

FRED: I used to see spots before my eyes.
PAUL: So what did you do?
FRED: I sold my leopard.

FIRST SALESMAN: I made some valuable contacts today.
SECOND SALESMAN: I didn't sell anything, either.

LOIS: Can you swim?
FRED: At times.
LOIS: What do you mean?
FRED: When I'm in the water.

LOIS: How come you don't laugh any more when the boss tells a joke?
RUTH: I don't have to—I'm leaving Friday.

FRED: How do you spell onion?
PAUL: O-n-y-u-n.
FRED: I think the dictionary spells it o-n-i-o-n.
PAUL: Sure, but you asked how *I* spell it.

FRED: Do you know the best place to find lobsters?
LOIS: Yes.
FRED: Where?
LOIS: On a dinner plate.

FIRST SPACE CADET: Meet you on Mars tonight.
SECOND SPACE CADET: How do I get there?
FIRST SPACE CADET: When you get to the moon, turn left.

344

LOIS: How are you doing with your driving lessons?
RUTH: Great! The road is beginning to turn when I do.

FRED: What's the most you ever weighed?
PAUL: One hundred and twenty pounds.
FRED: What's the least?
PAUL: Six and one-half pounds.

FRED: I can play the violin just like a great artist.
PAUL: In what way?
FRED: I use both hands.

DOCTOR: Hmmm, your pulse is as steady as a clock.
PATIENT: It *should* be; you've got your hand on my watch.

FRED: Last night while driving home I came to a washed-out bridge.
PAUL: Have trouble getting your car across?
FRED: Oh, no. I just sat down and *thought* it over.

LOIS: I've got a great idea for cooking the dinner.
RUTH: What?
LOIS: Let's add a spoonful of soap powder to the recipe.
RUTH: Soap powder? Why?
LOIS: Think of how much easier it will make dishwashing.

BOSS: I wish you wouldn't whistle while you work.
EMPLOYEE: Who's working?

FRED: Did you get invited to the party?
PAUL: I'll be out of town.
FRED: I didn't get invited either.

LOIS: So you and Fred are engaged? I thought it was only a mild friendship.
RUTH: So did Fred.

DINER: I can't eat this terrible food. Call the manager.
WAITER: Sorry, sir, but he won't eat it either.

345

SHOPPER: How much are your tomatoes?

GROCER: Twenty cents a pound.

SHOPPER: At the market down the street they're only ten cents a pound.

GROCER: Why don't you buy them there?

SHOPPER: They haven't any.

GROCER: Well, when we haven't any, our tomatoes are only five cents a pound.

FIRST DETECTIVE: Ah, I can tell that you have on green socks.

SECOND DETECTIVE: How can you tell?

FIRST DETECTIVE: You forgot to put on your shoes.

FRED: I'm a spy on a secret mission.

PAUL: What mission?

FRED: It's so secret they didn't tell me.

LOIS: Well, Fred, did they like your speech at the banquet?

FRED: Yes! When I finally sat down, they said it was the best thing I'd ever done.

LOIS: I'm going home.

FRED: Why?

LOIS: I live there.

FRED: Paul, I'm starving. How about a bite?

PAUL: I'm not so good at it myself, but I'll call my dog.

FRED: I had to buy five tickets to get into that new movie theater.

LOIS: How come?

FRED: Well, every time I stepped inside, they tore them up.

BOSS: You should have been here at nine o'clock.

EMPLOYEE: Why? What happened?

Section 9

Skits for Several Players

The fun in an act is multiplied by the number of players. A comedy skit with a cast of several actors of either sex is always a favorite.

Start by selecting a skit from the following pages. Next, assign your players to their roles. You can have a boy play a girl's part or vice versa.

You can keep the cast small, or you can expand it to include many players. For each speaking role, only one can be assigned, of course, but you can use as many extras as you like. For example, in *Food Fun* you can have a good many diners.

The steps supplied for each skit make it complete and ready for rehearsal. However, you can have lots of extra enjoyment by adding your own personal touches. For instance, in *The Gold Miners,* if your school is having a rally to win subscriptions to the school paper, one of the actors can add the line, "Once we find the gold, we can buy a thousand subscriptions to the school paper!"

An announcer should introduce the acts. He can state the background of the skit and hint briefly at the fun that is to come.

DEFINITIONS

This is just about as simple a stunt as you can imagine. It is especially good for players who are appearing before an audience for the first time, as it gives beginners a chance to develop their talents.

The master of ceremonies comes onstage to tell the audience, "Ladies and gentlemen, I am sure you are all interested in being educated. That is why we are presenting this act. We will give you some definitions of words. A number of our most intelligent

347

scholars have spent considerable time getting exactly the right definitions. I am quite sure you have not heard these before."

One by one the players come onstage. Each supplies a single definition and exits. Players should present different kinds of personal characteristics when giving the definition. One should be solemn, another gay, a third may shout with enthusiasm.

Here are some definitions:

1. *Time:* Time is something that passes slowly between meals.

2. *Parking space:* A parking space is what you see when you're not driving your car.

3. *Good judgment:* Good judgment is what you have when you think I am attractive and charming.

4. *Circle:* A circle is a straight line that got tired of lying down.

5. *Silence:* Silence is a successful substitute for brains.

6. *Happiness:* Happiness is when you enter a gift shop and see all the presents your friends haven't given you.

7. *Experience:* Experience is the polite name we give to our mistakes.

8. *Ant:* An ant is a busy creature who still has time to go to picnics.

9. *Tree:* A tree is something that jumps in front of a careless driver.

10. *Night watchman:* A night watchman is someone who earns his living without doing a day's work.

11. *Cold soup:* Cold soup is something that tastes better when you exchange it for cold ice cream.

12. *Bicycle:* A bicycle is something you take to bed so that you won't have to walk in your sleep.

13. *Will power:* Will power is the ability to eat only one salted peanut.

14. *Good sport:* A good sport is someone who lets you have your own way.

THE FUNNY BOX

This act keeps the audience in suspense. The suspense soon turns to laughter!

The comedian comes onstage carrying a box in which he has a wide assortment of items. The items can be almost anything, as we will discover in a moment. One by one, the comedian holds them up for the audience to see. He then makes a clever or surprising remark about each item.

To prepare yourself for this act, select some simple item. It may be a coin or a book or a ribbon. Now, try to think of a humorous comment to make about it. It is really amazing how you can take almost anything and turn it into a laugh!

Two comedians can perform the act. They merely take turns in commenting upon the objects. If you have a third actor, make him an assistant who hands the objects to the comedians, and makes faces as he works.

Here are enough items to get you started:

1. A love letter with blank pages—sent by a very bashful lover.

2. A piece of string once used to wrap a birthday present from Cleopatra to Julius Caesar. The reason the string is so long is that the present was a pyramid.

3. A leaf once blown into my back yard.

4. A new love song entitled, *Let's Take Another Romantic Stroll in the Moonlight Down by the Riverside, Only Next Time Please Don't Push Me into the Water*.

5. A transistor radio that was dropped from an airplane to see whether it could stand the shock.

6. A shoe. The other one is worn by a very annoyed man

now attracting considerable attention as he limps down Main Street.

7. A dab of grease from the calendar of a man who wanted the year to run smoothly.

8. A rock that absolutely will not sink—unless dropped into water.

9. A ball once bounced against the Great Wall of China by an idle shepherd boy.

10. A pepper shaker with no holes—for people who don't use pepper.

SECRET WISHES!

Here is an act that makes the most of the comedy trick of *surprise*. Your audience is held in suspense for a moment—then hit with something unexpected.

It goes like this:

A magician appears and announces to the audience that they are about to witness some astounding feats of magic. He gestures toward a screen, declaring it to be a truly magic screen. It has power to grant anyone's secret wish. All one needs to do is make the wish, then pass behind the screen and obtain it.

One by one, the players stand beside the magician. He asks each one, "And what is your secret wish?" As the player closes his eyes, the magician makes some mysterious movements over the player's head. The magician then declares, "Your secret wish is granted! Go—find it behind the magic screen!"

The player then disappears behind the screen. After a brief pause, he exits on the other side with his secret wish.

Start with these:

1. A young man exits while hopping along in imitation of a kangaroo. The magician shrugs and explains to the audience, "That's what he wanted—to be able to imitate a kangaroo."

2. A young lady exits while licking a lollipop and carrying as many more as she can. She cheerfully remarks to the audience, "Go ahead and laugh, but how many lollipops do *you* have?"

3. A young man walks out while frowning at the bulging wallet in his hand. He complains to the magician, "When I said I wanted a loaded wallet, I didn't mean with *gunpowder*."

4. Someone comes out, pauses and smiles at the audience as he says, "I had a very simple secret wish. I just wanted to play a small part in this act." He waves goodbye and exits.

5. The magician looks toward the screen and nods as if someone has just come out from behind it, although no one actually has done so. He explains to the audience, "You might have missed that one. He wanted to be an invisible man."

6. A girl smilingly exits holding hands with a boy who is well known to the audience.

7. Someone runs out looking upward and holding out his hands as if ready to catch a falling ball. He explains to the audience, "My secret wish was to toss a ball a mile high. It should be down here any minute." He exits while in position to catch the ball.

8. An actor comes out riding a scooter. He cheerfully remarks, "My secret wish was a trip to Alaska."

CLASSROOM COMEDY

A comedy set in a classroom is one of the easiest of all to prepare. You can have as few or as many players as you like. If you have a large number, each player speaks only a line or two.

The act starts with the pupils seated in the classroom, asking questions.

Your stock of jokes and stories can be easily strung together in the questions and answers. Just pass from one to another quickly. After the teacher gets a nonsensical answer, she might exclaim something like, "Tommy, please!" and then turn to another pupil with the next question.

The following ideas are typical of those you can use for your classroom comedy:

TEACHER: Eddie, where were you born?
EDDIE: In Minnesota.
TEACHER: What part?
EDDIE: Why, *all* of me.

TEACHER: Carol, if you subtract seventeen from four hundred and fifty, what's the difference?
CAROL: I don't think it makes much difference either.

TEACHER: Billy, would you like to visit the moon?
BILLY: Yes, but my mother told me to come straight home from school.

TEACHER: Helen, what are the names of your parents?
HELEN: Mom and Dad.

TEACHER: Norman, why were you late to school this morning?
NORMAN: It was too late when I started from home.
TEACHER: Why didn't you start earlier?
NORMAN: By the time I started it was too late to start earlier.

TEACHER: Virginia, do my questions bother you?
VIRGINIA: No, but the answers do.

FOOD FUN

Scene: A restaurant. Players are seated around a table.

1. The players look over the menu and comment about the food they want.

2. The waitress enters to take their orders.

3. The players ask for odd combinations, such as tomato and popcorn salad, peanut butter and chocolate chip ice cream on an English muffin, boiled cabbage with strawberry syrup, a pumpkin sandwich, coconut cake with mustard frosting.

4. The players add to the confusion by changing orders several times. The waitress rips off and tosses away several slips of paper.

5. A restaurant employee enters with a broom. He sweeps the floor, then goes on to sweep off the top of the table and the clothing of the players. They run away from him and he exits while still sweeping.

6. The waitress comes back with a tray of food (imaginary). Just as the players are about to eat, the waitress quickly takes everything back. She explains, "I decided to give this to a group on the other side of the room. They give bigger tips."

7. The waitress brings the food. She spills some of it on the players, and then wipes it off their clothes.

8. The players make exchanges. For example, someone calls out, "I'll trade a half-melted strawberry sundae for a soggy waffle!"

9. They pay their checks by scrambling around for nickels and pennies.

10. Someone asks, "Well, what shall we do now?" Someone shouts, "I know! Let's go get something to eat!"

ONION SOUP

Scene: The kitchen of a soup factory. Several tables are placed in a row across the front of the stage. They are set with various cooking utensils and ingredients.

1. The Chief Chef enters with several assistant cooks. He tells them that today they will make onion soup. He shouts en-

thusiastically, "But today we must set a new onion soup record! I want speed, gentlemen! Speed, speed, speed!"

2. The cooks nod. One of them shouts, "Right, Chief Chef!" He turns to the other cooks and leads them in shouting in unison, "Speedy, speedy, onion soup! Speedy, speedy, onion soup!"

3. As the cooks take their places behind the tables, the Chief Chef explains, "I will hand the first man in line a kettle of onions. Each of you will then do your part. Understand?" The cooks nod and again chant, "Speedy, speedy, onion soup! Speedy, speedy, onion soup!"

4. The Chief Chef explains to each man his particular task. The first cook mashes the onions, the second man adds salt and pepper, the third man stirs it, the fourth cook tastes the soup, and the last man rushes the kettle out to the cannery. More tasks can be assigned if the cast is large.

5. The Chief Chef shouts, "Remember, gentlemen, I want to see that kettle fly down the line from one man to the next! Understand?" The cooks again chant, "Speedy, speedy, onion soup! Speedy, speedy, onion soup!"

6. The Chief Chef blows a whistle and hands a kettle to the first man. The fun begins.

7. Everything goes swiftly but awkwardly. The salt shaker drops into the kettle and is pulled out by hand, the third man frantically stirs with his elbow, the last man crashes offstage, and so on.

8. More kettles go down the line. All the while the Chief Chef strides back and forth, blowing his whistle and screaming for more speed.

9. The Chief Chef calls for a halt. He points at his watch and

shouts, "Congratulations! We have a new onion soup record! You shall have a reward. Your reward is a kettle of onion soup!"

10. One by one the men taste the soup in the last kettle. As they finish they slowly turn to scowl at the Chief Chef. He screams for help as they chase him offstage.

THE GOLD MINERS

Scene: A mountain stream. It is being worked by gold miners of the early West. Several prospectors are at work with their equipment.

1. The miners *ad lib* about their chances of finding a fortune in gold, such as, "Maybe today we'll strike it rich," and, "I hear there was a big gold strike around here last week."

2. A new arrival asks a miner to show him how to pan gold. The miner goes through several fancy and nonsensical movements, such as standing with his back to the stream while swishing the pan. As the miner finishes, he sighs and explains, "Of course it doesn't give you any gold, but it's wonderful exercise."

3. The newcomer picks up some pebbles, glances at them, then amuses himself by tossing them back into the stream. When someone asks him what he is doing, he replies, "Oh, tossing back some diamonds and rubies." Someone shouts, "But *why?*" He shrugs and says, "You said we were looking for *gold.*" The miners dive after the gems.

4. A girl in modern dress comes on stage. The miners stop work and stare. She asks, "Pardon me, but I'm driving down to the television studio. Am I on the wrong road?" A miner drawls, "No, miss, you don't have the wrong road but you sure have the wrong act." Everyone smiles. She exits.

THE KING

Scene: The throne room of a royal palace. The king and queen are on their thrones. A table loaded with food is off to one side.

1. The king claps his hands. A servant comes onstage and bows. The king shouts, "I wish to be entertained! Bring on the royal comedians!"

2. The queen adds, "A royal prize shall go to the funniest act." She gestures toward the food and says, "The funniest entertainer shall be permitted to dine at the royal table."

3. A king's subject comes onstage and tells a joke: "Yesterday I went to the doctor. He told me, 'If you want to get well, the best thing for you to do is to give up eating so much.' I asked him what was the *next* best thing." The king and queen frown and shake their heads. The king remarks, "I've heard better than that on the royal television."

4. Another entertainer comes onstage and remarks, "You know, your majesties, I would be a great dancer if it weren't for two things—my feet." The king wails, "Where, oh where, can I find someone to make us laugh?"

5. A third comedian comes onstage and says, "I went out to dinner last night. I complained to the waiter, 'Say, you brought me a wet plate,' He said, 'That's your soup.'" The king holds his head in his hands as he wails, "A laugh, a laugh, my kingdom for a laugh!"

6. A fourth comedian enters and speaks: "Ranch life is hard work. Like the season when you brand the livestock. The cattle aren't so hard, but it's tough work rounding up and branding those bees." The king throws up his arms in despair. He comes downstage and groans, "I, the handsomest and most intelligent king in all the world, cannot find a laugh!"

7. The queen comes downstage and asks the king to repeat what he just said. The king shouts, "I am the handsomest and most intelligent king on earth!"

356

8. The queen bursts into hysterical laughter. She shouts, "That's it! That's the funniest joke of all time!"

9. The queen leads the king to the table, saying, "Eat, O handsome and intelligent king!"

10. The king meekly asks, "Is this all I get for being so funny?" As the queen leads him offstage by the ear she replies, "No, you also get to wash the royal dishes."

FIFTY GOOD IDEAS FOR SKITS

Here are fifty basic ideas that can be turned into comedy acts for several players. Just get your players together and have everyone work with an idea. In this way, an act will develop swiftly.

1. *School Song:* The players gather together to write a school song. They try to find words that rhyme with the name of their school, they compose a melody, and so on.

2. *Flight:* Passengers make funny remarks as they look out of their airplane. They mistake New York for Hawaii, they think that a small lake is the Atlantic Ocean (or vice versa), they mistake a bird for a space rocket. The hostess patiently corrects them.

3. *Beachcombers:* At the seashore. The players find all sorts of curious things on the beach, such as a bottle containing a letter written by Columbus and a pearl as big as a baseball.

4. *Vacation:* One of the players is leaving on vacation. His friends help him pack, but get all mixed up. Needed items are left out, while unnecessary items are packed.

5. *The Debate:* Two teams debate interesting questions, for example: *Boys Should Compliment Girls at Least Once a Day. Yes* or *No?* Players take turns in presenting their side of the question.

6. *Look Pretty:* A photographer tries to get a group to pose correctly, but has trouble. One of the players moves at the wrong moment, another munches peanuts, and so on.

7. *The Interview:* An actor takes the part of a famous explorer who has just returned from the jungles of South America. When he is interviewed by several reporters he gives unusual answers to their questions.

8. *The Applicant:* A player is preparing himself to apply for a job. His friends give him all sorts of hopeless advice. They show him how to act and tell him what to say.

9. *At the Zoo:* Players do and say funny things as they visit a zoo (imaginary animals). A zoo keeper tries to help them understand the animals.

10. *Laugh Time:* The actors and actresses show how many different ways there are to laugh. Some laugh with a deep rumble, others giggle, some roll on the floor.

11. *The Club:* Players are forming a new club. They try to think of an unusual name for it, such as *The Committee for Bigger Candy Bars,* or, *Club for Kindness to Homeless Homing Pigeons.*

12. *Play the Game:* A simple tossing gave is started by several performers. They do and say funny things as they toss buttons into a basket. One player rips buttons off his own coat (a discarded one) in order to make a higher score.

13. *Singers:* Players hold a tryout for singing roles in a musical play. Each player sings briefly—and humorously.

14. *Predict Your Future:* Players sit in a circle around a gypsy fortune teller who predicts their future. Players are told that they will do interesting things, such as becoming the king of a South Pacific island.

15. *Candidates:* Several candidates for office practice their speeches in front of their friends. The candidates make curious promises, such as a pair of fishing boots for everyone.

16. *Imitation Contest:* Performers hold a contest to see who can give the best imitation. They imitate a puppet, a policeman, an animal trainer, and so on.

17. *Lost Watch:* Someone has lost his watch at a picnic. Everyone has interesting adventures while searching around. Example: They chase a squirrel (imaginary) that they suspect has taken the watch.

18. *Homework:* A player needs help in finding answers to his homework problems. His friends look through books for him. After all sorts of wrong answers, they finally come up with correct ones.

19. *Shoppers:* Players are shoppers who stop to chat as they go through the market. They tell of a new dish they are preparing for dinner, such as macaroni and cheese with whipped cream and cherries.

20. *Western Act:* Indians and cowboys meet to trade their goods. Funny exchanges are made, such as an Indian feather for a box of animal crackers.

21. *The Secretary:* A secretary tries to keep several salesmen from charging into the office of her boss. She supplies them with magazines, suggests that they play checkers, and so on.

22. *Nature Hike:* Actors and actresses go on a nature hike. They try to identify different kinds of birds and trees, but get all mixed up.

23. *Song Quiz:* Someone sings or hums brief portions of familiar songs, while others try to identify them. Funny answers are given; for instance, someone mistakes *Home on the Range* for *Jingle Bells*.

24. *Treasure Hunt:* The performers have an old treasure map. They search around the desert and find old bottles and tires, but no treasure. Still, they have a good time.

25. *Comedy Show:* Players get together to write a comedy show. They rehearse scenes and tell jokes. (Use material from other pages of this book.)

26. *Forfeit Fun:* The skit opens with the announcement that the losers in party games must pay their forfeits before the audience. Players then do so with comical acts, such as trying to kiss their own elbows.

27. *Down with Noise:* A committee gathers to fight unnecessary noise in the city, such as forbidding dogs to bark. But members complain when another member makes too much noise writing with his pen.

28. *Hobbies:* Everyone has a different and unusual hobby. They display and explain them. One collects rubber erasers, another carves figures made of cake, a third collects drawings of Little Red Riding Hood.

29. *Fashion Show:* Players model some curious new fashions,

such as a coat with sleeves that reach the floor. Create the fashions from old clothing.

30. *Circus:* Circus acts are presented. Players are clowns, acrobats, jugglers, cowboys, and so on.

31. *Candy Factory:* Workers in a candy factory try to invent new kinds of candy. They come up with green chocolates, square jelly beans and other strange sweets.

32. *House for Sale:* A real estate agent shows prospective buyers around a house. They are dismayed to find that it is on the edge of a cliff, that the roof leaks, and so forth.

33. *The Cashier:* The cashier of a restaurant confuses diners as they pay their checks. She asks all sorts of pointless questions in adding up their bills, such as the color of their plate and whether they used the salt shaker more than once.

34. *Newspaper Office:* Reporters rush in to shout the latest news. Many of the jokes from Section 8 can be worked into this act.

35. *In the Museum:* Players make comical comments as they stroll about a museum. Some of the exhibits can be real items, such as vases, while others can be imaginary.

36. *At the Laundry:* Everything gets mixed up as the performers fold and sort the laundry. Some of the clothes are ripped, some of it is walked on. (Use discarded clothing as the laundry.)

37. *Gas Station:* A motorist in an imaginary car drives into an imaginary gas station. Attendants rush out to sell him tires, seat covers and anything else they can. They even try to charge him for air in his tires.

38. *Star Study:* Players use cardboard telescopes to study the stars and planets. They make funny remarks; for instance, an actor shouts that he sees a hot dog stand on Mars.

39. *Television Shop:* Customers come into the television repair shop to ask odd questions about their set. For example, a woman asks whether the trouble was in the carburetor or the spark plugs.

40. *Strange Island:* The skit takes place on a remote island where visitors run into all sorts of strange creatures. Costumes and masks from other skits will serve nicely here.

41. *Office Act:* Office employees rush around to get some work out for the boss. Papers fly about—and so do the employees.

42. *Pantomime Play:* In this skit some performers pantomime various games and sports. The others try to guess the sport. As soon a they do so, another pantomime is performed.

43. *Call the Plumber:* A plumber is called to fix a broken water pipe. The harder he tries to fix it, the more it squirts (imaginary) water all over everyone.

44. *Poetry Workshop:* Performers write out and read aloud their poems. The poems can be brief, just two or four lines. Write them on any subject and make them funny.

45. *Painters:* Several painters (using real brushes but imaginary paint) go to work on a table. They accidentally paint the floor, a clock and each other.

46. *The Experts:* Three or four performers are the experts on a television panel show. Others make up the audience who asks questions. The questions are odd—and so are the answers. Select a lively topic to discuss, such as how to build an attractive personality.

47. *Beauty Shop:* The beauty operator (using imaginary fluids) gets the wrong colors on the hair of her customers. One who wanted blonde gets purple; another who asked for red gets green. All colors are imaginary.

48. *News Exchange:* Several players sit around the room reading a newspaper. The comedy occurs when everyone wants to exchange sections. Pages get accidentally ripped, two or three players want the same section, and so on.

49. *Scenes from History:* Performers act out famous historical scenes, such as Washington crossing the Delaware. When it is guessed, another scene is presented.

50. *Sailing the Sea:* Players are passengers aboard a ship. They roll about in a stormy sea, they ask the captain whether they are likely to see pirates, they take turns at the helm.

Section 10

Let's Have a Comedy Show

Imagine yourself as part of an audience watching a comedy act. An actor and actress speak out:

FRED: I couldn't get to sleep last night.
LOIS: What did you do?
FRED: I ate candy and cake.
LOIS: Did that help you to sleep?
FRED: No, but it made me happier to be awake!

Sounds like a merry act, doesn't it? Comedy shows have been popular entertainment for thousands of years.

Your own comedy show will be great fun for both audience and performers as you learn how to put on humorous acts. In this section you will be given script ideas, sample material, lively jokes and advice on how to get started. See the preceding sections on "Pantomimes," "Monologues," and "Skits" to get the material for your show.

HOW TO START

A good show starts with a plan. Remember, your efforts should be organized from the very beginning to make things run smoothly.

Start your plan by assigning people to the different positions in the show. For a school production, your teacher may be the one who makes assignments, and acts as general director.

Besides actors and actresses, you may also need several people to serve as stage crew, costume designers, and publicity promoters. Cover every part of your show production, but keep everything as simple as possible. The smaller the program, the fewer assignments you need to make.

Another part of your planning is to consider the kinds of comedy you want to present. But remember that your audience really doesn't care what *type* of show you give—as long as it's funny! Therefore, select the acts that are easiest for you and that you like best to do.

FIVE RULES FOR COMICAL COMEDY

What makes us laugh?

Before we go into action, we should know a few rules for making people laugh. Use them in your show to have a *comical* comedy!

1. *Keep it clear:* For something to seem funny, we must know exactly what is happening, so keep your movements and your words clear and simple. Don't crowd too much material into too little space. Use your rehearsals to check for clearness. Ask yourself, "Will the audience know exactly what is happening?"

2. *Provide surprises:* Surprising your audience is a basic requirement for good comedy. Present something unexpected and unusual. For instance, a scene might have a mother ask her son, "Jimmy, have you filled the salt shaker yet?" Jimmy replies, "Not yet; it's pretty hard to push the salt into those little holes." This is funny because it's unexpected. In one way or another, all comedy must provide a surprise.

3. *Exaggerate it:* Comedy is often the exaggeration of everyday life. A stage action becomes funny if we can relate it to

something that has also happened to us. Since we have probably become mixed up when learning to dance, it is funny when an actor gets confused learning to dance. But to make an action clear, the actor must exaggerate it to some extent.

4. *Keep it innocent:* This means that nothing should be said or done that might embarrass or offend anyone in the audience. Keep the humor kindly.

5. *Have fun:* Whatever part you play in the show, have fun. Make it an interesting adventure. Your own enthusiasm will spill over to the audience and they, too, will have fun.

SPECIAL ACTS FOR EXTRA LAUGHS

Acts are something like a rubber band—you can stretch them out as long as you like. You will see what we mean as we go along.

An audience likes surprises, something unusual and unexpected. The material in this section will bring extra laughs by being illogical and unexplained.

The acts can be used in two different ways. They can be separate acts constituting a whole show. Or, you can insert them in certain places within another skit, in which case they become acts-within-an-act. Wherever you use them, you can be sure they will make your comedy more comical!

The Running Gag

You have probably seen a comedy show that is continually interrupted by someone who doesn't appear to be a part of it. The player pops in for a moment, does something odd and makes an exit. He may appear four or five times during the regular show. For example, he may plead each time with the master of ceremonies, "You *must* use me in this show. I've got great talent. Let me show you!" Then he goes into a silly dance or sings or does tricks of magic. He is so ridiculous that the announcer chases him off. Yet he persistently appears several times.

This is called a running gag. It runs along with the main show, yet is a separate act in itself. Use it only when there is a natural pause in the regular show, as, for instance, when the announcer is about to introduce another act.

The final appearance of the player should include a punch line, and all his appearances should build up to this climax.

The running gag builds up extra amusement in your show as the audience learns to expect the entrance of this special comedian and is ready to laugh at each appearance.

Here are some good ideas for building running gags:

1. A young lady pops in to ask directions for getting to a certain town. (Make it interesting by using the name of a neighboring town.) The announcer tries to help her, but she is just too confused to understand. On each appearance, she holds a sheet of paper, which she calls a map, and to which she pointedly refers. On her final appearance the master of ceremonies examines the paper and explains that it is not a map at all, but rather a restaurant menu. She frowns and nods, "You know, I

didn't *think* I could get there by crossing through a lemon cream pie!"

2. A blundering detective wanders around the stage as if looking for clues. He runs his magnifying glass up and down the announcer's leg, peers under his shoes, and so on. When he appears for the last time the announcer asks, "What crime are you trying to solve?" The man replies, *"Crime?* I'm looking for my lost cuff links!"

3. Someone enters with hand cupped to ear as if listening intently. The announcer asks him, "What do you hear?" Ignoring the question, the player continues to listen as he exits. Finally, when the master of ceremonies asks the player what he is hearing, the player replies, "Nothing at all—and it's been that way all day long!"

4. A man appears carrying a toy telephone and calling out to the audience, "Telephone for Dr. Green; telephone for Dr. Green." On his last appearance, the announcer asks, "How can Dr. Green get a call from an unconnected telephone?" The man replies, "Who said anything about a call? I just want to give this telephone to Dr. Green!"

Time to Rhyme

For a different kind of act, try rhyming answers.

Choose a scene, such as the living room or an office. Then build up rhymed dialogue around it, and end the act with a snappy line.

To prepare your act, write down as many rhymes as you can. Then think of questions that could go with them. Finally, arrange them in logical order.

Here is a rhymed skit that can be used exactly as it is. It should be introduced something like this: "Ladies and gentlemen, let's see what happens when a young man applies for employment:

"Do you have many bad habits?"

"Few."

"You are intelligent?"

"True."

"What are one and one?"

"Two."

"What does a cow do?"

"Moo."

"What do meat and vegetables make?"

"Stew."

"What color is the sky?"

"Blue."

"What fixes things?"

"Glue."

"Who do you think is handsome?"

"You."

"You know, young man, I think you'll *do!*"

The next can be introduced, "Ladies and gentlemen, we are about to watch a woman who wants to rent a house from a real estate agent. Let's listen!"

"What about the rent?"

"Low."

"Are the neighbors noisy?"

"No."

"How do the weeds grow?"

"Slow."

"How can we have fun on that lake?"

"Row."

"What kind of weather?"

"Snow."

"What does that river do?"

"Flow."

"What does the sunset do?"

"Glow."

"What is that bird up there?"

"Crow."

"You know, I can't think of any more rhymes so I'll just take the house!"

Telephone Talk

Funny gags over telephone lines are always a favorite. The staging is simple. Place a screen downstage center to separate the two players. Over the telephone, they fire funny lines back and forth. Much of the material found in other pages of this book can be used. Here is how one comedy team starts:

"Hello. Is this the medical office of Dr. Miller, Dr. Miller, Dr. Miller and Dr. Miller?"

"That's right."

"Well, I'd like to talk to Dr. Miller."

"Sorry, but he's on vacation."

"Then please let me speak with Dr. Miller."

"Dr. Miller hasn't come in as yet."

"In that case I'll talk to Dr. Miller."

"He's busy with a patient."

"Then let me talk with Dr. Miller."

"Dr. Miller speaking."

Try this one:

WOMAN ON TELEPHONE: Hello. Fish Market? Will you please send me a pound of cod?

VOICE: We don't have any cod.

WOMAN: Then make it mackerel.

VOICE: No mackerel.

WOMAN: How about some salmon?

VOICE: No salmon.

WOMAN: How come you're all out of fish?

VOICE: Because this is the fire station.

There is something fascinating about watching two people on the telephone. You see both sides of the picture, while in real life you see only one. This gives the players the opportunity to include some action comedy, as well as words.

Here is a good example of how action can add to the fun:

Player A asks player B a series of questions—the birth date of President Lincoln, the area of the Pacific Ocean, the location of England, and so on. After each question player B rushes about to get the answer. As he does so, player A lazily stretches out and munches candy. After four or five questions have been answered, player B asks, "Why all these questions? What are you doing?" Player A cheerfully replies, "I'm not doing anything. I just finished my homework!"

SECRETS FOR A SUCCESSFUL SHOW

A script is simply a map that guides the actors along the way. It includes both the dialogue and the directions to be followed. You will discover ways to build a good script quickly and easily. Although the examples apply to a skit for several players, the same basic rules can be used for other kinds of acts.

How do you start preparing your script? One good way is to get the players into a challenging situation. Give them a definite goal to be reached or a certain task to be performed. You then build your script around their efforts to achieve their goal. Here are ten examples of a *Challenging Situation:*

1. Win a contest
2. Find lost treasure
3. Apply for employment
4. Compose a song
5. Prepare a banquet
6. Learn to play golf
7. Win an election
8. Sell merchandise
9. Build an outdoor camp
10. Put on a comedy show

Have you noticed how many professional comedies are set in periods of history? It is lots of fun to have fun with history! As a second method for setting a comedy background, here are some ideas for a *Historical Period:*

1. Days of knighthood
2. The Stone Age
3. The American West
4. Ancient Egypt
5. Days of French royalty
6. Early American days
7. Time of the Vikings
8. Days of pirates
9. Early British Empire
10. Southern Confederacy

A third way to find a good setting is to place your players in an interesting location. Their surroundings will then suggest all sorts of comical actions. Look over these ideas for an *Interesting Location:*

369

1. Inside a candy factory   6. On shipboard
2. A television studio   7. An Arabian oasis
3. A paradise island   8. A newspaper office
4. At the zoo   9. A jungle
5. With a detective at work   10. On a strange planet

A Sample Script

Let's select the background of a faraway planet. See what you can do with this strange world which you may call by the name of Mysterioso. What might you run into when landing here? Well, you could discover all kinds of comical things. Obviously, the citizens of Mysterioso might have funny faces and even funnier costumes. Maybe their leader is a bumbling sort of fellow with peculiar manners. The furniture in the background might look like something from—well, from another world! The nice thing about the planet Mysterioso is that it can look just as peculiar as your imagination can make it.

Now you have an interesting background to serve as a springboard for some lively actions. So let's take the next step of building a story around it. Ask yourself, "What kind of a laugh-arousing story can take place?" Now, let your mind come up with a simple story line. Here is one outline:

1. Some Earthmen arrive on the planet Mysterioso. They wander around, staring at the strange background.

2. They reveal their mission to the audience by discussing it. Their objective is to buy some Magic Marshmallows. They have heard that these Magic Marshmallows will give beautiful singing voices to anyone who eats them.

3. A couple of players show how awful their voices are by singing a few sour notes. Their companions groan and plug their ears.

4. To the sound of music, the King of Mysterioso marches in, followed by his attendants. The King, a comical man, goes to his throne while happily munching marshmallows.

5. The Earthmen start to plead for some of the marshmallows, but the King hushes them. He eats a marshmallow, sings a couple of rounded notes, explains to the Earthmen, "Just in case you're wondering—up here that's called a beautiful voice."

6. The Earthmen plead to purchase some marshmallows. They

370

offer the King all sorts of trades, but he doesn't know what they are. Examples: He sets a silver coin on his head, remarking, "Your Earth kings must be very small people." He pretends to bite a necklace, saying, "Earth grapes are hard on the teeth—but delicious!"

7. The King finally agrees to give them some Magic Marshmallows in exchange for an autographed picture of a famous Earthman. He is handed a picture of some famous person, maybe a local man or woman who is well known to the audience. The King holds it up in admiration.

8. The King tells the Earthmen that their Magic Marshmallows are behind a screen, next to the throne. They rush in back of it and pretend to eat. They shout *ad libs,* such as, "Delicious! Magic Marshmallows! We'll sing like birds!" Empty boxes fly out.

9. They line up in front of the screen and try to sing in harmony, but it comes out an awful howl. Someone suggests, "More Marshmallows!" Once more they pretend to eat while shouting *ad libs*.

10. Again they line up. This time they pantomime the act of singing while a phonograph behind the screen plays a record. Everyone sings happily as they march offstage.

11. The King eats a marshmallow, sings a sour note, and puzzledly remarks, "I wonder why they don't work for me?" He exits while singing sourly, but happily. The curtain falls.

Just select your background and outline your action. Those two steps will build your script with surprising speed. You will find that funny details will pop into your mind like magic!

Building Funny Dialoque

If you have your background and story, what comes next? Funny lines! Put some amusing words into the mouth of an actor. Many good lines will occur to you as you map out your skit. But if suitable lines don't come to mind at any particular point, just write down any kind of temporary dialogue. Improvements will come as you work.

Picture yourself holding a toy clown made of soft clay. Imagine that it is a funny figure. But suppose that you want to make it *your own* funny creation? What would you do? Well, you would push and twist the clay into another shape, change the figure in any way you want.

That gives you a picture of how professional comedy writers work. They start with a collection of familiar jokes and gags. They then twist them this way and that, while adding their own original touch. That gives them fresh and enjoyable material.

Start by having everyone in your show collect a batch of jokes and funny stories. Your public library has books of humor. You can find more in magazines and newspapers. Still others can be written down from memory. The material in this book can be used.

Connect your material with your script. Suppose that while working on your Mysterioso script you came across this joke:

FRED: I'll pay you five dollars if you'll do all my worrying for me.
PAUL: All right. Where's the five dollars?
FRED: That's your first worry.

You can easily rework this to make it fit spacemen characters. It could be used shortly after they land on Mysterioso, like this:

FIRST SPACEMAN: This crazy planet gives me the shivers. I'll give you a thousand dollars to worry for me.
SECOND SPACEMAN: That's great, but when would I get the thousand dollars?
FIRST SPACEMAN: That is your first worry.

Look for opportunities to plant your jokes within the script, and you will find more spots than jokes. Remember, don't try to make every line a funny one. Very often, the characters must speak in order to explain something to the audience. At other times, their dialogue serves as a buildup to an explosively funny scene. Besides, much of your humor comes from elsewhere, such as from the situation and from the peculiarities of the characters. Plant your funny lines where there is very little physical action onstage.

Across the Bridge

What do you use when you want to cross from one side of a river to the other? A bridge. What do you use when you want to pass from one joke to another? The same thing: A bridge. But it is a special kind of bridge, one used by all comedians.

Your bridge is made up of a few words, or perhaps a sentence or two. The words themselves are not an important part of a joke. Their purpose is to let you cross from one joke to another. Your bridge of words helps you to drop one funny subject and take up an entirely new one.

Let's imagine that you and your partner are planning to work as a team. You have already gathered your material of jokes, stories and stunts. You decide to start your act with this dialogue:

FRED: I can prove to you that I'm not standing here on this stage.

PAUL: You can prove that you're not standing on this stage? I don't believe it.

FRED: All right. Am I in Mexico right now?

PAUL: No.

FRED: Then if I'm not in Mexico, I must be some place else. Correct?

PAUL: Correct.

FRED: And if I'm some place else, I can't be here on this stage. Right?

PAUL: Hmmm. That's right, all right.

You are now ready to move into the next joke. So you use a word-bridge. For instance, Paul looks down at Fred's socks and continues, "Well, Fred, I don't know whether you are here or not, but I see some funny-looking socks down there."

FRED: What's funny about them?

PAUL: Take a look. One is red and one's green.

FRED: Yes, and I've got another pair at home just like them.

They now cross into the next joke:

PAUL: Speaking of funny things, last night I dreamed I ate a twenty-pound marshmallow.

FRED: So what?

PAUL: So when I woke up my pillow was gone.

373

Whenever you finish the punch line of a joke, smoothly cross over to the next with your word-bridge. You can let any of the players supply it.

Funny Sights

Your audience laughs at what it *hears* and what it *sees* or imagines it sees. We have already talked about funny dialogue, so now let's find ways to create sight gags.

Go through your material and select items that can be turned into visual comedy. For instance, this story is told by a lecturer:

"A shopper entered a market and began selecting her groceries. At the end of the aisle was a horse who was stocking the shelves with cans and bottles. As the lady pushed her cart past the horse she stared in amazement. The horse turned to her and asked politely, 'Why look so surprised, miss—haven't you ever seen a horse before?' 'Why, yes,' replied the lady, 'but I was hoping to talk to the cow that worked here before you.'"

You can change the story in any way that fits your purpose. For instance, you can switch from a grocery store to a restaurant where the horse is a waiter.

Imagine the visual shock this story can give, if you can find a horse costume!

Comical Costumes

A truly funny costume is a funny sight! Many of your acts will become doubly entertaining by the use of comical clothing that has some relationship to the scene and material. It is one of the surest ways to make your audience look and laugh.

There is something else about costumes that makes them use-

ful. They turn *players* into definite *characters*. Instead of seeing actors and actresses, the audience sees policemen and Indians and nurses. And that makes the audience eager to see what they are going to do!

Character costumes can be just as simple or as fancy as you like. For short acts you need only simple ones, just to give a clear idea of the character being portrayed. A straw hat and work clothes give a good picture of a farmer. A fisherman can be shown wearing a raincoat and boots.

Exaggeration and surprise can make things funny. An ordinary situation becomes humorous when it is blown up to a ridiculous size. Remember this when you work on costumes. Take an ordinary article of clothing and make it extra large or extra bright or extra long. Picture in your mind a woman wearing a hat with a small feather on top. Now imagine the same lady wearing a hat with dozens of tall, fuzzy feathers.

Comical effects can be achieved by adding something unusual to an actor's street clothing. On one television show a prancing nature-lover had leaves and berries fastened to his clothing. On another show the comedian came out with two medals on his chest. He touched the smaller one and remarked, "I got that one for singing." Touching the larger one, he added, "I got that for stopping."

Don't forget masks! Have you ever noticed how differently you feel toward someone wearing a mask? The magical power of a mask is that it seems to turn a player into something strange, perhaps an elf or an animal or a monster. You can make your own masks to fit a special character, or you can buy ready-made ones. For a quick costume, there's nothing like a mask.

Rehearsal Ideas

Rehearsals can be as interesting as your comedy show itself. Besides developing your talents, rehearsals can give you an insight into how audiences react. Ask questions of your invited guests. It's best *not* to have the players act as a test audience. You want the guests to answer such questions as:

1. Are there scenes that moved too slowly?
2. Do the spoken lines need better timing?
3. Are the players acting too seriously?
4. Would funnier costumes add to the humor?
5. Are the lines clearly and easily heard?
6. Can certain jokes or stunts be sharpened?
7. Is the action confused or complicated?
8. Do the players display amusing personalities?

Suppose there are slow scenes. You can speed them up. For example, two young ladies are walking down the street. Instead of their chatting aimlessly, give them some funny lines, like this:

LOIS: I wonder what time it is?
RUTH: I know it's not three o'clock.
LOIS: How do you know?
RUTH: I'm supposed to be home at three and I'm not there yet.

Rehearsal offers many opportunities to squeeze in extra laughs. You can make a funny show even funnier. Take a scene where a player is handed a letter to read aloud. What can make it more comical? Try this: The player takes the letter and reads aloud: "Glub wuppy koo ranatig wog tok." Everyone acts puzzled at the strange language. Then, the reader grins as he sees what happened—he was reading upside down. He turns the letter upright and reads correctly.

Suppose the script calls for someone to be noticed as he comes onstage. Can you turn his entrance into an extra chuckle? Here is one way: The player comes onstage bent over and holding his head in his hands. Another player quickly notices him and the dialogue goes like this:

FRED: Hello, Paul. What's the matter?

PAUL: Oh, what a night. I ache all over.

FRED: What happened?

PAUL: When I went to bed I made a mistake in plugging in the electric blanket.

FRED: So?

PAUL: So I plugged in the automatic toaster by mistake. I kept popping out of bed every two minutes.

What you accomplish in rehearsal gives you added skill, self-confidence, and leads to a smooth performance.

Section 11

Puppet Plays

MAKING YOUR PUPPETS

Puppets can be the most interesting little people on earth. For thousands of years these lively performers have entertained and delighted audiences all over the world.

You too can build a fascinating puppet for yourself. You and your friends can put on puppet shows that will delight everyone, and you will have as much fun as your audiences! In this section you will find out exactly how to do it.

There are dozens of kinds of puppets to choose from. In the next few paragraphs you will be shown how to create several different types. All of them are easy to make, using materials found in the home or schoolroom.

Solid Puppet The head of this type of puppet is made from any solid object, such as an apple, potato, carrot, or perhaps a ball of tightly packed newspaper. Almost any kind of solid object can serve as a head so long as you can scoop out a hole

in the object. Make a channel large enough for your forefinger or for two fingers.

Next, turn your imagination loose to create a face. For example, you can make eyes out of colored thumbtacks and ears from pieces of cardboard. Make hair from strands of cotton or wool or from strips of paper and glue them to the head. Another way to make a face is to cover the head with a sock and then sew the features of the face onto the sock.

As a final step, drape a handkerchief over your hand and push your finger or fingers into the opening of the puppet head. The handkerchief should be large enough to act as a coat or dress that covers your hand and arm. All puppets of this type need a coat or dress.

Your puppet is all ready to perform!

The solid puppet is one of the most popular among the many kinds of puppets. There are endless ways you can use this easy method to create different kinds of interesting little people.

Sock Puppet You can turn an old sock into a puppet person in just a few minutes. Stuff the end of the sock with newspaper or cotton to form the head. Sew on the face using buttons or pieces of cloth of contrasting colors, or paint on a face. Slip your hand into the open end of the sock and extend one or two fingers into the stuffed newspaper or cotton. By bending your fingers you can make your puppet move his head and upper body.

Socks are especially good for making animal puppets, such as a cat or a whale.

FRONT   BACK

Stick Puppet Few types of puppets are as easy to make as the kind we call stick puppets. You can make one by drawing a figure upon a piece of thick paper or thin cardboard. Cut the figure free from the rest of the paper. If your audience will be seeing both sides of the puppet you should dress or cover both sides of the figure. Paste your puppet person to the end of a slender stick so that the stick serves as a handle. Make sure the stick is long enough so that the puppet can appear above the stage while your hand remains out of sight.

Paper Bag Puppet A small or medium-size paper bag can turn into an interesting puppet person. Draw a face on the bag, or paste on bits of paper to form the features. Cut a hole on each side of the bag, one for your thumb and one for your little finger. These are the arms of your puppet. If the bag is not long enough to cover your arm, paste on an extra piece of paper to serve as the rest of the coat or dress.

380

Leg Puppet Your own fingers will form the legs of this kind of puppet. He can actually walk and dance and hop merrily about the stage.

Draw a puppet person on a piece of cardboard. Color the figure and cut it out. Make two holes at the place where the legs should go. Push your forefinger and your middle finger down through the holes as legs. Your leg puppet is ready to dance!

Moving Object A moving object is any kind of a non-human and non-animal figure that moves while onstage. Here are some examples: train, boat, airplane, bicycle, balloon, kite, sun, moon, star, clouds, swaying building, rolling ball.

A moving object adds extra excitement to your puppet show. For instance, instead of having a puppet person walk onto the stage you can build a cardboard automobile for him to ride in. As another example, you could build a stunt around a tall tree that sways back and forth and almost topples over in a storm. A moving object can be flat, with a stick attached as explained in the section on stick puppets, or can be made round, and worn over your hand.

Some objects move through the sky, such as an airplane or the sun. Attach such an object to a stick and hold it downward from the top of the stage.

Give your audience an extra treat by including moving objects in your puppet show!

Your Puppet's Personality

Your puppet will be especially appealing to both you and your audience if you give it a definite personality. This means that your puppet person should have his own special character which is unlike any other performer on the stage.

The main idea is to make him an outstanding individual with his own mannerisms, with his special way of dressing, and with his particular way of walking and talking. For instance, he might be a *happy* and *lighthearted* type of person who laughs constantly, or he might be a puppet person who is outstanding because of his *mighty muscles* or because he wears the *costume of a spaceman,* or maybe he is noticeable because he is much *taller* than the rest of the puppets onstage.

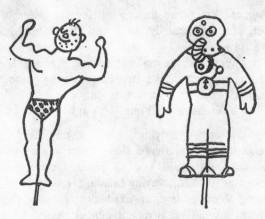

Use your puppet's costume to give him a special personality. Think of ways to dress him in an interesting style.

The facial features of your puppet will also help to make him outstanding in appearance. Remember to give him a face that attracts attention. The features of a puppet should be exaggerated. Give him an extra big nose or a very crooked mouth, so that the audience can recognize him easily.

Let your puppet speak and act according to the kind of a person he is. If he is supposed to be an excited and eager sort of person, have him talk and move around with enthusiasm. If he is in a sleepy mood, let him act as if he wants to go to bed.

The personality of your puppet is half the show! Show your audience an interesting personality!

Puppets in Action

When putting on any kind of a show or stunt with puppets, keep your actions clear and simple. In some cases you can help

INITIAL ACTS

Here is an interesting way to build short charade acts. Players build their secret words by using the initials in their first and last names. A player named Betty Lewis, for example, could use her initials of *B* and *L* to work out *beautiful lake* or *bouncy lions*. For the second time around the players could use their middle initials also. A performer named Charles Frank Dennis, for instance, could act out *cake for dessert.*

ADD-A-LETTER CHARADES

The pantomimist acts out a word, such as *tree,* which the viewers must guess. Once they have the sound of *tree,* they must add a single letter of the alphabet to reveal the secret word, while the actor tries to help them with gestures. In the case of *tree,* the proper letter to be added is T, thus making the secret word of *treat.* The sound (not the spelling) of the acted-out word, plus the sound of an added letter, completes the secret word.

1. treat (*tree* plus *T*)
2. single (*sing* plus *L*)
3. droop (*drew* plus *P*)
4. sticky (*stick* plus *E*)
5. tense (*ten* plus *S*)
6. ready (*red* plus *E*)
7. goat (*go* plus *T*)
8. short (*shore* plus *T*)
9. toot (*two* plus *T*)
10. slate (*sleigh* plus *T*)
11. yellow (*yell* plus *O*)
12. load (*low* plus *D*)
13. soak (*sew* plus *K*)
14. shine (*shy* plus *N*)
15. squawk (*squaw* plus *K*)
16. great (*gray* plus *T*)
17. hair (*hay* plus *R*)
18. arrow (*air* plus *O*)
19. cattle (*cat* plus *L*)
20. change (*chain* plus *G*)
21. slide (*sly* plus *D*)
22. cellar (*sell* plus *R*)
23. grope (*grow* plus *P*)
24. frenzy (*friend* plus *Z*)
25. pine (*pie* plus *N*)
26. hurry (*her* plus *E*)
27. hide (*high* plus *D*)
28. slipper (*slip* plus *R*)
29. spice (*spy* plus *S*)
30. storm (*store* plus *M*)

TAKE-AWAY CHARADES

This game usually moves along at a fast pace. Performers act out the listed one-syllable words, but the secret word for the audience to discover is obtained by taking away the first letter. Example: The performer acts out the word *cloud* and the viewers take away the letter *c* to end up with the secret word *loud*.

1. hear—ear
2. fall—all
3. ground—round
4. hair—air
5. star—tar
6. crow—row
7. bread—read
8. speak—peak
9. feast—east
10. farm—arm
11. feel—eel
12. broom—room
13. wink—ink
14. table—able
15. sport—port
16. trip—rip
17. steam—team
18. spill—pill
19. box—ox
20. wheel—heel
21. plate—late
22. flight—light
23. reach—each
24. sour—our
25. tape—ape
26. cup—up
27. bright—right
28. glove—love
29. flip—lip
30. flag—lag

CHARADE CONTEST

Two performers occupy the stage at the same time for a charade contest. The game leader swiftly calls out a number to each. The numbers should range between three and six. For instance, the leader might call out "Five!" to one player and "Three!" to the other one. Each player must think of a word containing the number of assigned letters, and immediately act out that word. The players compete simultaneously for the attention of the audience. A point is scored by the one whose word is guessed first by the viewers. Whoever first scores three points wins the contest. Another two contestants then take the stage.

BEGIN-END LETTERS

The listed words give the viewers an opportunity for fast answers. They are told that the secret word being acted out starts and ends with the same letter.

1. rooster
2. museum
3. label
4. treatment
5. clinic
6. eclipse
7. register
8. tonight
9. hurrah
10. lawful
11. classic
12. depend
13. elegance
14. target
15. overdo
16. level
17. triumphant
18. willow
19. napkin
20. refrigerator
21. typist
22. defend
23. cubic
24. nation
25. experience
26. regular
27. cosmetic
28. laurel
29. discard
30. maximum
31. glaring
32. northern
33. recover
34. elude
35. telecast
36. radar
37. tumult
38. liberal
39. yearly
40. transparent

HA!

Each performer in turn acts out one of the listed words, all of which begin with *ha*. Give each performer his word (or words) on a slip of paper before starting. The audience should be informed beforehand that all the words to be acted out begin with these letters. This makes it easier for both actors and viewers —and supplies a *ha* or two for all!

1. hammer
2. handshake
3. hat
4. hack
5. hail
6. hair
7. half
8. hawk
9. haunt
10. haul
11. handball
12. harvest
13. happy
14. harness
15. harmony
16. harbor
17. hard
18. hand
19. halo
20. handle
21. hay
22. handsome
23. ham
24. halt
25. handcuff
26. hairpin
27. hammock
28. halfback
29. hasten
30. handkerchief

NAME CHARADES

This one is fun for both beginners and experts. Below are lists of names of boys and girls which are especially good for charade play. The idea is to act out the sound of the first part of the name. This supplies the audience with a clue for guessing the complete name. The viewers should be informed in advance that they will be given only the first part of a name and that they must take it from there.

Girls	Boys
1. Lois (low)	1. Richard (rich)
2. Julia (jewel)	2. Gilbert (gill)
3. Lydia (lid)	3. John (jaw)
4. Mildred (mill)	4. Dennis (den)
5. Phyllis (fill)	5. Walter (wall)
6. Peggy (peg)	6. Woodrow (wood)
7. Patricia (pat)	7. Tony (toe)
8. Jane (jay)	8. Michael (my)
9. Doris (door)	9. Raymond (ray)
10. Grace (gray)	10. Donald (dawn)
11. Barbara (bar)	11. Orville (ore)
12. Sharon (share)	12. Cecil (see)
13. Gladys (glad)	13. Keith (key)
14. Sylvia (sill)	14. Lionel (lion)
15. Rose (row)	15. Chester (chest)
16. Sandra (sand)	16. David (day)
17. Harriet (hair)	17. Warren (war)
18. Joyce (joy)	18. Carl (car)
19. Irene (eye)	19. Eugene (you)
20. Hazel (hay)	20. Stuart (stew)

PARTNER CHARADES

This is played in the usual way except that each syllable in the secret word (or each word in the secret sentence) is acted out by a different player. Thus the three-syllable word *volcano* would be acted out by three partners, while the proverb *Better late than never* would need four players. As soon as one part of the word or sentence is guessed, the next member of the partnership takes over.

This can be played as a contest by assigning different words having an equal number of syllables to two teams. A timekeeper keeps track and at the end of each round announces which team completed its word in the shorter time, and awards them a point. The first team to score five points wins the contest.

147

THE SOUND OF T

Players take turns in acting out the listed words. Even though the viewers are informed that all the words end with the sound of *t* they may have to do some extra thinking in order to come up with the right answers.

1. activity	16. beauty
2. celebrity	17. serenity
3. curiosity	18. royalty
4. hilarity	19. perplexity
5. timidity	20. thrifty
6. university	21. authority
7. intensity	22. deputy
8. liberty	23. stability
9. oddity	24. property
10. personality	25. ability
11. mighty	26. velocity
12. captivity	27. popularity
13. poverty	28. immensity
14. piety	29. rapidity
15. electricity	30. prosperity

QUESTION AND ANSWER CHARADES

Two performers occupy the stage together. One of them asks a simple question (such as "What time is it?") which the other answers (by looking at his watch and holding up two fingers, for example). Both the question and the answer must be given in pantomime, of course; no words are spoken. Each player asks and answers just one or two questions, after which another couple takes the stage.

The viewers follow the performances by calling out as they get the questions and answers. This is a good charade with which to start off a large party.

KING CHARADES

Players act out these words which end in *king*. Viewers try to guess which kind of king is on the throne, or rather on the stage.

1.	waking	21.	soaking
2.	parking	22.	stacking
3.	shrieking	23.	shaking
4.	thinking	24.	ducking
5.	breaking	25.	stroking
6.	joking	26.	blocking
7.	hiking	27.	clicking
8.	packing	28.	hacking
9.	working	29.	wrecking
10.	talking	30.	kicking
11.	cooking	31.	quacking
12.	sneaking	32.	blinking
13.	backing	33.	basking
14.	choking	34.	licking
15.	raking	35.	thanking
16.	locking	36.	tracking
17.	poking	37.	sticking
18.	peeking	38.	tacking
19.	honking	39.	sinking
20.	smacking	40.	striking

NICKNAME CHARADES

Each player is given a comical nickname which he or she acts out for the others to guess. Try these examples:

1. Prince Charming
2. Twinkletoes
3. Angel Face
4. Big Hero
5. Muscles
6. Lover Boy
7. Princess Fair
8. Happy Farmer
9. Jumping Jack
10. Dragonfire
11. Beauty Queen
12. The Brain
13. Magnificent One
14. Champ
15. Personality Plus

TRIPLE CHARADES

This is a slightly more difficult game than the preceding ones. Three charade actors perform at the same time, each acting out a different word. However, the audience knows their words are all of one syllable and rhyme, like *leap, weep, peep*. The spectators try to guess any or all of the three as soon as possible. As soon as the viewers guess a word, its performer retires from the stage, while the others continue to act. Here is enough material for twenty rounds.

1. sing, sling, cling
2. knock, talk, walk
3. sigh, fly, pie
4. cake, ache, break

5. fall, haul, call
6. hum, drum, gum
7. swift, lift, gift
8. freeze, breeze, sneeze
9. east, feast, beast
10. strain, chain, cane
11. drink, blink, sink
12. girl, curl, pearl
13. fig, pig, twig
14. shine, nine, pine
15. tree, bee, sea
16. hat, bat, mat
17. boy, joy, toy
18. joke, oak, yoke
19. hay, clay, jay
20. giggle, wriggle, jiggle
    (tell the audience word has two syllables)

PERFORMING POET CHARADES

Players are allowed enough time to make up their own simple two-line poems. The verses are then acted out for the audience to guess. A poem can be on any subject the player prefers and can be just as sensible or nonsensical as he likes. Below is a pair of examples:

> I like summer and I like fall,
> But I like ice cream best of all.

> Oranges, apples, lemons and limes,
> It may not make sense but at least it rhymes.

151

RHYMING WORD CHARADES

Each player in turn is assigned one of the secret words listed below. Before the performer begins, the audience is told that the word suggested by the pantomimed action rhymes with the secret word. The idea is to guess both words. For instance, if the pantomimist pretends to saw a piece of wood the viewers would first have to guess the word *saw*. The players in the audience may shout as many guesses as they can as rapidly as they can. When a guesser shouts the word *saw*, the pantomimist nods to indicate that he has found the right word. The viewers now try to guess the secret word which rhymes with *saw*, which might be *law*.

This stunt is especially good for team play. Members of each team are each assigned a secret word. One at a time, they perform while their team guesses. The team that guesses the secret words in the shortest time is the winner. Here are some secret words with suggestions for pantomiming them.

1. cake (pretend to *shake* hands)
2. gold (shiver as if *cold*)
3. ball (hold hand at *tall* level)
4. leap (pretend to *sleep*)
5. ring (pretend to *sing*)
6. cook (pretend to read *book*)
7. sound (*pound* fist)
8. out (cup hands, *shout*)
9. blue (hold up *two* fingers)
10. sink (*blink* your eyes or pretend to *drink*)
11. drop (*hop* around)
12. match (*scratch* arm)
13. green (*lean* to one side)
14. toe (pretend to *row* boat)
15. ice (pretend to *slice* bread)
16. chair (pat *hair*)
17. burn (*turn* around in circle)
18. fine (pretend to *shine* shoes)
19. bush (*push* away)
20. calm (point to *palm*)
21. chance (*dance* about)
22. please (tightly *squeeze* arm)

23. ripe (pretend to *type*)
24. snow (pretend to *sew*)
25. haste (pretend to *taste*)

HINK-PINK CHARADES

Each player is assigned to act out for the audience to guess two single words which complete a little but not necessarily sensible rhyme. (More difficult would be "Hinky-Pinky" Charades—two rhyming words of two syllables each. Advanced players could try that. Then go on to "Hinkety-Pinkety!")

1. long song
2. small ball
3. pull wool
4. flat hat
5. my pie
6. keep sheep
7. hurl pearl
8. slow throw
9. fly high
10. red head
11. sweet wheat
12. warm storm
13. crush mush
14. I spy
15. shun sun
16. whole bowl
17. stop mop
18. see bee
19. grip lip
20. jump stump
21. munch lunch
22. scrub tub
23. love dove
24. sad lad
25. bake cake
26. blue shoe
27. clean screen
28. big fig
29. spill pill
30. house mouse
31. float boat
32. brown clown
33. sock clock
34. one gun
35. tug rug
36. throw snow
37. drink ink
38. chew stew
39. sour flower
40. toss sauce

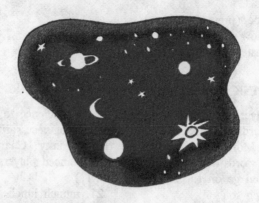

CHARADE NUMBERS

The idea of this game is for player to act out a word which is connected with a number. The viewers silently guess the word from which they guess aloud the number. For example, if the actor portrayed the word *alphabet* the audience would guess number 26—the number of letters in the alphabet. In this list of usable words and numbers, the charade words are in italics.

1. 7 days in a *week*.
2. 4 *seasons*.
3. 3 corners to a *triangle*.
4. 60 seconds to a *minute*.
5. 10 *fingers* on hands.
6. 24 hours to a *day*.
7. 31 days in *March*.
8. 9 *planets*.
9. 2 *ears* on a person's head.
10. 12 months in a *year*.

OPPOSITE ACTIONS

This is a tricky game of charades. The idea is for a performer to reveal his secret word by acting out its exact opposite meaning. For instance, for the secret word of *tall*, the player would act out the word *short*. Once the audience guesses the word *short*, it must keep guessing until it gets *tall*. The performer must not nod his head when and if the audience guesses the word acted out (*short* in this instance). The viewers are to keep guessing until they finally guess the exact secret word.

The charade performer acts out a word and the viewers call out, not the word acted, but that word spelled backwards. The audience must not call out the word, only the reversed word.

For example, if the performer acts out the word *nap,* a viewer would first discover that it is *nap,* then reverse its spelling and call out the secret word *pan.* Here are enough backward charades for 20 periods of play.

1. ton—not
2. peek—keep
3. tap—pat
4. deer—reed
5. nab—ban
6. trap—part
7. won—now
8. pool—loop
9. dial—laid
10. pin—nip
11. gulp—plug
12. yam—may
13. net—ten
14. no—on
15. war—raw
16. lap—pal
17. pit—tip
18. saw—was
19. nod—don
20. step—pets

THINK OF A QUESTION CHARADES

Here is a quiz contest with an unusual twist. The charade performer acts out one of the words supplied in the list below. Once someone in the audience guesses the word he must raise his hand, keep the answer secret, but ask a *question* that demands the same answer. For instance, if the secret word turns out to be *diamond* the guesser would ask the question, "What precious stone is mined in South Africa?" As another example, for the word *Paris* the question could be, "What city is the capital of France?"

The player who first indicates that he has guessed the secret word is allowed a few seconds to think up a question. If he succeeds he scores a point for his team. If his question reveals the wrong answer, and he has guessed an incorrect word, the charade simply continues. The game ends when one team has scored fifteen points. Here are enough charade words for several games.

1. diamond	30. pearl
2. Paris	31. forest
3. whale	32. cream
4. pepper	33. palace
5. Sweden	34. Tokyo
6. clock	35. cotton
7. river	36. squirrel
8. beaver	37. ocean
9. Delaware	38. letter
10. prince	39. Christmas
11. mountain	40. waterfall
12. treasure	41. igloo
13. bouquet	42. carpenter
14. tomato	43. root
15. salmon	44. detective
16. valley	45. Wednesday
17. Canada	46. bay
18. soldier	47. army
19. doctor	48. robin
20. collie	49. butterfly
21. village	50. fence
22. tunnel	51. book
23. snowstorm	52. carrot
24. Japan	53. rancher
25. cave	54. August
26. library	55. picture
27. college	56. pillow
28. Panama	57. meadow
29. tiger	58. wheel

59. volcano	80. candle
60. school	81. celery
61. Mexico	82. leopard
62. dinosaur	83. carnation
63. statue	84. Monday
64. zebra	85. sergeant
65. London	86. nutmeg
66. walnut	87. highway
67. farmer	88. pumpkin
68. mayor	89. fountain
69. bridge	90. Mars
70. comet	91. gorilla
71. rainbow	92. telegram
72. pineapple	93. bakery
73. Hawaii	94. iceberg
74. eagle	95. Boston
75. cloud	96. giant
76. pony	97. senator
77. coffee	98. medal
78. Australia	99. Indiana
79. emerald	100. blossom

SYNONYM CHARADES

The pantomimists (either individuals taking turns or teams alternating), keeping the list secret, act out the listed words for an audience (or for the other team) to guess. When someone in the audience (or a member of the guessing team) thinks he knows the word being acted out, he must call out two words, synonyms (words meaning more or less the same thing) which should correspond to those on this list. However, it's best not to be too exact in the requirements, as there are many words meaning the same thing. For example, the list calls for *quick* and *fast,* but *rapid* and *speedy* would be just as acceptable. If the guess is wrong, the pantomimist continues until he hears two correct words. Then the game continues with the next synonyms.

1. quick and fast
2. laugh and chuckle
3. strong and mighty
4. look and see
5. mystery and puzzle
6. drop and spill
7. fasten and tie
8. listen and hear
9. sleep and slumber
10. tune and melody
11. small and tiny
12. far and distant
13. shy and timid
14. brace and courageous
15. shout and yell
16. calm and peaceful
17. rich and wealthy
18. wise and intelligent
19. groan and moan
20. breeze and wind
21. beautiful and attractive
22. gay and merry
23. sad and gloomy
24. disappear and vanish
25. late and tardy
26. price and cost
27. dinner and supper
28. love and affection
29. hard and solid
30. heavy and weighty
31. work and effort
32. grab and grasp
33. honest and truthful
34. easy and simple
35. take and receive
36. throw and toss
37. run and sprint
38. keep and save
39. stone and rock
40. valuable and precious
41. want and desire
42. trip and journey
43. repair and mend
44. thin and slim
45. friend and chum
46. woman and lady
47. thought and idea
48. begin and start
49. new and fresh
50. talk and speak
51. shake and shiver
52. city and town
53. large and giant
54. empty and vacant
55. choose and select
56. umpire and referee
57. street and avenue
58. meadow and field
59. gift and present
60. game and sport

ANTONYM CHARADES

This is played just like the preceding game, except that the guessers try to think of the word being acted out and another that means the opposite.

1. open and close
2. north and south
3. agree and oppose
4. confident and afraid
5. believe and doubt
6. continue and cease
7. active and still
8. bright and dull
9. fancy and plain
10. freedom and slavery
11. gentle and rough
12. silence and noise
13. happy and sorrowful
14. gain and loss
15. famous and unknown
16. hit and miss
17. proud and humble
18. dangerous and safe
19. scarce and abundant
20. few and many
21. over and under
22. different and same
23. deep and shallow
24. accept and reject
25. collect and scatter
26. crooked and straight
27. melt and freeze
28. top and bottom
29. equal and uneven
30. separate and join
31. dry and wet
32. interesting and boring
33. serious and funny
34. wrong and right
35. all and none
36. cloudy and clear
37. stand and sit
38. mountain and valley
39. winter and summer
40. follow and lead
41. in and out
42. perfect and faulty
43. thrifty and wasteful
44. strange and ordinary
45. ready and unprepared
46. sweet and sour
47. build and destroy
48. tight and loose
49. on and off
50. backward and forward
51. left and right
52. best and worst
53. true and false
54. inhale and exhale
55. float and sink
56. often and seldom
57. nothing and something
58. most and least
59. ask and answer
60. increase and decrease

GO-TOGETHER WORDS

Each player in turn acts out a word which is commonly matched with another word, such as *salt* which is usually associated with *pepper*. The audience must guess the go-together words.

1. salt and pepper
2. up and down
3. hammer and nail
4. wash and dry
5. read and write
6. sun and moon
7. ham and eggs
8. day and night
9. soap and water
10. work and play
11. cup and saucer
12. fast and slow
13. enter and exit
14. bow and arrow
15. long and short
16. dog and cat
17. bread and butter
18. lock and key
19. bat and ball
20. east and west
21. black and white
22. knife and fork
23. hook and line
24. pail and shovel
25. pen and pencil
26. nut and bolt
27. shoes and socks
28. see and hear
29. arms and legs
30. land and sea
31. king and queen
32. aim and fire
33. first and last
34. give and take
35. stop and go
36. eat and drink
37. win and lose
38. yes and no
39. rich and poor
40. add and subtract
41. heel and toe
42. bride and groom
43. buy and sell
44. boy and girl
45. thick and thin
46. high and low
47. push and pull
48. teacher and student
49. hat and coat
50. brush and comb

ANAGRAM CHARADES

An anagram is a word built by rearranging the letters of another word. For this charade the exact letters in the first word are used to build the second word. For instance, from the word *swing* the anagram of *wings* could be built.

To begin, a player acts out the first word, and when this is guessed by one of the viewers, he (or his team) must rearrange its letters to find a word which contains the same letters. The first viewer (or team) to do this is awarded a point for himself (or for his team). If a blackboard is handy the game director can write out the first word (once it is guessed) so as to make it easier for viewers to rearrange it letters.

The first word in each of the following sets is the one to be acted out. The second word suggests an anagram answer, although in some cases there are several answers possible.

1. lamp (palm)
2. pear (reap)
3. stop (post)
4. read (dare)
5. stew (west)
6. eat (tea)
7. north (thorn)
8. petal (plate)
9. rope (pore)
10. sword (words)
11. taste (state)
12. throw (worth)
13. stab (bats)
14. race (care)
15. blow (bowl)
16. leap (peal)
17. grin (ring)
18. plum (lump)
19. tide (diet)
20. drop (prod)
21. shoe (hose)
22. golf (flog)
23. steam (meats)
24. wolf (flow)
25. smile (miles)
26. snap (naps)
27. stub (tubs)
28. owl (low)
29. heart (earth)
30. march (charm)

WORD-BUILDING CHARADES

This game is also an anagram one, and is best for contests between teams. Before the game begins, a scorekeeper is appointed. One performer then acts out any short word, like *time* or *rain*. The moment a member of the other team guesses the secret word he shouts it out. If he has guessed correctly his team is allowed a few seconds to rearrange the letters to form as many other words of two or more letters as they can. For example, from *time* they might get *tie* and *me* and *met*. The team scores a point for each word they are able to build from the letters in two minutes. The game continues until one team scores a total of twenty points.

WORDS WITH SIMILAR SOUNDS

Here is an opportunity for two pantomimists to perform side by side at the same time. Each acts out one of the paired words. Both words sound the same, although they have different spellings and different meanings. As soon as the viewers guess one of the words they will quickly find the other. It will be interesting to see which performer helps the audience the most.

1. beat, beet
2. cot, caught
3. tea, tee
4. blue, blew
5. meat, meet
6. sun, son
7. hair, hare
8. Sunday, sundae
9. sew, sow
10. four, fore
11. rode, road
12. see, sea
13. eight, ate
14. brake, break
15. clothes, close
16. soar, sore
17. hour, our
18. I, eye
19. knight, night
20. sale, sail
21. pear, pair
22. one, won
23. cent, scent
24. horse, hoarse
25. write, right
26. plane, plain
27. tide, tied
28. ball, bawl
29. pail, pale
30. rap, wrap
31. waist, waste
32. heal, heel
33. him, hymn
34. toe, tow
35. beach, beech
36. wait, weight
37. pain, pane
38. stake, steak
39. buy, by
40. board, bored

CHARADES ON SPECIAL SUBJECTS

Thinking up charades is often more difficult than acting them out. Here are handy lists of special topics to consult when you are stumped for an idea. The charade maker should indicate the category by gestures before acting. For instance, with *Precious Stones and Gems,* you might indicate a pendant on a necklace or a ring on your finger, until the audience guesses that the category is "jewel." Then each word should be split into syllables if the whole word is too difficult for the audience to guess. Take "opal" —split into an exclamation "oh" and a friend "pal."

Precious Stones and Gems

1. emerald
2. opal
3. diamond
4. sapphire
5. agate
6. amethyst
7. onyx
8. ruby
9. pearl
10. topaz
11. garnet
12. turquoise

Musical Instruments

1. clarinet
2. trombone
3. drum
4. harp
5. violin
6. flute
7. trumpet
8. piccolo
9. piano
10. tuba
11. organ
12. saxophone

Birds

1. oriole
2. swallow
3. bluebird
4. owl
5. eagle
6. wren
7. parakeet
8. sparrow
9. turkey
10. hawk
11. penguin
12. dove
13. cardinal
14. lark
15. duck
16. canary
17. robin
18. parrot
19. blackbird
20. chicken
21. raven
22. ostrich
23. goose
24. crow
25. mockingbird
26. sea gull
27. pheasant
28. pigeon
29. woodpecker
30. hummingbird
31. quail
32. swan
33. goldfinch
34. chickadee
35. stork
36. nightingale
37. thrush
38. crane
39. falcon
40. albatross

Fish

1. mackerel
2. bass
3. perch
4. salmon
5. sailfish
6. barracuda
7. trout
8. sardine
9. cod
10. shark
11. tuna
12. swordfish

Vegetables

1. carrot
2. spinach
3. celery
4. beet
5. lettuce
6. squash
7. artichoke
8. onion
9. potato
10. turnip
11. radish
12. garlic
13. corn
14. parsnip
15. cabbage
16. bean
17. tomato
18. pumpkin
19. peas
20. broccoli
21. asparagus
22. cauliflower
23. parsley
24. cucumber
25. pepper
26. eggplant
27. yam
28. horse-radish
29. rhubarb
30. okra

Fruits

1. peach
2. cherry
3. pineapple
4. apple
5. grape
6. watermelon
7. plum
8. orange
9. apricot
10. lime
11. pear
12. banana
13. fig
14. cantaloupe
15. grapefruit
16. pomegranate
17. date
18. lemon
19. persimmon
20. quince
21. nectarine
22. prune
23. crab apple
24. tangerine

Berries and Nuts

1. loganberry
2. almond
3. filbert
4. blueberry
5. coconut
6. strawberry
7. cashew
8. blackberry
9. cranberry
10. pecan
11. gooseberry
12. peanut
13. raspberry
14. mulberry
15. walnut
16. Brazil nut

Flowers

1. tulip
2. poppy
3. zinnia
4. carnation
5. lily
6. iris
7. rose
8. pansy
9. snapdragon
10. orchid
11. petunia
12. violet
13. lilac
14. daisy
15. chrysanthemum
16. hibiscus
17. cosmos
18. geranium
19. sunflower
20. daffodil

Trees

1. maple
2. cypress
3. oak
4. birch
5. willow
6. redwood
7. hemlock
8. fir
9. beech
10. cottonwood
11. elm
12. ash
13. cedar
14. palm
15. sycamore
16. pine
17. spruce
18. balsam
19. poplar
20. magnolia

Planets

1. Venus
2. Neptune
3. Mars
4. Earth
5. Jupiter
6. Mercury
7. Pluto
8. Saturn
9. Uranus

Famous Characters of the Bible

1. Samson
2. Ruth
3. Paul
4. Moses
5. Adam
6. Solomon
7. Esther
8. Abraham
9. Peter
10. Joshua
11. Cain
12. Rebekah
13. John
14. Elijah
15. Eve
16. Isaac
17. Noah
18. Andrew
19. Samuel
20. Joseph
21. Jonah
22. Sarah
23. David
24. James
25. Jacob
26. Benjamin
27. Lot
28. Aaron
29. Mary
30. Abel
31. Esau
32. Salome
33. Matthew
34. Gideon
35. Luke
36. Jonathan
37. Goliath
38. Rachel
39. Mark
40. Delilah
41. Daniel
42. Naomi
43. Jeremiah
44. Saul
45. Hannah
46. Leah
47. Isaiah
48. Ishmael
49. Nicodemus
50. Stephen

9. The host asks one of the guests to do an imitation. The guest imitates an animal. The others applaud.

10. The host invites everyone to have fun. The guests leap about, wrestle, run offstage and back, and have a wild time.

11. The guests remark that it is time to go. One by one they thank the host and exit.

12. As the last guest leaves, the host turns to the audience and thanks everyone for coming to the party. The host exits and the curtain falls.

Football Fans

1. The spectators at a football stadium come onstage while excitedly chatting about the forthcoming game.

2. As the game starts, they cheer loudly for their team.

3. They fall all over each other in frenzied excitement as their team scores.

4. The spectators cheer in unison, as a yell.

5. As their team fumbles the ball, they roll all over the stage while groaning and making gloomy remarks.

6. A hot dog vendor enters, spills his tray all over the protesting spectators.

7. An absent-minded spectator cheers loudly for the opposite team. As the others crowd around him with threatening glares, he again cheers the original team.

8. The spectators look upward while yelling that the football is sailing into the stands. As an offstage assistant tosses a toy ball onto the stage, the spectators scramble to catch it.

9. A spectator excuses himself several times, saying he needs a drink of water. He bumps into the others as he awkwardly exits and enters. They yell at him to sit down.

10. A spectator stretches and announces how tired he is. As he sleeps, the others try to arouse him with shakes and shouts, but without success. Another spectator then falls asleep; the others try to awaken him also. One by one, all fall asleep. All suddenly awaken in unison to cheer explosively for their team.

11. As their team wins, the spectators waltz around with each other.

12. While remarking about the tough game they had, the spectators drag themselves offstage wearily.

The Runners

1. Two or three runners enter from the right wing. They puff and stagger as if running a cross-country race.

2. In a series of actions they pass each other, fall behind each other, pass once more.

3. As they continue to pass and fall behind they yell out, loudly, "Wait for me!" and "Not so fast!" and "Here I come!"

4. The runners exit at the left wing, one another another. When they reappear at the right wing, they are in another order. This can be repeated several times throughout the play.

5. With odd and funny actions, the runners appear, cross the stage, disappear, and reappear. Here are a few examples: They run upside down. They flash back and forth as rapidly as the puppeteer's arm can move. They run into each other, collide, fall, and run once more.

6. The runners disappear at the left wing. When they reappear at right, one of the puppets is riding the shoulders of another. The next time across, the rider becomes the carrier.

7. The runner in front suddenly turns around and calls out, "Halt!" He then hands candy bars to the others, inviting, "Here, have some candy." While the others munch their candy, the leading runner speeds offstage. The others suddenly wake up, yell out, speed offstage after him.

8. The puppets halt suddenly and peer into the left wing. They yell that they are approaching the finish line with, "There's the finish line!" and "We're almost there!"

9. They repeat the wild antics mentioned at Step 5 above. They finally disappear into the left wing.

10. The stage is empty for a moment. Then, all puppets appear from right wing. They wearily stumble to the center of the

stage where they line up. The middle puppet says to the audience, "Sorry, we made a mistake. That wasn't the finish after all." Another puppet adds sadly, "It was just the beginning." The third puppet remarks, "So if you will excuse us, we have to be running!"

11. All puppets dash wildly around, repeating several of the previously listed actions.

12. All finally rush offstage as the curtain falls.

The School for Singers

1. The professor of the school for singers enters while singing off-key. He glances at his watch and remarks that it is time for his pupils to arrive.

2. One by one the pupils enter. They sing a happy greeting to the professor. He sings back a welcome.

3. The professor announces that practice will now begin. He leads them in singing the scale a few times.

4. A pupil requests that they be allowed to practice with a song. The professor agrees, then leads them in any familiar song, perhaps *Dixie* or *Sailing, Sailing*.

5. The pupils sing off-key and out of rhythm. The professor screams in dismay and rushes about in distress.

6. They sing the same song again, with the same off-key results.

7. The professor states that he will discover who is singing off-key. One by one he tests the pupils. All of them sing poorly. The professor rolls on the floor and groans.

8. The professor tells two of the pupils that he wants them to sing lower. They crouch down and sing briefly. He shouts that that was not what he meant.

9. The professor says that he will show them how to sing beautifully. He steps forward to the center of the stage and sings

sourly while gesturing wildly. He then tells the pupils that *that* is what he wants to hear. The pupils now sing as did the professor, with sour notes and wild gestures. The professor nods in pleasure and says that they are doing much better.

10. The pupils and the professor jump excitedly up and down as they sing a fast and lively song.

11. The professor tells the pupils that they will now sing a special song for the audience.

12. The pupils sing a familiar tune, singing in harmony. All puppets bow and exit.

SPECIAL FUN WITH PUPPETS

Puppets can perform so many exciting acts! They can entertain audiences in so many interesting ways!

This section will show you how to use your puppets in special ways for special fun. You will discover ideas for making your puppets dance. You will find the best way to build a comical puppet show. You will learn how to perform the kind of stunts that win enthusiastic applause from your audiences.

Some of the acts in this section run for just a minute or two. Some you can build into a performance that remains onstage for three or four minutes. You can choose the ones that run for the length of time you desire.

You can also use this material to present a variety show. Build up several short acts and then bring them onstage, one after another, with a short intermission between the acts.

"It Happened to Me"

To build this stunt the puppeteer thinks of something that happened to him. It can be anything exciting or funny or just plain interesting. The puppeteer then sends his puppet onstage to act out the event. As the puppet acts, the puppeteer narrates. That is, he explains the action as it goes along.

Suppose your puppet is showing how he learned to swim. He could perform and explain all sorts of actions. He could start off by showing how he shivered when first touching the chilly water. Next, he could act out his first dive—an awkward leap which ends with a thud on the stage floor.

410

You can also make your puppet swim comically along. Just move him slowly across the stage while dipping him up and down. Let his head appear above the stage floor and then disappear below it as he swims.

Here are fifteen good ideas. They are typical of the kind that make good solo acts.

1. Learning to swim.
2. Searching for a lost object.
3. Cooking dinner.
4. Repairing a bicycle.
5. Hiking through the woods.
6. Trying to study in a noisy room.
7. Playing baseball.
8. Walking to school in a heavy rain.
9. Washing dishes.
10. Learning to dance.
11. Fishing from a rowboat.
12. Building a tree house.
13. Watching an exciting television show.
14. Shopping in a busy market.
15. Learning to play a musical instrument.

Dancing Puppets

Puppets which dance bouncily around the stage can put on an attractive and amusing show. Very little practice is needed to make the puppet dancers move about in unison with music. Here are ten ideas for making the most of your dancing puppets:

1. Have a pair of puppets dance together, perhaps with a waltz.

2. Several puppeteers can take part by having some of the dancers exit as others enter.

3. In rhythm with exciting music, have a puppet or two perform a comical dance. They can leap, hop, dart across the stage, exit at the left wing and re-enter at the right.

4. Have the puppets sing as they dance.

5. The dancers can wear costumes of foreign lands.

6. Have a girl puppet dance gracefully about in harmony with soft music.

7. Have odd combinations of animals dancing as partners, such as a lion and a deer.

8. Change the pace of the dancing by speeding up or slowing down the music.

9. Build a short scene in which a girl teaches a boy to dance. At first he dances awkwardly, but grows increasingly skillful.

10. Finish your show of dancing puppets by having them dance offstage as the music concludes.

Animal Stunt

This is a humorous stunt which can be a popular part of your puppet show. Since the puppets occupy only a small portion of the stage, as many as six or seven animal puppets can take part.

Each puppeteer makes a puppet of an animal or a bird. Since this is a brief stunt, it is best to make stick puppets, for you can create one in just a few minutes. The puppeteer draws a picture of an animal or a bird (or clips a colored picture from an old magazine) and mounts it on a stick. The puppet should not be too large.

The show begins as one of the smaller puppets comes onstage while making appropriate animal sounds. For example, a cat could enter while *meowing*. Next, a somewhat larger animal enters and performs. For instance, a dog could run onstage while barking. One at a time the animals and birds continue to appear until the stage and the space above the stage is thick with puppets—all of them making their natural noises. The creatures run or fly about as best they can within their own small portion of the stage.

All the puppeteers watch for a signal from the teacher. At her signal everyone swiftly—and at the same time—pulls his puppet from the stage and becomes silent. When done in unison, this makes an interesting finish to the stunt.

Singing Puppets

Puppets can be merry singers! Anyone can sing well enough to make his puppet sound interesting and amusing. Audiences always enjoy musical selections. For these three reasons, use the following ideas for adding extra showmanship to your puppet plays:

1. While working up a performance, find a place or two where you can include a song. Use songs that fit in with the play, like *Yankee Doodle* in a scene with a background of American history.

2. Let your puppets act out the playing of musical instruments as they sing along. It is easy to make small drums and horns. You can play real music offstage, or use a phonograph.

3. Let the puppets lead the audience in the singing of popular tunes.

4. Have the puppets march around the stage as they sing lively songs.

5. As one of the characters in a play, have someone who bursts into song every once in a while.

6. Play a phonograph record with a solo singing voice. Let a puppet pretend to sing. You can also play a chorus of voices, while having several puppets onstage.

7. To make it appear as if a single puppet has several voices, have only one puppet onstage while several hidden voices sing.

8. Turn interesting puppet characters into singers. Examples: a giant, a tiger, an alligator.

9. As background music to a pantomime play, have a hidden chorus sing softly.

10. Build a complete show around singing puppets. Have several acts, some of them humorous and others of a more serious nature.

Puppets from Many Lands

Puppet acts that take place in a foreign land are always welcome. It is easy to dress your puppets in a costume of another country, and just as easy to work up some actions for them to perform.

First of all, select one of the countries listed below. All of them are familiar lands which offer good opportunities for costumes and customs.

Next, build an act around some typical or colorful custom of the

413

country. If you choose Switzerland you could show Swiss children playing in the snow of the Alps mountains. For a show taking place in Japan, your characters could cross a Japanese-style bridge over to an orchard of cherry blossoms.

1. Holland
2. Egypt
3. China
4. Spain
5. Switzerland
6. India
7. Japan
8. Italy
9. Ireland
10. Mexico

You Are the Star

In this show, you are both the puppeteer and the puppet! The idea is for you and your friends to play yourselves. The puppet does not have to look exactly like you, but you can dress it in the same kind of clothing that you often wear.

You can build the play around one of the other ideas found in this book. For instance, in the play called *The Singing Dragon* you and your friends could play the roles of the children. The main idea is for you to play yourself, whatever the play.

Another way to use this idea is for you and one or two friends to act out a scene based on your shared activities. Think of something that you do together, such as walking home from school. Ideas for dialogue and action will come very quickly once you start with a familiar activity.

It is important that the audience knows that you are playing yourself. This is best done just before the curtain rises. The teacher announces each person by name. Your puppet self then appears onstage for a bow. When everyone has been introduced, the play begins. To help the audience remember, the puppets address each other by name—the puppeteers' name of course—frequently.

414

Performing Puppets

This stunt is always good for a few minutes of fun at a puppet show and it usually produces some extra laughs. The announcer tells the audience that some of the puppets have been trained to obey any orders that anyone cares to give them. He invites members of the audience to command the puppets to perform.

The announcer stands aside as two or three puppets bounce onstage and bow. The audience then commands them to perform whatever stunts come to mind. The audience can ask them to run in a circle, to bump into each other, or sing a song. Half the fun of this stunt is that the audience will ask the puppets to do difficult or strange things. When the puppets try to obey the commands, the fun begins!

Funny Puppets

Puppets are natural comedians. They like nothing better than to have fun onstage. They can make the audience laugh, too. Here are ten good ideas for building comedy shows:

1. Dress your puppets in comic costumes, such as that of a clown and a scarecrow.

2. Have a puppet character tell about something funny that happened to him. Let him go through funny motions as he tells his story.

3. Remember that your puppets can perform some amazing stunts. Turn them loose. Let them dart back and forth swiftly. Have a puppet disappear into one wing and reappear almost instantly at the opposite wing. Let a puppet hang downward from the ceiling. As you practice, you will think of many more funny stunts.

4. Build funny dialogues by using jokes. The puppeteers can search books and magazines for jokes that can be added to a comical conversation.

5. Put on a humorous dancing act. The puppets can whirl and fly about the stage.

6. Have a puppet man who bursts into laughter all the time.

7. Have a puppet girl who giggles constantly.

8. Make one of your puppet characters an awkward sort of person who is always bumping into people and dropping things.

9. Speak with funny voices. Examples: a squeaky voice, a voice that sings its words, a shouting voice.

10. Give your comic characters interesting mannerisms. For instance, a puppet could bounce across the stage, instead of walking. Another character could always be eating something. A third puppet could have the habit of walking backwards, explaining that he likes to see where he has been.

Question Puppets

This idea gets the audience into the act. It also gives acting experience to the puppeteer. The puppet comes onstage and asks any kind of an interesting question for the audience to guess. If the audience comes up with the right answer, the puppeteer goes on to another question. If the listeners fail to come up with a correct answer, the puppeteer supplies it.

Each puppet can ask three or four questions. The quizzes should not be too difficult, nor too easy. The following ten are good examples of the kind that can make an exciting quiz-show.

1. Who is Henry Wadsworth Longfellow? (an American poet)

2. In what country is the city of Tokyo? (Japan)

3. What is the Mona Lisa? (a famous painting)

4. On what continent do gorillas live in the jungle? (Africa)

5. The picture of what man is on a five-dollar bill? (Abraham Lincoln)

6. The name of what planet begins with the letter v? (Venus)

7. What are the first names of the Wright Brothers? (Orville and Wilbur)

8. On what continent is the country of Bolivia? (South America)

9. The name of what precious stone begins with the letter *e?* (emerald)

10. What state of the union is directly north of California? (Oregon)

Salesman and Customer

Just get a salesman and a customer together! That is all you need for building a one-man show that includes two puppets.

The first thing to do is to build a pair of interesting puppet characters, one as the salesman and the other for the customer. Choose two characters who are unlike each other in appearance and manner. For instance, the salesman could be a talkative and brash sort of person, while the customer is shy and never finishes a sentence. Or, it could be the other way around, with the customer loudly demanding faster and better service from a meek and nervous clerk.

Next, decide upon the type of product which the customer is seeking to buy. It can be almost anything from an automobile to a pair of socks.

Before the play begins, tell the audience where it is taking place and who the two characters represent.

Finally, get your salesman and your customer onstage and let them act things out! You will be pleased at the way in which they build an interesting play for you. Let the customer ask questions about the product. Let the salesman show the customer how the product works. Have the customer complain that the price is too high. Before long you will have dozens of good ideas which you can develop into a lively act.

Puppets from History

You can build a very interesting act around great moments in history. Keep the performance fairly short and simple. It is best to choose scenes which do not require too many puppets. A few examples:

1. Thomas A. Edison works with one or two assistants to invent the electric light.

2. Christopher Columbus listens to the complaints of his sailors, but a few moments later they break into cheers as the New World is sighted.

417

Famous People

The idea is for a puppet or a group of puppets to impersonate famous people. The audience tries to guess who they are. The famous man or woman can be revealed by the puppet's words and actions. A single puppet could impersonate Benjamin Franklin by pretending to fly a kite while remarking about electricity. Two puppets could come onstage and act out a scene which revealed them as George and Martha Washington.

Dance and Joke

This is an old and favorite type of stage act which is just as popular today as it ever was. You can use it to put on an attractive act with puppets.

Two puppets take part. They can be two boys or two girls or one of each. The act proceeds as the puppets alternate between dancing and joking. In other words, the performers dance for a bit, then stop long enough to exchange funny conversation, then dance once more. They alternate between dancing and joking for as long as the act continues.

The dance can consist of almost anything, just as long as it is light and peppy. All sorts of varieties can be used, such as dancing back to back and by having them alternate back and forth with one stretching upward and the other crouching. The dancing part should be accompanied by music. The music starts and stops as the puppets dance and stop.

Two or three jokes are enough for exchange during each pause in the dancing. Jokes and riddles can be found in books and magazines.

Wild West Show

A show about the wild west is certain to be popular with your audience. It is especially suitable for a large group of puppeteers. A wide *Blanket Theater* (explained in the first pages of this section) is best for staging a western scene. Several types of puppets (also explained in the first pages) can be made and used.

Build your show around familiar actions of the wild west. The show could open as a pair of covered wagons bump onto the

419

stage. Next, some cowboys or soldiers could enter on horseback as guards. Bison could rush onstage briefly and disappear. Then, some Indians could attack the covered wagons. Simple actions like these will make an exciting show that can last for several minutes.

You can include the following characters and animals and moving objects:

1. cowboys	7. sheep
2. soldiers	8. bison
3. Indians	9. cattle
4. women	10. train
5. children	11. stagecoach
6. horses	12. covered wagons

What Language?

This one makes a fun-filled series of short acts in which the audience can take part. The viewers are told that the acts will include just two or three sentences of dialogue. While puppets will speak in English, the audience must try to guess the language which is correctly associated with the performance.

As an example of how an act might be worked out, two puppets come onstage. One of them starts working. The other puppet asks him, "What are you doing?" The working puppet replies, "I'm repairing this wall." The audience might then guess that the correct language is Chinese, inasmuch as the Great Wall is in China. As another example, one puppet might ask another, "Where do you live?" The other puppet answers, "In the city of the Eiffel Tower." Since the Eiffel Tower is in Paris, the language would be French.

420

The following languages will make good scenes:

1. Chinese
2. French
3. Italian
4. Dutch
5. Arabic

6. Spanish
7. German
8. Swedish
9. Egyptian
10. Japanese

Helpful Puppets

Puppet people are ready and willing to teach us the lessons we need to learn for healthy and happy living. Why not build a show or stunt around a useful idea? The stunt entitled *Crash* on another page of this section is a good example of how you can build one.

Here are twenty topics which can be developed into useful and attractive shows:

1. traffic safety
2. thriftiness
3. good study habits
4. forest preservation
5. fair play
6. correct eating habits
7. reading of books
8. self-reliance
9. dental care
10. friendliness

11. proper sleeping habits
12. patriotism
13. good manners
14. personal neatness
15. promptness
16. good working habits
17. cooperation
18. safety in the home
19. good posture
20. building of courage

PANTOMIME PLAYS FOR PUPPETS

You will be surprised at what superb pantomime artists puppets can be. The ideas in this section will show you how to present attractive puppet plays in pantomime.

No words are spoken by the actors or actresses during a pantomime act. They perform in silence. They tell the story of the play by their actions and gestures. However, it is always effective to include background music in the play. Also, you can add sound effects to help develop the drama.

Your puppets should perform simple movements that the viewers understand clearly. Puppeteers should check their play from time to time during rehearsal to make sure that the pantomime movements are easy to understand.

This section offers you a wide variety of acts. Some of them make use of a narrator who speaks to the audience as the actors perform in silence. The purpose of a narrator is to help the audience understand the onstage action.

Charade Puppets

Here is a very special way to have fun with puppets. Your audience takes part in the play. The idea is for the puppet (or puppets) to lead the audience in a game of charades. Charades is a game in which a secret word is acted out for the audience to guess. No words are spoken by the actor; he reveals the secret word by acts and motions.

For your puppet charades use very simple words. Also, choose words that the puppet can reveal through simple actions. For example, if the puppeteer chose the secret word of *whirl,* he would enter the stage and whirl around. If the audience guessed the word *spin,* or maybe *turn,* the puppet would shake his head and whirl some more. Before too long the audience will guess that the secret word is *whirl.*

Two puppets can come onstage and act out the same word. The audience should be told beforehand that both actors are going to be doing the same thing.

Here is a list of good words to use:

1. bounce
2. yes
3. sleep
4. dance
5. slow
6. run

7. bow	14. sway
8. jump	15. fast
9. no	16. stumble
10. retreat	17. leap
11. shiver	18. fly
12. fall	19. knock
13. hop	20. exercise

Tug-of-War

Here is a favorite picnic stunt that you can perform onstage with entertaining results. You can present the act using four puppets, or only two, so long as you have an equal number on both sides.

Before the puppets appear onstage fasten a length of cord to them in a way that makes it appear that the puppets are grasping the rope. This prevents the rope from slipping off during the tugging. Small safety pins will usually serve the purpose.

Use your imagination to think of clever actions for the puppet athletes. Here are some good suggestions:

1. Let them tug back and forth as if one side is winning, then the other.

2. Let one side pull so hard that they move backward into the wing and off the stage completely, then have their opponents struggle back to do the same in the opposite wing.

3. Let one side collapse so that the puppets are dragged across the stage for a while.

4. Let them tug in rhythm to offstage music.

5. Let one side pull its opponents offstage so swiftly that all of them shoot into the wing with a loud crash.

Ships at Sea

Your ships are the stars of this show! You can build a very entertaining pantomime act by sending to sea some boats of different shapes and sizes. There is something fascinating about ships that sail and dip upon the ocean—especially when you include background music and sound effects.

Draw several kinds of boats on thick paper or thin cardboard. Cut them out and color them brightly. (Or, you can clip pictures from magazines no longer being used.) Paste each ship onto the

end of a long and narrow stick. Hold the other end of the stick and let the ship appear above the stage as if sailing over the water.

Let your ships move around with various actions. Here are ten suggestions:

1. A pair of ships race each other.
2. A tugboat helps a passenger liner into port.
3. Ships struggle as if in a violent storm.
4. A man floats by on a raft.
5. A whale chases a ship around the stage.
6. A submarine comes up and goes down.
7. A speedy motorboat races around a slow sailboat.
8. A pirate ship and a modern ship pass each other.
9. Two ships turn and dip in unison.
10. Several ships speed onstage and off furiously.

Story Acts

In this type of pantomime a narrator tells a story to the audience at the same time that the puppets act it out. The narrator can remain hidden from the audience by standing behind the stage, or he can stand in view and to one side of the stage where he can see the action.

Fairy tales and ancient myths are especially good for story acts. Sound effects will help to make the acts interesting.

Busy Boulevard

Cars zip past each other!

A traffic policeman blows his whistle at a speeding motorist!

Pedestrians dodge the traffic!

That is the kind of exciting action you can expect when your pantomime show takes place on a busy boulevard. Stick puppets are best for this pantomime act because you will want to use a great many puppets. Here are a few kinds of puppet people you can place on the boulevard:

1. drivers in automobiles
2. drivers in trucks
3. men on motorcycles
4. pedestrians
5. policeman
6. policeman in police car
7. passengers on bus
8. firemen on fire truck

The best way for the puppeteers to build the act is to think of what actually happens in heavy traffic—and then exaggerate everything, including the speed of the vehicles. You can develop dozens of interesting movements, such as pedestrians dodging in and out, drivers shaking their fists at each other, and so on.

Sound effects are very important to the show. Assistants can stand in back of the puppeteers and add the sounds that you hear in heavy traffic.

The Magic Mirror

This idea will give you extra use of the puppets which you have made for other shows. It offers brief roles for ten or more puppets. This pantomime play employs a narrator who is a puppet himself.

The puppet who narrates the act is an inventor who is dressed in a smock. He enters and introduces himself as Gregory Q. Genius, the world-famous inventor. He announces that he has just invented a magic mirror. This magic mirror, he says, can instantly change a person into someone else. The only thing a person has to do is to walk in front of it and *bang!* The person is changed instantly into someone or something else.

The inventor then faces a screen which has been set up at the center of the stage. He says that the magic mirror is behind the screen. He tells the audience that his magic mirror has been set up on a busy sidewalk where lots of people pass by. "Let's see what happens," he says finally, "as people are changed by my magic mirror."

The inventor stands aside. A puppet enters from the right wing and passes in back of the screen. As soon as he disappears behind it he is quickly replaced by another puppet who comes out on the other side of the screen. He exits at the left wing.

One after another, several puppet persons walk in back of the screen where they are replaced by other puppet people. You can make all sorts of amusing switches. For instance, a man can turn into a prancing goat, or a horse can come out as a bouncing clown.

To finish the act, the inventor announces that he himself will also walk before the mirror. He then goes behind the screen and comes out as some funny sort of creature, perhaps a monkey. He shrugs and remarks to the audience, "All I can say is, be sure to watch out for the magic mirror!" He scampers offstage as the curtain falls.

The Chasers

For exciting action, there is nothing like puppets who chase each other around the stage! With a little imagination you can build a peppy play out of chasing performers.

The first step is to decide upon the kind of puppets who will chase each other. Here are five examples:

1. man and bear
2. dog and cat
3. cowboy and Indian
4. eagle and wolf
5. kangaroo and soldier

Next, think of different things that could happen as they run around. They might suddenly drop below the stage as if falling into a river. They can alternate in chasing each other. The puppet being chased might stop so suddenly that the pursuing puppet crashes into him. Once you get your puppets onstage you will be able to come up with lots of ideas for action.

Music is especially good for this type of show. Play a lively phonograph record as the puppets perform.

You can start the show with an introduction something like this: "Ladies and gentlemen, you will now see some exciting action as a cowboy chases an Indian—and as the Indian does some chasing, too!"

Fishing

The way in which a puppet theater is built is the reason why this amusing stunt is possible. Two or three puppets can take part. They are assisted by stagehands who also remain out of sight behind the theater.

The pantomime opens as the puppet fishermen sit or stand facing the audience. Their fishing lines are fastened to their arms so that they can swing them up and down. The lines are just long enough to reach out of sight below the stage floor. A piece of bent wire, serving as a hook, is attached to the end of each line.

The following kinds of actions make this a lively play:

1. The fishermen constantly catch all sorts of odd and funny items, such as a cookie, a peanut, a flower, a spool, and miniature toys.

These objects are attached to the hooks by the assistants when the puppets lean forward to lower the lines. As a puppet leans back, the line is raised to reveal the object to the audience. When the line is once more lowered the first object is removed and another hooked on.

The puppets can react to their strange catches by fainting, shaking, and turning to look at each other with shock.

2. For a second series of actions, have an assistant tug on a fishing line as if a large fish had caught his hook. They struggle back and forth. The puppet finally flies outward toward the audience for a few inches, then plunges downward and out of sight as if yanked by the fish. The puppet reappears and fishes once more.

You can use this idea in several ways. Have all the fishermen disappear at once. Have them disappear one after another in quick succession. Have one of them dip up and down rapidly several times.

For a humorous finish, have a large fish puppet poke its open mouth upward toward the fishermen. They jerk back and race offstage.

The Keep-Trying Man

This pantomime is narrated by a player who may stand in view of the audience or who may remain hidden. The important idea is for the narrator to speak clearly and in harmony with the onstage action.

The words and actions given below are written for a puppet performance. However, it is also suitable for real actors and actresses. In the puppet performance, the puppets appear and disappear from below the stage. In a show for real players, the performers crouch onstage as if hiding, then stretch up and down as directed in the instructions given below.

The narrator's words can be memorized or simply read from this book. As soon as he speaks a sentence, the players carry out the actions as instructed:

"Once upon a time there was a man with a camera . . ." (The puppet comes onstage, carrying a camera. He bows to audience, remains facing it.)

"He was a man who liked to keep trying to take pictures . . ." (He moves himself and his camera from left to right and back.)

"He was a man who liked especially to keep trying to take pictures of wild animals . . ." (As the puppet looks straight ahead toward the audience, the animals pop up in unison from below the stage just long enough for a bow, then disappear downward. There should be either two or four animals altogether, one or two on each side of the puppet man.)

"One day the man who liked to keep trying to take pictures of wild animals went for a hike in the woods . . ." (The man walks in a circle.)

"As the man who liked to keep trying to take pictures of wild animals walked in the woods he looked around for wild animals to take pictures of . . ." (The man walks in a circle, looking around.)

"He looked toward the east, but saw no wild animals . . ." (As the man looks toward the right, the animals pop up at the left, then disappear downward.)

"He looked toward the west, but saw nothing . . ." (As he looks toward the left, the animals pop up at right, then disappear.)

"He looked up into the trees, but saw no wild animals . . ." (As he looks upward, the animals pop up near his legs, then disappear.)

"He looked down into the caves, but saw nothing at all . . ."

(As he looks downward, the animals appear overhead by hanging down from the top of the stage, then disappear upward. Note: If the play is performed by real actors in pantomime, eliminate this action.)

"Wherever he looked, the man who liked to keep trying to take pictures of wild animals could see no wild animals that he could take pictures of . . ." (The man looks rapidly in succession toward the four previous directions.)

"This made him so very sad that he cried like this . . ." (He bends forward and shakes as if sobbing.)

"But because he was a man who liked to keep trying to take pictures of wild animals, he decided to keep trying to take pictures of wild animals . . ." (While keeping his back to the audience, the man searches around upstage.)

"And this is when something interesting happened . . ." (The animals pop up and huddle together downstage to talk.)

"The wild animals decided that because the man who liked to keep trying to take pictures of wild animals was the kind of a man who kept trying to take pictures of wild animals that they would help him to take pictures of wild animals . . ." (All the animals disappear downward.)

"So the next time the man looked toward the east he saw a wild animal . . ." (As he looks toward the right, an animal pops up.)

"When he looked toward the west he saw another wild animal . . ." (As he looks toward the left, an animal appears.)

"He looked upward and there was another one . . ." (As he looks upward, an animal appears by hanging overhead.)

"And when he looked downward he saw another wild animal . . ." (As he looks downward, an animal appears close to his face.)

"No matter where he looked, the man who liked to keep trying to take pictures of wild animals always saw wild animals . . ." (The animals appear anywhere onstage.)

"This made him so very happy that he laughed like this . . ." (He shakes back and forth as if laughing merrily.)

"This also made the wild animals so very happy that they also laughed like this . . ." (The animals also shake back and forth in merry laughter.)

"Everyone agreed that it is always a good idea to keep trying to do whatever you want to do . . ." (Everyone onstage nods toward the audience. The curtain falls.)

Marching Soldiers

It is a fascinating sight to watch puppet soldiers march around the stage! The audience is certain to like the way they step around in rhythm to peppy music. Try the following ideas for building a show of marching puppets:

1. Stick puppets make wonderful soldiers and are easy to create. Draw pictures of soldiers on stiff paper. Then cut the figures out and paste them on stick handles.

2. Have the soldiers march in time with the music by bouncing up and down as they march.

3. For humorous action, have your soldiers march down the left wall of the stage, march across the stage, then march up the right wall. When they reach the top of the wall, pull the puppets offstage and let them appear once more from the floor of the stage.

4. Have all the soldiers break formation and march individually in any direction. They march back and forth across the stage while passing each other.

5. Let all the soldiers line up facing the audience. Have them sway sideways, back and forth, in rhythm to the music.

6. Let the soldiers march around in single file.

7. Have them line up facing the audience, while bouncing up and down only slightly. The first soldier in line starts to bounce up and down vigorously. In turn, the other puppets do the same. As soon as all of them are bouncing with vigor, they march away into another stunt.

8. Let the soldiers march offstage and march back again. This can be performed two or three times.

9. Leave just two of the soldiers onstage to perform for a while. For one of their stunts, have them march straight toward each other and dodge a collision at the very last moment.

10. The soldiers march offstage as the music concludes.

The Wall

Prepare for this act by setting up a paper wall on the stage. Let it run from upstage to downstage, a short distance from the left wing. It should be somewhat higher than the puppets as they appear onstage.

A narrator explains the action to the audience as a pair of puppets act it out:

"Once upon a time there were two enthusiastic travelers . . ." (The puppets bounce merrily onstage from the right wing.)

"One morning the two enthusiastic travelers were traveling toward a big city when they suddenly came to a big wall . . ." (The puppets walk to the wall and stop.)

"The big wall was a big problem to the two travelers because they did not know how to get to the other side of such a big wall . . ." (The puppets look up to the top of the wall and shake their heads.)

"One of the travelers decided to try to get to the other side of the wall by digging beneath it . . ." (Puppet A bends back and forth at the base of the wall as if digging.)

"But the wall was much too thick for him . . ." (The puppet sags and falls to the ground.)

"The other traveler decided to try to jump over the wall . . ." (Puppet B runs and jumps in swift action in an effort to get over the wall.)

"But the wall was much too high for him . . ." (The puppet collapses and falls down.)

"But the enthusiastic travelers made up their minds that the thick and high wall was not going to defeat them . . ." (The puppets leap up and nod their heads vigorously.)

432

"They knew there had to be a way to get over the wall and they also knew that they could find it . . ." (The puppets nod with even more vigor.)

"They agreed to travel to a library and read a book entitled *How You Can Get on the Other Side of a Thick and High Wall* . . ." (The puppets exit at right.)

"They were very wise in reading that book because it told them exactly how to get on the other side of a thick and high wall . . ." (The puppets enter from right while nodding.)

"The enthusiastic travelers knew that they would only hurt themselves by trying to dig under the wall . . ." (Puppet A digs briefly, faces the audience and shakes his head.)

"And they knew that there was a much better way than to try to jump over the wall . . ." (Puppet B briefly tries to jump the wall, then faces the audience and shakes his head.)

"They discovered that there is a right way to do everything . . ." (The puppets nod in unison.)

"They discovered especially that there is a right way to get on the other side of a thick and high wall . . ." (The puppets nod with vigor.)

"So here is how they did things in the right way and got to the other side of that thick and high wall . . ." (The puppets crouch briefly, then crash through the paper wall and bounce offstage at left.)

Crash

Here is a short act which is especially good for teaching safety. The announcer tells the audience that they will be shown why they should not run while indoors. The announcer then stands aside as a puppet races in from the left wing, dashes across the stage and exits at right. Another puppet enters from the right and races across to exit at left. The first puppet enters from the right and races offstage at the left. The second puppet runs on from the left and exits at the right. Then, both puppets race onstage from opposite wings and crash together in the center, accompanied by the sound effects of a loud crash. They fall, slowly get up, and stagger dizzily offstage in opposite directions.

Pantomime Circus

Put on a puppet circus in pantomime! Back up the onstage action with a phonograph record that plays a lively military march. You are sure to have a hit.

Prepare as many puppets as you like in the costumes of circus performers. Here are a few you can use:

1. clown
2. acrobat
3. cowboy
4. Indian
5. lady dancer
6. popcorn salesman
7. horse
8. elephant
9. seal
10. lion and lion tamer

The puppet performers come onstage in any order and perform according to their characters. The clown bounces merrily around, the lion trainer snaps a whip at the lion, and the dancer glides gracefully about. They perform briefly, then exit, and then return for another brief performance. The action should be continuous. Two or three puppets can be onstage at the same time.

Best Friends

You can use puppets from other shows for this amusing act, both human figures and animals. The greater the variety you have, the better the act will be.

434

A puppet comes onstage as the announcer. He informs the audience that the puppets of this theater have formed some close friendships. He goes on to say that everyone in the group has found a best friend—and that some of the couples are very interesting to see. The announcer remarks that it might be fun to watch the couples as they meet each other. The announcer calls out, "Here they come!" and races offstage.

Here is an example of the action that now takes place: A puppet comes onstage from the right wing, looks into the left wing as if seeing someone, then waves happily. From offstage the announcer calls out, "Best friend!" Another puppet races in from the left wing and another voice offstage calls out, "Best friend!" They embrace each other and walk offstage together.

The above action is repeated several times with different pairs of puppets. In other words, a puppet enters, calls out, and waits expectantly. The other puppet then rushes onstage and returns the greeting. After embracing, the puppets walk offstage together.

The idea that makes the act amusing is the odd combinations of best friends, so be sure to make them as different as possible. Here are five examples:

1. A boy and a whale
2. A princess and a mule
3. A tall man and short man
4. A fish and a bird
5. A girl and a dragon.

The puppets can come onstage from the wings or from above or below the stage. Animals can appear from below the stage as if coming from underground, while birds can swoop down from the top of the stage.

The Quick-Change Artist

You would have to search long and far to find an act as delightful as this one. It makes full use of some of the advantages of using puppets as actresses and actors.

The show is based on the fact that a puppeteer can switch swiftly from one puppet to another. The change of puppets is seen by the audience as a change of costume by a single puppet who is a quick-change artist. In other words, although a number of puppets appear in the act, they are supposed to be the same puppet in different costumes and characters.

The program starts as the announcer (or the puppet himself in a one-man show) informs the audience that they are about to see a quick-change artist in action. The puppet enters and bows to the audience. He performs a little dance or stunt and meanwhile the announcer says that the performer will show how quickly he can change from one costume to another.

The puppet races offstage. Then he enters seconds later wearing a completely different costume and bows to the viewers. He then exits and, in his original costume, the puppet returns to the stage for another bow. He remains onstage for the next announcement.

Of course, the puppeteer doesn't have to change the puppet's clothes. He simply switches to another puppet with the same face and shape but wearing another kind of costume altogether.

For the second act the puppet can perform a whole series of speedy switches in costume. The puppet dashes offstage and back several times, each time in a different outfit. Two puppeteers can work together to make the changes rapid and smooth. In that way you won't need so many puppets. While one of the puppets is onstage, another actually gets a new costume. Finally, the original puppet returns and bows several times.

For act three, the puppet bows, runs offstage and returns a moment later as the very same puppet with no changes made whatsoever! The announcer explains with a smile that the puppet is so speedy that while offstage he changed into six other costumes and still had time to change back to his own. The puppet bows happily in several directions.

The grand finale is the most fantastic of all. Two or three puppeteers work at racing several different puppets onstage and off. They can enter from either wing, or hang down from the ceiling or pop up from below the stage. Two or three should appear at the same time. Some of them need not look like the original puppet at all. In fact, you can even include animals and birds. Finally, the original puppet appears alone onstage for final bows and the announcer leads the audience in applause.

Section 12

Short Plays from the Great Classics

(This section illustrated by Shizu)

The twelve short plays in this section are all easy to stage, fun to act out, and entertaining to watch. They are suitable for performing in a simple classroom or an elaborate auditorium, at a club meeting or a party at home. They may be used effectively during a Sunday school class or for a camp program, in front of a large audience or for just a few friends of the actors. Their main purpose is to entertain, and if they happen to instruct at the same time, that's just an added attraction.

Why these plays? The dramas here have been adapted from some of the best-loved classics of all time. Because actors and audience will probably be familiar with the original books, the plays will be especially attractive. The characters will seem like old friends given new life and the boys and girls who meet them

438

again in dramatic form will feel closer identification with them as they participate in the action. If there are some members of the group who haven't yet read the books, the plays should arouse their interest and curiosity.

Each play is easy to put on. You need only a few props and little scenery. Preparation and rehearsal can be kept to a minimum and even the most inexperienced actor and actress can do a good job.

Select a play that seems best for your group. This book contains a wide variety of plays, so you can select those that especially appeal to you and your group. Go through the pages and choose those that are the most appropriate.

Some plays are shorter than others, and you should consider the amount of time you will have. Youngsters who have had some rehearsal will perform a play in less time than those who have not become very familiar with it. Yet each play is short enough to be performed during a class period or as part of an assembly program. Two or three classes or groups might prepare different scenes, and present one play after another to offer a complete show of an hour or so.

Some plays may be more appealing to girls; others to boys. There are roles for both boys and girls in most of the plays. If necessary, girls may play boys' roles, and vice versa. In some cases, the sex of characters is not specified, so you may cast whatever actors are available. Even if all the roles are to be taken by boys, the girls in your group will be an enthusiastic audience.

There are at least ten roles in each play. Extras may be added or eliminated to meet casting requirements, but if your stage space is limited, you should not have an excessive number of extras.

Roles calling for players to appear as children should be filled by smaller performers, dressed according to the ages they represent.

The stage. The stage may be as simple or as elaborate as your facilities permit. It may be just the front of a classroom, a section of a living room, a clearing at a camp or a real stage in an auditorium.

All stage directions are given from the viewpoint of the actors

439

as they stand onstage and face the audience. This means that *left stage* is to the left of the actor, *right stage* is toward his own right. *Upstage* is toward the backdrop (real or imaginary); *downstage* is toward the audience. You can easily remember the difference between the two by picturing the stage as slanting downward toward the audience.

Actors should carefully follow the directions for entering or exiting from left or right wings (also real or imaginary), since they are usually significant to the action.

If you have no curtain, the stage may be set with characters and properties shortly before the audience is seated. Begin the action as soon as the narrator exits.

Stage properties and sound effects. Basic ideas for properties and backgrounds are supplied. Those which play an important part in the action should be located according to directions. However, you may make changes or additions with details, using your imagination to create the effect you want. All items such as tools and weapons should be made from cardboard or some other soft and safe material.

Use offstage sound effects, if possible, for they add much to the dramatic impact. Two or three boys and girls could study the script and devise suitable and interesting sound effects. But do not overdo them, lest they distract the audience from the scene itself.

In some of the scenes, offstage music (from a record player) can help to put the audience into the proper emotional mood.

Costumes. Costumes may be simple or elaborate. Quite often a hat or coat will be enough to establish the character—a sailor's cap or crown or feathers, for example. The narrator may appear in a costume representative of the period and country of the play. An old trunk will probably be full of wonderful costumes, and with a little ingenuity the cast can put together imaginative apparel.

Note to the Actor

Acting is fun! Whether your role is large or small, you have a great opportunity to discover and develop your dramatic talent and an excellent means for self-expression. Dramatics help you to build self-confidence, poise and leadership qualities. But let's get back to our first point—it's fun. You and your audience will enjoy and appreciate the entertainment provided by a play.

Consider the character that you will portray. Characterization is vital! First read the play through and take careful note of the character you will play. Notice at the same time the entrances and exits you will make, and the props you will use. Visualize how the character would say the lines, and if you are not going to read during the performance, learn your lines as quickly as possible. Then try to act as the person himself would act. For example, if you are portraying an old man, your movements should be somewhat slow and faltering. A young, bold man would be vigorous, decisive. Try to be the character, not yourself.

Rehearse your performance. While *you* may know that your character is supposed to be happy or sad, you must make these emotions clear to the audience. Make your gestures, your movements, and your facial expressions indicate a definite mood, but do not exaggerate them so much that they become unnatural and grotesque. It is often a good idea to exaggerate an emotion during rehearsal so that it becomes clearly fixed in your mind, and then tone it down during the performance.

When you rehearse with the rest of the cast, watch your timing. Observe the stage directions for pausing, turning, gesturing. Make sure that you enter and leave at just the right moment. Practice until you get it right. Ordinarily, pause two seconds after another actor has finished a line. Sometimes you need to pause longer. If you have a real stage for your performance, start your walk onstage several steps back inside the wing. This gives you the appearance of coming from *somewhere,* and not merely from offstage. Be sure the audience cannot see you while you are waiting for your cue to enter.

Remember that the more familiar you become with your role, the easier and more natural it will be. Finally, remain relaxed, confident, alert—and you will give a performance that will be pleasing to you and entertaining to your audience.

Now, Curtain Up. The play is about to begin . . .

441

THE TREASURE OF MONTE CRISTO

Characters

Narrator	Third Sailor
Jacopo	Fourth Sailor
Edmond Dantes	Fifth Sailor
The Captain	Sixth Sailor
First Sailor	Seventh Sailor
Second Sailor	Extra Sailors

Introduction by Narrator

Ladies and gentlemen, welcome to this evening's performance. Tonight we present a scene from one of the most exciting adventure stories ever written. Our play is entitled "The Treasure of Monte Cristo." It is adapted from the classic story *The Count of Monte Cristo,* written by the French author Alexandre Dumas.

Let us briefly review the events leading up to tonight's scene. Our hero is Edmond Dantes, a young sailor who was arrested and imprisoned on false charges brought against him by French officials. Edmond was sent to the Château d'If, a prison located on an island in the Mediterranean Sea. While at the Château d'If he found himself in a cell next to another innocent prisoner —a kindly old clergyman. The clergyman told Edmond of a fabulous treasure which was buried on the isle of Monte Cristo —a treasure that would be Edmond's if he could manage to escape.

After fourteen years in prison, Dantes *did* escape. He did this by sewing himself into a large sack which was tossed into the sea by his unsuspecting jailers. After several miserable hours in the cold water he was picked up by a shipload of smugglers. The captain called Edmond by the name of *Maltese* . . . and invited him to become one of the crew.

One day the captain decided to make camp on the deserted isle of Monte Cristo—the very place where the secret treasure was buried in a cave. As they landed, Dantes wondered if he could find the treasure without arousing the suspicions of the crew. Our story opens as Dantes and the smugglers make camp on the treasure island of Monte Cristo. (*Narrator exits. Curtain rises.*)

Setting at Rise of Curtain

The scene is a campsite near the shore. Nautical and general equipment, such as chests, crates and telescopes, along with a pile of sticks (representing rifles) are set in the background. A burned-out campfire is at stage center.

Jacopo, a sailor, sits at the fire and idly pokes at the ashes with a stick. He looks up as Dantes enters from right.

JACOPO (*in friendly greeting*): Ah, my Maltese friend, where have you been? Ever since landing you have been poking around the coastline. What do you expect to find in this dreary place?

DANTES (*shrugging, warming his hands over the fire*): Monte Cristo is a strange island. Who knows what I may stumble across? (*Glancing around.*) Where are the others?

JACOPO (*gesturing*): On shipboard, going over the charts. The captain is planning a new voyage. (*Grinning.*) Even smugglers must find new and profitable sources of plunder. (*He reaches into a nearby box, taking some bread.*) Sit awhile and share some bread and cheese.

DANTES (*taking a "rifle"*): Later, Jacopo. I want to explore the east coast.

JACOPO (*protesting*): But you've just come back. In and out, up and down. (*Gesturing.*) What's out there, anyway? (*Sighing, rising.*) Ah, well . . . maybe I can help you. Let's be off.

DANTES (*shaking head*): No, no; I prefer to go alone. You're such a clumsy fellow; you're liable to go lame on me. Stay here and keep us a warm fire.

JACOPO (*shrugging, sitting*): At least fetch us back a fresh goat for dinner. (*Breaking bread, scowling at it.*) The foul weather makes mold of our bread.

(*As Dantes starts to leave toward right, the Captain and the first six Sailors plus Extra Sailors, enter from left. They stand or sit around the fire.*)

FIRST SAILOR (*to Dantes, gruffly*): Hold on, Maltese sailorman. We've had enough of your wanderings. Get back here. (*To others, sarcastically, as he gestures toward Dantes.*) Here is a curious fellow. He would rather tramp around this bleak rock than make his fortune with us. (*Commanding Dantes.*) Get over here and explain a few things about yourself.

CAPTAIN (*to First Sailor, sternly*): I'm still captain of this crew,

443

Mister Watkins; and I'll give the orders. (*To Dantes, briskly but kindly.*) Why not spill yourself to us? Who knows?—maybe we can help.

SECOND SAILOR (*to Dantes who returns to fire*): You tell us that you are a seaman—and you are for sure. You skip the deck as spryly as any of us. But about your past we know nothing!

CAPTAIN (*to Dantes*): Do you know the Mediterranean?

DANTES: I've sailed it since boyhood.

CAPTAIN: You know the best ports?

DANTES: I could enter most of them blindfolded.

CAPTAIN (*watching Dantes closely*): And your last port of call . . . where was it?

DANTES: With all respect, Captain, I'll keep that to myself.

CAPTAIN (*chuckling*): You're not easily tricked, shipmate. We can use your sharp wits.

THIRD SAILOR (*to Dantes*): There is usually a woman mixed up in a man's secrets. (*Gesturing.*) Tell us, do you have a lady hidden out there in the caves? (*Crew chuckles.*)

DANTES (*nodding with good humor*): There is a lady . . . (*Soberly.*) A lovely lady named Mercedes . . . whom I haven't seen for fourteen years.

FOURTH SAILOR (*laughing*): Maybe our mysterious shipmate is a member of royalty. (*Bowing mockingly to Dantes.*) Hail to the count of Monte Cristo . . . or is it duke? Perhaps Napoleon Bonaparte himself! (*Others laugh good-naturedly.*)

FIFTH SAILOR (*jokingly*): No, shipmates; our Maltese friend is an agent of the French government. His specialty is smugglers. (*Grinning, holding out wrists to Dantes.*) I confess! Haul me away! Ha!

SIXTH SAILOR (*sarcastically eyeing Dantes*): I suspect the joke may be on us. I've been watching this sly mate of ours. He's keeping something from us . . . and I intend to find it out. (*The crew sobers somewhat.*)

CAPTAIN (*reproving Sixth Sailor*): You and your suspicious mind. (*To Dantes.*) Speak for yourself, Maltese. Answer these rascals.

DANTES (*boldly, confidently*): Keeping things from you?—of course I am—just as you guard your own secrets. You are wanted by the Paris police? (*Shrugging.*) That is your own

444

business. You owe a pile of debts to fifteen merchants in fifteen ports? That is your affair, not mine. Do I pry into your life? Not at all. And neither will I permit you to force my secrets. (*Gesturing.*) Fair enough, shipmates?

JACOPO (*applauding and grinning*): Well spoken! (*Glancing at others.*) We are desperate sea dogs at that. One step from pirates, every man of us.

CAPTAIN (*briskly business-like*): Enough of this. We've got plans to make. (*To First Sailor.*) Fetch the chart. (*As First Sailor obeys, Dantes takes a rifle.*)

DANTES (*gesturing*): I spotted a herd of goats on the far side. We'll have a roast joint for dinner.

FIRST SAILOR (*to others, suspiciously*): See what I mean? (*Sourly.*) I suspect he has more than a roast joint on his mind.

CAPTAIN (*shooing Dantes away*): Fresh meat—there's a tasty idea. Off with you.

JACOPO (*to Dantes who walks toward right wing*): Take care . . . the shore rocks are slippery. We want you back safely with our dinner. (*Dantes exits. All except First Sailor bend over the chart and talk in low tones. The First Sailor walks suspiciously toward right, pauses briefly while peering at the departing Dantes, finally follows him offstage.*)

CAPTAIN (*gesturing to crates*): Now . . . we have stocks of Turkish rugs . . . chests of fine spices from the Orient. We need ideas for selling them. Where can we get the best price for our plunder?

SECOND SAILOR (*growling*): The coast of France gets more dangerous by the hour. No matter where we try to get ashore we are likely to be greeted by the police. I'm for hiding out right here for a few days.

THIRD SAILOR (*protesting*): While our hard-earned loot spoils by the sea? (*Scowling.*) The weather is foul enough to eat the steel off our knives. Let's get away—take our chances.

FOURTH SAILOR (*glumly*): A smuggler's lot is a miserable one at that. I'm for abandoning the whole mess and turning into an honest man. (*Sighing.*) Ah, for the peaceful life with a quiet home and a loving wife. I think, shipmates, you have seen the last of me on board.

SEVENTH SAILOR (*entering from left with armful of clothing, glancing around*): Where is our new shipmate? I've brought him extra clothing. Those rags he wore when we fished him from the sea . . . fah! . . . not fit for a beggar.

SIXTH SAILOR (*suddenly, sourly, as he glares toward right wing*): I'm getting more suspicious by the minute. (*To Captain.*) Captain, think it over. After we pulled him from the water we heard a roar of cannon from the prison of Château d'If. That gun is fired only when there is an escape.

JACOPO (*shrugging, gesturing nonchalantly*): So he is wanted at the prison. (*To Sixth Sailor, sarcastically.*) How many jails want you, my innocent shipmate? (*Others roar with laughter.*)

SIXTH SAILOR (*angrily*): But that's not my point. Why does he make mystery of the Château d'If?

FIRST SAILOR (*entering from right, scowling*): Gave me the slip, he did. He's hunting all right. . . . (*Nodding knowingly.*) But not for goatmeat.

CAPTAIN (*somewhat annoyed*): We spend too much time talking about him. We have enough problems of our own.

JACOPO (*glancing over his shoulder, toward right wing*): We should have heard from his rifle by now. I warned him of treacherous rocks. (*Rising.*) I'll have a look. (*Jacopo exits at right.*)

SIXTH SAILOR (*forcefully*): I tell you, shipmates, there's something up. I've heard of buried treasure on Monte Cristo. Maybe that's his game.

SEVENTH SAILOR (*to Sixth Sailor, scoffing*): There's not a spot in the seven seas without its treasure tales. You show more greed than good sense.

FIFTH SAILOR (*staring toward right wing, leaping up*): He's hurt! (*Fifth Sailor races offstage at right, returns while helping Jacopo to support the injured Dantes. They place him near the fire as the others gather around.*)

SECOND SAILOR: What happened?

DANTES (*gasping painfully*): Inside a sea cave . . . lost my footing . . . fell on sharp stones. (*Adjusting his position.*) There now . . . let me be . . . I'll mend fast enough.

FIRST SAILOR (*to Dantes, suspiciously, sarcastically*): What kind of goat hangs around the sea caves?

SIXTH SAILOR (*peering suspiciously*): What do you say to that?

CAPTAIN (*gruffly*): Hold your tongues—the man is in pain enough. (*To Dantes.*) I've decided to set sail at once, before the weather ruins our prizes. If we wait until evening, you'll be in shape for moving aboard. All right, shipmate?

DANTES (*protesting*): No, Captain, don't wait on my account. Leave me with some biscuits and water—perhaps a pickax to defend myself.

FIRST SAILOR (*mockingly*): Or perhaps to dig with?

THIRD SAILOR: No, Maltese, we'll not abandon you. Smugglers we may be, but we're loyal to our comrades.

DANTES (*shaking head*): I'll be all right. Just send a ship for me as soon as you can. (*Shifting painfully.*) In a day or two I'll be able to move these aching bones.

JACOPO: There's just one way to settle things. (*Pointing to himself.*) I will stay with him. The rest of you rascals go and bring us a rich profit for our goods.

DANTE: (*to Jacopo*): You have a kind heart, Jacopo, but there's no need. I'm used to hardship, I assure you.

CAPTAIN (*to Dantes*): Have no worry. We'll send a ship for you within the week. (*To Sailors, authoritatively.*) Load the crates! We're off for the coast of France!

(*The action divides as follows: Jacopo sets small boxes of equipment next to Dantes; they chat in low tones. All Sailors—ex-*

447

cept the First and the Sixth—pick up equipment and exit at left. The First and Sixth Sailors sneak aside to upstage left, whispering furtively.)

FIRST SAILOR (*calling, beckoning*): Captain!

CAPTAIN (*approaching briskly*): Yes, what is it?

SIXTH SAILOR (*grasping Captain's arm, frowning toward Dantes*): What man in his right mind would insist on staying here alone? (*Fiercely.*) I'm for forcing his secret from him right here and now.

FIRST SAILOR (*greedily*): He may have a secret worth ten times our Turkish rugs.

CAPTAIN (*angrily jerking away*): You'd stab your own shipmate in the back? You're the worst scoundrels in the lot. (*Gesturing toward left.*) Get on board! (*Captain exits at left.*)

SIXTH SAILOR (*shaking his fist after the departing Captain*): The Captain's a bungler. (*Eagerly.*) Here's our plan. (*Gesturing toward upstage right.*) We'll hide out in the hills where we can watch the Maltese. Make no mistake, as soon as the ship sails he'll be up to something.

FIRST SAILOR (*greedily rubbing hands*): And whatever he finds we'll grab for ourselves!

SIXTH SAILOR (*laughing sarcastically*): When we are through with him he'll have no use for gold or anything else. Let's go! (*As they start to cross to right wing the Captain enters from left, curtly hails them.*)

CAPTAIN: Misters!

FIRST SAILOR (*viciously, as both Sailors halt and turn*): I warn you, Captain, stay out of this.

CAPTAIN (*grimly*): And I warn you, gentlemen. If you as much as touch the Maltese I'll have your hides. Understand me, misters. Now get on board. (*The Captain glares at them for a moment, exits at left.*)

SIXTH SAILOR (*as both scowl and hesitate*): Fah! It's not worth the risk. We'd better go along with the ship. (*They glumly exit at left.*)

JACOPO (*making final comforts for Dantes*): Take good care of yourself, Maltese. I need a friend like you.

DANTES (*nodding*): I need you, too, Jacopo. I'll not forget your kindnesses when we meet again.

JACOPO (*stepping back, grinning*): Just one thing . . . all this talk about buried treasure . . . I wonder if you really do have your secret. (*Waving cheerfully.*) Ah, well, that is still your affair. Good fortune, shipmate.

DANTES: Goodbye, Jacopo. (*Dantes watches Jacopo who exits at left. With difficulty, Dantes raises himself to his feet, picks up cardboard pickax, leans against a crate. Looking seaward— toward audience—he shades his eyes with his palm. He speaks slowly as he watches the ship sail away.*) Goodbye, friends . . . my griefs of the past sail with you. My future is in my own hands at last. (*Lowering palm, nodding, still looking seaward.*) Yes, shipmates, there is a rich treasure on Monte Cristo . . . and I shall find it. (*Turning, gesturing into right wing.*) It's out there somewhere . . . waiting for me. (*He walks with difficulty toward right.*) Then for France again . . . and Mercedes . . . and a new life. (*He exits at right. Curtain descends.*)

OLIVER TWIST ASKS FOR MORE

Characters

Narrator	Mr. Bumble
Oliver Twist	Mr. Limbkins
First Boy	Mr. Gamfield
Second Boy	First Magistrate
Third Boy	Second Magistrate
Cook	Extra Boys
Maid	

Introduction by Narrator

Ladies and gentlemen, welcome to this evening's performance. Our play is called "Oliver Twist Asks for More." No doubt you recognize that our story is based on the classic book *Oliver Twist*, written by that famous English author Charles Dickens.

You may recall that Oliver was an orphan boy who was lonely, frightened and hungry . . . especially *hungry*.

Our play takes place at a workhouse for homeless boys. Oliver and his friends have just finished their supper—that is, if you can call a small bowl of oatmeal a supper. (*Narrator exits. Curtain rises.*)

Setting at Rise of Curtain

Oliver and the three other poorly dressed boys, plus Extra Boys, are seated behind a long, plain table. The room is bare and cheerless.

The boys hungrily scrape the last bit of oatmeal from their bowls, then set them down while sighing.

FIRST BOY (*painfully*): I'm still hungry.

SECOND BOY (*licking spoon*): We are always still hungry. Not even a crust of bread tonight.

THIRD BOY (*to Oliver*): Don't forget your promise, Oliver. (*As the Cook enters from right, the Third Boy nudges Oliver, whispers.*) There he is. Go ahead. (*Oliver timidly hesitates as the Cook approaches table. The Cook snatches two or three bowls, grabs Oliver's.*)

COOK (*gruffly, sourly*): Get back to your work. No time for idleness around here.

OLIVER (*holding out hand*): Please, sir, may I have my bowl back? There's a spoonful left. . . .

COOK (*slamming bowl on table*): Finish and be off with you! (*The Cook turns away to collect other bowls.*)

FIRST BOY (*whispering anxiously to Oliver*): Hurry!

OLIVER (*rising, choking with fright as he speaks to Cook*): Please, sir. . . .

COOK (*sourly*): What do you want? Speak up, boy.

OLIVER (*miserably shaking head, sitting down*): Nothing . . . nothing, sir. (*The Cook growls and busies himself at a far end of the table. The boys turn hopefully toward Oliver.*)

SECOND BOY (*pleading with Oliver*): Oliver, please . . . you promised to ask for more supper. (*Oliver nervously fingers his bowl and spoon, finally picks them up, rises and circles to stand in back of the Cook.*)

OLIVER (*stammering*): Sir . . . could you please. . . .

COOK (*turning around, scowling, nodding, reaching for Oliver's bowl*): Through at last? All right, I'll take your bowl.

OLIVER (*holding bowl up with both hands*): Please, sir, I want some more. (*The stunned Cook is speechless for a moment. He claps a hand to his forehead.*)

COOK (*exploding*): What! What did you say?

OLIVER (*trembling*): Please, sir, I want some more supper.

COOK (*staring in horror at Oliver*): What! What's that? You have the nerve to stand there and demand more supper? Why, you ungrateful wretch! More indeed! I'll teach you! (*He swings at Oliver who dodges. The Cook whirls, screams into left wing.*) Mr. Bumble! Mr. Limbkins! We are betrayed! Treachery under our very noses! (*Mr. Bumble and Mr. Limbkins, two harsh, self-righteous characters, race in from left, glance around in alarm.*)

MR. BUMBLE (*excitedly*): What's happened?

MR. LIMBKINS (*anxiously*): Are we on fire? (*The Cook takes Oliver by the ear and leads him before the two men. Oliver cringes.*)

COOK (*slowly, emphasizing his words*): This boy . . . this miserable, wretched, ungrateful scoundrel has dared to push his empty bowl into my face. (*Shouting.*) He asked for more supper!

MR. BUMBLE (*horrified*): For more supper? Unbelievable!

MR. LIMBKINS (*gasping*): After all we have done for him! I am painfully shocked! (*Shaking Oliver.*) Young man, you are the worst of scoundrels! What evil within your heart rebels against our kindness?

OLIVER (*trembling*): I . . . I am not ungrateful for your many kindnesses, sir . . . but . . . I am still hungry. (*Gesturing to boys.*) We thought your generosity might spare another mouthful to fill our emptiness.

MR. LIMBKINS (*arrogantly*): Tell me, boy, how hungry would you be if we put you out on the streets where you belong? (*Painfully grimacing.*) How it grieves my kindly heart to witness such rash impudence.

MR. BUMBLE (*leering*): Perhaps a few days in a dark cellar will cleanse him of evil. (*Pompously nodding.*) Yes, yes, for the boy's own good we must punish him severely. (*He nods self-righteously in unison with Mr. Limbkins.*)

MR. LIMBKINS (*to Oliver, with dramatic hypocrisy*): How fortunate for your soul's welfare to find yourself in such merciful hands as ours. (*The two men again nod in solemn unison as Oliver backs away*.)

451

MAID (*entering from left*): Mr. Limbkins, sir, there is a Mr. Gamfield at the door. He wishes to hire an apprentice chimney sweep.

MR. LIMBKINS (*whispering brightly to Mr. Bumble*): Hear that? A heaven-sent opportunity to get rid of a certain trouble-maker. (*Greedily rubbing palms together.*) Think of the money we'll save. (*To Maid.*) Show him in. (*The Maid curtsies and exits as the two men greedily leer at each other.*)

COOK (*shouting to boys*): Clear the table! Get on with the kitchen work! (*The boys clear the table and start to exit at right.*)

MR. BUMBLE (*calling sharply to Oliver*): Oliver Twist! (*Jabbing a finger toward floor.*) Come here! (*Oliver hands his bowl to another boy as the boys and the Cook exit at right.*)

OLIVER (*timidly approaching*): Yes, Mr. Bumble?

MR. BUMBLE (*pompously*): Oliver, my lad, you shall see that our mercy is equal to our justice.

OLIVER (*bewildered*): I don't understand.

MR. LIMBKINS: Mr. Gamfield needs a strong, healthy boy to serve as an apprentice chimney sweep. You shall be a man of business! What do you say to that?

OLIVER (*gratefully*): Oh, sir, you are a kindly gentleman. (*Timidly asking.*) You have forgiven my rashness in asking for more supper?

MR. BUMBLE (*with false loftiness*): Our humble hearts are always ready to forgive a repentant sinner. (*Gesturing toward right.*) Go, put yourself into a clean shirt; prepare yourself for Mr. Gamfield.

OLIVER: Thank you, sir. (*As he exits at right, Mr. Gamfield stomps in from left.*)

MR. GAMFIELD (*snarling, shaking a fist at the two men*): Mind you, none of your usual tricks. I want a lad who'll give me a full day's work with little supper to show for it. (*Suddenly whining, hunching.*) I am a poor, poor man with scarcely a coat on my back.

MR. LIMBKINS (*eager to please*): Yes, of course. I'm sure you'll be pleased with our selection. (*Scowling toward right wing.*) Where is that boy? (*Shouting.*) Oliver! Oliver Twist! (*Oliver races onstage.*)

OLIVER: Sorry I took so long, sir.

MR. BUMBLE (*to Oliver, gesturing expansively*): Oliver, my

boy, meet Mr. Gamfield, a generous soul whose heart bursts with love for all mankind. (*Sternly.*) You do want to go with him, don't you?

OLIVER (*timidly, hesitantly*): I . . . I guess so.

MR. GAMFIELD (*roughly feeling Oliver's arm*): Humph! A scrawny lad. (*Sourly.*) I have no intention of feeding his hungry muscles from my poor, poor kitchen.

MR. LIMBKINS: Come, come, the boy is a prize package indeed! All he needs is a whack across the back now and then. (*Hypocritically.*) For his own good, of course.

MR. GAMFIELD (*viciously leering at Oliver*): There'll be plenty of whacks if you turn out to be a stubborn donkey. (*Nodding, grumbling.*) We have a bargain. Get the boy's papers.

OLIVER (*pleading*): Please, Mr. Limbkins, may I ask. . . .

MR. LIMBKINS (*roaring*): Silence, you rude rascal! Off to the corner with you! (*Sighing, as Oliver retreats to upstage right.*) I'm afraid, sir, you'll have to whip some manners into him. (*Briskly rubbing his palms together.*) One moment, gentlemen, while I fetch the legal papers. (*As he starts to leave toward left, the Maid appears at left.*)

MAID: Sir, the magistrates are here.

MR. LIMBKINS (*angrily shocked*): The magistrates! (*Sourly.*) Those busybodies.

MR. GAMFIELD (*puzzledly*): What do they want?

MR. BUMBLE (*scowling*): They are the law. No boy can leave here without their approval.

MR. LIMBKINS (*to Maid, in nervous confusion*): Uh . . . hold off those worthy gentlemen for a moment. (*The Maid curtsies and exits. Mr. Limbkins angrily beckons to Oliver who races over to the three stern men.*) Mind your manners, Mr. Oliver Twist, or you'll regret it.

MR. BUMBLE (*wagging a finger close to Oliver*): If they ask if you want to go with Mr. Gamfield you had better say yes.

OLIVER (*timidly protesting*): But, sir . . . (*Mr. Bumble misses a slap at Oliver as the two Magistrates enter from left, carrying legal papers. The Magistrates are elderly, kind and simple characters. The First Magistrate is so nearsighted that he blinks constantly. The Maid enters behind them, crosses stage to exit at right.*)

MR. LIMBKINS (*fawning, as the three men assume exaggerated airs of charm and friendliness*): Ah, honored gentlemen! What brings you to us today?

FIRST MAGISTRATE: We heard that Mr. Gamfield was seeking an apprentice. We wish to examine the boy.

MR. BUMBLE (*eager to impress*): Of course, of course. First and foremost we wish for the lad's happiness and welfare. (*Calling loudly but courteously into right wing.*) Young gentlemen, please bring table and chairs. Also pen and ink. Hurry, please, we mustn't keep our guests waiting. (*Four or five boys carry a small table and two chairs to center stage in front of the dining table. As they leave, Mr. Bumble assumes a broad smile and gestures in friendly fashion after them.*) Thank you for your kindly cooperation. (*To Magistrates, fawning.*) Notice the kindness and affection we extend to our young friends. (*He sighs hypocritically.*)

MR. LIMBKINS: Please be seated, sirs. (*As the Magistrates sit, Mr. Limbkins prods Oliver who steps before the table. The three men stand menacingly behind Oliver. The First Magistrate fumbles with his papers for a moment, finally looks up at Oliver.*)

FIRST MAGISTRATE (*smiling*): So you are the young man who wishes to become a chimney sweep. What is your name?

OLIVER: Oliver Twist, sir.

SECOND MAGISTRATE: Oliver Twist. Hmmmm . . . that's an interesting name.

OLIVER: The orphanage gave us names according to the alphabet. When I arrived they used the letter T.

FIRST MAGISTRATE: Would you like to be apprenticed to Mr. Gamfield? Hmmmm . . . (*As both Magistrates peer down at papers, Mr. Bumble shakes Oliver's arm, urging him to reply.*)

OLIVER (*hesitantly*): I . . . I . . . suppose so.

MR. GAMFIELD (*trying to explain*): As you can plainly see, the boy is so overwhelmed with gratitude that he can hardly speak. (*Pinching Oliver.*) Isn't that right, my boy? (*Oliver remains miserably silent.*)

SECOND MAGISTRATE (*to Mr. Gamfield*): I trust you will take good care of him?

MR. GAMFIELD (*laying a hand on Oliver's shoulders, groaning with a false air of compassion*): Care of him, indeed! Like a sparrow cares for a birdling! (*Oliver tearfully sniffs. He unsuc-*

cessfully tries to control himself as he is jabbed by one of the men.)

FIRST MAGISTRATE (*nodding as he fumbles for and takes the pen*): Well, then, I believe we can happily settle the boy's future. I'll sign him over to you, Mr. Gamfield. Hmmmm . . . where is that inkwell? (*He blinks, peers around for the inkwell but fails to find it because it is directly under his nose. In the course of his peering he chances to look up at the quietly weeping Oliver. He sets the pen down, peers with kindly curiosity at Oliver. Note: This is climactic action which should be clearly performed. The First Magistrate speaks to Oliver.*) My boy, you look pale and alarmed.

MR. GAMFIELD (*desperately trying to explain*): It's nothing at all, I assure you. So eager is he to go with me that he weeps with joy! (*Mr. Gamfield is so angry that his next jab at Oliver is clumsily obvious.*)

SECOND MAGISTRATE (*to the three men, sharply*): Stand back—all of you! (*To Oliver, gently.*) Now, boy, tell us what's the matter. Don't be afraid.

OLIVER (*bursting forth with sobs, pleading desperately to Mr. Limbkins*): Please sir—starve me, beat me, chain me in the cellar; do anything but please don't send me away with this cruel man.

MR. LIMBKINS (*indignantly throwing up arms, groaning painfully*): Oh, the cunning deceit of his young lips! (*To Magistrates, sorrowfully.*) I'm afraid his worthless character is exposed at last. (*Clicking tongue, bowing head.*) Tch, tch, tch. We must double our prayers for his poor misguided soul.

FIRST MAGISTRATE (*somewhat sarcastically*): A touching performance, sir. (*Rising, speaking gently to Oliver.*) Oliver, my decision is made. You need not go with Mr. Gamfield.

OLIVER (*gratefully relieved*): Thank you, thank you. (*To Mr. Limbkins, anxiously*). Mr. Limbkins, I hope I haven't offended you. Please, sir, I'm sorry. (*Mr. Limbkins glares furiously at Oliver.*)

SECOND MAGISTRATE (*soberly and sternly*): Gentlemen, we warn you against whipping this boy. Treat him kindly, for we shall be watching you.

MR. BUMBLE (*nervously, in fear*): Yes, sir, sorry, sir. You shall be watching us. (*The Magistrates go around the table to Oliver.*)

FIRST MAGISTRATE (*patting the sniffing Oliver on head*): There, there, young Mr. Twist. We shall find a suitable place for you. How would you like to ship out to sea? Or perhaps we can find a place for you in the countryside? Goodbye. (*To the men, sternly.*) Good day, gentlemen. I trust you won't forget our warning. (*As the Magistrates exit at left, the three men angrily surround the fearfully cowering Oliver.*)

MR. GAMFIELD (*starting to take off his coat, speaking fiercely to Oliver*): Now for you, my lad.

MR. BUMBLE (*gesturing with terror toward left wing*): No, no! They'll find out! (*Scowling in defeat at Oliver.*) Bah! He's not worth the beating. (*Mr. Bumble sourly stalks out at left.*)

MR. GAMFIELD (*snarling at Oliver*): At least I won't have to feed the rascal. (*Muttering as he stomps toward left.*) Probably eats like a young horse. (*He exits at left while growling.*)

MR. LIMBKINS (*wringing his hands in despair*): I am ordered to treat him with kindness! (*Weeping.*) How can a cruel creature like me treat anyone with kindness? (*Shrugging, sighing.*) Ah, well, perhaps I can learn. (*Dismally shaking his head, he exits at left. Immediately, the boys race in from right.*)

THIRD BOY (*clapping Oliver on back*): We heard everything! Oliver, you're saved!

FIRST BOY (*nodding*): It's a good thing that old gentleman looked up in time and saw you.

OLIVER (*eagerly*): Did you hear what he said? Maybe we can all ship out to sea!

MAID (*entering from right, shoving the reluctant Cook before her*): Which one of you boys asked for more supper?

SECOND BOY (*as boys turn toward Oliver*): Our brave friend, Oliver Twist!

MAID (*to Oliver*): The cook has something to say to you. (*Prodding the cook.*) Speak up!

COOK (*gruffly but not unkindly*): I've found a bit more supper in the kitchen. (*Grinning.*) For everyone. (*The boys cheer.*)

THIRD BOY (*to Oliver*): Lead the way, Oliver! And thanks for asking for more! (*The boys crowd around Oliver as all exit at right. Curtain falls.*)

JOHNNY APPLESEED IN DANGER

Characters

Narrator	Third Mother
Johnny Appleseed	First Indian
First Child	Second Indian
Second Child	Third Indian
Third Child	Fourth Indian
First Mother	Extra Children and Indians
Second Mother	

Introduction by Narrator

Welcome to our theater, ladies and gentlemen. Tonight we present for your enjoyment a short play entitled "Johnny Appleseed in Danger." It is adapted from the life and legend of a person who actually lived, for Johnny Appleseed was more than just the hero of a folk tale. His real name was John Chapman, and he lived during the pioneer days of America when there were log cabins, oxcarts, and savage Indian tribes.

When our play begins, Johnny Appleseed has been wandering through the wilderness for many, many years, stopping for short visits in Ohio, Indiana and Illinois. Perhaps some of you wonder why he wandered around so much. And maybe you'd like to know what he did when he visited a new section of the country. Our play will now answer your questions. (*Narrator exits. Curtain rises.*)

Setting at Rise of Curtain

Bushes, flowers and other plant life are set around the stage background. The rest of the stage is bare.

The three children, plus Extras if desired, are playing about, racing and shouting.

FIRST CHILD (*shouting to Second Child*): You can't catch me!
SECOND CHILD: I can, too! (*Second Child chases First Child around stage until they reach left stage. They suddenly halt, peer*

curiously into left wing.) Wait a minute! Who's that coming? (*All children stop playing to peer toward left.*)

THIRD CHILD: It's a funny old fellow with a sack over his shoulder. I wonder who he is.

FIRST CHILD: Let's hide back here! (*The children scramble behind the bushes at upstage right.*

As they watch, Johnny slowly enters from left. He is elderly, bearded, barefoot, and simply dressed. He wears an old hat and carries a sack over his shoulder. He looks around, sets the sack on floor, goes through motions of scooping a small hole in the ground. He takes a seed—imaginary—from sack and goes through motions of planting and covering it. He wanders around left stage, selects another spot, plants a second seed.)

SECOND CHILD (*curiously, in stage whisper*): What's he doing? (*Straining to see.*) What's in his sack? (*Johnny plants a third seed, wanders offstage at left while searching for another planting area.*)

THIRD CHILD (*straining to see Johnny*): There he goes again!

FIRST MOTHER (*entering from right with other mothers, glancing anxiously around, calling*): Sarah, where are you? Children, come here!

FIRST CHILD (*as children step out*): Here we are. (*Excitedly gesturing toward left wing.*) We're watching that old man over there. Do you know who he is?

FIRST MOTHER (*barely glancing at Johnny, grabbing First Child's hand*): Never mind that for now—it's not safe out here. (*The mothers quickly herd the children toward right stage; the children hang back.*)

SECOND CHILD (*to mothers*): What's the matter? (*Glancing toward Johnny.*) Is he a dangerous man?

SECOND MOTHER (*shaking head*): No, it's not that. We've just heard that unfriendly Indians are around. Hurry!

THIRD MOTHER (*to mothers, as she gestures toward the still-offstage Johnny*): We ought to warn him. (*Calling to Johnny.*) Sir! There are Indians lurking about . . . you'd better get back to the village. (*Frowning, shaking head.*) He didn't hear me. We should make sure he understands. (*All players hurry toward left.*) Sir! You're in danger. Come with us.

(*While they are turned toward left, three Indians, with Extras if*

desired, enter from right, carrying cardboard tomahawks and bows and arrows. They stand at right stage, blocking the way, fiercely scowling. The others turn around to exit at right, suddenly see Indians. The mothers gasp and grab the children. All react in fright.)

FIRST INDIAN (*accusingly*): You settlers have taken our lands and rivers; you have driven us from our homes. (*Stepping forward.*) We will take revenge.

FIRST MOTHER: Please, let us return to our village.

SECOND MOTHER: We mean you no harm.

SECOND INDIAN (*angrily*): Your soldiers have already done us great evil. (*Gesturing toward sky.*) Every moon we have less and less food for our women and children.

THIRD MOTHER: If you will return with us to our village we will give you food for your families.

THIRD INDIAN (*fiercely*): No! We will hunt our own food on our own lands. We will drive you from our hills and rivers.

(*As the Indians slowly and fiercely approach, Johnny enters from left. As he grasps the situation, he steps between the Indians and the settlers.*)

JOHNNY APPLESEED (*courageously, to Indians*): Stand where you are!

FIRST INDIAN (*scoffing, as he studies Johnny*): Ha! Where is your rifle, old man? All settlers carry rifles to hunt us down.

JOHNNY APPLESEED (*soberly shaking head*): I carry neither rifle nor hunting knife. I am a friend of your people.

SECOND INDIAN (*suspiciously, as he feels Johnny's sack*): Maybe

460

you carry a pistol in your sack. (*Frowning, as he feels it.*) What strange weapon do you have in here?

JOHNNY APPLESEED (*setting sack on ground, reaching inside*): I'll show you. (*With clearly defined movements he takes a seed, holds it up to Indians, digs a small hole, plants seed, steps back, gestures toward covered hole.*) In a few years a beautiful tree will blossom from this very spot. It will bear delicious apples— enough for both your people and mine.

THIRD INDIAN (*with a puzzled expression as he takes a handful of seeds from sack*): Apples? From these seeds?

THIRD CHILD (*to Johnny, as tension relaxes somewhat*): You must be Johnny Appleseed! We've heard all about you! (*The children and mothers smile and mutter in agreement.*)

FIRST INDIAN (*frowning in confusion*): Johnny Appleseed? (*To other Indians.*) We have not heard of such a man.

SECOND INDIAN (*sourly, suspiciously*): It's another trick to take more of our lands. (*Other Indians growl their agreement.*)

THIRD INDIAN (*scowling with finality as he takes the arm of one of the mothers*): You will come as our prisoners. Your warriors will be sorry for their wickedness.

JOHNNY APPLESEED (*to Indians, sternly, boldly*): You will return to your village alone. (*Surprised by such boldness, the Third Indian releases mother's arm. Johnny now appeals to the Indians' curiosity.*) Let me show you something. (*Taking a large, shiny apple from the sack, he holds it up.*) Here is a token of our friendship. (*Handing apple to an Indian.*) Here—taste it. (*One at a time, the curious Indians bite the apple, nod with pleasure.*)

FIRST INDIAN (*admiring the apple*): This is magic fruit! Where did you find it?

SECOND INDIAN (*reaching for sack which Johnny opens for him*): We'd like more. (*Second Indian takes another apple from sack.*)

JOHNNY APPLESEED: You can have all the apples you wish. But you must promise to live peacefully with your neighbors.

THIRD INDIAN (*doubtfully, suspiciously*): You are tricking us again. You hope to trade us a few apples for our forests and lakes. (*To other Indians.*) Let's take our prisoners!

JOHNNY APPLESEED (*calmly but sternly blocking the way to the right wing*): Stop! I may be old, but you'll think you've tangled

461

with a grizzly bear. (*As the Indians hesitate, the Fourth Indian enters from right, hailing Johnny.*)

FOURTH INDIAN (*in friendly greeting*): Johnny Appleseed! Welcome, old friend! (*Fourth Indian and Johnny exchange greetings by placing hands on each other's shoulder.*)

JOHNNY APPLESEED: How are you, Running Elk? It's been many moons since we planted your apple orchards.

FOURTH INDIAN (*commanding other Indians*): Get back! (*As the Indians retreat, the Fourth Indian explains to them.*) It's true that there are wicked settlers, just as there are evil warriors in our own tribes. But this man is our friend. He has shown my tribe how to grow great orchards that give us food and shelter. (*The other Indians turn curiously toward Johnny.*)

FIRST INDIAN (*to Johnny*): Will you teach us how to make the earth bloom with your magic trees?

FOURTH INDIAN (*to Indians*): Johnny has restless feet; he does not stay long in one valley. But my people will teach you of Johnny's magic. (*The three Indians briefly huddle to talk things over.*)

SECOND INDIAN (*holding up palm*): We are friends from this day on. Together we will share the land.

JOHNNY APPLESEED (*to Fourth Indian*): Thank you for bringing peace between our peoples. (*Throwing sack over shoulder.*) Goodbye for now. (*The Indians wave and happily exit at right. The settlers crowd around Johnny, murmuring:* Thank you . . . Please return . . . Johnny Appleseed!)

SECOND CHILD: Think of all the wonderful things that his trees give us—like apple pies and apple juice!

THIRD CHILD: And cool shade on hot days!

FIRST CHILD: And what's more fun than swinging from an apple tree!

JOHNNY APPLESEED (*smiling, giving a handful of seeds to a child*): Perhaps you will help me by planting these. A hundred years from now folks may have apples descended from these very seeds. (*Waving goodbye, he wanders toward left while looking around for planting areas.*)

FIRST MOTHER (*as all wave goodbye to Johnny*): Goodbye . . . we'll always remember your wonderful work.

SECOND CHILD: Goodbye, Johnny Appleseed! (*Curtain falls.*)

SIR GALAHAD AND THE MAIDENS

Characters

Narrator	First Brother
Sir Galahad	Second Brother
Old Man	Third Brother
Young Man	Fourth Brother
First Maiden	Fifth Brother
Second Maiden	Sixth Brother
Third Maiden	Seventh Brother
Fourth Maiden	Castle Extras

Introduction by Narrator

Ladies and gentlemen, we are about to journey back to the exciting times of King Arthur and his knights of the Round Table. Perhaps you remember some of the characters who appeared in these famous tales: Merlin the Magician, Queen Guinevere, and those dashing knights named Sir Lancelot and Sir Tristram.

Tonight's scene tells the story of one of the most gallant of all the knights privileged to sit with King Arthur at his Round Table. We shall witness one of the thrilling adventures of Sir Galahad, that brave, heroic, and courteous knight in armor. Our scene is entitled "Sir Galahad and the Maidens."

Late one morning, after winning several battles for his king and after rescuing some fair maidens in distress, Sir Galahad found himself riding along a strange and silent valley. Before him there suddenly appeared a mysterious-looking castle. He was surprised to find himself at its gates, for he had expected to discover nothing more in this quiet valley than a few wild birds or perhaps a woodcutter or two. Our story begins as Sir Galahad dismounts from his horse and stands in astonishment at the entrance to the mysterious castle. (*Narrator exits. Curtain rises.*)

Setting at Rise of Curtain

The setting is a courtyard just outside the castle's main gate. Plans, crockery, and a bench or two may be set in the background. Other items common to the Middle Ages, such as lances, shields, and buckets, may also be displayed. Sir Galahad stands near the left wing, with shield and drawn sword. (All swords are made of cardboard.)

SIR GALAHAD (*calling toward opposite wing*): Ho, there! A stranger bids to enter your castle! I am Sir Galahad, knight of the Round Table. I bring you greetings in the name of noble King Arthur! (*After a brief pause, the Old Man totters out from right, followed by the Young Man.*)

OLD MAN (*peering closely at Sir Galahad, shaking his head*): Son, I beseech you to seek lodgings elsewhere. The brave champion of King Arthur will find only sorrow here.

SIR GALAHAD: Pray tell me, sir, what is the name of this silent castle?

YOUNG MAN: It is silent because it is sorrowful. It is called the Castle of Maidens. All the fair ladies who dwell here are captives within its walls. . . .

(*The four Maidens stealthily enter from right, glancing anxiously over their shoulders. They are followed by Extras. The Young Man gestures toward the Maidens.*)

OLD MAN: From their own lips you will hear of their distress.

FIRST MAIDEN (*as Maidens approach Sir Galahad*): Brave knight, sir, please turn aside from this wicked place.

SECOND MAIDEN: At once! We implore you! You are in mortal danger.

SIR GALAHAD: What is the mystery here? Why do you warn me against the Castle of Maidens?

THIRD MAIDEN (*glancing fearfully about, she inquires of the others*): Is it safe to speak? (*Asking in stage whisper.*) Where are the seven wicked brothers?

FOURTH MAIDEN (*gesturing furtively*): I think . . . I think they are on the far side repairing their armor. We cannot linger here for long.

OLD MAN (*to Sir Galahad*): All of us who live within the Castle of Maidens are prisoners of the seven wicked brothers. We cannot leave as we wish . . . nor can strangers enter its walls without peril to their lives.

SIR GALAHAD: So this is a captive castle.

OLD MAN (*sadly*): Yes . . . our chains grow heavier every day.

SIR GALAHAD: I wish to hear more.

YOUNG MAN: It all started many years ago when the seven brothers came here as guests of Duke Lianor. They betrayed the good duke and took possession of the castle and its inhabitants. (*Sternly.*) They are hard and angry men without a trace of mercy. (*Reminiscently.*) But one day something happened which frightened them. The duke's daughter prophesied that on some bright day a gallant knight would overcome their wickedness and restore freedom to the people.

OLD MAN: That is why you must leave at once. The wicked brothers are desperately afraid of visitors. If they should find you here. . . .

FIRST MAIDEN (*quickly glancing toward right wing, holding up a hand for silence*): Listen! I hear the sound of their armor. (*In alarm.*) They are coming! (*Pleading.*) Please, sir knight, turn and flee. To remain here means your very life. (*As the seven Brothers angrily enter from right, the Maidens and the Extras cry out and race offstage at left. Sir Galahad stoutly faces the Brothers.*)

FIRST BROTHER (*standing with spread legs before Sir Galahad, contemptuously eyeing him up and down*): You will wish, sir intruder, that you had heeded the warning of our fair ladies. Now you may find it too late.

SECOND BROTHER (*smirking, as all Brothers approach Sir Galahad in a threatening manner*): Unless, of course, you choose to show us the speed of a frightened deer. Be off with you!

OLD MAN: Please obey his command, Sir Galahad.

YOUNG MAN: We would not think you cowardly, sir. Your single sword cannot fairly match their seven.

THIRD BROTHER (*laughing*): Ah, the young squire speaks the truth. One puny sword against seven of the mightiest blades in all the land. Ho! (*The Brothers swiftly draw their swords, holding them ready for action.*)

SIR GALAHAD (*calmly, bravely*): One sword against seven? I tell you, sirs, it would be an unfair match indeed. I am used to doing battle with at least ten swords. (*Holding his sword in position for attack.*) However, if you insist upon battle, I must take unfair advantage of you. (*Crouching.*) Are you ready, sirs? (*The Brothers are somewhat shaken at Sir Galahad's calm confidence.*)

465

FOURTH BROTHER (*to his brothers, sourly and with amazement*): A bold fellow we have here . . . the likes of which we have not seen before. Shall we finish with his insolent words?

FIFTH BROTHER (*shaking his sword*): Let's be done with him! (*Jeering.*) King Arthur will soon find a vacant chair at his Round Table.

SIXTH BROTHER (*shaking his head, holding up a restraining arm before his brothers*): Wait, brethren. I am enjoying this comical fellow. It is a long time since we have had so much amusement. A court jester—that's what he is—the king's clown! (*The Brothers laugh, relax somewhat.*)

SEVENTH BROTHER (*looking at the sky, pointing toward the sun with his sword*): Sir Clown, you may continue to amuse us until the sun reaches the top of the sky. (*Growling.*) But take heed, if we find you still here at noon of day you will have a chance to prove your sword. You will think yourself struck by seven bolts of lightning. (*Laughing, waving sword.*) By all means entertain our fair maidens. (*Jeering.*) But take care that we do not entertain ourselves with you. (*The Brothers replace their swords and start to exit at right while chuckling and ad libbing remarks, such as:* Ha! . . . One sword against seven . . . Foolish knight. *As they exit, all the previous characters enter cautiously from left. Sir Galahad replaces his sword in scabbard.*)

SECOND MAIDEN (*with admiration*): Sir Galahad! You are the first noble knight to tame those wicked men!

THIRD MAIDEN: Welcome, brave sir! (*Tilting head in sudden wonder, speaking to others.*) Is it possible that he is the answer to the prophecy? Can we hope to be saved at last?

OLD MAN (*nodding soberly*): It is the right time of the year for the prophecy to be fulfilled. It may well be that Sir Galahad is our champion and deliverer.

SIR GALAHAD: I know not whether I have been sent here as an instrument of justice, but I assure you that I will not depart until freedom and honor have been restored. (*The others murmur their admiration.*)

YOUNG MAN (*glancing nervously at sky*): The hour of noon approaches. . . .

SIR GALAHAD: Then I beg all of you to return to your rooms within the castle. I will not have you endanger your lives.

466

OLD MAN (*indicating himself and the Young Man*): We shall remain . . . perhaps we can help in some small way. It is our battle, too.

SIR GALAHAD (*gallantly*): Thank you, sirs, but no. Please escort the ladies to safety.

FOURTH MAIDEN (*nodding emphatically, speaking with certainty*): Truly he is the one sent to deliver us. Heaven's greatest

467

blessing upon you, brave knight. (*The others agree by ad libbing:* Brave Sir Galahad . . . Stout heart . . . Our champion.)

SIR GALAHAD (*swiftly drawing his sword, waving it*): Into the castle! Hasten! (*As they reluctantly start to exit at right, the Old Man lingers, holding up arms toward Sir Galahad in blessing.*)

OLD MAN: Righteousness shall be your sword and shield! (*Others exit as Sir Galahad glances at sun, walks cautiously about. He turns toward right wing, as if expecting the Brothers to appear there.*)

FIRST BROTHER (*unexpectedly leaping onstage from left, waving sword*): Welcome to my blade, foolish knight! (*They duel, while working their way toward right wing. First Brother staggers offstage, holding his wounded side. The moment he exits the Second Brother leaps in from right.*)

SECOND BROTHER (*shouting*): Perish! (*They duel furiously; the Second Brother, wounded, crawls offstage at right while groaning. The Third Brother charges in immediately from opposite wing. After a brief duel he also falls offstage at right. Sir Galahad leaps to stage center as the Fourth and Fifth Brothers appear at left wing and the Sixth and Seventh Brothers appear at right wing.*)

FOURTH BROTHER (*as Brothers slowly close in on Sir Galahad*): Our brothers shall be avenged!

SIXTH BROTHER (*as Brothers charge Sir Galahad*): At him! Give him our steel! (*A furious duel takes place. Sir Galahad is driven backward at first, but manages to nick the Fourth Brother who howls and reels offstage. At this point Sir Galahad takes the offensive; as he thrusts with quickened energy the remaining three brothers are driven backward toward the left wing. The Fifth Brother tosses aside his sword and flees offstage at left; the remaining pair fight desperately for a moment longer, then also turn and race off at left. Lest they return, Sir Galahad remains on guard for a moment. He then replaces his sword, turns away from left wing. All the previous characters joyously troop in from right. They surround Sir Galahad.*)

FIRST MAIDEN: Well done, sir!

SECOND MAIDEN (*gesturing toward right wing*): I was watching from the tower window. The seven wicked brothers are riding away as if pursued by an army!

468

THIRD MAIDEN: We are free at last. We are forever grateful to you!

OLD MAN (*gesturing toward right wing*): Come and lodge with us in our captive . . . I mean in our free castle. We welcome you as our honored guest.

FOURTH MAIDEN: Yes, please tarry with us for a while.

SIR GALAHAD: Thank you, kind people, but there are many more adventures yet to come. I must ride on once more. Who knows what other castles may be in need of King Arthur's knights? (*Raising arm.*) I bid you all a fond farewell. (*The others wave goodbye while ad libbing:* Peace be with you . . . Farewell, noble champion . . . We shall always remember your brave deed. *Sir Galahad exits at left as the others continue to wave. Curtain descends.*)

HAPPY HOLIDAYS FOR LITTLE WOMEN

Characters

Narrator	Mother March
Jo March	Laurie
Amy March	First Young Man
Beth March	Second Young Man
Meg March	Third Young Man

Introduction by Narrator

Welcome, ladies and gentlemen. One of the most beloved classics of American literature is a story written by Louisa May Alcott. It is entitled *Little Women.* I'm sure that many of you have read this book about the four March sisters—Jo, Amy, Beth, and Meg. Tonight, our actors and actresses will present a scene which is based on several incidents in the lives of our little women. The time is evening, shortly before Christmas of 1864. The place is the parlor of our four young heroines.

Setting at Rise of Curtain

The parlor is set with the usual furnishings of a home during the Civil War period. A table is set at center stage. A few simple,

469

homemade Christmas ornaments, such as holly wreath and a picture of Santa Claus, are displayed in background.

Jo is lying on the rug with a book propped up in front of her.

AMY (*entering from right with a dress and sewing equipment*): Jo, what do you think of this old dress? How can I fix it up for Christmas? (*Jo ignores her, continuing to read.*) Jo March! I spoke to you! (*As Jo still ignores her, Amy sighs indignantly, sits and works on the dress. Beth and Meg enter from right carrying dresses and sewing baskets. Amy holds her dress up to them.*) Meg, you're the one with all the imagination around here. Do some imagining for me on this.

MEG (*setting down her basket, examining Amy's dress, sadly shaking head*): I can't imagine this for Christmas. It's hopeless. (*Fingering her own dress.*) And just look at mine. It's so dreadful to be poor.

JO (*looking up from book*): Christmas won't be Christmas without something new and pretty.

BETH (*sewing*): Mother thinks it best that we go without presents this year. After all, it won't be much of a holiday season for father. (*Hopefully.*) Maybe the army will let him come home for a visit. Wouldn't that be wonderful!

AMY (*sadly*): When will this frightful war end? I guess President Lincoln is doing his best to bring peace.

JO (*cheerfully*): Someday I'll write an exciting book that everyone will want to read. Then we'll have plenty of Christmas presents!

MEG (*to Jo*): Why don't you stop dreaming and get out and really earn some money? Take me—teaching stubborn little children their lessons. (*Sighing.*) I pay a high price for being the eldest of the four March sisters.

BETH (*reproving Meg*): You can just stop feeling sorry for yourself, Miss Meg March. And the rest of us, too. Christmas is supposed to be a merry season, no matter how poor you are. (*Examining her sewing.*) At least we can make it a merry Christmas for mother, even it it's only a pair of gloves. (*There is silence for a moment as Jo reads and the others sew.*)

JO (*while looking at book*): When will mother be home?

AMY: Soon, I think. (*Holding up an oddly shaped piece of cloth.*) Now what in the world can I do with this rag?

470

MEG (*giggling*): Make a witch's mask. At least it's something you can wear.

AMY (*indignantly, as the others giggle*): You're so funny. Just you wait. I'll turn it into some lovely handkerchiefs. You'll see how clever I am. (*They again fall into silence.*)

JO (*snapping book shut, rising, stretching*): We need something active to do. (*Brightly.*) I know! We'll rehearse the Christmas play. Let's see who's the best actress.

BETH: How?

JO: We'll take turns acting out the same scene. Like this! (*Clasping hands, staggering across the room, pleading dramatically.*) Roderigo! Save me! Please, Roderigo! Save me! (*To Beth, in normal voice.*) Your turn.

BETH (*shyly, reluctantly*): Must I? (*The others firmly nod. Beth acts out the scene shyly and self-consciously, without much dramatic expression.*) Roderigo. Save me. Roderigo. Save me. (*Shrugging apologetically.*) That's the best I can do.

MEG (*stepping confidently forward*): I'll show you how a real actress does it. (*With exaggerated dramatics she acts out the scene.*) Roderigo! Roderigo! Save me! Please, sir! Save me! (*Demanding of others.*) Applause, please.

AMY (*clapping once only, stepping to stage center*): I'll try it. (*She performs stiffly, primly.*) Roderigo. Please save me. Roderigo, do you hear me? Roderigo. (*To others in self-defense.*) Anyway, I don't claim to be an actress. (*Returning to her basket.*) Let's get on with our sewing. (*There is a short silence once more as Jo reads while the others sew.*)

JO (*looking up*): We do want to make it a merry Christmas for mother. Here we sit around and complain while mother has more problems than the rest of us put together. (*Tilting ear toward wing, leaping up.*) Here she comes! Hide your sewing! (*The girls quickly set their baskets in back of chairs.*)

MOTHER (*cheerfully entering from left*): Glad to find you so merry, my girls!

BETH (*running to Mother who puts an arm around her*): Mother!

MOTHER (*inspecting the girls*): Jo, you look tired. Mustn't study too hard. How is your cold, Meg? (*As Amy rushes offstage at right, the others help Mother with her coat, lead her to a chair at center table.*)

AMY (*returning with tea on tray*): We kept the tea hot for you, Mother. (*All sit around table as Amy pours tea.*)

MOTHER (*smiling*): After supper I'll have a surprise for you.

MEG (*excitedly*): A surprise! (*Pleading.*) May we have it now? Please?

JO (*soberly sighing*): We want a surprise so badly.

BETH (*eagerly asking*): Is it something about Christmas? (*Explosively.*) I know what it is! Father's coming home! (*Almost weeping.*) Will father be here for Christmas?

MOTHER (*taking a letter from her handbag on table*): No, children, I'm afraid the army still needs him. (*Cheerfully waving envelope.*) But he did write us a nice long letter. We'll have to be satisfied with that for now. (*She slowly takes letter from envelope.*)

AMY (*impatiently*): Hurry, mother!

MOTHER (*unfolding letter*): You can read the details later on, but your father tells of his days around the campfires and on the battlefield. A soldier's day is hard and dreary, but he's not one to complain.

MEG: That's just like him. No matter how dreadful, he tries

472

to make things sound easy. That's so we won't worry too much. Dear, dear father.

JO (*indignantly*): Why did they have to take him, anyway? He's so much older than the others.

MOTHER (*explaining*): The army needs chaplains just as much as it needs captains and generals. Your father reads the Bible to wounded men; tries to give them hope and courage. They need him almost as much as we do. (*Indicating letter.*) I'll read you the part of his message especially for you. (*Reading.*) Give them all my dear love and a kiss. Tell them I think of them by day, pray for them by night, and find my best comfort in their affection at all times. I know that when I come back to them I may be fonder and prouder than ever of my little women. (*All girls sniffle, as two of them touch handkerchiefs to eyes.*)

AMY (*sobbing, hiding her head on Mother's shoulder*): I'm so ashamed of my selfishness. (*Reproving herself.*) Fussing over a Christmas dress when father is out there!

BETH (*with determination*): We'll try very hard to make him proud of us.

MOTHER (*tenderly patting nearest girl*): Of course you will. (*Changing the mood to cheeriness.*) Now, then, suppose we have our tea while we make some plans. After all, we have both Christmas and New Year's Day to celebrate! (*Smiling, peering at baskets behind chairs.*) Do I see sewing baskets? Suppose you bring them out where I can help. (*As the girls take baskets there is a knock on the door.*) Jo, get the door. (*Jo lightly races off at left.*)

MEG (*brightly*): Maybe it's Santa Claus!

AMY (*to Meg, grinning*): Silly goose! (*Jo enters from left with Laurie, a pleasant and somewhat shy young man in his teens.*)

LAURIE: Good evening, Mrs. March . . . Meg, Beth, Amy.

MOTHER: How are you, Laurie? Join us in tea?

LAURIE (*sitting, somewhat bashfully*): I can stay only a few minutes. I . . . I just wanted to ask about New Year's Eve. Are . . . are you girls doing anything?

MEG (*grinning, posing with dramatic gestures*): I don't know about my poor sisters, but I am attending the royal ball!

BETH: Meg, stop it! (*To Laurie, eagerly.*) We're not doing anything that we can't set aside!

AMY (*expectantly*): If it's a party invitation our answer is yes.

MOTHER (*smiling, reproving*): Girls!

LAURIE (*nodding*): I've been asked to help with a New Year's party.

JO (*eagerly*): Who will be there?

LAURIE (*gesturing toward left wing*): Three of the fellows are waiting outside right now.

MOTHER (*surprised*): Out in the chilly night? (*To Jo.*) Jo, you get them in here at once. (*Smiling at Laurie as Jo exits at left.*) You needn't fear that my daughters will bite them.

LAURIE: It isn't that, Mrs. March. They're afraid they're not dressed properly. They just came from their work at the factory.

BETH (*to her sisters in dismay*): Dressed! (*Gasping, glancing at her dress.*) How awful we look!

LAURIE (*studying Beth*): You look good to me.

AMY (*as the three sisters leap up and start toward right*): We just can't entertain guests looking like this! (*The girls squeal while racing offstage at right. Mother smiles at the surprised Laurie.*)

MOTHER: That's the way little women behave sometimes. You'll just have to get used to them. (*Jo enters with the three young men. Greetings are ad libbed between Mother and the young men.*)

FIRST YOUNG MAN (*to Jo, glancing around in disappointment*): Where are your sisters? I was hoping they'd be here.

MOTHER (*rising*): They'll be back in a moment. Please take off your coats while I prepare tea and cakes. You must be frozen. (*The young men remove their coats as Mother exits at right with the tea tray. The boys stand or sit.*)

JO (*eagerly*): I understand you fellows will be at the New Year's party. (*Hinting.*) Are you taking anyone special? (*The offstage girls giggle as if excitedly primping. The boys exchange surprised glances and stare toward right wing. Jo tries to distract them.*) Uh . . . cold weather we're having for winter. (*The giggles grow louder.*)

SECOND YOUNG MAN (*somewhat absently, as the boys blink toward right wing.*) Uh . . . yes . . . funny that it's colder in winter than in summer.

THIRD YOUNG MAN (*staring, absently nodding*): Yes . . . lovely weather we're having this summer. (*As the giggles abruptly cease, the three girls enter. They are more colorfully dressed, with additions of hair ribbons and jewelry.*)

MEG (*assuming surprise at seeing the boys*): Well! Hello! (*Apologizing.*) Sorry we missed you when you first came; we were in the other room.

JO (*somewhat sarcastically*): Yes, we heard you. (*All exchange ad lib greetings.*)

FIRST YOUNG MAN: Mrs. Gardiner is giving a New Year's party. If you'd like to come, there'll be all kinds of fun. Do you like to dance? (*The girls eagerly ad lib together:* Yes! . . . Very much! . . . I do!)

SECOND YOUNG MAN (*grinning, stepping to center stage*): How about practicing right now? That is, if it's all right with your mother.

MOTHER (*entering, nodding, placing tray on table*): You young folks go right ahead and have a good time. Be sure to try my fruit cookies. (*Mother exits at right.*)

THIRD YOUNG MAN (*bowing playfully to any one of the girls*): May I have this dance? (*For the next few minutes they pair off to dance, chat, laugh, munch cookies, and have a good time in general. If desired, one of the couples may perform an exhibition dance which the others applaud. Offstage music may accompany their dancing. Finally, Laurie takes his coat.*)

LAURIE (*calling*): Come on, fellows; time to go.

MEG (*disappointed*): Oh, no! Can't you stay a little longer?

FIRST YOUNG MAN: Wish we could, Miss Meg, but we've got to get up early tomorrow morning. The war makes lots of extra work for everyone.

SECOND YOUNG MAN (*to girls*): Just you wait till New Year's Eve. We'll make up for lost time. (*The girls help the boys with their coats as all ad lib pleasant remarks, such as:* Don't catch cold . . . Thank you for the invitation . . . Come again, soon.)

THIRD YOUNG MAN (*as boys are ready to exit at left wing*): Goodbye. Please thank your mother for us.

LAURIE (*holding up finger*): Don't forget—New Year's Eve! (*As the boys exit at left, the girls follow them offstage as both groups again ad lib their farewells. Mother enters at right, looks toward left wing, smiling as she hears the offstage chatter. As she places the teacups back on the tray, the girls joyously race back, laughing and shouting ad libs, such as:* Happy holidays! . . . Three cheers for Christmas! . . . Won't it be fun? . . . Hooray! *They suddenly notice Mother.*)

AMY (*bursting with joy, hugging Mother*): Guess what, Mother?

BETH (*also bursting*): We're invited to a New Year's party! I'm sure Mrs. Gardiner will want you, too.

MOTHER (*gently smiling*): Your shining faces are enough for me. I'm sure it will be happy holidays for my little women.

MEG (*gasping*): Our party dresses! We've got to get busy!

JO: Let's see what we can find in the closet. (*To Mother.*) Will you help us, Mother?

MOTHER: Of course, dears. A little needle and thread will turn you into four lovely princesses. (*The girls gaily race off at right as Mother sighs and picks up the tea tray.*)

BETH (*poking head onstage*): Hurry, Mother! (*Beth disappears.*)

MOTHER (*calling toward right*): Coming, girls! (*She replaces the tea tray on the table, picks up a sewing basket, smiles, nods, sighs deeply as she walks toward right.*) Yes, I'm sure it will be happy holidays for the four little women . . . my precious little women. (*Mother exits. Curtain descends.*)

DAVID AND GOLIATH

Characters

Narrator	Second Woman
David	Third Woman
Goliath	Fourth Woman
First Soldier	Fifth Woman
Second Soldier	King Saul
Third Soldier	Extra Soldiers
First Woman	

Introduction by Narrator

Good evening, ladies and gentlemen, and welcome to tonight's play. You are about to see a short drama entitled *David and*

476

Goliath which is based on the classic story from the Old Testament.

Perhaps you recall that the armies of Israel and the forces of the Philistines were camped on opposite mountains, ready for battle. Perhaps you also remember that when they finally clashed in the valley between them, the Israelites drove the Philistines back in defeat. Tonight's play will show you how and why the armies of Israel were able to conquer their enemies. The time of our play is shortly before the beginning of the battle. (*Narrator exits. Curtain rises.*)

Setting at Rise of Curtain

The background is set with shrubbery, grass, and rocks. The rest of the stage is bare, except for small clusters of bushes.

The three Israelite soldiers creep cautiously onstage from right, armed with shields and cardboard swords. They motion to each other as they silently work toward the left. When reaching left stage they crouch behind shrubbery and peer anxiously into left wing.

FIRST SOLDIER (*in dismay*): The Philistine army appears as ten thousand ants. How shall we stand before them?

SECOND SOLDIER (*continuing to peer*): Fear not; the Lord is mightier than all their arms. He shall give us the victory. (*The five women, plus Extras if desired, cautiously enter from right.*)

FIRST WOMAN (*calling softly to soldiers*): How goes it? Does the enemy advance?

THIRD SOLDIER (*angrily gesturing toward the women*): Back— stay back! (*The women retreat a step or two, huddling fearfully.*)

FIRST SOLDIER (*rising, gesturing toward left wing in astonishment*): Look! A single Philistine approaches!

SECOND SOLDIER (*amazed, as soldiers stare*): A giant of a man —as tall as a sycamore! Back! (*The soldiers retreat to stage center where they crouch toward left wing in battle postures.*)

DAVID (*entering from right, carrying a sack of food*): Brethren, I bring bread and cheese to strengthen your arms. . . .

THIRD SOLDIER (*whirling to David, interrupting*): Drop your sack and be off! This is no place for a shepherd boy. (*To soldiers, as he gestures toward left.*) He comes!

(*David sets sack down, remains near right wing, apart from the women. Goliath struts heavily onstage from left, plants his feet wide apart, arrogantly looks around. He is tall, darkly bearded, clad in armor, and carrying a blunt spear made of wood or cardboard tubing. The women gasp.*)

GOLIATH (*booming defiantly*): Hear me, men of Israel! I am Goliath, champion from the camp of the Philistines! I challenge you to send me your mightest warrior for combat. If I slay your champion your people shall become our slaves. But if I fall before your warrior, my people shall be your servants. Ho! (*He makes an X mark on the ground with his spear.*) Choose your champion and send him here within the hour! (*Goliath looks contemptuously around, laughs viciously, thumps his spear against the ground, struts offstage at left.*)

SECOND WOMAN (*in distress*): What shall we do? We have no giant equal to the fierce Philistine.

DAVID (*confidently*): Brethren, have no fear of the heathen giant. Whoever fights him shall have the strength of the Lord's right arm.

THIRD WOMAN (*to David, somewhat scornfully*): Why do you linger, shepherd boy? Return to the safety of your flock.

DAVID (*boldly stepping forward*): This is the hour of our deliverance. I, David, son of Jesse, will go and fight him. (*The others mutter and jeer somewhat.*)

FOURTH WOMAN (*looking into right wing, gesturing*): King Saul approaches!

(*King Saul, dressed in bright, royal garments, enters with great dignity from right. If desired, he may be followed by Extra Soldiers. The Israelites bow, open the way for him to pass through.*)

FIRST SOLDIER (*saluting King Saul*): King Saul, the mighty Goliath has challenged us to send a champion against him. Where will we find a man strong enough to slay him?

KING SAUL (*looking around*): Is there not a single man of courage among you? (*The soldiers hang their heads.*) Is there not one of you with the heart of a giant?

DAVID (*bowing to King Saul*): Let your servant David go forth for you. I have no fear of the Philistine. (*The crowd mutters its disapproval.*)

FIFTH WOMAN (*shaking head at David*): Can a sparrow slay a hawk?

KING SAUL (*with kindness, nodding to David*): You are but a frail youth, while the giant is the mightiest warrior in his camp.

DAVID (*eagerly holding up hands*): When a lion and a bear attacked my father's flock I slew them with my bare hands. So shall I do to the Philistine. The Lord who delivered me from the lion and the bear shall deliver me from this wicked one. (*King Saul ponders for a moment while studying David.*)

KING SAUL (*suddenly exclaiming*): So be it! (*To Second Soldier.*) Give him your sword and shield!

SECOND SOLDIER (*protesting, shaking head*): King Saul, I fear we are lost. Let us at least send forth our mightiest captain.

KING SAUL (*decisively*): The choice is final. David shall be our champion. (*To David.*) Go with our prayers. (*Second Soldier offers his sword to David.*)

DAVID (*refusing sword*): I wish neither sword nor shield. (*He opens a small bag tied to his waist and takes out a sling.*) My weapons shall be this sling and five smooth stones. (*He quickly searches about and picks up five imaginary stones which he places in the bag. Goliath roars Ho! from offstage.*)

479

FIRST WOMAN (*alarmed, motioning toward left*): Goliath comes! (*The Israelites gasp and fearfully cluster behind King Saul at right stage. King Saul himself stands tall and unafraid. David takes imaginary stone from bag, sets it in sling, ready for action at center stage.*)

GOLIATH (*strutting arrogantly onstage from left, glancing disdainfully around, shouting*): Where is your mighty champion? I see but a lowly shepherd boy before me. (*To David, laughing.*) Am I a dog that you meet me with sling and stone? Ha!

DAVID (*boldly taking a quick step forward*): You come to me with a stout spear, but I stand before you in the name of the God of Israel. This very hour shall you fall before me!

GOLIATH (*approaching, raising spear, jeering*): The champion shepherd boy! Ha! (*For a few seconds they shift positions around stage, preparing to attack. Goliath strikes out several times toward David who nimbly leaps aside. As Goliath snarls and again prepares to lunge, David adjusts the imaginary stone in the sling, whirls it around and overhead and lets it fly. Goliath cries out, clapping a hand to his forehead as he staggers toward downstage left. He collapses, falling outstretched on his back. David races over, raises his arms overhead in a gesture of victory as he stands astride Goliath.*)

DAVID (*victoriously*): The Lord has given victory to His people!

SECOND WOMAN (*triumphantly*): The shepherd boy has conquered our enemy! Hail, David! (*All cheer.*)

THIRD WOMAN (*peering into left wing, motioning, shouting*): Look! The Philistines scatter like straws in the wind!

FOURTH WOMAN (*as all joyously look into left wing*): Without their champion they are lost!

FIFTH WOMAN: The battle is ours! (*All cheer.*)

KING SAUL (*commanding soldiers, gesturing broadly*): Blow the trumpets! Sound the advance! Our armies shall finish the enemy! (*As an offstage trumpet blows, the soldiers wave their swords, shout triumphantly and charge offstage at left. King Saul calls to David.*) Riches and honor shall be your reward. (*Motioning toward left wing.*) Go! Give us the full victory! (*David raises a palm in recognition of King Saul's command, turns and races offstage at left. The women cheer as the curtain falls.*)

THE RETURN OF RIP VAN WINKLE

Characters

Narrator
Man who Whittles
Man with Newspaper
Rip Van Winkle
First Child
Second Child
Third Child
The Mayor
First Citizen
Second Citizen
Third Citizen

Fourth Citizen
Fifth Citizen
Sixth Citizen
Seventh Citizen
Eighth Citizen
Ninth Citizen
Tenth Citizen
Old Woman
Old Man
Extra Citizens

Introduction by Narrator

Good evening, ladies and gentlemen. You are about to witness a scene from one of the great classics of American literature. This will be a dramatic presentation based upon the story of *Rip Van Winkle,* written by Washington Irving. Our scene is entitled "The Return of Rip Van Winkle."

Washington Irving opens his tale with a description of the countryside in which the events take place. Rip Van Winkle and his family lived in a small village at the foot of the Catskill Mountains in New York State. This region was originally settled by Dutch colonists who tilled the soil, gathered their crops, and taught their children to read, write, and live as liberty-loving Americans.

The early part of Washington Irving's story also tells us something about the character of Rip Van Winkle himself. This likable fellow enjoyed nothing better than roaming the hills and valleys in search of adventure. He always carried his old-fashioned rifle, and his faithful dog Wolf accompanied him wherever he went. It was during one of these hunting expeditions that a very strange thing happened to Rip Van Winkle. It seems that he fell asleep. Now this isn't so strange in itself, but no one—before or after—ever had such a peculiar sleep as Rip Van Winkle. For one thing, he slept for twenty years! And when he finally woke up . . . well, this is where our exciting story begins. (*Narrator exits. Curtain rises.*)

Setting at Rise of Curtain

The scene opens on the main street of a small mountain village, shortly after the American Revolution. A vacant bench is at upstage center. On another bench at upstage right sit the Man who Whittles and the Man with Newspaper.

MAN WHO WHITTLES (*lazily stretching*): Lazy day . . . lazy day. . . . (*To Man with Newspaper.*) What's the news today? What has General Washington been doing? I suppose our Congress is busy making new laws for the new nation. (*Nodding in appreciation.*) Bless those brave lads who went through Valley Forge. Bless our free and independent country.

MAN WITH NEWSPAPER (*after reading a moment longer*): I see that we'll be holding some more elections. Now that the war of guns is over we'll be having a war of words. (*Closes paper, stretching.*) Already our war for independence seems far away and long ago. As you say, squire, it's just another lazy day. (*Looks around.*) Nothing much seems to happen in our peaceful little village.

MAN WHO WHITTLES: Yesterday the baker's horse ran wild and trampled the mayor's garden . . . if you can call that exciting. (*Looks up, sees Rip Van Winkle, who is still offstage left, approaching.*) Well, who is this stumbling old fellow coming into town?

MAN WITH NEWSPAPER (*also peering offstage left*): A peddler, most likely. He doesn't seem to have anything to sell. (*They fall into silence, continue to whittle and read.*)

(*Rip Van Winkle, bearded and carrying a rusty rifle, slowly enters from left wing. He gazes around in bewilderment, falters, moves forward a few steps, rubs his eyes. A man and woman enter from right wing, cross toward him.*)

RIP VAN WINKLE (*speaking hopefully to couple*): Good day, neighbors. (*They stare blankly at him, pause briefly, pass by. He speaks as they pass.*) Please, can you tell me . . . (*He breaks off as they ignore him and exit at left. He wanders about, inspecting the street. He looks around, trying to find familiar sights, mutters as he fails to do so.*) Everything seems so strange, so different . . . so many new houses. (*Looking upward.*) Where are all the familiar old rooftops I used to look upon from my mountaintop?

(*First, Second, and Third Child gaily enter from right, catch sight of Rip Van Winkle, curiously approach him.*)

FIRST CHILD (*greeting Rip pleasantly*): Hello. Are you a stranger to our village?

SECOND CHILD: Maybe you are the grandfather of one of our schoolmates.

THIRD CHILD: My grandfather's beard is not nearly as long as yours.

FIRST CHILD: When I am a grandfather I will want to have a beard just as long and fine as yours.

SECOND CHILD: Sir, you look very tired and hungry. (*Reaches into pocket, pulls out piece of bread.*) Here, take a piece of bread. It will make you strong and healthy. (*Second Child stuffs piece of bread into Rip Van Winkle's pocket as the old man nods his thanks. The three children playfully exit at left.*)

RIP VAN WINKLE (*again looking around, speaking sadly*): Even the faces are strange . . . (*Suddenly remembering, speaking with spirit.*) And where is my dog, Wolf? (*Turns around, calling.*) Here, Wolf, come boy! (*Shakes head.*) Has my faithful Wolf forgotten me, too? (*Again calling, louder.*) Here, Wolf, here, Wolf, come here, old friend! (*His loud calls attract a number of citizens who enter from both wings to surround him at a moderate distance. They examine him up and down, discuss him among themselves.*)

MAYOR (*striding authoritatively toward Rip Van Winkle*): Look here, my good fellow, you cannot disturb the peace and quiet with all this shouting. As mayor of this village I'd like to know who you are and what you want.

RIP VAN WINKLE (*confused*): You want to know who I am? Please, sir, don't you recognize me?

MAYOR: Well, now, we recognize only an old fellow with a gray beard. Tell us who you are and why you have caused such an uproar. We have no time for loafers, sir; you may be sure of that. (*Rip, more confused than ever, hesitates.*) Come, Mr. Graybeard, speak up!

FIRST CITIZEN (*as he examines Rip Van Winkle's old rifle*): I think it most likely that he is a soldier of King George of England. (*Nodding vigorously.*) That's who he is—an enemy spy! (*The crowd angrily repeats the word* Spy.)

SECOND CITIZEN (*laughing at Rip Van Winkle*): A spy? Ha! Come, old man, don't you know the war is over? If you are a spy you are a bit too late to do King George any good. (*The crowd chuckles at the joke.*)

RIP VAN WINKLE (*searching faces in the crowd*): Mr. Vedder . . . Nicholas Vedder . . . are you here? (*To crowd.*) Mr. Vedder will tell you that I am no English spy.

THIRD CITIZEN: Mr. Vedder has been gone from us these last eighteen years. Don't tell us that you and the good Nicholas Vedder were friends?

RIP VAN WINKLE (*searching faces of other citizens who now enter from both wings*): Where is Brom Dutcher? Many days we spent together hunting in the Catskills. Brom Dutcher, here is your old friend.

FOURTH CITIZEN: Brom Dutcher no longer hunts for squirrels. Some say he was a hero at the battle of Stony Point. Others say he was lost in a storm. No one knows—he never came back. That was a long, long time ago, old man.

RIP VAN WINKLE: Maybe . . . maybe Derrick Van Bummel, the schoolmaster, can help me. (*As his distress deepens he pauses, sighs and again searches the crowd.*) Can you tell me where I can find him?

FIFTH CITIZEN (*as crowd shakes heads, muttering*): We have no schoolmaster by that name. (*Nods as he remembers.*) Come to think of it, there used to be a fellow who called himself Van Bummel. He, too, marched off to war. I've been told he got elected to Congress. At any rate, you're not likely to find him among us any more.

MAYOR (*sternly*): Enough of this! Tell us your name, old fellow . . . that is, if you have one.

RIP VAN WINKLE: My name, sir? (*Sighing.*) I was hoping that one of you would call me by name. Please, friends, my name is . . . Rip Van Winkle. (*Citizens shrug, repeat his name, shake heads as if his name is unfamiliar.*)

SIXTH CITIZEN: Rip Van Winkle, you say? And why might Rip Van Winkle ask so many questions about us? No one seems

to know you, and you seem to know no one. (*Chuckles, winks at crowd.*) I think our old fellow has mistaken us for some of his mountain squirrels. (*The crowd chuckles.*)

RIP VAN WINKLE (*looks offstage right, where his former home was located, walks expectantly toward it.*) My home . . . there! Here is where I live. (*He stands at stage right, staring into wing; he calls.*) Good wife! Dame Van Winkle, are you here? Good wife, your husband has returned. . . . (*He droops as he sees that his home is vacant.*) All is empty . . . quiet. Dame Van Winkle has gone . . . and my children.

SEVENTH CITIZEN: If memory serves me rightly, I do remember something of a Dame Van Winkle. She used to keep an enormous tea kettle in her window. Proud she was of that immense tea kettle.

EIGHTH CITIZEN (*shaking head*): No, no, you are mistaken. You are probably thinking of Dame Van Horn who owned an enormous yellow cow. It used to wander into my potato patch at least twice a week.

NINTH CITIZEN (*shaking head, gesturing to right wing*): I am afraid both of you are wrong. This humble home was occupied by the preacher Peter Hudson. How well I remember his fiery sermons on the Sabbath day.

MAYOR (*holds up arms for silence, addresses Rip Van Winkle*): You claim to be our neighbor, Mr.—what do you call yourself—Mr. Rip Van Winkle? (*Addressing crowd.*) Fellow citizens, is Mr. Graybeard Van Winkle your neighbor? (*Crowd shouts No.*) Does he speak the truth when he says he lives in our village? (*Crowd shouts No.*) Have we ever set eyes upon him before? (*Crowd shouts No and Never.*)

TENTH CITIZEN: That should be enough to take care of you, Mr. Graybeard Van Winkle. Suppose you take yourself and your fanciful stories back to your cave in the mountain. I think you will be far more at home among a village of wild squirrels! (*Crowd nods agreement, chuckles.*)

RIP VAN WINKLE (*sighing*): Friends, please let me tell you a strange story . . . a story so peculiar that I must confess that I hardly believe it myself. (*Crowd grows quiet and attentive.*) It must have been twenty years ago that I set out to the Catskills with my faithful dog, Wolf. After bagging a few squirrels and pigeons I started back to my good wife and my warm fireside. As I was about to descend the mountain I heard a strange voice calling my name. I asked myself, who could be calling for Rip Van Winkle upon this lonely mountaintop? Upon turning around I saw an odd little creature who barely resembled a man. He was a short, square-built old fellow with thick, bushy hair and a grizzléd beard. When I asked him why he called my name, he

486

motioned for me to follow him. I was so amazed by his fantastic appearance that I went along with him until we reached a flat valley. Here I sighted many more of these fanciful creatures who were playing a game of tenpins. The roar of the balls as they crashed against the pins echoed like great peals of thunder. . . .

FIRST CITIZEN (*scoffing*): Come, come, your imagination has taken flight indeed. Little men who bowl at tenpins! Ha! (*Crowd laughs.*)

SECOND CITIZEN (*holding up arms for silence*): No, no, let us hear him out. Go on with your adventurous tale, Mr. Van Winkle. (*The crowd grows quiet.*)

RIP VAN WINKLE: My little companions then invited me to join in their festivities, which I did. But I must confess that I was not used to such violent activity, so I soon grew drowsy. Finally, I could stay awake no longer. I fell into a deep, overpowering sleep.

THIRD CITIZEN (*as all eagerly listen*): And then what happened?

RIP VAN WINKLE: When at last I woke up I looked around for my strange companions. But they had disappeared. The tenpins were nowhere to be seen. All was silent. The grass had overgrown everything around me, my rifle was covered with rust, my faithful hound had disappeared. (*Pauses briefly, gestures.*) Call it my dream or call it my fanciful imagination, but that is what happened to me.

FOURTH CITIZEN (*in amazement*): Twenty years ago. . . .

FIFTH CITIZEN: You mean that you actually slept for twenty long years? (*Rip nods.*)

SIXTH CITIZEN (*boldly*): Well, fellow citizens, what do we think of this fellow's strange tale? (*Crowd is of mixed opinions, mutters in confusion.*)

SEVENTH CITIZEN (*boldly*): A fanciful tale indeed! I, for one, do not believe a word of it!

RIP VAN WINKLE (*wearily*): It is all right, good neighbors. You don't believe me, and I cannot blame you. Perhaps you are right . . . maybe I belong (*gestures toward left wing*) out there. (*He sighs, slowly turns toward left stage. He suddenly catches sight of a young lady, peers closely, exclaims as he approaches her.*) Young lady . . . your face . . . I know who you are. Yes, you are my daughter; I am your father. Young Rip Van Winkle once—old Rip Van Winkle now! (*As the puzzled girl hesitates, Rip looks desperately around once more.*) Does nobody recognize old Rip Van Winkle? No? (*He droops, falters toward left wing.*)

OLD WOMAN (*totters out from crowd, shades her brow with palm, peers closely at Rip's face*): Somewhere I have seen those eyes before. . . . (*She gestures toward the Old Man who also approaches.*) My good husband, do you remember a fellow like this who used to bring us berries and nuts from the hillside? Remember how he would urge us to fill our baskets? A generous soul he was.

OLD MAN (*studies Rip*): Yes, I do remember such a happy sort of fellow who used to wander about doing whatever he pleased. He always had a fine hound at his heels. Yes, his dog's name was Wolf all right.

OLD WOMAN (*brightly*): Sure enough! It is Rip Van Winkle. Yes, yes, we know you, sir! (*Gently pats Rip Van Winkle's arm.*) Welcome home, old neighbor! (*Rip bursts into smiles.*)

MAYOR (*as crowd cheers, gathers closer to Rip*): Welcome home, friend and neighbor! (*Crowd joins a little bashfully in the welcome.*)

EIGHTH CITIZEN (*taking Rip's arm*): Welcome! Come, sir, we want to hear more of your adventure! (*Crowd opens the way as the Eighth Citizen escorts Rip to bench at upstage center. He sits, surrounded by citizens; his daughter stands at his side.*)

NINTH CITIZEN (*shouting*): We believe Rip's story—and we hope it will be told as long as there are stories to tell! We want strangers who pass through our village to hear of the twenty years' sleep of Rip Van Winkle.

TENTH CITIZEN (*shouting*): It shall be heard all over the world!

MAYOR: The fantastic adventures of Mr. Rip Van Winkle! . . . did he dream them or did he live them? It makes no difference. He is not only our friend and neighbor—but he is also a legend who will live forever! (*Mayor and crowd turn to Rip.*) Rip Van Winkle—a legend forever! (*Curtain falls.*)

THE STRANGE TALE OF KING MIDAS

Characters

Narrator	Second Princess
King Midas	Third Princess
First Servant	First Prince
Second Servant	Second Prince
The Weary Traveler	Third Prince
Bacchus	Extra Court Members
First Princess	

Introduction by Narrator

Ladies and gentlemen, welcome! We believe we have a treat for you this evening. Our class will act out for you one of the most famous of the ancient Greek myths. Perhaps you have read the strange story of King Midas who ruled the kingdom of Phrygia . . . tonight you will *see* his story. Our dramatic presentation is entitled "The Strange Tale of King Midas."

There was one thing in life which King Midas treasured above everything else. This one thing was an obsession with him; he craved it more and more . . . but I had better not give away the story! (*Narrator exits. Curtain rises.*)

Setting at Rise of Curtain

The scene is a royal room in the king's palace. Suitable furniture is set in background. King Midas is seated upon his throne at upstage center. On a low table before him is a large box labeled "Treasure." The box is filled with a variety of riches, such as necklaces, rings, bracelets, gold and silver cups. King Midas eagerly holds them up, admires them.

KING MIDAS: Gold! Silver! Precious stones sparkling with light! They are mine, all mine! I am the richest king in all the kingdoms of the world. (*Clapping his hands.*) Hasten, royal servants! (*First Servant quickly enters.*)

FIRST SERVANT (*bowing deeply*): Yes, O royal king?

KING MIDAS (*gesturing nervously*): Gold, more gold! Fetch me another royal treasure chest. Quickly!

FIRST SERVANT: At once, your majesty. (*First Servant backs away while bowing, exits.*)

SECOND SERVANT (*entering, bowing*): O great King Midas, there is a weary traveler at the palace gate who begs for food and rest. Shall I send him on his way?

KING MIDAS (*somewhat annoyed*): Can't you see that I am counting my gold? (*Shrugging impatiently.*) Ah, well, send him to me. (*Second Servant bows and exits as King Midas greedily continues to enjoy his treasure.*)

(*The Weary Traveler enters, falls on his knees before King Midas.*)

WEARY TRAVELER (*gratefully*): May all good things come to you, O kindly king. I beseech but a dry crust of bread and a stone upon which to lay my weary head.

(*First and Second Servants enter with a heavy box labeled "Gold." They set it on the table before King Midas.*)

KING MIDAS (*ignoring the Weary Traveler as he greedily digs both hands into gold coins and other golden objects*): My precious gold! How it warms my hands! I shall spend the rest of the day counting my golden treasures! (*Greedily chuckling.*) Ha-ha-ha!

FIRST SERVANT (*coughing, to attract the king's attention*): A-hum . . . a-hum!

KING MIDAS (*looking up in annoyance*): Yes, yes, what is it?

FIRST SERVANT (*gesturing to the kneeling Weary Traveler*): Pardon, your majesty, but . . .

KING MIDAS (*sighing*): Oh, yes. (*Briskly, but with kindness.*) Take this weary fellow to the royal dining hall. Give him everything he needs. (*He again fondles his gold.*)

WEARY TRAVELER (*backing away, bowing with upraised arms*):
The blessing of heaven upon your kindly majesty. Great praise
to noble King Midas.

(*King Midas ignores the Weary Traveler and the servants as
they exit. He greedily ad libs as he lets his treasures slip from his
fingers to fall back into the chest. Bacchus, who wears bright
garments and a wreath on his head, steps onstage at right and
silently faces King Midas. Bacchus is more or less hidden from
King Midas—by a stage property—but is clearly visible to
audience.*)

KING MIDAS (*slowly looking up and around in suspicion*): I
sense a stranger . . . who is there? (*Standing, he angrily jerks
his head about.*) Who dares to enter the royal chambers without
permission?

BACCHUS (*approaching King Midas slowly and with great dignity*): I am no stranger to you, King Midas.

KING MIDAS (*in astonishment*): Bacchus! One of the gods
come down from Mount Olympus! (*Bowing.*) I am honored by
the presence of mighty Bacchus!

BACCHUS: I have observed your mercy and kindness to the
weary traveler. That needy man was Silenus, my foster father.
Because you have shown him compassion, I will grant you your
fondest wish. Whatever you ask I will grant immediately.

KING MIDAS (*tilting head, thinking deeply*): My fondest wish!
Hmmm. What shall I choose? Hmmm. (*Exclaiming, suddenly.*)
I know. Please, great Bacchus, I wish that everything I touch
should turn to gold! I wish to have the golden touch.

BACCHUS (*solemnly*): I do not approve of your wish, King
Midas, but it is hereby granted. (*Raising arms toward King
Midas.*) Henceforth, everything you touch shall turn instantly to
gold! (*Lowering arms.*) I leave you with your golden touch.
(*Bacchus exits.*)

KING MIDAS (*jubilantly holding up and admiring his hands*):
My golden touch! (*Eagerly.*) I must test it! (*He touches an apple
in a fruit basket, holds up a golden apple.*) A golden apple!
(*Racing to a potted plant he plucks off a twig, holds it up.*)
Gold, gold, pure gold! (Note: *The apple and twig, which are
covered with gold-colored paper, should be originally placed out
of sight of the audience, so that when held up they will appear to*

have turned to gold. King Midas now calls excitedly into both wings, gestures inward.) Come, lords and ladies of the royal court! Witness the magic of King Midas! (*The three Princesses and three Princes, plus Extras, quickly enter from both wings. They bow.*)

FIRST PRINCESS: We await your majesty's pleasure.

KING MIDAS (*shouting*): Then behold, as my royal chambers turn to pure gold! (*He races to two or three small objects, holding them up while ad libbing:* Gold! . . . Look! . . . The golden touch! *The others gasp in astonishment while also ad libbing:* Amazing! . . . How can this be? . . . Look, it turned to gold!)

FIRST PRINCE: Congratulations, O king! Your fame will spread to the far corners of the earth! (*The two servants enter with trays loaded with fruits, vegetables, cakes.*)

FIRST SERVANT (*bowing*): The royal dinner hour, your majesty.

KING MIDAS (*annoyed by the interruption*): What's that? . . . oh, yes. Set them down and be off with you. (*The servants set trays on a table and exit.*) Come, royal lords and ladies; we must celebrate my good fortune. (*The Princes and Princesses gather*

492

around the trays, while King Midas lingers, still admiring his gold.)

SECOND PRINCESS (*biting a small cake, nodding appreciatively*): The baker has outdone himself with his sweetcakes. (*To King Midas.*) Come, your majesty, the royal dinner awaits. (*As King Midas approaches, the Second Prince hands him a small cake.*)

SECOND PRINCE: Try this tasty sweetcake.

KING MIDAS (*grimacing as he tastes*): What kind of a joke is this? (*Staring in horror at cake.*) A cake of gold! (*He tosses the cake aside, quickly reaches for a grape, fearfully stares, tosses it aside while groaning. Note: the cake and the grape are also previously wrapped in gold-colored paper. As King Midas first takes them he covers them with his hand so that they cannot be seen by the audience. Then, as he holds them up in horror, the audience sees that they are golden. King Midas shouts in terror.*) My dinner itself has turned into gold!

THIRD PRINCESS (*sympathetically*): Poor, poor King Midas. Everything you touch turns into hard, cold metal. What shall you do for your dinner? (*King Midas dismally shakes his head, walks droopily to his throne, sits and leans forward with head cupped in hands.*)

THIRD PRINCE (*to others*): We must help our king.

FIRST PRINCESS (*gesturing hopelessly*): But how?

FIRST PRINCE: Yes, how can we help him? He cannot eat his gold, neither can he drink it.

SECOND PRINCESS: Nor can he ride throughout his kingdom upon a golden horse.

SECOND PRINCE (*as all gaze sympathetically at the dejected King Midas*): It was a sorry hour that our king acquired the golden touch. (*Gesturing.*) Come, let us leave him to his sorrow. Perhaps we can devise some magic which will relieve him of his curse. (*All except King Midas exit.*)

KING MIDAS (*standing, after a brief pause, pleading as he sadly looks around*): Bacchus, god of Mount Olympus, hear my humble prayer. I beseech you to take away my grief. (*Nodding.*) I have been a greedy man. (*Closing his eyes, he bows his head.*)

BACCHUS (*entering, holding upraised hands over King Midas*): Because you repent of your greed, I take pity upon you. (*King*

493

Midas hopefully raises his head.) Go to the River Pactolus and plunge yourself into its cleansing waters. Do this and you will be healed of your golden touch. And may you always remember that there are far more precious treasures in life than gold. (*Bacchus exits. The Princesses and Princes enter.*)

THIRD PRINCESS (*glancing about*): We heard a strange voice, your majesty. . . . (*Brightly, as she sees the joy on the face of King Midas.*) Your majesty . . . your face is bright with joy . . . what has happened?

KING MIDAS (*nodding gratefully as he descends from throne*): My golden curse will vanish as I bathe in the waters of the River Pactolus. Come, lords and ladies, this is a happy day for all of us. Your king has lost his golden touch . . . but has won a great deal of wisdom.

THIRD PRINCE (*as all start to leave*): We rejoice with you, King Midas. Hail to our king, who is rich in peace and honor. (*Others bow to King Midas who then leads them offstage. Curtain falls.*)

AROUND THE WORLD—BY WAY OF AMERICA

Characters

Narrator	Mrs. Grant
Phileas Fogg	Mr. Grant
Passepartout	Mr. Fix
Aouda	Captain Smith
Train Conductor	Station Master
First Child	Mr. Mudge
Second Child	Indians
Third Child	Extra Passengers

Introduction by Narrator

Ladies and gentlemen, you are about to see a two-act drama entitled "Around the World—by Way of America." Our play is taken from a portion of the classic book *Around the World in Eighty Days*, a great adventure story written by the French novelist, Jules Verne.

494

Our principal character is Phileas Fogg, an Englishman with a sense of daring. One evening Mr. Fogg attended a meeting of the Reform Club in London. There he told his fellow club members that he believed it was possible to travel around the world in eighty days. His friends thought he was joking—for at that period of history the only means of transportation were horses, sailing ships and slow locomotives.

But Mr. Fogg was not joking. He insisted that he could circle the world in eighty days. When his friends challenged him to prove it, Phileas Fogg left London that very night to begin his perilous journey. He was accompanied by his French servant, Passepartout.

Tonight's play includes two other principal characters. One of them is Mr. Fix, a detective who believes that Mr. Fogg is a fleeing criminal and follows him wherever he goes. Another character is Aouda, a young lady who was saved from tragedy in India by Mr. Fogg and his servant.

Our story opens as Mr. Fogg and his companions reach the western prairies of the United States—almost the last lap of their trip—and time is running out. They are on board a train headed for New York. So here we go—around the world! (*Narrator exits. Curtain rises.*)

Act I
Setting at Rise of Curtain

The scene is a railway lounge car. To give the actors enough room for movement—while maintaining the appearance of a train—the stage is set as follows: The car runs lengthwise from right stage to left stage, with the front of the car at the left. A row of passenger chairs is set along the back curtain, facing left stage. The rest of the car contains lounge-car equipment, such as a bookcase and a table set with food and drink. From time to time during the action, a bell, whistle or other offstage sounds typical of a train may be used.

Mr. and Mrs. Grant—plus Extra Passengers if desired—are quietly sitting on upstage chairs. Phileas Fogg and Passepartout sit at a small table at stage center.

MR. FOGG (*holding up a map to Passepartout*): Look, Passepartout, we are exactly on schedule. The prairies will be behind us within a few more hours—if all goes well.

PASSEPARTOUT (*nodding at map*): We should make it to the port of New York in plenty of time. And then for a fast ship back to London!

MR. FOGG (*lowering map*): I shall ever be grateful to you, Passepartout. Never did a man have a more faithful friend and servant. Wherever we have struggled—India, China, the Pacific Ocean—you have been my extra strength.

PASSEPARTOUT (*smiling*): The adventure itself is reward enough for me. Just think—the first men to circle the globe in eighty days!

(*Aouda, dressed in East Indian costume, enters from right.*)

MR. FOGG: Ah, Aouda, what do you think of this strange land? Is it far different from your native India?

AOUDA (*glancing and gesturing over heads of audience*): Very different, truly. Wherever I look I can see nothing but flat prairies and rolling hills. I haven't seen a single human being out there all morning . . . (*Anxiously.*) Except for those feathered savages charging about on their wild ponies. Are we in danger?

PASSEPARTOUT: Bows and arrows are always dangerous. The savages are American Indians—called the Sioux tribe.

AOUDA: I shall try not to be frightened. (*Conductor enters from left.*)

MR. FOGG: Conductor, please, are we on time?

CONDUCTOR (*glancing at watch, gesturing toward left wing*): The engineer says we'll make it to Omaha on schedule unless snow blocks the track. But we shouldn't have much trouble with the weather.

AOUDA (*anxiously gesturing*): What about the Indians? They seem to be following us.

CONDUCTOR: The Sioux is a warlike tribe, miss, but I wouldn't worry. We're not far from the army garrison at Fort Kearny. (*Aouda sits at table with Mr. Fogg and Passepartout. The three children noisily race in from right. They ad lib: Run, run . . . The redskins are coming! . . . Watch out for the Indians! The conductor grins, speaks to Aouda.*) You see, our children are more terrifying than our Indians. (*Speaking playfully to the children.*) That's enough war-whoops for my train. (*Gesturing toward*

upstage passengers.) Maybe they have some cakes for you over there. (*Conductor exits*.)

FIRST CHILD (*curiously wandering to Mr. Fogg*): You don't look like an Indian. Are you an Indian in disguise?

MR. FOGG (*chuckling in amusement*): No indeed, little friend. I am what you call an Englishman.

SECOND CHILD (*puzzledly*): What's an . . . an Englishman?

THIRD CHILD (*innocently, to second child*): Maybe an Englishman is a savage without feathers. (*The adults chuckle in amusement*.)

MRS. GRANT (*calling*): Children! Come here!

MR. GRANT (*calling apologetically to Mr. Fogg*): Sorry, sir; they have Indians on their minds.

FIRST CHILD (*to Passepartout*): We're going to Chicago. Where are you going?

PASSEPARTOUT: Our home is in London.

SECOND CHILD (*gesturing toward right wing*): The man in the next car said something about London. (*Frowning.*) That's funny, but he said that you folks might never get there.

MR. FOGG (*tilting his head curiously*): You heard a man say that? What did he look like?

THIRD CHILD (*shrugging*): Well, he didn't look like an Indian. I guess he looked more like . . . like what you call an English-man.

AOUDA (*sighing*): It's our detective friend, Mr. Fix. He's still with us.

MRS. GRANT (*calling to children*): Children, come over here. We'll play a quiet game for a while. (*The children join their parents upstage where they sit and play silently.*)

AOUDA (*to Mr. Fogg*): What a terrible injustice that you should be hounded halfway around the world by that Mr. Fix. What does he want with you?

MR. FIX (*entering from right*): Mr. Fix himself can give you an answer. (*Indicating vacant chair at table.*) May I?

MR. FOGG: As you wish. (*Mr. Fix sits.*)

MR. FIX (*to Mr. Fogg, somewhat apologetically*): As I've told you before, sir, I'm only doing my duty. A bank was robbed just before you left London in such a hurry. You'll admit, sir, it looks suspicious. What do you say to that?

MR. FOGG (*shrugging*): I doubt if your suspicious mind would accept my explanation. If it is your duty to follow me around the world, I have no objection—but I must warn you against arresting an innocent man. I assure you that I shall soon return to London. Why not hold off until we both return home?

MR. FIX: It's part of my job to have a suspicious mind, Mr. Fogg. For all I know you may not be planning to return to England. That's why I'm sticking close.

PASSEPARTOUT: All we ask is that you do not delay our journey. Mr. Fogg cannot afford to waste hours, or even minutes. (*Indians suddenly shriek offstage.*)

MRS. GRANT (*rising, screaming, gathering her children*): It's the Indians! They're here! (*All players leap up, startled.*)

MR. FOGG (*taking command, gesturing toward left wing*): Throw up a barricade. Hurry! (*All rush about, shouting, piling boxes near left wing. If Extra Passengers are used, they immediately rush offstage at right.*)

498

PASSEPARTOUT (*to the Grants*): Let's get the children away! (*The Grants and Passepartout hustle the children toward the right, while ad libbing:* Run! . . . Hurry! . . . Over there! *Just as they are about to exit at right Indians—three or more—dash in from right to grab Passepartout and Mr. and Mrs. Grant. The children scream, elude the Indians, race over to safety at the left where the others still are. Mr. Fogg and Mr. Fix grab clubs and start to dash toward right, just as the Indians drag their three prisoners offstage.*)

CONDUCTOR (*entering, climbing around barricade of boxes, shouting to Mr. Fogg and Mr. Fix*): Come back! It's hopeless! The train's surrounded.

MR. FOGG (*as he and Mr. Fix reluctantly halt*): But we've got to do something!

AOUDA (*comforting the children who cling whimperingly to her*): There, there; everything will turn out all right. Come with me. (*She takes the children offstage at left.*)

MR. FOGG (*agitated*): My old friend Passepartout . . . and the Grants . . . taken by those savages. (*Firmly.*) Gentlemen, we've got to go after them.

CONDUCTOR (*shaking head*): You don't realize what we're up against. (*Gesturing.*) Come here. (*Conductor leads others to a downstage position where he gestures outward toward audience.*) Look out the window. They're across the river already. Only a miracle can save them. (*Offstage hoofbeats sound.*)

MR. FIX (*tilting head*): I hear hoofbeats. (*Tensely.*) Another attack?

CONDUCTOR (*looking out*): We're all right. It's the troops from Fort Kearny—at least fifty men. But too late to save the others, I'm afraid. (*Gesturing toward left wing.*) Here comes Captain Smith.

CAPTAIN SMITH (*striding onstage, glancing around*): Any wounded?

MR. FIX: We're all right. But three passengers were taken.

MR. FOGG (*to Captain Smith*): Your men must ride at once! Perhaps there is time.

CAPTAIN SMITH (*shaking head*): About one chance in a million.

MR. FOGG (*insisting*): Then you must take that chance!

CAPTAIN SMITH (*politely but firmly*): I can't risk the lives of fifty men on the bare hope of saving three. You don't know the tricks the Sioux have—perhaps an ambush is already set for us. Believe me, sir, if anything could be done I would do it.

MR. FOGG (*with determination*): Very well. I will go alone.

MR. FIX: Be reasonable, Fogg. If it's hopeless for the army, it's doubly useless for you.

CONDUCTOR: He's right. They'd pick you off the minute you hit their hills.

MR. FOGG: My mind is made up. Captain, I want to borrow a horse.

CAPTAIN SMITH (*giving in*): All right, if you want to give it a try I'll give you a horse and five of my best men. But you'll only find out how impossible it is. Come along. (*Captain Smith and Mr. Fogg exit at left. Mr. Fix and Conductor watch them leave.*)

MR. FIX: A brave fellow, that Phileas Fogg.

CONDUCTOR (*nodding in admiration*): We could use more of his kind of courage.

MR. FIX (*reflectively*): I wonder if I'm wrong about him? He doesn't seem to be a criminal.

CONDUCTOR: A few minutes ago his only goal was to get to New York quickly. Now he's sacrificing hours and days—perhaps even his life.

MR. FIX (*nodding toward left*): Yes, maybe I've made a mistake. (*After a brief pause he suddenly gestures, speaks briskly.*) Come along; perhaps the others need help. (*They exit. Curtain falls.*)

Introduction by Narrator to Act II

Phileas Fogg wanted to go around the world in eighty days, but at this point it looks more like *one hundred* and eighty. There are so many hazards . . . he may be captured by the Indians . . . perhaps he'll get lost on the prairie. London—and the completion of the journey—is still a long way off. But perhaps things will take a turn for the better. Act II takes place several hours later at a prairie railway station. Let's see how things turn out. (*Narrator exits. Curtain rises.*)

Act II
Setting at Rise of Curtain

The railway station is indicated by a sign reading *Fort Kearny Station*. Typical items, such as luggage and benches, are set in the background.

If Extra Passengers are used, they sit or stand at various upstage positions. The Station Master is making notes in his book.

AOUDA (*entering, anxiously approaching Station Master*): Is there any word of Mr. Fogg? (*Looking outward.*) Isn't there some way we can find out what's happening?

STATION MASTER (*shaking head*): It was a dangerous attempt, Miss. Your Mr. Fogg was brave enough, but . . . (*He looks toward right as bell sounds.*) Here comes the next train. I suggest that you and the others make plans to leave on it. (*Sympathetically.*) Sorry, Miss.

AOUDA (*shakily*): No, I can't leave . . . not until I know what has happened.

STATION MASTER: That could mean a long wait. (*Glancing toward right.*) Excuse me, Miss; the train's pulling in. (*As the bell rings the Station Master calls out.*) All aboard for Omaha and points east! All aboard! (*The Station Master exits at right. Some of the Extra Passengers, if any, gather their belongings and follow the Station Master offstage.*)

MR. FIX (*racing in from left, shouting, gesturing toward right wing*): The troops are coming back!

AOUDA (*anxiously*): What about Mr. Fogg and the others?

MR. FIX: I don't know. They may be with the soldiers. Captain Smith will bring us word in a minute.

STATION MASTER (*entering, remaining at right wing, calling*): All aboard for Omaha! (*To Aouda and Mr. Fix.*) Last call, folks.

AOUDA (*to Mr. Fix*): Are you staying, too?

MR. FIX (*nodding*): I must find out what has happened to Mr. Fogg.

STATION MASTER: Coming, folks?

MR. FIX (*to Station Master*): Tell the engineer to go ahead. (*The Station Master waves toward right wing as if signaling the engineer. The bell rings several times as the Station Master resumes writing.*)

501

AOUDA (*gesturing toward left wing*): There goes the train.

MR. FIX (*gesturing excitedly toward right wing*): And here they come!

AOUDA (*eagerly, to Captain Smith who enters from right*): Are they all right? (*Looking toward right.*) Please, are they here? (*The Captain smiles, gesturing toward right wing. Mr. Fogg, Passepartout, and Mr. and Mrs. Grant enter. Aouda gasps in relief, hurries toward them.*)

MRS. GRANT (*anxiously*): Where are our children?

STATION MASTER: They're quite safe. I'll take you to them in a moment.

MR. FOGG (*briskly, breathlessly*): The train. We heard it from a distance. How soon will it arrive?

STATION MASTER: Sorry, sir, it has come and gone. You missed it by seconds.

AOUDA: But you are safe, Mr. Fogg; that's all that matters. What happened out there?

MR. FOGG: We battled the Indians ten miles south of here. They rode off after a short, hard fight. (*Anxiously.*) But I'm many hours behind schedule; I've got to make it up. (*To Station Master.*) When does the next train come?

STATION MASTER: Not until late this evening. (*To Mr. and Mrs. Grant.*) Come, I'll take you to your children. (*The Grants follow the Station Master offstage.*)

MR. FOGG (*desperately*): I've got to reach New York in time to catch the ship for London. (*Swinging around to Captain Smith.*) Captain, what about horses?

CAPTAIN SMITH: Too much ice on the ground between here and Omaha. Besides, the horses would tire after a few hours.

PASSEPARTOUT (*apologetically*): It's all my fault, sir. You wouldn't be here if I had been more careful.

MR. FOGG: Never mind, friend. Let's concentrate on our problem. (*Emphatically.*) There must be a way.

MR. FIX (*to Mr. Fogg*): Is it absolutely necessary for you to reach New York by the eleventh of this month?

MR. FOGG: Absolutely.

MR. FIX: Suppose I provided the way. Would you promise not to escape?

PASSEPARTOUT: Mr. Fogg has no wish to escape anywhere but to the east coast, and then home. You can be sure of that.

AOUDA: Why do you ask these questions, Mr. Fix?

MR. FIX (*to Mr. Fogg*): If I have your word, I believe I can help.

MR. FOGG (*impatiently*): You have my word, sir! Out with it!

MR. FIX: I had an idea you wouldn't be stopped by those Indians so I made plans to regain your lost time. At least we can try. (*Calling into wing.*) Mr. Mudge!

MR. MUDGE (*appearing at right wing*): All set, Mr. Fix? Shall I bring it out?

MR. FIX: At once. (*To Passepartout and Captain Smith as he gestures toward Mr. Mudge.*) Will you be so kind as to give Mr. Mudge a hand? (*Passepartout and Captain Smith follow Mr. Mudge offstage.*)

AOUDA (*curiously peering into wing*): What is it?

MR. FIX: You shall see. Ah, here it comes.

(*The three men push a low, wide sled onstage. The sled may be simply made by attaching wooden or cardboard runners to a wheeled wagon. By covering the wheels with overhanging canvas, the sled will appear to slide on the runners. The sled should look large enough for several persons. To achieve this, extend a cardboard platform over the sides and beyond the rear wheels. A sailing mast stands upright toward the front of the sled.*)

MR. FOGG (*staring, gasping*): What kind of a joke is this?

MR. FIX: No joke, I assure you. (*To Mr. Mudge.*) Mr. Mudge, please explain it.

MR. MUDGE (*enthusiastically*): Gentlemen, here is your perfect vehicle for speeding across the icy prairies. Believe me, you will win your race.

PASSEPARTOUT (*in bewilderment as he studies the sled*): You mean we are to push our way along? Or are we to be pulled by horses?

MR. MUDGE: Neither. Let me show you a power ten times that of a team of horses. (*Mr. Mudge picks up a sail from the sled, places it on the mast. The others gasp, mutter in appreciation. Mr. Mudge steps back, gesturing toward the sail.*) There you are! The power of the winter wind!

MR. FOGG (*enthusiastically*): A ship of the prairie! It just might work!

AOUDA: We can short-cut across the plains!

CAPTAIN SMITH (*nodding*): The winds may speed you into Omaha well ahead of the train itself.

MR. MUDGE: You should reach a speed of at least forty miles an hour. Keep yourself bundled up—the wind is as cold as it is mighty.

MR. FOGG (*triumphantly*): We'll win after all! (*Gesturing to Mr. Fix and Mr. Mudge.*) Thanks to you gentlemen.

CAPTAIN SMITH: You need have no fear of Indians. Should they sight your strange vehicle they'll ride for their lives.

MR. FIX (*chuckling*): What a sight that will be.

PASSEPARTOUT: We've journeyed by boat, train, oxcart—even on elephant-back—but this is the strangest yet.

MR. MUDGE (*glancing at sky*): The wind is rising. Better sail with it.

MR. FOGG: Right! We have no time to lose. (*Getting onto sled, steering it.*) Give me enough start to catch the breeze. Once I'm started the rest of you can hop aboard. (*The others quickly toss small pieces of luggage onto the sled while happily ad libbing, such as:* We're on our way . . . Let's go . . . I'll push back here. *They push the sled so that it slowly rolls toward the left.*)

PASSEPARTOUT (*shouting, as they push*): Around the world!

MR. FOGG (*shouting triumphantly*): In eighty days! (*Guided by Mr. Fogg, the sled is pushed offstage. Passepartout, Aouda, and Mr. Fix chase offstage after it.*)

MR. MUDGE (*reflectively to Captain Smith, as they look toward left wing*): You know what I think, Captain Smith?

CAPTAIN SMITH: What, Mr. Mudge?

MR. MUDGE: I think they'll make it.

CAPTAIN SMITH: You know what I think?

MR. MUDGE: What?

CAPTAIN SMITH: I think you are absolutely right. (*Curtain falls.*)

GULLIVER WINS HIS FREEDOM

Characters

Narrator	Army Captain
Gulliver	Prime Minister
First Lilliputian	Emperor
Second Lilliputian	First Prince
Third Lilliputian	First Princess
Fourth Lilliputian	Second Prince
Fifth Lilliputian	Second Princess
Sixth Lilliputian	Extras, Archers, Pages

Introduction by Narrator

Good evening, ladies and gentlemen. We welcome you as our guests to a short drama in two acts. Our play is called "Gulliver Wins His Freedom." It is adapted from the classic *Gulliver's Travels,* by Jonathan Swift.

Our play takes place in the land of Lilliput. As you may remember, the Lilliputians were tiny folks, no larger than Gulliver's thumb. Although we searched for actors and actresses of thumb-size, we just couldn't find any! So you can help us out by imagining that our Lilliputian actors are just about six inches tall.

In the year 1699 Gulliver set sail from England with the intention of voyaging to the South Seas. During a violent storm his ship was driven off course—and Gulliver was cast into the sea, near the coast of a strange little island. He managed to swim to shore, but was so exhausted by the effort that he immediately fell into a deep sleep. He was still sleeping the next morning . . . and here is where our story begins. (*Narrator exits. Curtain rises.*)

Act I
Setting at Rise of Curtain

The setting is the seashore. Gulliver is lying asleep at stage center, his head and feet toward the wings. Note: The smallness of the Lilliputians as compared to Gulliver can be emphasized in three ways: (a) By casting the tallest actor (wearing hat and boots) in the role of Gulliver. (b) By casting the smallest players as Lilliputians, and having them appear without hats, wearing low shoes or sandals. (c) By having Gulliver stay on an elevated area—such as a covered platform—so that it is necessary for the Lilliputians to look upward to him. His elevation also gives the audience a clear view of the reclining Gulliver.

The action begins as the First and Second Lilliputians enter with fishing poles. They suddenly notice Gulliver.

FIRST LILLIPUTIAN (*gasping with astonishment*): What is this? It appears to be some great monster from the sea! (*They cautiously edge closer.*) No! It's a human giant! See his enormous arms—like trees from the forest! (*Stage whispering.*) Shhhhh . . . he's asleep!

SECOND LILLIPUTIAN (*as they look with awe at Gulliver's great length*): A Man Mountain indeed! (*In alarm.*) Why, this immense creature could clutch us between his very fingers! (*Gulliver rolls over heavily, groans loudly.*)

FIRST LILLIPUTIAN (*in terror*): He shakes the very earth with his groans!

SECOND LILLIPUTIAN (*beckoning*): Come, let us call out the army before he awakens. (*They hurriedly exit. Gulliver groans and rolls, but remains asleep. The following characters now enter: Army Captain; Prime Minister; Third, Fourth, Fifth and Sixth Lilliputians; a few Extras and Archers. They carry lengths of string, representing ropes. For a moment they are paralyzed at the sight of Gulliver.*)

ARMY CAPTAIN (*giving commands in stage whisper*): Quickly,

506

men! Bind him! Make sure of your knots! (*All except Prime Minister race silently, tossing and tying ropes around Gulliver who stirs and groans.*) Hurry! Faster! The Man Mountain awakens! (*As they complete their task the Army Captain waves his cardboard sword and shouts triumphantly.*) We have captured the Man Mountain! All cheer! (*The Lilliputians dance around Gulliver, shouting and cheering. Gulliver slowly awakens, tugs puzzledly at his ropes, lifts his head and stares dazedly around. As he suddenly understands that he is tied down he roars, struggles against the ropes, reaches with a free arm for the Lilliputians. They shriek in terror, retreat a few steps.*)

THIRD LILLIPUTIAN (*taunting Gulliver*): Tug and strain, O mighty giant, you shall not get free!

FOURTH LILLIPUTIAN (*boasting to others*): We Lilliputians are no larger than his thumb—yet he is our slave! (*Gulliver angrily roars, claws at Lilliputians who once more shriek and retreat.*)

GULLIVER (*who has moved his upper body enough to sit up on his elbow*): Tiny people, what harm have I done that you should bind me? I may be a giant to you, but I am not your enemy.

PRIME MINISTER (*stepping forward, shaking walking stick at Gulliver*): Silence! As the Prime Minister of his great and majestic emperor of Lilliput, I decree that you shall be carried to the gates of the royal palace. His royal highness shall decide your fate. (*The Prime Minister is a somewhat fumbling and comical character.*)

GULLIVER (*politely*): I shall be most pleased to meet your royal emperor, but . . . (*Frowning.*) I have not eaten since yesterday. Surely you are a hospitable people who will not deny food and drink to a hungry visitor.

PRIME MINISTER (*doubtfully*): Hmmm . . . very well. (*To others.*) Fetch our unexpected guest some breakfast. (*A pair of Extras race offstage as the others make sure that Gulliver's ropes are secure. Gulliver again roars and clutches, somewhat playfully. The Lilliputians dance about him at a safe distance, laughing triumphantly. The Extras return with several small saucers containing bits of bread.*)

ARMY CAPTAIN (*raising sword to Gulliver*): Give us your word that we may serve you with safety.

GULLIVER (*nodding, licking lips*): Only let me taste your Lilliputian food. I am famished! (*The Lilliputians pass food to Gulliver who hungrily finishes within a few moments. He looks around, complainingly.*) But I have had but a bare morsel. Where is the breakfast you promised?

FIFTH LILLIPUTIAN (*in dismay*): He will eat our country clean. The giant has an appetite of . . . of . . . a giant.

ARMY CAPTAIN (*to Gulliver, gruffly*): Exactly what do you require?

GULLIVER (*cheerfully*): Suppose we start off with a dozen boiled eggs. . . . (*Frowning.*) Since they are Lilliputian eggs, better make it three dozen.

ARMY CAPTAIN (*sighing*): Three dozen eggs. What an omelet that will make. What else?

GULLIVER (*brightly*): Suppose we say six loaves of bread.

ARMY CAPTAIN (*sourly*): Suppose we say three loaves. Is that all? . . . I hope.

GULLIVER: I am fond of fruit for breakfast.

ARMY CAPTAIN: Very well. We'll include a dozen grapes.

GULLIVER: Please . . . make that a dozen bunches of grapes. (*Gulliver nods in satisfaction.*) That ought to give me a good start.

PRIME MINISTER (*sourly*): A start for you and the finish of us. (*To Lilliputians, impatiently.*) His royal majesty is anxious to see this gigantic fellow. Come, let us prepare to carry him to the palace.

GULLIVER (*amused*): Carry me? Ha! Why, I am fifty times the weight of all of you!

SIXTH LILLIPUTIAN: We are small in size but mighty in wisdom. (*Gesturing to others.*) Let us prove ourselves to the Man Mountain! (*The Army Captain and the Prime Minister ad lib orders to the others who rush offstage and return again with building materials, such as lumber, nails, hammers, wheels. Gulliver struggles and roars, but they ignore him as they go about their work. Curtain falls.*)

Introduction by Narrator to Act II

The little Lilliputians were clever at that. They built an immense, flat platform which was made movable with dozens of tiny wheels. It wasn't easy to lift the Man Mountain, but with the aid of long, stout poles they managed to get him upon the rolling platform. Fifteen hundred tiny horses then hauled him to the gates of the Lilliputian city. There Gulliver was freed from his ropes, but he was chained by his left leg to a pillar.

The Man Mountain has mountains of problems all right. Let's find out whether he solves them. (*Narrator exits. Curtain rises.*)

509

Act II
Setting at Rise of Curtain

The scene is the city gates. Gulliver sits on a platform, surrounded by all the previous characters, plus new Extras. His left leg is chained (with cardboard links) to a pillar. Outdoor objects, such as small bushes and crockery, may be set in background. In order to maintain the appearance of great size Gulliver remains on his platform at all times.

GULLIVER (*complaining indignantly as the Lilliputians stare at him and discuss him among themselves*): What is this? Am I to be stared at like an elephant in a zoo? In my own land I am but one of thousands who are of my own size. You, my puny folks, are an amazing sight to me! I once owned a pet puppy who could have carried the lot of you upon his back! (*The Pages enter, blowing trumpets and beating drums.*)

PRIME MINISTER (*rapping his walking stick against the ground*): All hail! All hail his royal majesty, the emperor of Lilliput!

(*The Emperor majestically enters to the beat of the trumpets and drums. He is followed by the two princes and two princesses, plus other Extras if desired. All except Gulliver bow deeply and ad lib greetings to the Emperor. As the cheers die down, the Emperor walks about with great dignity, haughtily examining Gulliver.*)

EMPEROR (*shouting to Gulliver, as he suddenly remembers his own importance*): Where is your respect for royalty, Man Mountain? Bow to your emperor!

GULLIVER (*apologizing, though somewhat amused*): Forgive me, mighty king of Lilliput, but I was surprised that so great an emperor should be so tiny. (*Gulliver grins, bows from his sitting position several times with exaggerated courtesy.*) Hail to your great but small majesty!

EMPEROR (*sputtering indignantly*): For one in chains you are a saucy fellow. Take care that I do not turn my archers upon you.

GULLIVER (*respectfully*): Little king . . . I mean great king, I'd like to talk to you about my chains. (*Plucks chains.*) To put it frankly, I'd like them removed. (*Gestures.*) Surely I should be as free as the rest of your loyal subjects.

FIRST PRINCE (*objecting fearfully*): No, no, father; he must not be turned loose. Why, with his left hand alone he could sweep us all into the sea!

PRIME MINISTER (*to himself, weepingly*): And I'm such a poor swimmer. (*The crowd nods, muttering ad lib agreement to the First Prince's argument.*)

FIRST PRINCESS (*anxiously*): His enormous appetite could bring famine to Lilliput. He requires six loaves of bread just to get warmed up for breakfast! (*The crowd again mutters agreement.*)

EMPEROR (*briskly, decisively*): Yes, yes, it is quite impossible. You must remain our prisoner.

PRIME MINISTER (*baffled*): Yet, what shall we do with him, your majesty? We have no ship great enough to send him on his way. What to do with him?

GULLIVER (*brightly*): I know what to do with him . . . I mean with me. It is true that I am as powerful as a hurricane . . . but this enormous strength can be of great service to you. Look! (*Gulliver slowly rises, stands with legs set somewhat apart, flexes his arms overhead. The Lilliputians gasp in awe, fall back.*)

ARMY CAPTAIN (*waving his sword toward Archers*): Watch out for treachery! (*The Archers crouch for action.*)

GULLIVER (*pleadingly*): Believe me, tiny folks, I want nothing more than liberty and peace. (*Gestures.*) Come close; let's talk as friends. (*Somewhat convinced of his good intentions, they cautiously draw closer. Gulliver smiles.*) That's better. (*He gestures toward a wing.*) Now take your fields and orchards out there. I could gather and store your crops in less time than it takes to whistle a tune. (*Lilliputians nod as the idea appeals to them. Gulliver gestures toward other wing.*) I could also build you a great highway over the mountaintop. Think of the advantages of a broad, smooth road that reaches the opposite sea! (*Lilliputians nod even more approvingly; they ad lib enthusiastically. Gulliver flexes muscles.*) I am powerful, indeed, citizens of Lilliput. Why not let my strength work in your behalf?

EMPEROR (*gesturing for Prime Minister and Princes to approach him, then speaking to Gulliver*): Ahem . . . we will meet in grand council to discuss your proposals. (*Huddling, they ad lib and gesture as if considering the good and bad features of Gulliver's proposal.*)

GULLIVER (*cheerfully, as the discussion continues*): Don't forget—I make a much better friend than enemy!

ARMY CAPTAIN (*calling over to Emperor*): He has a good point there, your majesty.

EMPEROR (*to Lilliputians*): Loyal subjects, your royal emperor will hear your opinions on the matter. Let us consider the advantages and disadvantages of freeing the Man Mountain. Speak up!

FIRST LILLIPUTIAN (*happily*): Look at his mighty frame. The very sight of him would be enough to scare away our enemies!

SECOND LILLIPUTIAN (*shrugging glumly*): But the very sight of him also scares us.

THIRD LILLIPUTIAN (*cheerfully*): As he promised, he could pick our apple crops within an hour!

FOURTH LILLIPUTIAN (*sourly*): And gobble them up within the same hour.

512

FIFTH LILLIPUTIAN (*happily gestures skyward*): He could carry us across the sky! In his palm we could soar like birds!

SIXTH LILLIPUTIAN (*timidly*): But what if we fall? (*The Lilliputians gather in small groups to discuss the matter with animation. After talking briefly with the Emperor, the Prime Minister steps off to one side to scribble furiously on a long sheet of paper.*)

EMPEROR (*holding up hands to crowd*): Silence, loyal subjects. (*They quiet down. The Emperor addresses Gulliver.*) Ahem . . . you are quite sure about all this business of harvesting our crops and building broad highways?

GULLIVER (*enthusiastically*): That would be just the beginning. I could even build a grand new palace for your majesty!

EMPEROR (*brightening*): A new palace . . . hmmm. (*Clears throat, speaks decisively to Lilliputians.*) I have come to my royal decision. The Man Mountain shall be set free. (*Shrugging.*) After all, you do want your imperial emperor to have a new palace. (*The crowd cheers in agreement.*)

GULLIVER (*happily*): I'd like to add my cheers. (*Waves arms.*) Three cheers for the emperor's wise decision!

EMPEROR (*gesturing to Prime Minister who is still scribbling*): Man Mountain, you will please notice that my Prime Minister is hard at work. (*To Prime Minister.*) Are you ready?

PRIME MINISTER (*dashing off final lines*): Coming! (*He approaches Gulliver, clears his throat.*) Giant visitor, attend to our royal decree. Your chains shall be loosened upon the following conditions. (*Again clearing his throat, he reads from the paper.*) First, you shall not depart from Lilliput without our permission.

GULLIVER: Agreed!

PRIME MINISTER (*reading*): Next, you shall not lie down in our fields of corn. (*Looks up.*) I guess you know why.

GULLIVER (*holding up palm in oath*): Not a stalk will I trample.

PRIME MINISTER (*reading*): While we will provide you with ample food and drink, you will please control your appetite.

SECOND PRINCE (*quickly*): In plainer language—no second helpings.

GULLIVER (*laughing*): Agreed, as long as the first servings are big enough.

PRIME MINISTER (*reading*): You shall assist our workmen as they beautify our country.

GULLIVER (*flexing muscles*): Agreed!

PRIME MINISTER (*pleased, as he folds paper*): You are a most agreeable fellow.

SECOND PRINCESS (*stage whispering to Prime Minister*): Don't forget the new palace . . . complete with a royal ballroom.

PRIME MINISTER (*reopening sheet*): Ah, yes . . . a new palace, complete with a royal ballroom. (*Folds paper.*)

GULLIVER: I agree to everything! (*Smiling, shrugging.*) As the Prime Minister said, I'm a pretty agreeable fellow, once you get to know me.

EMPEROR (*shouting*): Set him free! (*Several Lilliputians quickly unchain Gulliver. Gulliver rubs his ankle, waving gratefully. The Lilliputians dance around Gulliver, cheering and applauding him. If desired, background music may be added to the march-around. If used, Gulliver also claps time. The curtain falls on the celebration.*)

THE SWISS FAMILY ROBINSON—RESCUED

Characters

Narrator	Jenny Montrose
Father Robinson	Captain Littlestone
Mother Robinson	Mr. Wolston
Fritz Robinson	Mrs. Wolston
Ernest Robinson	Mary Wolston
Jack Robinson	Martha Wolston
Franz Robinson	Extra Sailors

Introduction by Narrator

Good evening, and welcome, ladies and gentlemen. Our actors and actresses are about to whisk you off to an island adventure. You will see a two-act drama adapted from the classic book written by Johann Wyss, *The Swiss Family Robinson.* Our dramatized portion of this book is called "The Swiss Family Robinson—Rescued."

Before the curtain rises, let's get acquainted with the Robinsons, a family that was shipwrecked on the island they call New Switzerland. The family consists of father and mother Robinson and their four sons—Fritz, Ernest, Jack and the youngest boy, Franz. What kind of folks are they? Well, the kind that makes an interesting story of adventure. The parents are courageous and resourceful—as we shall see. As for the boys, they are pretty much like . . . like normal, fun-loving boys—as we shall also see.

What a fascinating place New Switzerland was! It was rich with the natural beauties of forests, mountains, rivers, and flower-scented meadows. As for the wildlife, the land swarmed with wild creatures of every sort, including elephants, ostriches, boa constrictors, lions, and tigers.

Act I takes place several years after the Robinson family first found themselves on New Switzerland. They have brought some of their camping equipment—taken from the wrecked ship—down for a day at the seashore.

Act I
Setting at Rise of Curtain

The scene is the Robinson family's camping quarters by the shore. The sea is toward the left wing, inland is toward the right. Plant life is set along the background. General equipment, such as fishing poles, nets, boxes, cooking utensils, fruits and vegetables are in view. A small tent may be pitched at upstage right. Large rocks—made of cardboard—are set onstage near left wing.

Jack is sitting on a box with a basket of oysters (cardboard) in his lap. He takes the oysters, one at a time, pulls them apart, examines them, frowns and tosses them aside. Ernest enters with a coconut, peers curiously at Jack.

ERNEST (*approaching Jack*): What are you up to now, Jack? (*Looking into basket, laughing.*) Oh . . . more oysters.

JACK (*indignantly, as he continues to examine oysters*): Yes, more oysters, my dear brother Ernest. And someday I will have pearls. Just you wait.

ERNEST (*chuckling*): I've been waiting for years. So has mama. I doubt if you'll ever get her that pearl necklace. (*Holding coconut to lips.*) But here's a real treasure. (*Drinking.*) Hmmm . . . delicious.

515

(*Father and Franz enter from left with baskets.*)

JACK: What do you have in there, Father? And you, Franz?

FATHER (*smiling, wagging finger*): When Franz and I go fishing we catch fish. (*To Franz.*) Let's set them over here. Mother will want to bake them for dinner. (*They set baskets off to one side. Father idly takes one of Jack's oysters, pulls it apart, shrugs, pats Jack's shoulder.*) Patience, son . . . maybe tomorrow. (*Looking around.*) Where's mother?

ERNEST (*gesturing toward left*): Waiting down at the boat landing. She's worried about Fritz. He's been gone five days now.

FRANZ (*scoffing*): No need to worry about him. He said he was going to sail along the north coast. I feel sorry for any sharks who get in his way.

FATHER: Come on, boys, we've had our day at the seaside. Time to bundle up and get home. (*The boys busy themselves by gathering up the equipment. Mother worriedly enters from left, Father approaches her, touches her cheek with his finger.*) Here, now, what's the meaning of this teardrop? (*With mock sternness.*) Just wait till that boy gets home . . . I'll teach him to wander off.

MOTHER (*worriedly*): It's not like Fritz to be gone so long. So many things could happen.

FATHER (*comforting her*): There, there . . . just let him catch a whiff of your marvelous fish dinner and he'll run all the way home. (*To boys.*) Have you been watching from the lookout station?

FRANZ: (*nodding*): No sign of Fritz or of a rescue ship or anything else. I'll take another look tomorrow morning.

FATHER (*sighing, closing a box*): It's been a full day; suppose we get along home.

JACK (*quickly*): Wait a minute; I've got just three more to go in this batch. (*He eagerly breaks open the oysters, scowls, tosses them aside, sighs.*) Oh, well, the sea is full of oysters . . . and pearls, too, I hope. (*Franz wanders toward left with a telescope as the others gather equipment.*)

FRANZ: One last look. I wouldn't be surprised to see Fritz with a boatload of mermaids. (*He swings the telescope around, looking in various directions toward the left, suddenly halts, reacts with surprise.*) Wait! There is someone out there! In a canoe.

Doesn't look like Fritz. (*Others race to left stage, Father takes telescope, peers.*)

FATHER: He's paddling toward us . . . appears to be a savage of some sort . . . a fierce-looking creature. (*Gesturing toward right wing.*) Get back! He may be a scout for a war tribe. (*All quickly retreat toward right wing while grabbing cardboard rifles and clubs.*)

MOTHER (*tensely*): He's coming . . . be careful. . . .

(*Fritz, in savage costume, stealthily creeps in from left, crouching behind the rocks. He peeps around the rocks at the others.*)

ERNEST (*taking a couple of steps forward, aiming his rifle*): Just one more step, Mister Savage, and I'll split you like a log.

MOTHER (*alarmed*): Ernest . . . no . . . stay back. (*Fritz continues to duck and peep.*)

FATHER: Perhaps he speaks our language. (*Calling with authority.*) You! Come out where we can see you! Out! (*Fritz pauses briefly, steps into full view with folded arms.*)

FRITZ (*grinning broadly*): So you want to see me. (*Holding arms out.*) How's that? See enough?

FRANZ (*exclaiming*): Fritz! You big ape!

MOTHER (*relieved, but reproving Fritz who advances*): Shame on you. Scaring us like that! Where have you been?

JACK (*grimly approaching Fritz*): I'll take care of this savage. (*Jack tries to shove a basket over Fritz's head, but Fritz laughs and nimbly dodges aside.*)

FATHER (*trying to be stern with Fritz*): You'll have lots of explaining to do when we get you home. (*Gesturing.*) But for now, grab a basket of fish and let's be on our way.

FRITZ (*shifting uncomfortably*): Father, mother . . . I can't leave just yet. You see . . . (*Gesturing toward left.*) You see, while I was paddling around . . . I . . . uh . . .

MOTHER (*anxiously*): What's the matter, son?

ERNEST (*as Fritz hesitates*): Out with it. What happened out there? Meet up with a prehistoric monster or something?

FRITZ (*still befuddled*): Not exactly a monster. As a matter of fact, it was something rather attractive. I mean . . . (*Throwing up arms.*) I mean it's so unbelievable.

FATHER (*impatiently*): Just what do you mean?

FRITZ: It's a sort of surprise . . . at least a surprise to me. You see . . . (*Shrugging, sighing.*) Instead of trying to tell you, maybe I'd better show you. (*Turning toward left.*) I'll be right back. (*He quickly exits at left.*)

FRANZ (*as all exchange baffled glances*): What do you suppose it is? I've never seen him act like this before.

JACK (*shrugging*): Maybe it's a mermaid after all. (*Fritz returns with Jenny in tow. The others gasp.*)

ERNEST (*exclaiming*): What . . . I mean who is this?

FRITZ: This is what I mean . . . I mean this is who I mean. (*To Jenny.*) Jenny, I'd like you to meet my mother and father— and my brothers. (*Grinning weakly, speaking to his family.*) My mother and my father and my brothers, please meet Jenny. Miss Jenny Montrose.

JACK (*rubbing his eyes in amazement*): But . . . but she's a girl.

FATHER (*smiling at Jack*): Such sharp eyes.

FRANZ (*to Jenny*): Are you a girl mermaid? I mean a mermaid kind of a girl? If you are, you're the prettiest thing I've ever seen come out of the sea.

MOTHER (*sharply*): Stop this nonsense! (*Holding out hand to*

Jenny.) Come here, Jenny. Don't mind them. It's just that it's been so long since they've seen anything as lovely as you. Please tell us about yourself. Where did you meet Fritz?

ERNEST (*as he, Franz and Jack stare in wonderment at Jenny*): Think of it . . . a real, live girl.

FATHER (*nodding*): I guess dinner can wait. (*Beckoning*.) Come, Jenny. We'll feast on your story, instead. (*Jenny sits on a box at stage center. The others surround her*.)

JENNY: Years ago I lived in India with my father. He was a British officer. When he was recalled to England we took separate ships. My ship capsized in a storm, but I managed to make my way to shore. For three years I lived alone in the woods. Fritz was the first human being I had seen in three years. (*Gratefully*.) It's wonderful to be here.

MOTHER: What about your father?

JENNY (*doubtfully*): His ship probably reached England safely, but I don't know. Is there any way I can find out?

FRITZ (*shaking head*): This is the only world we have known for many years.

ERNEST (*trying to cheer up Jenny*): But it's an exciting life, Jenny. For instance, I can show you how to tame a wild monkey!

FRANZ (*eagerly*): And I'll help you to build your own tree house!

MOTHER (*smiling tolerantly at the boys*): That shows how little you boys know about a young lady like Jenny. It's a pretty new dress and a colored ribbon for her hair that she'll be wanting.

JENNY (*eagerly*): I'll make myself helpful to everyone. I can work in the kitchen and tend the garden . . . what fun it will be to share myself with friends again!

FATHER: Welcome to our family, Jenny. Your bright face will give additional strength to all of us. (*To Mother*.) Mother, why don't you show her around New Switzerland while we get our things back home? (*The boys load themselves with equipment as Mother escorts Jenny toward the right wing*.)

JACK (*calling*): Jenny, wait a minute! I may have a welcoming gift for you. (*Jack races to a basket of oysters, furiously breaks open two or three, scowls and tosses the shells aside. The others laugh*.) Just you wait, Miss Jenny Montrose; I'll find a pearl necklace for both you and mother. (*Scowling and gesturing*

519

toward basket.) If those oysters would only cooperate. (*All chuckle once more and exit at right wing. Curtain falls.*)

Introduction by Narrator to Act II

So a new and an interesting citizen has taken residence in the domain of New Switzerland. To the cry of the wind and the call of wild birds is added another sound—the pleasant voice of the lovely young lady named Jenny Montrose.

Time again passes as the Robinson family works, plays, and hopes for the day when a ship from the outer world will anchor off their island. As happy as they are, they wish for news of friends they used to know so long ago and await the time when they can let their old friends know they are alive and well.

One spring afternoon, after the day's work was done, they voted to take a stroll along the cool, refreshing beach. They enjoyed the seashore all the more because it offered them a view of the immense ocean—where a ship might be passing. Ladies and gentlemen, we present the second act of our drama.

Act II
Setting at Rise of Curtain

The seashore scene is somewhat similar to that of Act I. General camping equipment is set in background. The rocks used in Act I may be shifted to various upstage areas. Jenny is seated on a bench or box at stage center. Mother stands behind, combing Jenny's hair.

MOTHER: What lovely hair you have.

JENNY: Thanks to your expert grooming. (*Sighing.*) How I used to struggle with it when I was all alone. (*Three or four cannon roars sound. An offstage soundman can use a drum to represent the cannon. Jenny tilts her head toward right.*) What is that?

MOTHER: The menfolk are testing one of the cannons taken from our wrecked ship. We use it for long-distance signaling. Someday, perhaps, it may reach a passing ship.

520

JENNY: Mother, do you really think we'll ever be rescued? It's nice to hope, but maybe we're deceiving ourselves.

MOTHER: Hope is a great source of strength, Jenny, as long as you work with it.

JENNY: What do you mean by working with it?

MOTHER: By keeping busy, by making the best of things, by doing everything possible to make your hopes come true. I don't believe in the kind of hope that just sits around waiting for things to happen. Hope must be kept busy.

JENNY (*nodding*): That's why you folks have built such a rich life for yourself on this island. You hoped while working. (*In silence for a few moments, Mother continues with Jenny's hair. Father enters from right.*)

FATHER (*admiring Jenny*): As pretty as a poppy! No wonder the boys race back from their hunting trips. (*Cannon again sounds.*)

FRITZ (*entering from right, holding a fur over his head, growling*): Grrrrr . . . grrrrr . . . (*peeking through opening in fur.*) Surprise, Jenny! This will make a jacket—a fine fur for a fine lady. (*Stretching.*) Now, if you don't mind, I'll take my afternoon snooze. (*Lying down on back, raising head somewhat.*) Wake me in time for supper!

JENNY (*scolding playfully*): Lazybones! (*Ernest and Jack enter from right.*)

ERNEST (*scowling, wiping hands on a rag*): Keeping the rust off that old gun is a day's work in itself. (*Poking a foot at the dozing Fritz.*) As if you need to rest.

JACK: I'm the only one around here who doesn't take time off. I've got to work all the time.

JENNY: Doing what?

JACK (*grinning*): Doing this. (*Taking a basket, he again breaks open oysters. The cannon roars louder than before.*)

FATHER (*curiously*): Who's firing the gun?

MOTHER (*counting the others with her finger*): Fritz, Ernest, Papa . . . all here except Franz.

FRANZ (*entering from left*): Someone call Franz? Here I am, as handsome as ever. (*As the others exchange startled glances, Franz looks puzzled.*) What's the matter?

521

ERNEST: Did you come from the cannon?

FRANZ: Not me. I've been swimming in the bay.

FATHER (*with puzzled expression*): Must have been thunder.

JENNY (*glancing at sky*): On a clear day like this? (*As cannon again roars they mutter and exchange startled glances.*) There it is again!

FRITZ (*jumping to his feet*): A ship! It must be a ship! (*All race to various positions near left stage, peer excitedly into wing.*)

ERNEST: Look! The English flag!

FATHER: It's from England, all right.

MOTHER: After all these years.

JENNY: Here come the captain and some others.

(*Captain Littlestone, Mr. and Mrs. Wolston, their two daughters and Extra Sailors, if desired, enter from left.*)

CAPTAIN (*shaking hands with Father*): How do you do? I am Captain Littlestone. (*Indicating the others behind him.*) Mr. and Mrs. Wolston and their daughters, Mary and Martha—my passengers.

FATHER: We are the Robinson family—my wife and four sons. . . .

CAPTAIN (*breaking in, as he notices Jenny*): And you must be Jenny Montrose. (*Jenny nods.*) Your father sent us to find you.

JENNY (*happily*): Then he's all right! I'm so grateful for the news.

MR. WOLSTON (*looking around*): Where are we? What is this place?

MOTHER: We call it New Switzerland. It's a pleasant and abundant land.

MRS. WOLSTON (*to Mother*): What healthy sons you have. This must be a wonderful place to live.

MARY (*in delight*): What an adventure this turned out to be!

MARTHA (*excitedly glancing around*): I can hardly wait to scout around. (*Somewhat bashfully to the Robinsons.*) Would one of you be so kind as to take us on a tour? (*All four boys step forward, eagerly ad libbing:* I will . . . Allow me . . . Come along . . . Let's go. *The others chuckle.*)

CAPTAIN: I suggest we get better acquainted before seeing the sights. (*To Robinsons.*) Mr. Wolston hasn't been feeling too well

the last several days. Perhaps you folks could put him up for a while.

MOTHER: Of course. Please be our honored guests.

CAPTAIN: My ship is at your disposal. Do you wish to return home as soon as possible? What are your plans?

FATHER: We have already decided what to do in case of rescue. Franz and Fritz will return to Europe. Later, they will come back to visit the rest of us who have decided to remain on New Switzerland.

MR. WOLSTON (*breathing deeply, appreciatively*): The fresh, clean air makes me feel better already. (*To Mrs. Wolston.*) Perhaps we, too, should consider becoming citizens of this fine country.

MRS. WOLSTON: If the Robinsons will let us stay awhile, we can see if the life agrees with us.

MARY (*to Robinsons*): Please, would you let us join you?

MARTHA: We'd be helpful citizens—we promise.

ERNEST: Make yourselves welcome. It's no longer just our island—it belongs to you, too.

CAPTAIN: I suggest we celebrate this happy occasion with a banquet. Our ship has an ample supply of all that we need.

JACK (*eagerly*): And we have a storehouse loaded with fine foods!

JENNY (*with enthusiasm*): Mother Robinson bakes the tastiest cakes ever!

MR. WOLSTON (*rubbing his hands*): On with it! My appetite is restored already.

MRS. WOLSTON: Why don't we build a barbecue pit right here on the shore?

MARTHA (*clapping hands*): How romantic!

MARY (*brightly*): How romantic! (*All engage in task of clearing the center stage and arranging a barbecue pit with stones and firewood. As they work, Jack separates himself from the others by walking downstage right. He bends over a basket and quickly breaks and examines oysters, throwing the shells over his shoulder. Finally, he jerks upright, stares in amazement at the pearl between his fingers.*)

JACK (*shouting jubilantly, holding up the pearl*): Look! Everyone look! (*Racing back to others who silently crowd around him.*) A pearl! Look—at last! A precious pearl! Mother! Jenny! Do you know what this means? Pearl necklaces! For both of you! (*Almost hysterically.*) My first real pearl! (*Others smile, chuckle.*)

MARY (*with wide eyes*): Do you think you can find enough for us, too? (*Sighing dreamily.*) A pearl necklace. Oh. . . .

MARTHA (*eagerly*): I like pearls, too!

JACK (*proudly posing*): From now on please call me the Pearl Prince. (*Pleased with the idea.*) That's a clever title—the Pearl Prince of New Switzerland!

FRANZ (*grinning at Jack*): Yes, Pearl Prince . . . all you need is about three hundred more. (*Gesturing to the ladies.*) Yes, three hundred more ought to make necklaces for our five ladies.

JACK (*frowning, suddenly dismayed, scratching his head*): Just three hundred more?

JENNY (*grinning*): That's all, my proud prince, just three hundred more pearls.

JACK (*dismayed, shocked*): What have I gotten myself into?

MARY (*wagging a finger at Jack*): A promise is a promise.

JACK (*shrugging good-naturedly as the others chuckle*): Oh, well . . . back to work. (*He sadly returns to the basket, sits down, digs into it, resumes breaking open the oysters.*)

FATHER (*gesturing broadly*): This is a great day for New Switzerland! Long may she flourish!

FRITZ: A wonderful day for everyone! On with the celebration! (*Players busily prepare for the banquet. The curtain falls.*)

DON QUIXOTE SAVES THE DAY

Characters

Narrator	First Guard
Don Quixote	Second Guard
Sancho Panza	First Lady
Roque Guinart	Second Lady
First Bandit	Third Lady
Second Bandit	Fourth Lady
Third Bandit	Extra Bandits
Fourth Bandit	

Introduction by Narrator

Ladies and gentlemen, tonight we have for you an adventure story that is delightfully different. We believe you will find it amusing. Yes, you might call our drama an adventure in humor . . . a tender kind of humor that warms your heart at the same time that it makes you laugh. Our play is entitled "Don Quixote Saves the Day." It is adapted from the classic story *Don Quixote de la Mancha,* written by Miguel Cervantes.

Perhaps you remember that Don Quixote was a Spanish gentleman who fancied himself a dashing knight-in-armor. Assisted by his squire, Sancho Panza, Don Quixote galloped about the countryside seeking to conquer castles held by wicked men and to rescue fair ladies in distress. I'm afraid the Don wasn't exactly a heroic figure as he sat upon his scrawny horse, but he is at least a sincere, kindly, and intensely interesting adventurer.

Our play opens just after Don Quixote has charged with his horse against an enemy. Perhaps the enemy was a windmill which he mistook for a swinging giant, or maybe it was a flock of sheep that appeared to be an attacking army. But anyway, we shall see what happened to him after his ferocious charge.

Setting at Rise of Curtain

The scene takes place along a country road. Bushes and rocks are set in background. A sign with an arrow reads "Barcelona." A large bush stands apart from the others near stage center; however, it should be placed so as to allow room for action at stage center. Sancho Panza is hidden behind the bush, unseen by the audience.

Don Quixote is sprawled motionless in an awkward and comical position at downstage. Stunned, as if spilled from his horse, his arms and legs are flung out from his body. His sword and shield (both cardboard) are scattered about. After remaining motionless for a few seconds he stirs, slowly raises his head.

DON QUIXOTE (*groaning*): I, Don Quixote de la Mancha, spilled to the earth like an acorn in the wind. My enemies have worked their evil black magic against me. Never mind, I shall rise and charge once more. (*Painfully rising, hobbling toward sword, picking it up, shouting defiantly in several directions.*) Ho! Show yourself, cowards! My blade is ready! (*Suddenly groaning loudly, painfully holding his side, sitting on a rock.*) If only my faithful squire were here. (*Thinking.*) Whatever happened to my faithful Sancho Panza? (*Remembering.*) Ah, yes, I appointed him governor of an island.

SANCHO PANZA (*calling from behind the bush*): Help! Who's up there? I need your assistance! (Note: *Panza is trapped in a cave supposedly behind the bush. He remains unseen behind the bush until indicated otherwise in the stage directions.*)

DON QUIXOTE (*startled, tilting his head*): That voice! Where have I heard it before?

SANCHO PANZA: I am Sancho Panza, most faithful squire to the gallant Don Quixote de la Mancha. I am trapped down here in a cave. Whoever you are, please come to my rescue.

DON QUIXOTE (*angrily leaping up, waving his sword*): No, no!

It can't be! It's the voice of an evil magician! (*Whirling about in an effort to find source of voice, shouting a challenge.*) On guard, evil one! Taste the blade of Don Quixote de la Mancha! (*Suddenly groaning, painfully holding his side, staggering back to the rock.*) The wicked wizard has stabbed me with his curse. Ohhhhh!

SANCHO PANZA (*joyously*): Master! By all that's pure and noble, it's the voice of my master! Don Quixote, attend to the cries of your humble squire. Truly it is I, Sancho Panza!

DON QUIXOTE (*delighted*): My day of good fortune! It is indeed his voice! (*Peering, searching around.*) Sancho Panza, where are you?

SANCHO PANZA: Down here! In the cave behind the bush! (*Quixote confusedly hobbles to two or three of the smaller bushes and calls Panza's name, but gets no reply. Note: To make it appear that Panza is down in a cave, Quixote looks and calls downward. He finally goes to the correct bush.*)

DON QUIXOTE (*calling*): Sancho! Answer me, squire!

SANCHO PANZA (*calling*): Here I am!

DON QUIXOTE (*wagging a reproving finger down at Panza*): Ah, there you are, my foolish rabbit. It's the duty of a squire to assist his master, not the other way round. (*Sighing.*) Ah, well, give me your hand. (*Quixote stretches over and extends a hand. Panza's hand appears from behind the bush to grasp Quixote's. They struggle for a moment, then instead of Panza coming up, Quixote is pulled, shrieking, behind the bush as if down into the cave. Both ad lib distressed cries from behind the bush, such as: Sancho, you clumsy ox! . . . Sorry, sir . . . A miserable hole . . . Let's try again. Panza finally crawls into view at the side of the bush. He extends his hand to Quixote, and after another struggling tug, both again fall out of sight. The confused cries are repeated. Finally, both crawl out on opposite sides of the bush, not seeing each other. Both yell downward.*)

SANCHO PANZA (*calling, extending hand*): Grab my hand, master!

DON QUIXOTE (*calling, extending hand*): Sancho, take my hand! (*Both frown in bewilderment.*)

SANCHO PANZA: Master, look up here!

DON QUIXOTE: No, Sancho, you look up here! (*Both look up at sky, shaking heads. They crawl around the bush in the same direction, exchanging sides of the bush. They cannot see each other, of course, because of the bush between them.*)

SANCHO PANZA (*on his knees, calling down*): Noble knight, are you all right? (*As he continues to call, Don Quixote circles around the bush to stand in back of Panza, eyeing him sternly. Not noticing Quixote, Panza again calls.*) Please, sir, give me your hand!

DON QUIXOTE (*angrily raising his hand as if to strike*): I'll give you my hand all right, foolish squire! (*Panza whirls, Quixote holds arm in striking position, both stare, suddenly embrace while ad libbing happy greetings, such as:* Old friend! . . . How are you? . . . Together again! . . . I've missed you!)

DON QUIXOTE (*breaking away, snatching his sword, shouting dramatically*): Enough! Prepare to mount! We must ride on to Barcelona!

SANCHO PANZA (*eagerly*): There is adventure in Barcelona?

DON QUIXOTE (*dramatically, with hand over heart*): The sweetest adventure known to the human heart—the adventure of love. We must ride on to the castle of my fair Lady Dulcinea.

SANCHO PANZA (*spiritlessly, somewhat bored*): Oh, yes, that woman you call Lady Dulcinea.

DON QUIXOTE (*angrily raising his sword*): Say that again, squire—with purity and reverence.

SANCHO PANZA (*shrugging, sighing, holding hand over heart, trying to please Quixote*): Your fair and fragile flower—the Lady Dulcinea.

DON QUIXOTE (*lowering sword, satisfied*): Much better. Now let us find our horses and be off.

(*As they separate to walk toward opposite wings, Roque Guinart and his four bandits appear, three at one wing, two at the other. The bandits, armed with toy pistols and cardboard swords, silently watch as Quixote and Panza approach. Panza sees them, shouts in alarm.*)

SANCHO PANZA (*fearfully*): Master, we're surrounded by bandits!

DON QUIXOTE (*proudly drawing himself up, shaking his sword*): No, indeed, it is I who have surrounded the bandits! (*To Roque, who steps forward.*) Surrender, you prince of scoundrels! Drop your evil weapons before the feet of your royal knight.

(*Roque is so surprised that he drops his sword and laughs.*)

ROQUE (*to his men, chuckling*): You heard his command. Drop them! (*The bandits grin, drop their weapons as Roque speaks to Quixote.*) And to whom do we have the honor of surrendering? Your name, sir?

SANCHO PANZA: My master is Don Quixote de la Mancha—the bravest knight in all the kingdom.

DON QUIXOTE (*proudly, hand over heart*): In the service of the fair Lady Dulcinea.

ROQUE (*bowing, grinning*): At your mercy, sir. Pray do not deal harshly with us.

DON QUIXOTE (*frowning at the bandits*): A more miserable band of cutthroats I have not set eyes upon. Who are you—how dare you interfere with my journey?

ROQUE: Sir, I am called Roque Guinart. Some do indeed call us cutthroats and thieves. (*Sighing regretfully.*) Most distasteful titles to be sure, but very true, I'm afraid. (*Bowing.*) I assure, you, however, that I am most respectful to knights in armor such as you. Permit my comrades in crime to introduce themselves. (*Grinning, commanding his men.*) Scoundrels, show your respect!

FIRST BANDIT (*bowing to Quixote*): I am called by many names, most of them quite unkind . . . such as pickpocket, blackmailer, smuggler.

SECOND BANDIT (*gesturing to First Bandit*): Add "highwayman" to all that and you have my identity, sir.

THIRD BANDIT: My specialty is forgery. (*Bowing.*) Sorry, sir.

FOURTH BANDIT: Your prisoner is an all-around no-good. Your honesty makes me ashamed to admit it.

SANCHO PANZA (*wide-eyed and frightened*): Master, I fear we are in undesirable company.

ROGUE (*business-like*): And now that we understand each other, gentlemen, suppose we get on with our business. (*Gesturing to his men, who seize Panza. Panza struggles, finally gives up.*)

DON QUIXOTE (*angrily shaking his sword at Roque*): Release him at once or I shall run you through! (*Rogue grins, again gestures to his men who also seize Quixote. Quixote struggles and screams.*) Villains! Thieves! Unhand me! (*Quixote and Panza are forced to sit on rocks alongside each other. The bandits stand guard over them.*)

ROQUE (*to Quixote*): You see, sir, I am somewhat of a knight of the road myself. However, I lack the gallantry of a champion such as you—I require payment for my services. (*Holding out palm.*) Your purses, please. (*Quixote and Panza leap up but are shoved back. Roque smiles pleasantly.*) I am glad to see that you have regained your self-control. Shall we again discuss the matter of money, that is, your money?

SANCHO PANZA (*pleading*): Of a truth, sir, we haven't a coin between us. Search our pockets if you like.

DON QUIXOTE (*to Panza, somewhat startled*): Are we indeed as poor as all that? (*Panza sadly nods as Quixote speaks proudly to Roque.*) Our only wealth is honor and honesty.

SANCHO PANZA: We are also rich in pride. (*Muttering to himself.*) Oh, for less pride and more money.

DON QUIXOTE (*reproving Panza*): Silence! You tarnish the noble profession of knighthood with your greed.

FIRST BANDIT (*cupping an ear toward left wing*): Listen! I hear an approaching carriage. (*Grinning.*) Perhaps our new guests have heavier purses.

ROQUE (*nodding*): Ah! Suppose you give them our customary greeting. (*The first three bandits snatch up their weapons and vanish into left wing. The Fourth Bandit remains on guard over Quixote and Panza.*)

FOURTH BANDIT (*to Quixote and Panza*): Where are you bound for, noble knight and faithful squire?

DON QUIXOTE (*bewildered*): Bless me, but I've quite forgotten.

SANCHO PANZA (*sadly*): We rarely know where we are going.

DON QUIXOTE (*to Roque*): Turn into an honest man, sir, and I shall ride with you upon your adventures . . . or rather, I shall permit you to ride with me. (*Rising.*) Come, Sancho, we must find our horses. (*Roque and the Fourth Bandit shrug and let them go.*) I hope my fiery steed has not wandered too far. (*Hobbling toward right, calling.*) Rosinante, where are you? Rosinante! (*Quixote and Panza exit at right.*)

ROQUE (*staring after them in amused disbelief*): Do my eyes deceive me or have we just witnessed an amazing fellow who calls himself Don Quixote de la Mancha? (*Shrugging, then briskly rubbing his palms together as he looks toward left.*) Ah, our guests have arrived! (*The four ladies and their two guards are escorted onstage by the three bandits.*)

FIRST BANDIT (*with exaggerated courtesy to the captives*): Here you are, ladies and gentlemen, safe in the camp of Roque Guinart and his comrades. (*To Roque.*) Please meet our captives —I mean our guests.

FIRST GUARD (*angrily*): When word of this reaches the governor he'll have your heads!

SECOND BANDIT: Come now, no need to be upset. (*To Third Bandit.*) Show our guests how considerate we are.

THIRD BANDIT: Ah, yes, we must extend our usual courtesies. For example, we must relieve our weary travelers of their weighty baggage. (*Holding up forefinger.*) I'll show you what I mean. (*Snatching money bags from the guards, he weighs them in his palm, grinning.*) See! We relieve you of all your unnecessary weight! (*The bandits laugh. The Third Bandit steps behind the First Lady, fingers the back of her necklace while smiling.*) Surely I should offer you the same courtesy.

FIRST LADY (*slapping in back of her*): Insolent thief!

SECOND LADY (*indignantly, to guards*): Don't just tremble like frightened rabbits . . . do something.

SECOND GUARD (*miserably*): What would you have me do, my lady?

THIRD LADY (*gesturing*): Uh . . . whatever you're supposed to do . . . slap their faces, pull their hair . . . do anything.

FOURTH LADY: After all, guards are supposed to guard. Start guarding us!

531

ROQUE (*laughing, handing a sword to Second Guard*): The ladies are perfectly right. You must strike in their behalf. (*The guard miserably eyes the sword.*) Come, man, protect your fair ladies!

SECOND GUARD (*weakly*): Yes, sir. (*He looks sadly around, slowly and spiritlessly raises the sword, groans, almost weeps, drop sword to ground. The bandits roar with merriment.*)

ROQUE (*approaching ladies*): Sorry ladies, but we must earn our daily bread. (*Holding out palm.*) May I?

FIRST LADY (*indignantly drawing herself up*): You may not. Take my jewels and I shall scream. (*Nodding.*) Quite loudly.

FOURTH BANDIT (*sighing dreamily*): Ah . . . it's been weeks since I heard the delightful scream from a fair throat. Like music it is. (*Wagging finger to First Lady as he steps up to her.*) Don't forget your promise—a piercing, full-throated unlady-like scream. (*To other ladies.*) Perhaps you will join her—make it a harmonious chorus! (*Bandits chuckle.*)

SECOND LADY (*nodding primly to other ladies*): We shall scream indeed! Perhaps a fearless champion will ride to our rescue.

ROQUE (*grinning, snapping fingers as he glances toward right wing*): A champion, you say? I think it quite likely your prayers may be answered. (*Eyeing necklace of any lady.*) Such a lovely lady has no need for this ornament. (*The ladies scream, race toward right, scream again as the bandits follow.*)

DON QUIXOTE (*racing furiously onstage from right, shaking his sword*): Don Quixote to the rescue! (*He trips, sprawls awkwardly, sword flying. Panza races in, gently picks him up.*)

SANCHO PANZA: Easy, master.

DON QUIXOTE (*pushing Panza away, glancing angrily around*): What contemptible betrayal is this? (*To Roque.*) I warn you, sir! Release these fair flowers of womanhood at once! At once, sir, or you'll answer to the sword of Don Quixote de la Mancha!

SANCHO PANZA (*tugging at Quixote's coat*): Master . . . please.

FIRST BANDIT (*amusing himself with Quixote*): You don't understand, fearless one. We are merely relieving the burdens from our weary guests. Surely we must be good hosts to them.

DON QUIXOTE (*taken in by the double talk, relieved*): Well, now, that is worthy enough. (*Peering closely at faces of ladies.*) Do I see the fair face of the Lady Dulcinea among you? (*Brightly.*)

532

Ah, yes . . . my heart bows to you. (*Bowing to First Lady.*) My fondest affection, Lady Dulcinea. (*Bowing to Second Lady.*) My heart melts before you. (*Bowing to Third Lady.*) Lady Dulcinea, I love you as always. (*Bowing to Fourth Lady.*) I ask only your tender smile, fair one. (*The ladies exchange puzzled glances.*)

SANCHO PANZA (*explaining with embarrassment*): To my master, all ladies are his fair Lady Dulcinea.

THIRD LADY (*in confusion as she gestures toward Quixote*): This . . . this is our fearless champion? Dear me.

ROQUE (*placing a kindly hand on Quixote's shoulder*): Perhaps he's not the dashing knight you wish for, ladies, but I assure you he is nevertheless a fine friend. (*Shrugging.*) As a matter of fact, I am inclined to let you go for his sake.

SECOND BANDIT (*protesting*): But the jewels . . . we've rightly earned them.

ROQUE (*quietly*): Perhaps Don Quixote has also earned our guests the right to keep them. (*To bandits.*) Stand back, comrades. (*The bandits shrug and retreat from the ladies.*)

FOURTH LADY (*to Roque, gratefully*): You have a spark of goodness after all. Thank you.

THIRD BANDIT (*to ladies, while gesturing toward Quixote*): You had best thank Don Quixote de la Mancha who has softened five of the hardest hearts in the land.

FOURTH BANDIT: It's not often that we give mercy in place of the sword.

FIRST BANDIT (*to ladies and guards*): Come along before we change our minds. I'll escort you to your carriage.

FIRST LADY (*to other ladies*): First we must pay our debt. (*Stepping before Don Quixote, with bow or curtsy*): Your Lady Dulcinea thanks you.

SECOND LADY (*doing likewise*): Bless you. Truly you are a noble knight.

THIRD LADY (*doing likewise*): Your Lady Dulcinea shall remember your kindness forever. (*The Fourth Lady also bows, then kisses her fingertips, touches them tenderly on Quixote's cheek. Quixote almost weeps at their spontaneous show of affection for him. As the ladies, guards, and the First Bandit exit at left, he raises a limp and weary hand in farewell.*)

ROQUE (*beckoning to Panza who approaches, speaking quietly*): Help your master to his horse. (*Placing a friendly hand on Panza's shoulder.*) Take good care of him. (*Nodding at the still-stunned Quixote whose hand is still upraised.*) Take very good care.

SANCHO PANZA (*gently taking Quixote's elbow*): Come, sir, Lady Dulcinea awaits your arrival in Barcelona. (*Panza leads the dazed Quixote a few steps toward the right. Quixote pauses, slowly raises his fingers to touch the spot where his cheek was kissed.*)

DON QUIXOTE (*a pathetic but sympathetic figure, he whispers in wonderment as he stares outward*): Did you see, Sancho? . . . did you see my Lady Dulcinea? (*Looking at his fingers.*) She kissed my cheek. My lady kissed my cheek.

534

SANCHO PANZA (*tenderly, emotionally*): Yes, master . . . she kissed you. Your lady truly loves you. She will always love you. Come. . . . (*Panza slowly leads the weary Quixote offstage. The bandits, who are quieted and humbled by the emotional experience, gaze after them as Roque speaks.*)

ROQUE (*also gazing, speaking soberly, philosophically*): A foolish man, Don Quixote de la Mancha? Perhaps. But also a sincere soul who does the best he knows how. A blundering, awkward clown? Yes, but also a human being who yearns desperately to be loved. That, I suppose, is all that the rest of us really want—just to be loved by someone. Perhaps, my friends, if a man is loved enough he will be a good man . . . which is all that really matters. What difference does it make if a man is foolish or clumsy? . . . as long as he is a good man. (*After gazing toward the right wing a moment longer, Roque gestures to his men. All quietly and soberly exit at left. The curtain falls.*)

Index

537

542